Business

22 Years 2025-2004

ISC

CHAPTERWISE QUESTION BANK

Business Studies

Class 12

Author
Apeksha Agiwal

arihant
SUCCESS AND NOTHING LESS

arihant
SUCCESS AND NOTHING LESS

ARIHANT PRAKASHAN
(School Division Series)

卐 ADMINISTRATIVE & PRODUCTION OFFICES
Regd. Office
'Ramchhaya' 4577/15, Agarwal Road, Darya Ganj, New Delhi -110002
Tele: 011- 47630600, 43518550
Head Office
Kalindi, TP Nagar, Meerut (UP) - 250002, Tel: 0121-7156203, 7156204

卐 SALES & SUPPORT OFFICES
Agra, Ahmedabad, Bengaluru, Bareilly, Chennai, Delhi, Guwahati, Hyderabad, Jaipur, Jhansi, Kolkata, Lucknow, Nagpur & Pune.

卐 **PO No :** TXT-XX-XXXXXXX-X-XX

Published By Arihant Publications (India) Ltd.

For further information about the books published by Arihant, log on to www.arihantbooks.com or e-mail at info@arihantbooks.com

卐 **PRICE** ₹255.00

Follow us on

Achieving 99+ Marks in Board Exams

Achieving 99+ marks in board exams is definitely an ambitious goal, but with the right approach and these 7 tips from toppers, you can definitely increase your chances of success!

Here are the 7 Topper Tips to ace your board exams:

1. Master the art of consistency

Consistency builds understanding and confidence, both crucial for excelling in exams.

2. Build a winning study strategy

Create a personalised timetable that prioritises subjects based on your strengths and weaknesses.

3. Befriend the syllabus

Focus on high-weightage topics and prioritise mastering core concepts before moving on to advanced ones.

4. Embrace active learning

Explain concepts to yourself or in study groups to solidify understanding.

5. Conquer the past

Solve Past Years' Papers and Sample Papers under timed conditions to practice time management and understand paper pattern.

6. Seek help, when needed!

Don't hesitate to clarify doubts with teachers, tutors, or study groups. Asking questions strengthens your understanding and prevents confusion.

7. Prioritise well-being

Eat nutritious meals, get enough sleep, regular exercise and practice stress management techniques like meditation to stay calm and focused during exams.

These tips are just a starting point, and you can personalise them to fit your learning style and preferences.

Description of

Newly Added Features

01

Introduction to HRM & Job and Manpower Planning

TREND ANALYSIS

		Average No. of Questions Across all Sets					
		Types of Questions	2023	2020	2019	2018	2017
01	HRM	1 Mark	1	–	–	–	–
		2 Marks	–	–	–	–	–
		4 Marks	–	–	1	–	–
		6 Marks	–	–	–	–	–
		8 Marks	–	–	–	–	–

Trend Analysis

At the start of each chapter, Trend Analysis is given to indicate the types of Questions asked from different topics of the chapter. This feature helps students to know the importance of different topics of the given chapter from exam point of view and helps them to prepare accordingly.

1. Write an explanatory note on job analysis.

Ans In simple words, job analysis may be understood as a process of collecting information about a job. It is a systematic investigation of tasks, duties and responsibilities to perform a job.

The process of job analysis results in two sets of data

(i) Job description

(ii) Job specification

Value Points

For getting maximum marks, following points can be included in the answer

- Meaning of job analysis
- Components of job analysis

Value Points

'Value Points' are given with selected questions with the purpose to help students to know the key points to be covered in the answer to get full marks.

(iv) **Customer service** By improving physical work environment, employing supportive workforce and use of appropriate service delivery system, HRM enhance customer service.

Common Mistake Generally, students misunderstand this question in hurry and answer the question by giving common significance of HRM. Students are advisable to read question carefully and write correct significance of HRM related to category asked as it is categorised in different contexts.

Common Mistakes

It focuses on some of the general but critical mistakes that students commit while solving the questions. This feature helps students to develop the habit of avoiding mistakes while solving questions

14. One of the objective of human resource management is *Sem I Specimen 2021*

(a) development of people

(b) punishment of people

(c) adoption of people

(d) None of the above

Ans (a) development of people

15. Job enrichment involves *Sem I Specimen 2021*

(a) increasing the depth of a job

(b) increasing the width of a job

(c) describing the nature and content of a job

(d) a formal and detailed study of the job

Ans (a) increasing the depth of a job

Concept Enhancer Job enrichment is that motivational tool which allows more decision making power and work related authority to employees.

Concept Enhancer

Concept Enhancer gives the brief description of the concept, which has been used to solve the question. This feature provides revision of important concept along with practice of question solving.

Most Important Topics

from each Chapter

On the basis of analysis of last 5 Years' Board Examination Papers, we have identified Important Topics from each chapter.

Chapter Name	Important Topics	Weightage in Last 5 Years' Boards				
		2025	2024	2023	2020	2019
Introduction to HRM & Job and Manpower Planning	HRM	1M, 2M	1M	1M		4M
	Job and Manpower Planning	1M, 2M	1M	1M,4M	2M,4M	
Staff Recruitment and Selection	Staff Recruitment	1M, 1M	4M	8M	8M	2M,4M
	Staff Selection	4M	4M	1M,4M	2M,4M	8M
Staff Training	Meaning and Types of Staff Training	2M, 4M	1M		4M	2M,4M
	Methods and Hindrances of Staff Training	1M, 1M, 2M	2M,2M	4M		
Staff Morale	Meaning and Factors Affecting Staff Morale				2M	
	Methods of Raising Staff Morale, Morale Productivity Matrix	4M, 4M	8M	1M		8M
Staff Motivation	Motivation and Types of Incentives	1M, 1M				
	Maslow's Need Theory and Herzberg's Two Factor Theory	4M	4M	1M,4M	8M	2M
Staff Remuneration	Remuneration	1M, 1M	1M			
	Various Staff Benefits and Types of Leaves	1M, 2M, 2M, 2M	2M,2M	1M	2M,4M	2M,8M
Staff Leadership	Leadership, Quality of Good Leader					2M
	Leadership Styles and Situational Leadership	1M	1M,2M	1M,4M	8M	4M
Staff Appraisal	Meaning of Performance and Potential Appraisal	1M	2M	2M	2M	
	Methods of Performance Appraisal	4M	1M	2M		8M
Staff Promotion, Transfer and Separation	Staff Promotion	4M	4M	2M,6M	8M	2M,4M
	Staff Transfer and Separation	1M, 4M	1M,1M,2M		4M	4M
Emerging Trends in Human Resources	Energing Trends in HR	2M	1M,1M,2M	4M	4M	
Business Communication: Concept, Methods and Types	Communication			1M	2M	8M
	Types and Barriers of Communication	1M, 1M, 4M	8M	1M,1M	6M	
Business Correspondence (Business Letters & Reports) and Current Trends	Business correspondance and Letter	2M, 2M, 8M	8M	8M	2M,8M	8M
	Business Reports and Current Trends in Business Communication	1M	1M,1M,2M	1M	4M	8M
Business Size and Finance	Various Business Entities	1M, 2M	1M	4M	2M	
	Sources of Business Finance	1M, 2M, 2M	8M	8M	4M	8M
Globalisation and Recent Trends in Business	Globalisation	4M	1M,4M	1M	2M	4M
	E - business	2M	1M,4M	4M	8M	2M,4M
	Outsourcing		4M	1M,4M	8M	2M,2M
Business Regulators and Intermediaries	Business Regulators		1M,2M	1M,4M	1M	2M
	Business Intermediaries	1M			1M	

Dream, Believe, Achieve — Insights from ISC Toppers

Follow all the 5P's

• Persistence • Passion • Perseverance • Purpose • Practice

MANYA GUPTA
ISC Topper (99.75%)

Aim for high marks, that's what I was doing. I convinced myself that if I aim for 100 I will at least get a 95. That was my logic, but I ended up getting a 100.

I studied with the help of my school and tuition classes. I didn't study daily much, but before the exams, I used to pull all-nighters and study.

ARYAAN
ISC Topper (99.75%)

Studying for 3-4 hours every day along with six hours of school helped me secure 399 out of 400 marks, scoring 99.75%.

I'm very active on all social media platforms but it has never hindered my studies. I strike a balance between hard work and fun.

The degree of toughness of any subject is merely a subjective outlook. I made sure that I incentivised myself at times when I didn't feel like sitting at my study table, especially for theoretical subjects.

I simply believe in revising the concepts which were taught at school or tuitions that very day and minimise backlogs as much as I could.

POOJA KEJRIWAL
ISC Topper (97.5%)

I believe there is no substitute to hard work. There was no fixed hours of preparation. I read a topic till the time I completely understood it. I had to be satisfied with the topic covered.

See it is important to take breaks and everyone has their own way of entertainment. I do chat with friends on social media. I think it is fine until it becomes an addiction.

There is no secret formula as such, but one should not panic and have faith in his/her preparation.

DEVANG KUMAR
ISC Topper

DIMPLE KOTHARI
ISC Topper (97.5%)

- Don't run behind marks, crave for knowledge, experience because ultimately that's gonna help you.
- Don't let peer pressure dominate you.
- If you want to obtain good marks, leave all social media-This is a myth. I was active on Instagram & WhatsApp before my examinations, and even during my examinations. It's just that you need to remember that everyone has the same 24 hours, it's how you utilize it as well as enjoy it better than others.
- Both early morning and late night studies are best ~ you need to choose what's better for you.
- Don't hesitate to ask questions. If you have any doubts, please clarify. Everyone has different learning styles and speed, so it's nothing to be ashamed of.
- Never give up.

Please Note that all the information is collected from different websites.

Contents

ISC Chapterwise Question Bank 2025-2004

Latest Syllabus

Class XII (2025-26)

There will be two papers in the subject.

Paper I Theory : 3 Hours 80 Marks

Paper II Project Work 20 Marks

PAPER I THEORY 80 Marks

1. Human Resource Management

(i) Introduction to Human Resource Management

Meaning and definition of Human Resource Management; Characteristics of Human Resource Management: people oriented, comprehensive function, staff function, pervasive, challenging, continuous, individual oriented, development oriented, action oriented, future oriented, interdisciplinary, art as well as science, young discipline; Importance of human resource management.

(ii) Job and Manpower Planning

Meaning, relevance and difference between the following: Job Analysis, Job Specification, Job Description, Job Enrichment and Job Enlargement, Manpower Estimation.

(iii) Staff Recruitment

Meaning, definition and characteristics of staff recruitment; sources of recruitment: internal sources (promotion, transfer, ex-employees, recommendation by employees); external sources (advertisements, campus recruitment, casual callers, gate hiring, employment exchanges, placement agencies, labour contractors). Differences between internal and external sources of recruitment, their merits and demerits; e-recruitment: concept, benefits and limitations; sources of e-recruitment: internet and intranet (their benefits and limitations).

(iv) Staff Selection

Meaning and definition of staff selection; Selection procedures (preliminary screening, application blank, selection test, Group discussion, final interview, medical test, reference check, final approval, placement; brief explanation and importance of each step of the selection procedure); distinction between recruitment and selection.

(v) Staff Training

Meaning and definition of training; distinction between training, education and development; types of training (induction, job, remedial, safety, promotional, refresher- brief explanation of each.); methods of training: on the job and off the job (vestibule, apprenticeship, internship, classroom); Distinction between on the job and off the job training. Hindrances to training: brief explanation. Benefits of training to employer and employees.

(vi) Staff Morale

Meaning, definition and characteristics of staff morale; Morale Productivity Matrix (brief explanation of the four situations); factors influencing morale (morale depressants and stimulants: an understanding of how the same factor may lower or boost morale); methods of raising morale; indicators of low and high morale; advantages of high morale; disadvantages of low morale.

(vii) Staff Motivation

Meaning, definition and characteristics of staff motivation; difference between motivation and morale; importance of staff motivation to the employer and the employee ; factors influencing motivation: monetary and non-monetary incentives; differences between monetary and non-monetary incentives; Maslow's theory of the Hierarchy of Human Needs (explanation of the theory with the help of the pyramid, assumptions and criticism of the theory); Herzberg's Two-factor Theory (Motivation and Hygiene Factors).

(viii) Staff Remuneration

Meaning and definition of Staff remuneration, Methods of wage payment – Time Rate and Piece Rate System (An explanation of the two systems along with their merits, demerits and suitability, differences between the two); Pay Slip and Payroll - Meaning, Differences, Components, Specimens of both. Various staff benefits: Employee Provident Fund, National Pension System, Group Insurance (medical and life), encashment of leave, gratuity, (basic understanding only). Types of leaves (casual, medical/sick, earned / privilege, maternity/ paternity, sabbatical/ study, leave without pay: basic understanding only)

(ix) Staff Leadership

Meaning and definition of staff leadership; Distinction between Leadership and Management; Leadership styles: Autocratic, Democratic, Laissez-Faire (brief explanation, advantages, disadvantages and comparison between each style); Leadership continuum (brief description); Situational leadership (brief description); Blake & Mouton Managerial Grid (brief explanation).

(x) Staff Appraisal

Meaning and definition of Performance Appraisal and Potential Appraisal; Distinction between the two; Objectives and importance of Performance Appraisal, Methods of Performance Appraisal - merit grading, appraisal by results, appraisal by superior staff: self-appraisal; 360° appraisal (brief explanation of each method and their respective advantages and disadvantages).

(xi) Staff Promotion and Transfer

Staff Promotion - Meaning, definition, benefits and limitations of promotion; Open and Closed policy of promotion (meaning and differences); a brief understanding of the concept of Dry promotion and upgrading and distinction between the two; requirements of a sound promotion policy; Basis of promotion: seniority, merit, seniority-cum-merit (brief explanation of each and the advantages, disadvantages, comparison between seniority basis and merit basis.)

Staff Transfer: Meaning, definition and need for transfer; Types of transfers: replacement, versatility, remedial, production (meaning and relevance of each type).

(xii) Staff Separation

Meaning of Staff separation; means of staff separation: Retirement (Compulsory and Voluntary), Lay off, Retrenchment, Resignation, Suspension (Meaning and distinction only), Dismissal: grounds for dismissal, procedure for staff dismissal.

Exit Interview-Meaning and importance.

(xiii) Emerging trends in Human Resources

Flexible Hours, Permanent part time, Work from home, Retainership, Virtual teams, Self-managing teams (SMTs) - only meaning of the above terms.

2. Business Communication and Correspondence

(i) Business Communication

Meaning and definition of communication; importance of communication in business, elements of the Communication Process, Methods of communication: Oral, Written, Gestural, Visual (Meaning, advantages and disadvantages of all these methods), Difference between oral and written communication, Types of communication: On the basis of area of operation (Internal and External), on the basis of relationship (Formal and Informal), on the basis of direction (Horizontal, Vertical-upwards and downwards, Diagonal), Meaning, Advantages and Disadvantages of each; distinction between - Internal and External; Formal and Informal; Horizontal and Vertical Communication; Barriers to Communication (Semantic, Physical and Mechanical, Organisational, Socio-Psychological: meaning only, detailed explanation not required); overcoming the barriers to communication.

(ii) Business Correspondence

Need and functions of business correspondence.

Business Letters

Elements and contents of various business letters; types of letters: solicited and unsolicited letters of application for a job, along with drafting of biodata; Interview letter, Offer of Appointment, Letter of resignation, Letter of enquiry, Quotation letter, Order letter, Complaint letter, Reply to Complaint letter.

NOTE: Candidates should be able to draft all of the above types of letters, using the appropriate format.

Reports

Meaning and definition of Reports; types of reports: statutory, non- statutory, private, public, informational, interpretative, routine/periodic, special; brief explanation of each type of report; differences between statutory and non-statutory, private and public, informational and interpretative, routine/periodic and special report. Format of report (report writing not required).

(iii) Current trends in Business Communication: e-mail and video conferencing.

Meaning and uses of e-mail and video conferencing.

3. Business Size and Finance

(i) Various business entities

Meaning, definition and distinction between sole proprietorship, partnership, private limited company and public limited company.

(ii) Sources of business finance

A basic understanding of the following: Equity and preference shares, debentures and bonds, retained profits, public deposits, loans, trade credit, discounting of bills of exchange, global depository receipt, Angel investors, venture capitalists, crowd funding, peer to peer funding, factoring.

4. Globalisation and Recent Trends in Business

(i) Globalisation

Meaning, nature, opportunities and threats of globalization for business; brief understanding of how globalization has been instrumental in transforming the manner in which Business is conducted.

(ii) e-Business

Meaning, nature and importance of e- business to the buyer and to the seller.

(iii) Outsourcing

Concept of outsourcing; Parties involved – the outsourcer, the outsourced and the service provider – the respective advantages and disadvantages of each of the above.

(iv) Types of Outsourcing

Business Process Outsourcing (BPO), Knowledge Process Outsourcing (KPO), and Business Legal Process Outsourcing (LPO).

Basic understanding of the above.

(v) Online means of conducting business

Business to Consumer (B2C), Consumer to Consumer (C2C), Business to Business (B2B), Intra Business (Intra B) and, Business to Government (B2G), Government to Business (G2B).

Basic understanding of the above with a few examples.

5. Business Regulators and Intermediaries

(i) Regulators and Intermediaries

Meaning of the terms Regulators and Intermediaries.

(ii) Role of Regulators and Intermediaries

(a) Reserve Bank of India (RBI): Indian banks, foreign banks, Non-Banking Financial Companies (NBFC).

(b) Securities and Exchange Board of India (SEBI): stock exchanges, stock brokers, merchant bankers, depositories, mutual funds and credit rating agencies.

(c) Insurance Regulatory and Development Authority of India (IRDA): insurance companies, insurance agents and insurance brokers.

(d) Food Safety and Standards Authority of India (FSSAI): food processors, food packers.

(e) Bureau of Indian Standards (BIS): ISI mark given to industrial goods, consumer electrical goods, steel manufacturers.

Only a basic understanding of the roles of the above regulators and intermediaries.

PAPER II PROJECT WORK

20 Marks

Candidates will be expected to have completed two projects from any topic covered in Theory.

The project work will be assessed by the teacher and a Visiting Examiner appointed locally and approved by the Council.

Mark allocation for each Project [10 marks]:

Overall format	1 Mark
Content	4 Marks
Findings	2 Marks
Viva-voce based on the Project	3 Marks

Analysis of Pupil's Performance:
ISC Business Studies

Topics found difficult/confusing by candidates

TOPICS FOUND DIFFICULT BY STUDENTS

- Expansion of acronyms
- Gratuity
- Situational Leadership
- Appendix in a report
- Permanent Part Time
- E-Recruitment
- Morale productivity Matrix
- Selection as a negative process
- Group Insurance
- Assertion and reason
- Ways in which barriers to communication can be overcome
- Role of BIS
- Venture capitalist

CONCEPTS IN WHICH CANDIDATES GOT CONFUSED

- Types of Reports.
- Limitations/Need of Promotion
- Human Needs as given by Maslow
- Permanent Part Time/Flexible Hours/Part time
- Venture Capitalist/Angel Investors
- e-Recruitment/External Recruitment/e-Business
- Types/Methods of Communication
- Performance Appraisal/Potential Appraisal
- Hindrances/demerits of training
- G2B/B2G

SUGGESTIONS FOR CANDIDATES

- Gain conceptual clarity through practical examples.
- Read and understand the questions clearly before attempting to answer.
- Understand the requirements of the question (whether the answer is to be stated,explained, or named) and answer accordingly.
- Practice answering questions within the allocated time frame to improve time management during examinations. This involves strategizing which questions to attempt first and allocating appropriate time to each.
- Prior to the actual examinations, take mock tests under exam conditions to simulate the exam environment and gauge your preparedness.
- Regularly assess your progress, identify areas for improvement, and adapt your study strategies accordingly.
- Maintain a growth mindset and stay motivated throughout your preparation journey.
- While it is advisable to search on the internet, students must NOT forget the scope of syllabus as given by CISCE.
- Engage in group discussions with peers or join study groups to exchange ideas, clarify doubts, and reinforce learning. Teaching concepts to others can deepen your own understanding.
- Don't hesitate to seek guidance from teachers or online forums if you encounter difficulties with specific topics. Clearing doubts promptly prevents misconceptions from persisting.
- Stay informed about current affairs, business news, and case studies relevant to Business Studies. This not only enhances understanding but also prepares you for application-based questions in exams.
- Practice the previous years' ISC Question papers and Specimen Papers, and inculcate time management.

01

Introduction to HRM & Job and Manpower Planning

TREND ANALYSIS 5 YEARS

Average No. of Questions Across all Sets

		Types of Questions	2023	2020	2019	2018	2017
01	HRM	1 Mark	1	—	—	—	—
		2 Marks	—	—	—	—	—
		4 Marks	—	—	1	—	—
		6 Marks	—	—	—	—	—
		8 Marks	—	—	—	—	—
02	Job and Manpower Planning	1 Mark	1	—	—	—	—
		2 Marks	—	1	—	—	—
		4 Marks	1	1	—	—	—
		6 Marks	—	—	—	—	—
		8 Marks	—	—	—	—	—

Meaning and Definition of Human Resource Management (HRM)

Human resource management refers to that part of management which manages the people at work. It is the process which coordinates people within an organisation and helps both people and organisation to achieve each other's goal.

It is the comprehensive set of managerial activities and tasks concerned with procuring, developing, compensating, integrating and maintaining a workforce in ways that contribute to organisational effectiveness.

According to **Dale Yoder**, "The management of human resources is viewed as a system in which participants seek to attain both individual and group goals."

Characteristics of Human Resource Management

The following are the features or characteristics of human resource management

(i) It is people oriented. It covers all types of people at all levels in the organisation.

(ii) It is inherent in all organisations and at all levels.

(iii) It is a challenging job due to the dynamic nature of people.

(iv) It is an ongoing or never-ending exercise.

(v) It is individual oriented, i.e. under HRM every employee is considered as an individual.

(vi) It is concerned with developing potential of employees so that they get maximum satisfaction from their work.

(vii) It focuses on action rather than on record keeping or procedures.
(viii) It is future oriented.
(ix) It involves application of knowledge drawn from several disciplines like sociology, psychology, economics, etc.
(x) It is both science as well as an art.
(xi) It is relatively a new specialised area as compared to manufacturing and marketing.
(xii) Human resource managers contribute to the success and growth of an organisation by advising the operating department on human resource matters.
(xiii) It is the process of bringing people and organisation together, so that the goals of each are met.

Importance/Significance of Human Resource Management

The importance of human resource management can be seen in four contexts

Organisational	Professional	Social	Nation
Organisational effectiveness	Maximise the working potential	Enhance the dignity of labour	Overall economic growth
Employee commitment	Provide healthy working environment	Raise the standard of living	Increases GDP
Occupational safety	Effective team-work	Employment opportunities multiply	Utilisation of natural, physical and financial resources
Customer services	Boost confidence of people	Eliminate waste of human resources	Better employment rate

Meaning and Definition of Job and Manpower Planning

It is a continuous process of identifying human resource requirements for an organisation in terms of quality and quantity.

According to **Strainer**, "Manpower planning is a strategy for the acquisition, utilisation, improvement and preservation of an enterprise's human resources. It relates to establishing job specification or the quantitative requirements of job determining the number of personnel required and developing sources of manpower."

Components of Job and Manpower Planning

The following are the components of job and manpower planning

1. Job Analysis

In simple words, job analysis may be understood as a process of collecting information about a job. It is a systematic investigation of tasks, duties and responsibilities to perform a job.

According to **Flippo**, "Job analysis can be defined as the process of studying and collecting information relating to the operations and responsibilities of a specific job."

Relevancy/Importance of Job Analysis

Following points highlight the relevance of job analysis
(i) Job analysis determines the number and kind of people required in future.
(ii) It helps in selecting right employee and in right number.
(iii) It helps performance appraisal through fixing standard for work performance.
(iv) Compensation package of employee depends upon job evaluation that is done through job analysis.
(v) It ensures that all the duties that have to be done, are assigned to particular position.

Components of Job Analysis

The following are the two components of job analysis
(i) **Job Description** It gives information about the scope of job activities, major responsibilities and positioning of the job in the organisation. This information gives the worker analyst and supervisor with a clear idea of what the worker must do to meet the demand of the job.
According to **Edwin B. Flippo**, "The first and immediate product of job analysis is job description. As its little indicates this document is basically descriptive in nature and constitutes a record of existing and pertinent job facts."
It includes
- Job title/name of the job
- Working hours
- Duties and responsibilities
- Working conditions
- Salary and incentives

Relevancy/Importance of Job Description
- Orientation of new employees
- Clear explanation of requirement
- Differentiate the job from other jobs
- Better recruitment and selection

(ii) **Job Specification** It translates the job description in terms of the human qualifications, which are required for the performance of a job.

They are intended to serve as a guide in hiring and job evaluation. It includes knowledge, skill, ability, etc.

According to **Edwin B. Flippo**, "A job specification is a statement of minimum acceptable human qualities necessary to perform a job properly."

Relevancy/Importance of Job Specification

- Selection of most appropriate candidate
- Analysis of candidates
- Helpful in decision-making
- Fixes the responsibility

Difference between Job Description and Job Specification

Basis	Job Description	Job Specification
Meaning	It describes the job in terms of its title, duties and responsibilities.	It describes the requirement of job in terms of human qualification, needed for job.
Content	It includes job title, duties, responsibilities, working conditions, etc.	It includes knowledge, skills, abilities, qualification, etc.
Measures	It measures the tasks and responsibilities attached to the job.	It measures the capabilities that the job holder must possess to perform the job.
Benefit	It helps the worker analyst with a clear idea of what the worker must do to meet the demand of the job.	It helps the job seekers to analyse whether they are eligible for a particular job or not.

2. Job Enrichment

It is a way to motivate employees by giving them more responsibility and variety in their jobs. It includes the addition of some works previously executed by the supervisory level.

According to **Sirota** and **Wolform**, "Job enrichment is the designing of a job to provide a worker with great responsibility, more autonomy in carrying out that responsibility, closure a complete job and more timely feedback about his performance."

Relevancy/Importance of Job Enrichment

Following points highlight the relevance of job enrichment

(i) It motivates the workers to work more effectively by using their skills, capacities and abilities.
(ii) It improves the decision-making ability of employees in a systematic manner.
(iii) It reduces the workload of seniors.
(iv) It is a powerful method of employee empowerment.
(v) It reduces labour turnover, grievances and absenteeism in the organisation.
(vi) It creates 'sense of belonging to the organisation' among the employees.

3. Job Enlargement

It is developed to increase the total number of tasks that workers perform. It is an alternative to job specialisation that involves giving the employee more task to perform. It is horizontal in nature. It is done to keep workers from getting bored. It is different from job enrichment. Many organisations have used job enlargement, including IBM, AT &T, The U.S. Civil Service, etc.

Relevancy/Importance of Job Enlargement

Following points highlights the relevance of job enlargement

(i) It helps the organisation to improve and increase the skills of the employees.
(ii) It provides wide range of activities for employees.
(iii) It helps in full utilisation of both physical and mental abilities of employees.
(iv) It increases the degree of satisfaction among the employees of an organisation.
(v) It is an economical technique for organisation.

Difference between Job Enrichment and Job Enlargement

Basis	Job Enrichment	Job Enlargement
Meaning	It is the designing of a job to provide a worker with great responsibility.	It is the designing of a job to increase the total number of tasks that workers perform.
Supervision	Comparatively, less supervision of employee is required.	More supervision is required.
Purpose	It makes job more challenging.	It reduces boredom and monotony.
Nature	It is vertical in nature.	It is horizontal in nature.

4. Man Specification

It describes attributes (i.e. qualification, skills, experience, knowledge, etc) desired in a potential employee. It should be derived from job description. It is similar to a job description, but more specific. Once the man specification is complete, it becomes necessary to consider the sources from where such personnel will be forthcoming.

Relevancy/Importance of Man Specification

Following points highlight the relevance of man specification

(i) It allows the management to communicate the exact traits which company find desirable in their candidate.
(ii) It enables the management to assess each candidate fairly and objectively.
(iii) It helps job seekers to match themselves to the job role before applying for job.
(iv) It is the key tool of successful recruitment.
(v) It is helpful in organising and designing the new staff member's induction and training programme.

5. Manpower Estimation

It is very essential for HR manager to estimate the structure of its organisation at a given point of time. It involves the estimation of the quantity and quality of right kind of people or human force. It helps an organisation to retain the employees for long period and keep them functioning more efficiently and more productively and also at the reasonable cost. It is very useful to manage human resources in a better way with dynamic situations.

It includes

(i) Estimation of short, medium and long-term manpower needs.
(ii) A detailed job description.
(iii) Employees presently available in organisation.

Relevancy/Importance of Manpower Estimation

Following points highlight the relevance of manpower estimation

(i) It emphasis both the quantitative and the qualitative dimensions of human resources.
(ii) it provides smooth working even after expansion of the organisation.
(iii) It provides right people for right job.
(iv) It helps in achieving and maintaining production levels in an organisation.
(v) It facilitates organisations in devising training programmes to meet the diverse needs of employees.
(vi) It plays an active role in manpower planning.

PYQs Previous Years' Questions

1 Mark Questions

1. Which part of the management is concerned with the employees and their interrelationship within the organisation? *ISC 2023*

Ans Human resource management is concerned with the employees and their interrelationship within the organisation.

2. .... involves planning the requirement for staff in near future by the organisation. *ISC 2023*

Ans Manpower planning

3. Job specification is a written statement of the .... required for performing a job. *ISC Specimen 2023*

Ans skills, knowledge, abilities and other characteristics

4. The data collected through job analysis provides the basis for .... *ISC Sem I 2021*

(a) job description (b) job specification
(c) job enlargement (d) job enrichment

Ans (a) job description

5. Which one of the following is not a feature of human resource management? *ISC Sem I 2021*

(a) Pervasive function (b) Interdisciplinary function
(c) Staff function (d) Job oriented

Ans (d) Job oriented

6. Which one of the following is not a significance of human resource management? *ISC Sem I 2021*

(a) Professional significance
(b) National significance
(c) Social significance
(d) Environmental significance

Ans (d) Environmental significance

7. The role of human resource management in professional growth is to *ISC Sem I 2021*

(a) secure the willing co-operation of employees
(b) provide maximum opportunities for personal development of each employee
(c) help in speeding up the process of economic growth
(d) provide employment to people

Ans (b) provide maximum opportunities for personal development of each employee

8. Which one of the following options is a feature of human resource management? *ISC Sem I 2021*

(a) It is a method by which an organisation collects, maintains and reports information on people and jobs
(b) It aims to optimise the use of natural resources
(c) It is a process of bringing together people and an organisation so that the goals of both are achieved
(d) It benefits only the employer

Ans (c) It is a process of bringing together people and an organisation so that the goals of both are achieved

9. .... helps management to have the right number and the right kind of people at the right time and at the right place doing the right thing. *ISC Sem I 2021*

(a) Manpower estimation
(b) Recruitment
(c) Training (d) Placement

Ans (a) Manpower estimation

10. Job specification is another name for *ISC Sem I Specimen 2021*

(a) job analysis
(b) job description
(c) manpower estimation
(d) manpower specification

Ans (b) job description

11. A statement that describes the nature and contents of a job is called *ISC Sem I Specimen 2021*

(a) job analysis (b) job description
(c) job specification (d) job explanation

Ans (a) job analysis

12. .... includes compilation of qualifications and attributes needed for the job. *ISC Sem I Specimen 2021*

(a) Job analysis
(b) Job description
(c) Job specification
(d) Manpower estimation

Ans (c) Job specification

13. Human resource management is significant for an enterprise as *ISC Sem I Specimen 2021*

(a) it accelerates the process of economic growth
(b) it provides social and psychological satisfaction to people
(c) it helps develop a team of competent and dedicated employees
(d) All of the above

Ans (d) All of the above

14. One of the objective of human resource management is *ISC Sem I Specimen 2021*

(a) development of people (b) punishment of people
(c) adoption of people
(d) None of the above

Ans (a) development of people

15. Job enrichment involves *ISC Sem I Specimen 2021*

(a) increasing the depth of a job
(b) increasing the width of a job
(c) describing the nature and content of a job
(d) a formal and detailed study of the job

Ans (a) increasing the depth of a job

Concept Enhancer Job enrichment is that motivational tool which allows more decision making power and work related authority to employees.

16. Human resource management focuses on .... rather than on record keeping or procedures. *ISC Sem I Specimen 2021*

(a) action
(b) methods
(c) principles
(d) objectives

Ans (a) action

2 Marks Questions

1. Define human resource management. *ISC Specimen 2020, 2019*

Ans Human resource management is the comprehensive set of managerial activities and tasks concerned with procuring, developing, compensating, integrating and maintaining a workforce in ways that contribute to organisational effectiveness.

According to **Byars** and **Rue**, "Human resource management encompasses those activities designed to provide for and coordinate the human resources of an organisation."

2. List any two uses of conducting job analysis. *ISC 2020*

Ans Two uses of conducting job analysis are

(i) It determines the number and kind of people required in future.
(ii) It helps in selecting right employee and in right number.

4 Marks Questions

1. State any four differences between job enlargement and job enrichment. *ISC 2023*

Ans Differences between job enlargement and job enrichment are as follows

Basis	Job Enlargement	Job Enrichment
Meaning	It is the designing of a job to increase the total number of tasks that workers perform.	It is the designing of a job to provide a worker with great responsibility.
Nature	It is horizontal in nature.	It is vertical in nature.
Purpose	It reduces boredom and monotony.	It makes job more challenging.
Supervision	More supervision is required.	Comparatively, less supervision of employee is required.

2. State any two professional and any two social significances of human resource management. *ISC Specimen 2023*

Ans The professional significances of humnan resource management are

(i) It helps in maximising the working potential of the employees by providing a healthy working environment.

(ii) It boost the confidence of the people by placing them at the right place at the right time according to their qualification and work experience.

The social significances of human resource management are

(i) It raises the standard of living of the people by increasing the employment opportunities.

(ii) It eliminates the waste of human resources and enhance the dignity of labour by placing the right person at the right job.

3. What is meant by manpower estimation? Explain its relevance in human resource management. *ISC 2020*

Ans **Manpower estimation** It is very essential for H.R. manager to estimate the structure of an organisation at a given point of time. It involves the estimation of the quantity and quality of right kind of people or human force.

It helps an organisation to retain the employees for long period and keep them functioning more efficiently and more productively and also at the reasonable cost. It is very useful to manage human resource in a better way with dynamic situations.

The following points highlight the relevance of manpower estimation

(i) It emphasises both the quantitative (numbers) and the qualitative (nature of personnel) dimensions of human resources.

(ii) It provides smooth working even after expansion of the organisation.

(iii) It provides right people for right job.

(iv) It helps in achieving and maintaining production levels in an organisation.

(v) It facilitates organisations in devising training programmes to meet the diverse needs of employees.

(vi) Manpower estimation plays an active role in manpower planning.

4. Briefly explain the significance of human resource management to an enterprise. *ISC 2019*

Ans Significance of human resource management to an enterprise is as follows

(i) **Organisational effectiveness** It coordinates people within an organisation that helps in achieving organisational goals.

(ii) **Employee commitment** Through training, good compensation and motivation, human resource management system focuses on increasing employee commitment.

(iii) **Occupational safety** HRM hires reliable, trained and knowledgeable people to ensure occupational safety especially in case of manufacturing unit.

(iv) **Customer service** By improving physical work environment, employing supportive workforce and use of appropriate service delivery system, HRM enhance customer service.

Common Mistake Generally, students misunderstand this question in hurry and answer the question by giving common significance of HRM. Students are advisable to read question carefully and write correct significance of HRM related to category asked as it is categorised in different contexts.

Additional Questions

4 Marks Questions

1. Write an explanatory note on job analysis.

Ans In simple words, job analysis may be understood as a process of collecting information about a job. It is a systematic investigation of tasks, duties and responsibilities to perform a job.

The process of job analysis results in two sets of data

(i) Job description

(ii) Job specification

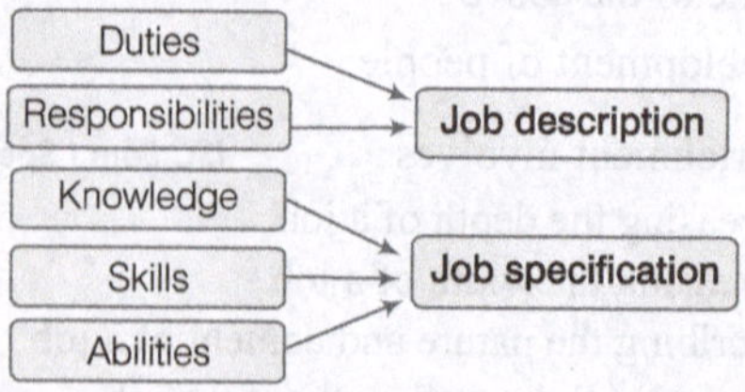

Job Analysis

Value Points

For getting maximum marks, following points can be included in the answer

- Meaning of job analysis
- Components of job analysis

2. Explain the term 'man specification'.

Ans It describes attributes (i.e. qualification, skills, experience, knowledge, etc) desired in a potential employee. It should be derived from job description. It is similar to a job description, but more specific in nature.

The area in which a detailed man specification can be outlined are

(i) Education and experience
(ii) Physical makeup
(iii) Level of general intelligence
(iv) Special aptitudes
(v) The degree of acceptability to others

3. State the features of human resource management.

Ans The following are the features of human resource management

(i) It is a continuous and never ending process.
(ii) It is a challenging job, due to dynamic nature of people.
(iii) It covers all levels of management and all categories of employees.
(iv) It is concerned with the employees both as individuals and as a group in attaining goals.
(v) It is concerned with developing the potential of employees.

4. Explain briefly the relevance of job analysis.

Ans The following points highlight relevance of job analysis

(i) **Human resource planning** Job analysis determines the number and kind of people required in future. It provides for the proper human resource planning.

(ii) **Recruitment and selection** It provides information regarding the required skills, qualifications, etc, for getting job. Therefore, job analysis helps in selecting right employee and in right number.

Relevance of Job Analysis
- Human resource planning
- Recruitment and selection
- Performance appraisal
- Compensation
- Safety and health
- Ensure complete assignment of duties

(iii) **Performance appraisal** It helps performance appraisal through fixing standard for work performance. Actual performance is compared with standards and becomes base for promotion and training.

(iv) **Compensation** Job evaluation is done through job analysis. Compensation package of employee depends upon job evaluation.

(v) **Safety and health** It provides an excellent opportunity to uncover and identify hazardous conditions and unhealthy environmental factors so that corrective measures can be taken.

(vi) **Ensure complete assignment of duties** It is also useful for ensuring that all the duties that have to be done are in fact assigned to particular positions.

5. Explain the importance of job specification.

Ans The following points highlight the importance of job specification

(i) Job specification helps in selecting the most appropriate candidate for a particular job.
(ii) Job specification helps candidates analyse whether they are eligible to apply for a particular job or not.
(iii) Job specification helps in selection process because it offers a clear set of minimum qualification for an individual to be hired for a particular job.
(iv) Job specification helps the H.R. manager to take decision regarding transfer, promotion, training and giving extra benefits to the employees.
(v) Job specification helps in fixing the responsibility which includes supervision of other employees, responsibility for production, responsibility for the safety of others and responsibility for preventing any other losses.

6. Write a short note on job specification.

Ans Job specification translates the job description in terms of the human qualifications, which are required for the performance of a job. They are intended to serve as a guide in hiring and job evaluation. Job specification is a written statement of qualifications, traits, physical and mental characteristics that an individual must possess to perform the job duties and discharge responsibilities.

Usually, this information includes the following

(i) **Knowledge** A collection of discrete, but related facts and information about a particular domain, acquired through formal education or training or accumulated through specific experiences.
(ii) **Skill** A practiced act.
(iii) **Ability** The stable capacity to engage in a specific behaviour.
(iv) **Other characteristics** Personality variables, interests, training and experiences.

7. Explain the meaning and relevance of job description.

Ans **Meaning of job description** It gives information about the scope of job activities, major responsibilities and positioning of the job in the organisation.

This information gives the worker, analyst and supervisor with a clear idea of what the worker must do to meet the demand of the job.

(i) The job description should indicate the scope and nature of the work including all important relationships.

(ii) The job description should be clear regarding the work of the position, duties, etc.

Relevance of job description The relevance of job description are as follows

(i) Job description helps in orientation of new employees, to learn duties and responsibilities of job.

(ii) Job description clearly explains all the requirements, objectives and goals that company wants from the employee to perform the job.

(iii) The main relevance of writing a job description is to differentiate the job from other jobs and state its outer limits.

(iv) It helps in the development of job specification.

(v) It helps in better recruitment and selection.

6/8 Marks Questions

1. What is meant by HRM? Explain any three importance of human resource.

Ans **Meaning of human resource management** Human resource management is the comprehensive set of managerial activities and tasks concerned with procuring, developing, compensating, integrating and maintaining a workforce in ways that contribute to organisational effectiveness.

Importance of human resource Following are the importance of human resource

(i) Human resources along can produce an output larger than the input. It is often said that all development comes from the human mind. It is possible due to creative skills of manpower.

(ii) Human resources are the only assets that appreciate over a period, while physical assets (i.e machine, equipments, etc) just depreciate with years.

Human resources are the game changer for every organisation in their growth.

(iii) It handles all physical (i.e. machine, building, etc) and financial (i.e. capital) resources in an organisation.

The plan and policies framed by the organisation from time-to-time are translated into reality by human resources only because they are active resources while others are inactive.

2. On behalf of a company, draft a job description for the post of junior accountant.

Ans A job description for the post of junior accountant as

Ram Industries Limited www.ramindustries.com

Job title	Junior Accountant	Job Number-815
Department	Finance	Grade -C
Reporting	Finance Manager	Date - 01-05-2023 Location - Delhi
Job summary	The junior accountant reports to finance manager and will be responsible for the function of accounting duties pertaining to organisation - creditors, debtors, cash, banking account, statutory returns and monthly reporting.	
Tasks and responsibilities	• Customer invoicing • Supplier payments and expenses • Reconciliations of key accounts • Processing of payroll • Budgets and other financial statements	
Required knowledge, skills, abilities	• Computer knowledge • Mathematical skills • Sound written and verbal communication skills • Self directed	
Education and work experience	• Degree in commerce/finance • Approximately 4-6 years proper accounting experience	
To apply	Interested candidates with relevant experience are to e-mail their CV's and covering letter to hr@ril.org	
Salary	INR ₹ 3,00,000 - 4,00,000 p.a.	

3. What is the importance of job enrichment and job enlargement?

Ans The following points highlight the importance of job enrichment

(i) It motivates the workers to work more effectively by using their skills, capacities, abilities, etc.

(ii) It improves the decision-making ability of employee in a systematic manner.

(iii) It reduces the workload of seniors.

(iv) It is a powerful method of employee empowerment.

(v) It reduces labour turnover, grievances and absenteeism in the organisation.

(vi) It creates 'sense of belonging to the organisation' among the employees.

The following points highlight the importance of job enlargement

(i) It helps the organisation to improve and increase the skills of the employees.

(ii) It provides wide range of activities for employees.

(iii) It helps in full utilisation of both physical and mental abilities of employees.

(iv) It increases the degree of satisfaction among the employees of an organisation.

(v) With job enlargement, the employee rarely needs to acquire new skills to carry out the additional task. So, it is economical technique for organisation.

4. State the relevance of man specification and manpower estimation.

Ans The following points highlight the relevance of man specification

(i) It allows the management to communicate the exact traits which company find desirable in their candidate.

(ii) It enables the management to assess each candidate fairly and objectively.

(iii) It helps job seekers to match themselves to the job role before applying for job.

(iv) It is helpful in organising and designing the new staff member's induction and training programme.

For relevance of manpower estimation, refer to Q. No. 3 of 4 marks questions on page 6.

Case Based Question

Case 1

Madhu and Suman are working for ABC and Co. as associate partners. Madhu has been promoted as partner. Suman continues to be an associate partner. However, Suman has been given charge to business all over India.

ISC Sem I 2021

(i) The change in Madhu's job profile is termed as ....

(a) job enlargement (b) job enrichment
(c) job analysis (d) job specification

Ans (b) job enrichment

(ii) The change in Suman's job profile is termed as ....

(a) job enlargement (b) job enrichment
(c) job analysis (d) job specification

Ans (a) job enlargement

(iii) One of the features of job enlargement is that

(a) it is a formal and detailed study of a job.
(b) it facilitates training of people.
(c) it involves adding more tasks of a similar nature to the job.
(d) it makes the job more challenging and satisfying.

Ans (c) it involves adding more tasks of a similar nature to the job.

(iv) One of the features of job enrichment is that

(a) it is a formal and detailed study of a job.
(b) it facilitates training of people.
(c) it involves adding more tasks of a similar nature to the job.
(d) it makes the job more challenging and satisfying.

Ans (d) it makes the job more challenging and satisfying.

CHAPTER TEST

01 Mark Questions

1. Which of the job design tool is defined as a portrayal of the tasks, responsibilities, duties and functions of a job?

2. Mr. Kavish Kumar has been working as 'team-lead' of the product development department of an MNC for 7 years. In order to increase the scope of his job, the company decided to get him involved in the process of designing the market strategies for a new product being launched by the company. What is this type of job design adopted by the company known as?

3. The process of bringing people and organisations together so that the goals of each are met, is called ....
   (a) career planning
   (b) employee welfare
   (c) human resource management
   (d) training

4. Job descriptions should be reviewed by ....
   (a) supervisors
   (b) human resource department
   (c) job incumbents
   (d) All of the above

5. .... helps the organisations in utilising human resources better through effective planning and timely execution.
   (a) Performance appraisal (b) Organisational analysis
   (c) Job analysis
   (d) Manpower planning

6. State whether the following are true or false.
   (i) Human resource management is future oriented.
   (ii) Job analysis is an informal examination of jobs.
   (iii) Job specification tells what kind of person to recruit and for what qualities that person should be tested.
   (iv) Manpower estimation involves the estimation of the quantity and quality of right kind of people.

7. .... provides information on the human attributes in terms of education, skills, aptitudes and experience necessary to perform a job effectively.

8. The survival and growth of the organisation depends largely on the competence and ....

02 Marks Questions

9. State any two uses of manpower-estimation in an organisation.

10. 'Man specification and job description, both are same'. Comment.

11. State any two relevance of job enlargement.

04 Marks Questions

12. Give any four differences between job specification and job description.

13. Explain the relevance of the following in job and manpower planning
    (i) Job analysis
    (ii) Manpower estimation

14. State any four characteristics of HRM.

06/08 Marks Questions

15. With reference to job analysis, explain the following
    (i) Duties
    (ii) Responsibilities
    (iii) Knowledge

16. (i) Explain human resources management.
    (ii) State any three significance of human resources management to organisation and to nation.

17. Explain any four components of job and manpower planning.

Answers

1. Job description
2. Job enlargement
3. (c) human resource management
4. (d) All of the above
5. (d) Manpower planning
6. (i) True (ii) False
(iii) True (iv) True
7. Job specification
8. effective management

02

Staff Recruitment and Selection

TREND ANALYSIS 5 YEARS

Average No. of Questions Across all Sets

		Types of Questions	2023	2020	2019	2018	2017
01	Staff Recruitment	1 Mark	—	—	—	—	—
		2 Marks	—	—	1	1	—
		4 Marks	—	—	1	—	—
		6 Marks	—	—	—	—	—
		8 Marks	1	1	—	—	—
02	Staff Selection	1 Mark	1	—	—	—	—
		2 Marks	—	1	—	—	—
		4 Marks	1	1	—	—	—
		6 Marks	—	—	—	1	1
		8 Marks	—	—	1	1	—

Recruitment and selection are the two crucial steps in human resource process and are often used interchangeably. There is, however a fine distinction between the two steps.

Recruitment is the process by which a large number of prospective candidates are attracted by various methods to apply for the jobs, while selection is the process of choosing the right candidate from the pool of many individuals.

TOPIC 1

Staff Recuitment

Meaning and Definition of Staff Recruitment

Staff recruitment is a process of discovering the source of manpower to meet the requirements of an organisation. It is considered as a positive process. It means the process of searching for prospective employees and stimulating them to apply for jobs in an organisation. In recruitment process, the potential candidates are discovered and attracted to fill the vacant positions of an organisation.

Appropriate sources of employees are identified and more-and-more people are encouraged to apply for the post, and thus, it is considered as a positive process. Its aim is to develop and maintain adequate sources of manpower from which selection can be done.

According to **Dale Yoder**, "Recruitment is a means to satisfy the manpower requirements of the organisation.

It involves locating various sources from where the required worker can be obtained and then using all possible tactics to obtain as many applications for the jobs as possible, because more the number of applicants, better would be the selection of the employees."

Characteristics of Staff Recruitment

The following are the characteristics of staff recruitment

(i) It attracts and encourages more-and-more candidates to apply in the organisation.

(ii) It determines present and future requirements of the organisation for manpower.

(iii) It is a positive approach because it attracts as many candidates as possible.

(iv) It is the process which links the employers with employees.

(v) It is a complex job that involves lots of factors i.e. nature of job, company profile, etc.

(vi) It searches the talent globally and not just within the country.

(vii) It increases the pool of prospective candidates at minimum cost.

(viii) It can be done either from inside or from outside the organisation.

Sources of Staff Recruitment

Employee may be recruited either from within the organisation or from outside. Therefore, there are two main sources of recruitment, *viz.* internal sources and external sources.

1. Internal Sources

Recruitment which is made from the organisation's existing workforce is called 'internal recruitment'. Some of the prominent sources of internal recruitment are given below

(i) **Promotion** It refers to shifting of an employee to a higher job position. It provides greater autonomy and boosts the morale of employees. However, time bound promotions may make the employees complacent.

(ii) **Transfer** It refers to shifting of an employee from one job to another or one department to another. It helps in training of workers and fulfil the deficiency of one department by the surplus of another. But frequent transfers may sometimes lead to reduced productivity.

(iii) **Ex-employees** Ex-employees of the organisation may be re-employed. An advantage with this source is that the performance of these people is already known.

(iv) **Recommendation by employees** The present employees may recommend their neighbours, friends and relatives for vacant job positions. Such candidates are reliable and proved to be good employees for the organisation. They get easily adjusted and acts as a costless source of recruitment for the company.

Merits of Internal Recruitment

The main merits of internal recruitment are

(i) It offers wonderful opportunities for the current staff to further enhance their careers.

(ii) Internal recruitment could also be a great way of retaining those workers who may have been considering to resign from the company.

(iii) This is advantageous because the cost of training and selection is less.

(iv) It helps to motivate employees and enhance their loyalty towards the organisation.

Demerits of Internal Recruitment

The main demerits of internal recruitment are

(i) It places heavy burden on training, if an unsuitable person is transferred to an important department.

(ii) The spirit of competition is hampered among the employees.

(iii) Lesser choice in case of existing firm, while a new enterprise cannot use internal source.

(iv) There may be favouritism and thereby creating an environment of politics.

(v) There is no infusion of new blood and creative ideas into the organisation.

2. External Sources

Recruitment which are made from the sources outside the organisation is called 'external recruitment'. Some of the prominent sources of external recruitment are specified below

(i) **Advertisements** Large organisations usually prefer advertisements as a source of attracting large number of candidates for a vacant job position. It is useful when the company wants a wide choice for selection, fresh talent and employees for blue collar jobs. But it suffers from the limitation of high cost.

It also generates a large number of ineligible candidates, increasing cost and time involved in their screening.

(ii) **Educational institutions/Campus recruitment** Many big organisations have close contact with colleges, universities and institutions, from where they get fresh candidates in a cost-effective manner.

(iii) **Casual callers** Many business organisations keep a database of unsolicited applicants, i.e. casual callers in their files. This source of recruitment is generally resorted by manufacturing organisations to fill up vacancies at the labour level. It is an inexpensive method of recruitment.

(iv) **Gate hiring** It is low cost method to fill casual vacancies. Under this method, job seekers present themselves at the factory gate and offer their labour services on a daily basis. It is used by small-scale sector in India.

(v) **Employment exchange** These are set up by the Government of India to match personnel demand and supply. But the records of such exchanges are often out of date.

(vi) **Employment agencies/Placement agencies** Private employment agencies provide eligible candidates to the organisation and job information to candidates for a nominal fee.

(vii) **Labour contractors** They have close contact with labourers in rural areas and supply large workforce on demand. But if the organisation gets into a dispute with the contractor, the whole workforce quits.

Merits of External Recruitment

Following are the merits of external recruitment

(i) With the availability of large pool of qualified candidates, the selection process becomes more competitive in choosing the best suited candidate.

(ii) External recruitment facilitates the entry of fresh talent in an organisation. It encourages the inflow of new ideas, knowledge and skills required to perform the tasks.

(iii) External recruitment creates an environment for healthy competition in between internal employees and external members, who are supposed to be more trained and efficient.

(iv) There is introduction of new idea and fresh blood in the organisation.

Demerits of External Recruitment

Demerits of external recruitment are

(i) External recruitment is expensive in the sense that it requires an extra cost for vacancy announcement, arrangements for employment, etc.

(ii) External recruitment follows a long process. Various activities such as vacancy announcement, application collection, review of application forms, selection process, etc need to be performed before the placement of the candidate.

(iii) The fresh candidates may not be suitable for the job, due to the limited information about outsiders.

(iv) There may be dissatisfaction among existing staff, as their chances of promotion extincts.

Difference between Internal and External Sources of Recruitment

Basis	Internal sources	External sources
Meaning	It refers to recruitment from within the organisation.	It refers to recruitment from outside the organisation.
Time involved	It involves lesser time of managers.	It involves more time of managers.
Cost	It is an inexpensive method of recruitment.	It is a costly method of recruitment.
Effect on existing staff	It enhances morale and motivation of the existing staff.	It creates dissatisfaction among the existing staff.
Scope of new blood	There is no scope of introducing fresh talent into the organisation.	There is a greater scope of introducing fresh talent into the organisation.
Training requirement	Induction training is not required.	Induction training is required.

E-recruitment: Concept

E-recruitment is the process of stimulating people to apply through web based resources (i.e. internet) for a vacant job position in the organisation. Now-a-days, e-recruitment is widely used by both recruiters and job seekers across the world. It is also referred to as online recruitment or internet recruiting.

According to **Wolfswinkel, Joost** and **Furtmuller, Elfi** and **Wildersom, Celeste (2010)**, "E-recruitment is the online attraction and identification of potential employees using corporate or commercial recruiting websites, electronic advertisements on other websites, or an arbitrary combination of these channels including optional methods such as remote interviews and assessments, smart online research agents or interactive communication tools between recruiter and applicant."

Benefits of E-recruitment

The following are the benefits of e-recruitment

(i) **Cost reduction** E-recruitment reduces the cost of recruitment because it does not use paper while traditional method is paper based.

(ii) **Save time** Job posting, applicant response and processing of resumes is done faster under e-recruitment.

(iii) **User satisfaction** It increase the efficiency of recruitment process which includes user satisfaction (i.e. recruiters as well as job seekers).

(iv) **Global reach** It attracts the job seekers from any part of the world.

(v) **More opportunities** Opportunities are unlimited for both recruiters as well as employees and can be grabbed within a fraction of clicks.

(vi) **Focus on other issues** It enables human resource manager to focus on other strategic issues like planning and policy formulation.

(vii) **Confidentiality** Both recruiters and job seekers can elect to maintain their confidentiality.

Limitations of E-recruitment

The following are the limitations of e-recruitment

(i) **Impersonal** E-recruitment lacks a personal touch between employers and job seekers. There are a lot of specialised jobs that require one-to-one meeting.

(ii) **Increasing number of applicants** Employers spend a great deal of time in screening the candidates through resumes.

(iii) **Fraudulent candidates** Some applicants may be fake. They may want to get information about the company.

(iv) **Quality of website** If website is poorly designed, outdated or slow speed, the candidates will not even bother responding to company notification.

(v) **Outdated job postings** Often, outdated jobs are not removed from website which misleads to job seekers.

(vi) **Knowledge of internet** E-recruitment may exclude who do not have access to internet and employers may lose some of the most potentially effective candidates.

Sources of E-recruitment

The following are the sources of e-recruitment

1. **Internet** (External Source) It is a network of computers which is available for all. Internet is the main source of e-recruitment.

   Benefits of internet are

   (i) Time saving (ii) Global reach
   (iii) Filters according to criteria
   (iv) Abundance of opportunities

   Limitations of internet are

   (i) Technical issues
   (ii) Fradulent candidates
   (iii) Rise in competition
   (iv) Lack of personal touch

2. **Intranet** (Internal Source) It is private network available only to those with the company. It can be considered as internal source of e-recruitment. It is accessed through login details i.e. user id, password, etc.

   Benefits of intranet are

   (i) Help employees to find information
   (ii) Provide organisational clarity
   (iii) Improves employees engagement
   (iv) Better sharing of information

   Limitations of intranet are

   (i) Security breach
   (ii) Heavy load of information
   (iii) Complex implementation process
   (iv) High maintenance

PYQs Previous Years' Questions

1 Mark Questions

1. Which one of the following is a benefit of e-recruitment? *ISC Specimen 2023*

   (a) The cost of recruitment per candidate is high
   (b) It requires investment in creating websites and portals
   (c) It weeds out the unqualified candidates through filters in the system
   (d) Trade unions support e-recruitment

Ans (c) It weeds out the unqualified candidates through filters in the system

2. Which one of the following is a limitation of internal source of recruitment? *ISC Sem I 2021*

   (a) It leads to high labour turnover
   (b) It leads to low labour turnover
   (c) It is an expensive source of recruitment
   (d) It is an incomplete source of recruitment

Ans (d) It is an incomplete source of recruitment

3. Identify the limitation of e-recruitment from the following options. *ISC Sem I 2021*

   (a) The cost of recruitment per candidate is low
   (b) Less time is required for recruitment
   (c) Both the employer and job seeker must have access to the internet
   (d) People with desired qualities cannot be recruited

Ans (c) Both the employer and job seeker must have access to the internet

4. .... is suitable for filling the vacancies for higher positions. **ISC Sem I 2021**

(a) Direct recruitment (b) A labour contractor
(c) Campus recruitment (d) A placement agency

Ans (d) A placement agency

5. Under which source of recruitment, does an organisation maintain a data base of unsolicited applicants? **ISC Sem I 2021**

(a) Direct recruitment (b) Casual callers
(c) Labour contractors (d) Advertisement

Ans (b) Casual callers

6. Recommendations by employees is a good source of recruitment as **ISC Sem I 2021**

(a) this method gives a wide choice
(b) preliminary screening is not required
(c) this method reduces labour turnover and absenteeism
(d) it is a two-way process

Ans (b) preliminary screening is not required

7. Recruitment is a .... process. **ISC Sem I 2021**

(a) day-to-day (b) negative
(c) positive (d) derogatory

Ans (c) positive

8. .... is undertaken through the organisation's own website. **ISC Sem I 2021**

(a) Internal recruitment (b) External recruitment
(c) Recruitment through internet
(d) Recruitment through intranet

Ans (d) Recruitment through intranet

9. Gate hiring is done for .... workers. **ISC Sem I 2021**

(a) unskilled and semi-skilled
(b) semi-skilled and skilled
(c) highly skilled (d) experienced

Ans (a) unskilled and semi-skilled

10. A linking activity that brings together those with jobs and those seeking jobs is called **ISC Sem I Specimen 2021**

(a) recruitment (b) selection
(c) employment (d) advertisement

Ans (a) recruitment

11. Under which of the following methods of recruitment, a notice is placed on the notice board of the enterprise specifying details of the job available? **ISC Sem I Specimen 2021**

(a) Casual callers (b) Advertisement
(c) Direct recruitment (d) Web publishing

Ans (c) Direct recruitment

12. Which of the following is also known as 'unsolicited applicants'? **ISC Sem I Specimen 2021**

(a) Casual callers
(b) Placement agencies
(c) Employment exchange
(d) None of the above

Ans (a) Casual callers

13. Campus recruitment proves to be beneficial for **ISC Sem I Specimen 2021**

(a) the institute where the student is studying
(b) the students
(c) the organisation appointing students
(d) All of the above

Ans (d) All of the above

14. The external sources of recruitment suffer from which of the following limitations? **ISC Sem I Specimen 2021**

(a) It is time consuming and expensive
(b) No fresh ideas are brought in
(c) It is an incomplete method of recruitment
(d) None of the above

Ans (a) It is time consuming and expensive

15. Employment exchanges run by the government are a good source of external recruitment because **ISC Sem I Specimen 2021**

(a) they have updated records of candidates
(b) they are a good source of recruitment for professionals
(c) they are a cheap source of recruitment
(d) the government takes guarantee of the candidates enrolled in the employment exchange

Ans (d) the government takes guarantee of the candidates enrolled in the employment exchange

16. One of the major benefits of internal recruitment is that **ISC Sem I Specimen 2021**

(a) it provides a wide choice
(b) it is an incomplete source of recruitment
(c) it is a two way process
(d) it is a cheap source of recruitment

Ans (d) it is a cheap source of recruitment

17. E-recruitment is gaining popularity because **ISC Sem I Specimen 2021**

(a) it can be done for any kind of job – unskilled, semiskilled and professionals
(b) a wide choice of candidates is available
(c) no amount of money needs to be spent by the recruiter and or candidate
(d) it boosts the morale of the existing employees

Ans (b) a wide choice of candidates is available

2 Marks Questions

1. Name the two sources of e-recruitment. Briefly explain any one of them. **ISC 2019**

Ans Sources of e-recruitment are

(i) Internet (External source)

(ii) Intranet (Internal source)

Intranet is the private network available only to those with the company. It is accessed through login details, i.e. user id, password etc.

> **Common Mistake** Students misunderstand between source of recruitment and sources of e-recruitment. Many students answer this question by writing two sources *viz.* internal and external but this question asks about the sources of e-recruitment that are-Internet and Intranet.

2. What is meant by unsolicited applications? **ISC 2018**

Ans Candidates who keep approaching companies for work are called at the time of recruitment. It is also referred to as 'casual callers'.

This provides a costless source of recruitment to organisation.

The number of such applications depends on

(i) Image of company

(ii) Economic condition of company

(iii) Job seeker's perception about company

(iv) Nature of job

3. Define recruitment. **ISC 2016**

Ans According to **Dale Yoder**, "Recruitment is a means to satisfy the manpower requirements of the organisation. It involves locating various sources from where the required worker can be obtained and then using all possible tactics to obtain as many applications for the jobs as possible because more the number of applicants, better would be the selection of the employees."

4. 'Recruitment is a two way process'. Explain. **ISC 2015**

Ans Recruitment is a two way process. It involves a recruiter and a recruitee. Just as the recruiter has a choice whom to recruit or not, similarly the prospective employee can choose for which organisation to apply for a job.

> **Value Points**
> For getting maximum marks, following terms should be included in the answer
> • Recruiter • Recruitee

5. What are the benefits of campus recruitment? **ISC 2015**

Ans Following are the benefits of campus recruitment

(i) This method helps in the recruitment of well-educated young persons.

(ii) It is an inexpensive method of recruitment.

6. Give two points of distinction between external sources and internal sources of recruitment. **ISC 2014**

Ans Difference between internal source and external source are

Basis	Internal source	External source
Meaning	It is concerned with recruiting people internally through transfers and promotions.	It is concerned with recruiting people externally through advertisements, employment exchange, etc.
Time taken	It is a quick process.	It is a lengthy process.

7. Explain the importance of campus recruitment as one of the sources of recruitment. **ISC 2013**

Ans In search of professionals, companies rely on campus recruitment. It is a new method introduced for recruiting professionals from campuses of technical and management institutes. The recruits have technical knowledge, are talented and infuse fresh blood for the growth of an organisation. This source is economical too.

8. State two merits of internal recruitment. **ISC 2010**

Ans Merits of internal recruitment are

(i) It offers wonderful opportunities for the current staff to further enhance their careers.

(ii) Internal recruitment could also be a great way of retaining talent pool and minimise labour turnover and absenteeism.

9. State two disadvantages of using advertisements as a source of recruitment. **ISC 2009**

Ans Disadvantages of using advertisement as a source of recruitment

(i) Recruiting through advertisements prove to be costly.

(ii) Sometimes, it creates a pool of applications of irrelevant and unwanted persons thus, results in being time consuming.

10. Justify how recommendations from current employees are an excellent source of recruitment. **ISC 2009**

Ans Selection is a very crucial process, but if the candidates capabilities, skills, aptitude and strength is known by someone, then it proves to be fruitful for an organisation.

Recommendation from existing employees helps in creating trust and also facilitates a fast hiring process in an organisation.

11. Define internal source of recruitment. *ISC 2007*

Ans Internal source of recruitment is the process of finding employees from the existing workforce. This can be done in the organisation with the help of two methods *viz.* transfers and promotions.

12. List any two differences between promotion and transfer. *ISC 2006*

Ans Two differences between promotion and transfer are

(i) Promotion is vertical shifting of employees, while transfer is horizontal shifting of employees.

(ii) Promotion involves change in authority and remuneration as well, while transfer involves only a change in work.

4 Marks Questions

1. What is campus recruitment? How does campus recruitment benefit the students as well as business houses? *ISC 2019*

Ans Campus recruitment is the external source of recruitment where senior managers of organisations visit professional colleges, technical institutes and educational institutes to recruit students who are pursuing their studies and about to complete the course as fresh candidate with latest knowledge.

Benefits to business

(i) They get fresh candidates in a cost-effective manner.

(ii) Candidates can be moulded according to requirement of organisation.

Benefits to students

(i) They get exposure just after the studies.

(ii) They get nurture their existing skill set.

Value Points

For getting maximum marks, few key-words should be included in the answer

- Colleges and institutes
- students pursuing studies and about to complete

2. Write an explanatory note on 'campus recruitment'. *ISC 2008*

Ans Many big organisations have close contact with colleges, universities and institutions, from where they get fresh candidates in a cost-effective manner. Candidates are selected after a rigorous selection process including a series of tests, group discussions and interviews.

It is ideal for entry level managerial and professionals jobs in management, engineering, pharmacy, biotechnology, etc.

Campus recruitment is most popular with many of the western countries. e.g. The USA, UK, etc. Now a days, large and medium organisations in India, send their teams to various universities and professionals institutions for selecting the fresh graduates.

3. Discuss any two advantages and disadvantages of external method of recruitment. *ISC 2004*

Ans Advantages of external recruitment are

(i) With the availability of large pool of qualified candidates, the selection process becomes more competitive in choosing the best suited candidate.

(ii) External recruitment facilitates the entry of fresh talent in an organisation. It encourages the inflow of new ideas, knowledge and skills required to perform the tasks.

Disadvantages of external recruitment are

(i) External recruitment is expensive in the sense that it requires an extra cost for vacancy announcement, arrangements for employment, etc.

(ii) External recruitment follows a long process. Various activities such as vacancy announcement, application collection, review of application forms, selection process, etc need to be performed before the placement of the candidate.

4. Discuss any two advantages and disadvantages of internal method of recruitment. *ISC 2004*

Ans Advantages of internal recruitment are

(i) It offers wonderful opportunities for the current staff to further enhance their careers.

(ii) Internal recruitment could also be a great way of retaining talent pool and minimise labour turnover and absenteeism.

Disadvantages of internal recruitment are

(i) It places heavy burden on training, if an unsuitable person is transferred to an important department.

(ii) It may lead to favouritism as one gives chances or opportunities to his or her favourite employee.

6/8 Marks Questions

1. Explain any four methods of external recruitment. *ISC 2023*

Ans Prominent sources of external recruitment are

(i) **Advertisements** Large organisations usually prefer advertisements as a source of attracting large number of candidates for a vacant job position.

It is useful when the company wants a wide choice for selection, fresh talent and employees for blue collar jobs. But it suffers from the limitation of high cost. It also generates a large number of ineligible candidates, increasing cost and time involved in their screening.

(ii) **Educational institutions/ Campus recruitment** Many big organisations have close contact with colleges, universities and institutions, from where they get fresh candidates in a cost-effective manner.

> **External Sources of Recruitment**
> - Advertisements
> - Educational institutions/Campus recruitment
> - Casual callers
> - Gate hiring

(iii) **Casual callers** Many business organisations keep a database of unsolicited applicants, i.e. casual callers in their files. This source of recruitment is generally resorted by manufacturing organisations to fill up vacancies at the labour level. It is an inexpensive method of recruitment.

(iv) **Gate hiring** It is low cost method to fill casual vacancies. Under this method, job seekers present themselves at the factory gate and offer their labour services on a daily basis. It is used by small-scale sector in India.

2. Briefly explain the four internal sources of recruitment. *ISC 2020*

Ans The important internal sources of recruitment are

(i) **Promotion** It means shifting an employee to a higher post carrying higher salary, status and responsibility. It is a vertical shift of employees.

(ii) **Transfer** It refers to shifting an employee to a similar job with no change in salary, status and responsibility. It is a horizontal shift of employees.

(iii) **Ex-employees** Ex-employees of the organisation may be re-employed. An advantage with this source is that the performance of these people is already known.

(iv) **Recommendation of employees** The present employees may recommend their neighbour, friends and relatives for vacant job positions. Such candidates are reliable and prove to be good employees for the organisation. They get easily adjusted and acts a costless source of recruitment for the company.

3. What is meant by e-recruitment? Briefly explain any three benefits and any three limitations of the same. *ISC Specimen 2019*

Ans E-recruitment is the process of stimulating people to apply through web based resources (i.e. internet) for a vacant job position in the organisation.

Now-a-days, e-recruitment is widely used by both recruiters and job seekers across the world. It is also referred to as online recruitment or internet recruiting.

The following are the benefits of e-recruitment

(i) **Cost reduction** E-recruitment reduces the cost of recruitment because it does not use paper while traditional method is paper based.

(ii) **Save time** Job posting, applicant response and processing of resumes is done faster under e-recruitment.

(iii) **User satisfaction** It increase the efficiency of recruitment process which includes user satisfaction (i.e. recruiters as well as job seekers).

The following are the limitations of e-recruitment

(i) **Impersonal** E-recruitment lacks a personal touch between employers and job seekers. There are a lot of specialised jobs that require one-to-one meeting.

(ii) **Increasing number of applicants** Employers spend a great deal of time in screening the candidates through resumes.

(iii) **Fraudulent candidates** Some applicants may be fake. They may want to get information about the company.

4. Filling vacancies from within the organisation has some merits as well as demerits. Briefly explain any four such merits and any four demerits. *ISC 2016*

Or State three advantages and three disadvantages of internal recruitment. *ISC 2008*

> **KEY IDEA**
> Filling vacancies from within the organisation is referred as internal recruitment.

Ans Filling vacancies from within the organisation is referred to as 'internal recruitment'.

Four merits of internal recruitment are discussed below

(i) **Motivation to employees to improve their performance** Internal recruitment through promotion helps in improving the motivation, loyalty and satisfaction level of employees because a promotion to a higher level may lead to boost employee's morale.

(ii) **Simplifies the process of selection and placement** Internal recruitment simplifies the process of selection and placement by evaluating the candidates, who are already working in the organisation more accurately and economically. This is a more reliable way of recruitment as the candidates are already known to the organisation.

(iii) **Less costly** It is a less costly source of recruitment, as no time and money has to be spent on advertising vacancies or on conducting tests and interviews. Also, people recruited from within the organisation don't need induction training.

(iv) **Helps in retaining competent workers** This form of recruitment helps an organisation to retain competent workers as they expect growth in their careers through promotions.

Four demerits of internal recruitment are discussed below

(i) **Suitability** Internal sources of recruitment are not suitable for new enterprises.

(ii) **Restriction in choice** When vacancies are filled through transfers and promotions, there is restricted choice and less scope for getting fresh talent in the organisation.

(iii) **Spirit of competition hampered** The spirit of competition among the employees may be hampered as they are likely to expect automatic promotion because of seniority.

(iv) **Encourages favouritism** This form of recruitment encourages favouritism, as seniors tend to promote employees on the basis of their personal equation and not on the basis of their performance. This also creates an environment for office politics.

5. Why are advertisements in the newspaper, the most popular source of recruitment? *ISC 2014*

Or Write a note on advertisement as a source of recruitment. *ISC 2011*

Ans It is a popular method of recruitment, as many recruiters prefer advertisements because of their wide reach. It clearly describes the job benefits, about the employer and give instructions about how to apply.

Newspaper is the most common medium which is adopted by many recruiters to invite the pool of applications because of its wide circulation. Not only in newspaper, it can also be placed in professional or business journals. Advertisements must contain proper information like the job content, working conditions, location of job, compensation including fringe benefits, job specifications, growth aspects, etc.

The advertisement has to sell the idea that the company and job are perfect for the candidate. It is also very advantageous as it is cost effective. This source has got an important place in the recruitment procedure.

The biggest advantage of advertisement is that it covers a wide area of market and scattered applicants can get information from advertisements.

6. Discuss the internal and external source of recruitment. *ISC 2004*

Ans **Internal sources** These refer to employing persons from within the organisation.

Four internal sources Refer to Q. No. 2 on page 18.

External sources These refer to the recruitment of candidates from outside the organisation.

Four external sources Refer to Q.No. 1 on page 17 and 18.

Concept Enhancer Placement agency has access to a large talent pool of high qualified and experienced candidates. Thus, using a recruitment/placement agency increase the ability to meet high-quality candidates with the relevant skills and expertise in the sector.

Additional Questions

8 Marks Question

1. Define e-recruitment. Discuss the various sources of e-recruitment.

Ans **Meaning of E-recruitment** According to **Wolfswinkel, Joost** and **Furtmuller, Elfi** and **Wildersom, Celeste (2010),** "E-recruitment is the online attraction and identification of potential employees using corporate or commercial recruiting websites, electronic advertisements on other websites, or an arbitrary combination of these channels including optional methods such as remote interviews and assessments, smart online research agents or interactive communication tools between recruiter and applicant."

Various sources of e-recruitment are as follows

(i) **Internet** (external source) It is a network of computers which is available for all. Internet is the main source of e-recruitment. Following are the basic categories of the e-recruitment through internet

(a) **General purpose job board** It provides online recruiting solution to both employers and job-seekers, e.g. Monster, hot jobs, etc.

(b) **Niche job board** It provides highly specialised job markets, e.g. Journalismjobs.com, Marketingjobs. com, etc.

(c) **Social networking services** These are used by most job seekers and human resource professionals, e.g. Facebook, Linkedin, etc.

(d) **Video platforms** Now-a-days, video platforms are used for e-recruitment, e.g. Youtube.

(e) **Blogs** These are personal editorial spaces which allow company to publish job description.

(f) **Social professional networks** They provide potential employees to corporate, e.g. CA club India, MBA club India, etc.

(ii) **Intranet** (internal source) It is private network available only to those with the company. It can be considered as internal source of e-recruitment. It is accessed through login details, i.e. user id, password, etc.

TOPIC 2

Staff Selection

Staff selection is the process by which all applicants are divided into two groups, *viz* those selected in company and those rejected from process.

Meaning and Definition of Staff Selection

It refers to the process of choosing the right candidate from the pool of many individuals. It is considered as a negative process because more candidates are rejected than employed.

According to **Dale Yoder**, "Selection refers to the negative process of eliminating from among all the candidates considered for possible employment, those who appear unpromising."

It involves making decision, as to which number of candidates for given positions, are to be given an opportunity to work.

Selection Procedure

The important steps in the selection process are as follows

1. **Preliminary screening** It helps the manager to eliminate unqualified or unfit job seekers, based on the information supplied in the application forms.

   Importance

   (i) Helpful in decreasing the number of candidates for next step of selection process.

   (ii) Helpful in reducing the cost of selection procedure.

   (iii) Helpful in increasing the efficiency of selection process.

2. **Application blank** The candidates who clear the preliminary interview are required to fill application blank. It contains data record of the candidates such as details about age, qualifications, reason for leaving previous job, experience, etc. It provides a base of records about the candidate to the organisation.

   Importance

   (i) Helpful in providing the written record of the candidates.

   (ii) Helpful in shortlisting the candidates for test and interview.

   (iii) Helpful in reducing the cost of selection procedure.

3. **Selection test** An employment test is a mechanism (either a paper and pencil test or an exercise) that attempts to measure certain characteristics of individuals. These characteristics range from aptitudes, such as manual dexterity, to intelligence, to personality, etc.

   Importance

   (i) Helpful in judging the technical and theoretical competence of the candidate.

   (ii) Helpful in scientific selection of candidates.

   (iii) Helpful in eliminating the unqualified candidates from the selection process.

4. **Group discussion** Now-a-days, group discussion is conducted alongwith interview as a criteria or procedure for the final selection of candidates in a college or company.

   It is basically conducted to check candidates communication skills and knowledge of a topic as well as the team spirit in a group. Through this, a candidates can create a good impression on penalists or invigilators to show his candidature.

   Importance

   (i) Helpful in judging the candidates personality traits i.e. leadership, awareness, reasoning, etc.

   (ii) Helpful in reducing the cost of final interview because it eliminates the unqualified candidates from the process.

   (iii) It is more helpful for managerial jobs in organisation.

5. **Final interview** Interview is a formal, in-depth conversation, conducted to evaluate the applicant's suitability for the job. Through an interview, an interviewer seeks to obtain maximum information about the interviewee and the interviewee seeks information about the job and the company.

   Importance

   (i) Helpful in obtaining supplementary information.
   (ii) Helpful in determining the suitability of candidates for the job.
   (iii) Helpful in judging the personality traits of the candidates.

6. **Medical test** After the selection decision and before the job offer, the candidate is required to undergo a medical fitness test. The job offer is given to the candidate, only if the candidate is physically and mentally fit for the job.

   Importance

   (i) Helpful in disclosing the physical characteristics of the candidates.
   (ii) Helpful to both employers and employees.
   (iii) Helpful in reducing the labour turnover ratio in company.

7. **Reference check** Many employers request names, addresses and telephone numbers of references for the purpose of verifying information and gaining additional information of an applicant. These references can be teachers, lecturers, previous employers and professors, who can give additional information about the candidate.

   Importance

   (i) Helpful in providing the index of personal strengths and weaknesses of candidates.
   (ii) Helpful in accessing the right candidate for right job.
   (iii) Helpful in minimising the cost associated with failed probation periods.

8. **Final approval** The final decision has to be made from among the candidates, who pass the tests, interviews and reference checks. A letter of job offer is issued to selected candidate which contains the details like basic pay, allowances, date of joining, terms and conditions. When candidate accepts the job offer, the contract of employment is made.

   Importance

   (i) Helpful in accessing the end-result of selection process.
   (ii) Helpful in eliminating the dispute between employers and employees regarding term and conditions of job.
   (iii) Helpful in providing the placement of employee.

9. **Placement** It is the act of assigning jobs to the selected candidates.

   Pigors and **Myers** have defined placement as, "The determination of job to which an accepted candidate is to be assigned, and his assignment to that job. It is a matching of what the supervisor has reason to think he can do with the job demand (job requirement) and what he offers in form of payrolls, companionship with others, promotional possibilities, etc."

   Importance

   (i) Helpful in reducing the labour turnover ratio in company.
   (ii) Helpful in improving the morale of employees.
   (iii) Helpful in reducing the absenteeism, accidents in factory and dissatisfaction among employees.

Difference between Recruitment and Selection

Basis	Recruitment	Selection
Meaning	It is the process of stimulating people to apply for a vacant job position in the organisation.	It is the process of selecting the best candidate from those who have applied for the job.
Objective	The objective of recruitment is to create a pool of eligible candidates for the purpose of selection.	The objective of selection is to get the best candidate selected for the job.
Nature	It is a positive process as it attracts people towards the organisation.	It is a negative process as it involves rejection of candidates at every stage of it.
Sequence	It takes place before selection.	It takes place after recruitment.
Number	No restriction.	Only limited number of candidates are selected.
Method	Economical.	Expensive.

PYQs Previous Years' Questions

1 Mark Questions

1. "Staff selection is a negative process". State is true or false. **ISC 2023**

Ans True

Concept Enhancer In staff selection process, more candidates are rejected than employed.

2. At which stage of selection procedure is the minimum qualification of recruited candidates' checked? **ISC Specimen 2023**

Ans Preliminary screening

3. Which one of the following is not a step of a selection procedure? **ISC Sem I 2021, Sem I Specimen 2021**
   (a) Recruitment (b) Medical examination
   (c) Checking references (d) Placement

Ans (a) Recruitment

4. .... provides a detailed and permanent record of the candidate who has applied for a job. **ISC Sem I 2021**
   (a) Preliminary interview (b) Application blank
   (c) Tests (d) Final interview

Ans (b) Application blank

5. What is the significance of the final interview in a selection procedure? **ISC Sem I 2021**
   (a) It checks if the candidate fulfills the minimum qualification required for the job
   (b) It helps in getting basic information about the candidate
   (c) It allows the crosschecking of information obtained through earlier steps of the selection procedure
   (d) It reveals whether the candidate is mentally and physically fit to do the job

Ans (c) It allows the crosschecking of information obtained through earlier steps of the selection procedure

6. Group discussion is an important step in the selection procedure for filling vacancies at the higher level because **ISC Sem I 2021**
   (a) it judges the job skills of the candidate
   (b) it helps in revealing the leadership abilities and team spirit of the candidate
   (c) pay package of the candidate can be discussed by a team of managers
   (d) the employer and the candidate get an opportunity to develop interpersonal relations

Ans (b) it helps in revealing the leadership abilities and team spirit of the candidate

7. Selection is the process of **ISC Sem I 2021**
   (a) searching for applicants
   (b) identifying different sources of recruitment
   (c) eliminating unwanted candidates
   (d) inviting applications

Ans (c) eliminating unwanted candidates

8. Selection is a complex process as **ISC Sem I Specimen 2021**
   (a) it eliminates all unsuitable candidates
   (b) it is a negative process
   (c) the candidates are required to cross several hurdles
   (d) it involves choosing the candidates having necessary qualifications

Ans (c) the candidates are required to cross several hurdles

2 Marks Questions

1. State any two reasons to justify 'medical examination' as an integral part of good selection procedure. **ISC 2020**

Or Explain the relevance of medical examination in a selection procedure. **ISC 2014, 2009**

KEY IDEA
This question asks the two reasons to justify 'medical examination' as an integral part of a good selection procedure. This means students need to write its relavancy or significance as why it is a good selection procedure.

Ans The relevance of medical examination in a selection procedure are as follows
   (i) It is helpful in disclosing the physical characteristics of the candidates.
   (ii) It is helpful in reducing the labour turnover ratio in company.

2. What is the significance of application blank in a selection procedure? **ISC 2016**

Or Give two advantages of using 'application blank' in the selection procedure. **ISC 2009**

Ans Application blank is a highly useful selection tool as it is
   (i) helpful in providing the written record of the candidates.

(ii) helpful in shortlisting the candidates for test and interview.
(iii) helpful in reducing the cost of selection procedure.

3. What is meant by halo effect in interviewing? **ISC 2015**

Ans It is a type of error, in which a single prominent characteristic of the candidate affects the judgement of the interviewer on all other traits. For example, an interviewer may conclude that a poorly groomed candidate is stupid or alternatively, he may over rate the candidate's qualifications just because of his pleasing personality.

4. Explain any two limitations of recruitment interview. **ISC 2013**

Ans Limitations of recruitment interview are

(i) **May be biased** The interviewer has certain predisposition, according to which, he judges the performance. There can be certain favouritism towards a particular candidates.

(ii) **Only checks the personality, not the skills** In an interview, one can judge a candidate from his looks and he cannot judge the hidden qualities and skills in one single interaction.

5. "Recruitment and selection are interdependent. Both are meaningless without each other." Explain. **ISC 2012**

Ans In human resource management, recruitment and selection are two interdependent functions that are performed to meet the process of identification, attraction and choosing the most suitable candidate in an organisation. In the process of recruitment, one invites application from candidates, with the help of which selection is possible and on the other hand, recruitment has no value, if selection is not done. Thus, it can rightly be said that these two are interdependent.

6. Why is recruitment a positive process, whereas selection is a negative process? **ISC 2008**

Ans The process of recruitment invites application from prospective candidates, thus, it is a positive process, whereas, selection is the process of choosing right candidates i.e. eliminating and rejecting the unsuitable candidates out of many applicants. Thus, it is considered as a negative process.

4 Marks Questions

1. Explain the relevance of the following in a selection procedure. **ISC 2023**

(i) Preliminary screening
(ii) Final interview

Ans Refer to text on page 20 and 21.

2. With reference to the selection procedure, explain the significance of **ISC Specimen 2023**

(i) Application blank (ii) Medical examination

Ans Refer to text on page 20 and 21.

3. State any four distinctions between recruitment and selection. **ISC 2020**

Or Distinguish between recruitment and selection. **ISC 2006**

Ans Refer to text on page 21.

4. Discuss the reference of preliminary screening and medical examination in a selection procedure. **ISC Specimen 2019**

Ans Refer to text on page 20 and 21.

6/8 Marks Questions

1. Define staff selection. Explain the meaning and relevance of checking references and placement in a selection procedure. **ISC 2019**

Ans Staff selection is the negative process of eliminating from among all the candidates considered for possible employment, those who appear unpromising. It refers to the process of choosing the right candidate from the pool of many individuals.

Checking references The process of verifying information and getting additional information of an applicant by references (such as teachers, previous employers) given by applicant in the application.

Relevance

(i) Helpful in providing index of personal strengths and weakness of candidates.
(ii) Helpful in accessing right candidate for the right job.

Placement It is the act of assigning jobs to selected candidates. It is the matching of what the supervisor has reason to think he can do with the job demand (job description) and what he offers in form of payrolls, companionship with others, promotional possibilities etc.

Relevance

(i) Helpful in reducing labour turnover ratio in company.
(ii) Helpful in improving the morale of employees.

2. Name and explain any three types of interviews. **ISC 2018**

Or Discuss any three types of recruitment interviews. **ISC 2017**

Ans Three types of recruitment interviews are

(i) **Informal interview** This type of interview is not planned and may be conducted anywhere. It is used when staff is required urgently.

In this type of interview, only general questions are asked, such as candidate's name, date of birth, previous experience, etc.

(ii) **Formal interview** This type of interview is planned beforehand and is held in a formal atmosphere. The date, time, venue and panel of interviewers are all decided in advance.

(iii) **Patterned or structured interview** This type of interview is pre-planned with a high degree of depth and accuracy. A list of questions is prepared and these questions are asked in a pre-determined sequence. The time allowed for each interview is also fixed. The candidate is only required to answer the questions put forth in a direct manner. This interview is also referred to as directed or guided interview.

3. With reference to selection process, explain the significance of the following

(i) Preliminary interview (ii) Application blank

(iii) Medical examination (iv) Final interview *ISC 2018*

Ans (i) **Preliminary interview** It is used to eliminate those candidates who do not meet the minimum eligibility criteria laid down by the organisation. The skills, academic and family background, competencies and interests of the candidate are examined during preliminary interview.

Significance

(a) Helpful in ensuring whether the candidate is fit for job.

(b) Helpful in eliminating the unsuitable candidates from the process.

(ii) **Application blanks** The candidates who clear the preliminary interview are required to fill application blank. It contains data record of the candidates such as details about age, qualifications, reasons for leaving previous job, experience, etc.

Significance

(a) Helpful in providing a base of records about the candidate to the organisation.

(b) Helpful in shortlisting the candidates for tests and interview.

(iii) **Medical examination** Medical tests are conducted to ensure physical and mental fitness of the potential employee. It will decrease chances of employee absenteeism.

Significance

(a) Helpful in determining an applicant's ability to perform the job.

(b) Helpful in minimising the injuries or accidents during employment.

(c) Helpful in reducing the medical budget of the company.

(iv) **Final interview** It is a one-to-one interaction between the interviewer and the potential candidate. It is used to find out whether the candidate is best suited for the required job or not.

Significance

(a) Helpful in obtaining the relevant information from the candidates.

(b) Helpful in judging the personal traits of candidates.

(c) Helpful in selecting the right candidate for right job.

4. State and explain any three steps involved in the selection procedure. *ISC 2015*

Or Explain any four important steps that may be adopted by an organisation in its staff selection procedure. *ISC 2011*

Ans Selection is the process of carefully screening the candidates to choose the most suitable persons for the job vacancies to be filled in.

Following steps involved in the selection procedure are

Step 1 Scrutiny of application Applications are received from various sources. These are scrutinised and irrelevant ones are discarded in this step on the basis of information provided in their application forms.

Selection Procedure Steps

- Scrutiny of application
- Preliminary interview
- Application blank
- Selection test

Step 2 Preliminary interview It is used to eliminate those candidates who do not meet the minimum eligibility criteria laid down by the organisation. The skills, academic and family background, competencies and interests of the candidate are examined during preliminary interview.

Preliminary interviews are less formalised and planned than the final interviews.

The candidates are given a brief summary about the company and the job profile, and it is also examined how much the candidate knows about the company. Preliminary interviews are also called 'screening interviews'.

Step 3 Application blank The candidates who clear the preliminary interview are required to fill application blank.

It contains data record of the candidates such as details about age, qualifications, reason for leaving previous job, experience, etc. It provides a base of records about the candidate to the organisation and helps in shortlisting the candidates for tests and interview.

Step 4 Selection test An employment test is a mechanism (either a paper and pencil test or an exercise) that attempts to meausre certrain characteristics of individuals.

These characteristics range from aptitudes, such as manual dexterity, to intelligence, to personality, etc.

5. What is an interview? Explain any two advantages and any two disadvantages of conducting recruitment interview. **ISC 2014**

Ans **Meaning of interview** It is a one-to-one interaction between the interviewer and the potential candidate. It is used to find out whether the candidate is best suited for the required job or not.

But such interviews consume time and money both. Moreover, the competencies of the candidate cannot be judged. Such interviews may be biased at times.

Such interviews should be conducted properly. No distractions should be there in room. There should be an honest communication between the candidate and the interviewer.

Advantages of interviews are as follows

(i) It helps to confirm that information supplied in application blank is true and accurate.

(ii) It provides a clear picture about the job and organisation to the candidate.

Disadvantages of interviews are as follows

(i) It involves a lot of time and money.

(ii) Decision of the interviewer may be biased.

6. Why are tests conducted in a selection procedure? State any two advantages and two limitations of such tests. **ISC 2013**

KEY IDEA

Write the relevancy of tests in a selection procedure.

Ans Various written tests are conducted during selection procedure such as aptitude test, intelligence test, reasoning test, personality test, etc.

These tests are used to objectively assess the potential candidate and this would also be very helpful in making the right choice during selection.

Advantages of such tests are as follows

(i) **Judge capabilities** These are designed to judge intellectual performance of an applicant.

(ii) **Right choice** This would help in making right choice and an employee can be more productive in other areas of the company.

Disadvantages of such tests are as follows

(i) **Personal bias** There may be bias in terms of evaluation of tests.

(ii) **Not reliable** It is not a reliable source as practical experience is different from the theoretical one.

7. "Psychological tests help to predict, how successful a candidate could be on the job." Explain any three types of tests that would help the management to judge the capability of a candidate. **ISC 2012**

Ans Psychological tests are very much necessary to conduct as these are helpful in objective and standardised measure of individual's performance on task. Three such types of tests are as follows

(i) **Personality tests** It assesses the degree to which a person has certain traits or dispositions which predicts the likelihood that a person will engage in certain conduct or not.

(ii) **Emotional Quotient** (EQ) It is the ability of an individual to understand his or her own emotions and the emotions of others. Testing job applicants for their emotional intelligence in the form of psychological based tests is a growing employment trend.

(iii) **Ability and aptitude tests** Ability and aptitude tests measure specific skill sets and the resultant score gives an indication of existing ability or potential to learn skills required for the job.

They evaluate a particular ability such as numerical, verbal, diagrammatic, etc. Often the tests are multiple choice and administered under exam conditions.

8. Chalk out a detailed selection procedure for an organisation which has to fill up vacancies arising out of expansion of business. **ISC 2007**

Ans Selection is the process of carefully screening the candidates, so as to identify and choose the most suitable persons for the jobs.

Steps of selection process Refer to text on page 20 and 21.

Common Mistake Students get confused among various steps of selection procedure and their relevancy as few steps sound similar. So students are advised to give proper attention and understand each step with the help of its keywords.

Case Based Questions

Case 1

Big Zenith Ltd. is a highly reputed company that has recently made some new appointments.

The new employees were very happy on being recruited. In an informal gathering, they shared how they were recruited by the organisation. Mr. Abrar Ahmed, Senior Sales Manager said that he was vertically shifted to the post. Mr. Aman Varma said that he was introduced to the company by the present Sales Manager Mr. John D'Costa. Ms. Renu Arora said that she had applied through the newspaper and was appointed as Assistant HR Manager. Ms. Sarah Johnson said that she was directly recruited from IIM Ahmedabad when she was in the last semester of PGDBM.

Identify and briefly explain the source of recruitment used for *ISC Specimen 2023*

(i) Mr. Abrar Ahmed (ii) Mr. Aman Varma
(iii) Ms. Renu Arora (iv) Ms. Sarah Johnson

Ans (i) **Mr. Abrar Ahmed**

Promotion It refers to shifting of an employee to a higher job position. It provides greater autonomy and boosts the morale of employees. However, time bound promotions may make the employees complacent.

(ii) **Mr. Aman Varma**

Recommendation by employees The present employees may recommend their neighbours, friends and relatives for vacant job positions. Such candidates are reliable and proved to be good employees for the organisation. They get easily adjusted and acts as a costless source of recruitment for the company.

(iii) **Ms. Renu Arora**

Advertisements Large organisations usually prefer advertisements as a source of attracting large number of candidates for a vacant job position. It is useful when the company wants a wide choice for selection, fresh talent and employees for blue collar jobs. But it suffers from the limitation of high cost. It also generates a large number of ineligible candidates, increasing cost and time involved in their screening.

(iv) **Ms. Sarah Johnson**

Educational institutions/Campus recruitment Many big organisations have close contact with colleges, universities and institutions, from where they get fresh candidates in a cost-effective manner.

Case 2

SPEED, a reputed automobile company has 100 employees. Sakshi was appointed by the Managing Director as she is his daughter. Rahul, an engineer, was selected by the company directly from his college to work on the shop floor. *ISC Sem I Specimen 2021*

(i) What was the source of recruitment used while appointing Sakshi?
(a) Advertisement (b) Campus recruitment
(c) Promotion
(d) Recommendation by employees

Ans (d) Recommendation by employees

(ii) What was the source of recruitment used while appointing Rahul?
(a) Advertisement (b) Campus recruitment
(c) Promotion
(d) Recommendation by employees

Ans (b) Campus recruitment

Case 3

Sherlock detective agency put up an advertisement in the newspaper for the post of security guards for their office which holds valuable information as well as equipment. They received 200 applications and the appointment needs to be done as soon as possible. *ISC Sem I Specimen 2021*

(i) Which source of recruitment was used by the agency?
(a) Internal source (b) External source
(c) Internet (d) None of these

Ans (b) External source

(ii) Which is the most important selection procedure step that cannot be missed in this case?
(a) Application blank (b) Selection test
(c) Group discussion (d) Reference check

Ans (a) Application blank

(iii) Which of the following will help the organisation shortlist from the 200 applicants for the next round?
(a) Preliminary screening (b) Medical examination
(c) Selection test (d) Reference check

Ans (b) Medical examination

(iv) Which of the following is not a feature of recruitment?
(a) It is a linking activity (b) It is a pervasive function
(c) It is a one way function (d) It is a positive function

Ans (c) It is a one way function

CHAPTER TEST

01 Mark Questions

1. In today's rapidly changing business environment, organisations have to respond quickly to requirements for people. In this context, which step starts the process of acquiring and retaining employees for an organisation?

2. Name the external source of recruitment in which students get recruited in their colleges and institutions.

3. What is the act of assigning jobs to the selected candidates in staff selection procedure called?

4. ……… refer to shifting of an employee to a higher job position.

5. ……… is the process of stimulating people to apply through web-based resources.

6. Which of the following recruitment sources is likely to have the widest reach?

(a) Campus recruitment (b) Advertisement
(c) Promotion (d) Employment exchange

7. What is the first step in the process of selection?

(a) Medical test (b) Group discussion
(c) Preliminary screening (d) Reference check

8. Which of the following is true in case of group discussion?

(a) They are used when the time available is more
(b) They are used when the number of applications is high
(c) They are used to select candidates for high end technology and high skills job
(d) They do not use a pre-determined framework of questions

9. Recruitment is a negative process. State true or false.

10. The selection process takes place after recruitment. State true or false.

02 Marks Questions

11. What are the sources of e-recruitment?

12. What is meant by selection of employees?

13. Why is selection called a 'negative process'?

14. Discuss in brief the first and last step of the selection process.

04 Marks Questions

15. Explain the significance of following in the selection process

(i) Interview (ii) Medical test

16. "External sources of recruitment are better than internal sources." Do you agree? If yes, specify any four reasons.

17. Why is it important to check the reference details given by a candidate in the application form?

18. Explain any four internal sources of e-recruitment.

06/08 Marks Questions

19. (i) Define e-recruitment.

(ii) State any three benefits and any three limitations of e-recruitment.

20. What is recruitment? Discuss any six external sources of recruitment.

21. XYZ Synergy Pvt. Ltd. wants to hire a plant manager for the company.

Explain the process adopted by the company to select a suitable candidate for this vacant job position from a large pool.

Answers

1. Recruitment *2.* Campus recruitment
3. Placement *4.* Promotion
5. E-recuitment
6. (b) Advertisement
7. (c) Preliminary screening
8. (b) They are used when the number of applications is high
9. False
10. True

03

Staff Training

TREND ANALYSIS 5 YEARS

	Types of Questions	Average No. of Questions Across all Sets				
		2023	2020	2019	2018	2017
01 Meaning and Types of Staff Training	1 Mark	—	—	—	—	—
	2 Marks	—	—	1	1	—
	4 Marks	—	1	1	1	—
	6 Marks	—	—	—	—	—
	8 Marks	—	—	—	—	—
02 Methods and Hindrances of Staff Training	1 Mark	—	—	—	—	—
	2 Marks	—	—	—	—	1
	4 Marks	1	—	—	—	—
	6 Marks	—	—	—	—	—
	8 Marks	—	—	—	—	—

Meaning and Definition of Staff Training

Staff training is described as an attempt to improve the current or future employee performance by increasing an employee's ability to perform through learning. To succeed in business or in career, it is necessary to provide training, as the work environment is constantly changing. At every point of time, a new technology is waiting as a challenge and requires new work skills and constant improvement.

According to **Edwin B. Flippo**, "Training is the act of increasing the knowledge and skill of an employee for doing a particular job."

Difference among Training, Development and Education

Basis	Training	Development	Education
Type	It is job-oriented process.	It is career oriented process.	It is knowledge oriented process.
Facilitates	It enables employee to do a job better.	It develops the overall knowledge of an employee.	It develops and improves the general knowledge of an employee.
Focus	It focuses on technical skills.	It focuses on conceptual skills.	It focuses to develop logical and rational mind.
Scope	Its scope is narrow.	Its scope is wider.	Its scope is wide.

Types of Staff Training

Various types are there for training, depending upon the need of the organisation.

Out of them, the popular ones are specified below

(i) **Induction** It is concerned with introducing a new employee to the company and its procedures, rules and regulations.

It is provided immediately after the selection of employees. It is also known as orientation training programme.

(ii) **Job Training** It is provided to employee to handle a specific job. It generates minimum skills and confidence among employees to do a specific job. It includes
(a) All information about machines, equipments, etc.
(b) Instructions (c) Process of production
(d) Methods (e) Safety measures

(iii) **Remedial Training** It is provided to reduce the shortcomings in the behaviour and performance of old employees in the organisation due to the invention of new technology or process of production. Generally, such type of training is conducted by psychological experts or human resource experts.

(iv) **Safety Training** It is provided to minimise the number of accidents due to mishandling of machines or other equipments. Under this training, the employees are given the safety instructions. So that, they may safely use the machines or other dangerous devices.

(v) **Promotional Training** It is provided to develop the skills of existing employees to make them fit for undertaking higher job responsibilities. It is given to the potential employees, who may be promoted to the senior position in the company.

(vi) **Refresher Training** It is provided to familiarise the existing employees with the latest methods of performing their jobs and improve their efficiency. It is also known as 'retraining programme'.

It includes
(a) Up-to-date information about working procedures.
(b) Rapid technological changes.
(c) New pattern of demand for goods in market.

Methods of Staff Training

Training methods are generally classified by the location of instruction.

These are broadly categorised in two groups

(i) **On-the-job Training** Trainings which are provided to the employees to enhance their learning opportunities in the course of work are referred to as on the job training. It is most effective tool for operative personnel. Under this method, training is given at the work site and in context of the job under the supervision and guidance of a trained employee or instructor.

Following are on-the-job training methods

(a) **Apprenticeship Programme** In this method, a trainee is put under the guidance of a master worker for a period of 2-5 years, to learn work related to crafts and technical trades such as electricians, plumbers, iron-workers, etc.

(b) **Internship Training** Under this method, selected candidates are sent to factories and offices to get knowledge of the practical aspect of work. It provides a good balance between theory and practice.
It is mostly used in professionals courses e.g. MBBS, MBA, CA, etc.

(ii) **Off-the-job Training** Trainings that are imparted away from the actual work floor, to enhance the capabilities of employees are referred to as off-the-job training. It is not a part of everyday job activities. It is an expensive method for the organisation and more suitable for non-manufacturing firms.

Off-the-job training consists of

(a) **Vestibule Training** Artificial environments are created and employees are made to work to get the experience of real working situations. It is an expensive, yet an effective method.
There is more emphasis on learning rather than production. It is a more suitable method where a large number of workers need to be trained at the same time for same kind of job.

(b) **Classroom training** Under this method, training is given in company's classrooms or in educational institutions.
It includes
- Lecturers
- Group discussions
- Case studies
- Audio-visual aids
- Instructor materials

Difference between On-the-job Training and Off-the-job Training

Basis	On-the-job training	Off-the-job training
Principle	Learning while doing.	Learning before doing.
Place of Training	Conducted at workplace.	Conducted away from the workplace.
Instructor	Superiors are the instructors.	Experts are the instructors.
Contribution	Employees contribute towards work.	Employees do not contribute towards work.

Basis	On-the-job training	Off-the-job training
Techniques of Training	Apprenticeship training and internship training are some of the popular techniques.	Lectures, film, case study and vestibule training are some of the popular techniques.
Approach	Practical	Theoretical
Cost	Inexpensive	Expensive

Hindrances to Staff Training

Hindrances in training programmes are as follows

(i) **Lack of support from supervisors or trainers** Generally, trainers does not provide adequate support to trainees which is essential due to
   (a) language problem (b) age
   (c) professional status
   (d) individual barriers to learning.

(ii) **Rapid change in technologies** It can made difficult to adequately prepare training material for trainees.

(iii) **Lack of funds** Small and medium organisations may not be able to afford high training cost.

(iv) **Absenteeism** Few trainees are not being presented regularly into the training programmes which can lead to worst results.

(v) **Business schools are unable to serve the purpose of industry** In India, business schools are often seen as not responding to labour market demands.

Benefits of Training

Training is beneficial for both, i.e. employer as well as employees.

Benefits to the Employer

(i) Training is a systematic learning, always better than hit and trial methods, which leads to wastage of efforts and money.

(ii) It enhances employee productivity both in terms of quantity and quality and leading to higher profits.

(iii) Training equips the future manager, who can takeover in case of emergency.

(iv) Training increases employee morale, reduces absenteeism and employee turnover.

(v) It helps in obtaining effective response to fast changing environment.

Benefits to the Employees

(i) Improved skills and knowledge due to training leads to better career of the individual.

(ii) Increased performance by the individual helps him to earn more.

(iii) Training makes the employees more efficient to handle machines, thus, less prone to accidents.

(iv) Training increases the satisfaction and morale of employees.

PYQs Previous Years' Questions

1 Mark Questions

1. Job training is given to the new employees to familiarise them with the organisation. State true or false. *ISC Specimen 2023*

Ans False. Job training is provided to generate minimum skills and confidence among employees to do a specific job. While, induction training is provided to new employees to familiarise them with the organisation's rules, regulations and policies, etc.

2. Which one of the following options is a set of types of training? *ISC Sem I 2021*
   (a) Vestibule training, Classroom training, Internship training, Apprenticeship training
   (b) On-the-job training, Off-the-job training, Orientation training, Induction training
   (c) Job training, Promotional training, Remedial training, Refresher training
   (d) Orientation training, Remedial training, Safety training, On-the-job training

Ans (c) Job training, Promotional training, Remedial training, Refresher training

3. Theoretical instructions and practical learning are provided under training where classroom lectures are followed by practical work. *ISC Sem I 2021*
   (a) Induction (b) Classroom
   (c) Apprenticeship (d) Internship

Ans (c) Apprenticeship

4. Off-the-job training is more suitable where *ISC Sem I 2021*
   (a) a large number of persons are to be trained every year
   (b) quantity of goods produced is more important than quality
   (c) the organisation does not have enough funds for training

(d) supervisors take an active part in training the subordinates

Ans (a) a large number of persons are to be trained every year

5. Anuj is appointed through campus recruitment. He is required to work on expensive and sophisticated machines. Which one of the following training methods is most suitable for him? ***ISC Sem I 2021***

(a) Classroom training (b) Apprenticeship training
(c) Vestibule training (d) Internship training

Ans (c) Vestibule training

Concept Enhancer In vestibule training, artificial environment will be created for candidate to get the experience of real working situation, so that he can do work on sophisticated machines in a proper manner.

6. One of the major hindrances to a good training programme is ***ISC Sem I 2021***

(a) the training is often systematic and organised.
(b) there is a lack of faith in the usefulness of training.
(c) the trainees may cause damage to costly equipment.
(d) there is a disciplined approach to work.

Ans (b) there is a lack of faith in the usefulness of training.

7. Refresher training involves ***ISC Sem I 2021***

(a) giving refreshment to the trainees
(b) imparting updated knowledge and skills to the trainees
(c) rectifying the mistakes of the employees
(d) introducing new employees to the organisation

Ans (b) imparting updated knowledge and skills to the trainees

8. Which one of the following is a benefit of training to an employer? ***ISC Sem I 2021***

(a) Training improves self-confidence of employees.
(b) Training helps employees to earn quick promotion.
(c) Training leads to economical usage of material and machinery.
(d) Training secures higher earnings for employees.

Ans (c) Training leads to economical usage of material and machinery.

9. Which one of the following is a hindrance to vestibule training? ***ISC Sem I 2021***

(a) Training cost is very high
(b) It combines theory and practice
(c) It is often haphazard and unorganised
(d) It is difficult to concentrate due to the noise at the workplace

Ans (a) Training cost is very high

10. Which of the following is a long-term process and takes place throughout the life of a person? ***ISC Sem I Specimen 2021***

(a) Education (b) Development
(c) Training (d) Internship

Ans (b) Development

11. ………… provides immediate feedback, permits quick correction of errors and provides extra practice when required besides learning in actual work environment. ***ISC Sem I Specimen 2021***

(a) On-the-job training (b) Classroom training
(c) Vestibule training (d) Internship training

Ans (a) On-the-job training

12. Learning by doing is also called ***ISC Sem I Specimen 2021***

(a) on-the-job training
(b) vestibule training
(c) apprenticeship training
(d) internship training

Ans (a) on-the-job training

13. Which of the following is not a method of training? ***ISC Sem I Specimen 2021***

(a) Vestibule training
(b) Apprenticeship training
(c) On-the-job training
(d) Refreshers training

Ans (d) Refreshers training

14. Which of the following is a characteristic of vestibule training? ***ISC Sem I Specimen 2021***

(a) Training is given in a replica model
(b) Training is given by expert trainers
(c) Training is given in an accident free environment
(d) All of the above

Ans (a) Training is given in a replica model

15. A process that involves improving the general knowledge and the overall development of a person is called ***ISC Sem I Specimen 2021***

(a) procurement (b) education
(c) development (d) training

Ans (b) education

16. The training designed to correct the mistakes and short comings in the work behaviour and job performance of employees is known as ***ISC Sem I Specimen 2021***

(a) job training
(b) remedial training
(c) refresher training
(d) versatility training

Ans (b) remedial training

17. One of the major limitations of on-the-job training is that **ISC Sem I Specimen 2021**

(a) the training situation is somewhat artificial

(b) it is an economical method of training

(c) there is no damage to costly equipment

(d) this method is often haphazard and unorganised

Ans (d) this method is often haphazard and unorganised

2 Marks Questions

1. State any two differences between training and development. **ISC 2019**

Or

Distinguish between training and development. **ISC 2015**

Or Give any two points of distinction between training and development. **ISC 2012, 2011**

Ans Difference between training and development are

Basis	Training	Development
Type	It is a job-oriented process.	It is a career oriented process.
Facilitates	It enables employee to do a job better.	It develops the overall knowledge of an employee.

2. State the significance of conducting refresher training. **ISC 2018, 2013**

Ans Significance of refresher training are as follows

(i) It helps in relearning the concepts.

(ii) It keeps pace with the technological changes in the field.

3. State any two hindrances to staff training **ISC 2017**

Ans Two hindrances to staff training are stated below

(i) Lack of resources on time.

(ii) Lack of support from supervisors or trainers.

Common Mistake In this question, students misunderstand the term 'hindrances' and write limitations of staff training. Hindrances and limitations of training are different. Hindrances are the barriers, while limitations are the disadvantages. So understand the question first, then give answer.

4. Training helps in reducing supervision of employees. Justify. **ISC 2010**

Ans The statement is true as training describes the formal, ongoing efforts of organisations to improve the performance and self-fulfillment of employees through a variety of methods and programmes. Thus, they become self-sufficient in doing their jobs.

Value Points

Following keywords should be used by students to get maximum marks

- Performance improvement
- Self-sufficient in doing job

5. Explain one major hindrance to a good training programme. **ISC 2009**

Ans Most companies do not provide budget allocation to training programmes on time. Budget allocation to training is the first item to be cut when company faces a financial problem.

6. Write any two advantages of orientation training. **ISC 2008**

Ans Two advantages of orientation training are

(i) Orientation helps in familiarising the employee with the ways of company and helps him to learn all aspects of his job.

(ii) An orientation training programme helps an employee to adjust easily in the working environment.

7. What is orientation training? **ISC 2006**

Ans This training is provided to the new employees with basic information about the company, employer and ways of working. This training ensures that the employees have all basic knowledge acquired to perform the job satisfactorily.

8. What is vestibule training? What is its purpose? **ISC 2004**

Ans Vestibule training is an off-the-job training method. In this, employees learn their jobs on the equipment/machine, they will be using, but the training is conducted away from the work floor. Actual work environment is created in a classroom or other area and the employee uses the same material, files, machines. Main purpose is to equip people to use complex and sophisticated machinery. It also ensures safety of employees by training them properly.

Value Points

For getting maximum marks, following keypoints should be used

- Actual work environment is created
- Training is conducted away from the work floor or factory

4 Marks Questions

1. Briefly explain any two methods of off-the-job training. **ISC 2023**

Ans Refer to text on page 29.

2. State any four differences between training and education. *ISC 2020*

Or Explain any three points of difference between training and education. *ISC 2018*

Ans Difference between training and education are

Basis	Training	Education
Type	It is a job-oriented process.	It is a knowledge oriented process.
Facilitates	It enables employees to do a better job.	It develops and improves the general knowledge of an employee.
Focus	It focuses on technical skills.	It focuses to develop logical and rational mind.
Scope	Its scope is narrow.	Its scope is wide.

3. What is meant by induction training? State any two objectives of this training. *ISC 2019*

Ans Induction training is the practice of introducing a new employee to the company and its procedures, rules and regulations. It is provided immediately after the selection of employees. It is also known as orientation training program. Proper induction enables new employee to have a good start and develop his/her overall effectiveness on job.

Objectives of induction are

(i) To develop confidence, sense of belongingness and loyalty in a new employee.

(ii) To develop cordial relationship between newcomers and old employees and superiors.

4. Why is induction training important in an organisation? *ISC 2010*

Ans Induction training is important in an organisation due to the following reasons

(i) Provides accurate information to the new employees.

(ii) Employees are kept focussed and feel busy from the day one.

(iii) Clear expectations are established to help improve employee performance.

(iv) Good work habits are quickly implanted in the employees.

(v) It helps employees in settling down quickly.

(vi) It is a short-time training, thus an employee would not feel bored or overburdened.

Concept Enhancer Induction training is concerned with introducing a new employee to the company and its procedures, rules and regulations. It is provided immediately after the selection of employees.

5. Explain in brief the advantages of 'on-the-job training'. *ISC 2008*

Ans Advantages of on-the-job training are

(i) **Simple** On-the-job training is simple and easy to learn by watching and doing. This will help in explaining and analysing the job details in a very simple and easy manner.

(ii) **Economy** On-the-job training is very economical in the sense that it does not require any extra cost or burden for arranging training needs.

(iii) **Immediate productivity** Training is provided on the actual work floor thus, quick learning and immediate productivity will be obtained from the workers.

(iv) **Multi-skill** On-the-job training is a practical approach. Thus, it develops multiple skills in an individual.

Common Mistake Generally, students consider on-the-job training and job training as the same, but they are totally different. "On-the-job training" is a method of staff training while "job training" is a type of staff training. Students are advisable to read question carefully and then give answer.

6. Define training. Distinguish it from education. *ISC 2007*

Ans **Meaning of training** It is the act of increasing the knowledge and skills of an employee for performing the job assigned to him. It is a short-term process that helps in improving performance on the current job in a very short time.

According to **Jucius**, "The term 'training' is used to indicate only a process by which the aptitude, skills and abilities of the employees to perform specific jobs are increased."

Differences between training and education

Basis	Training	Education
Focus	It focuses on technical skills.	It focuses to develop logical and rational mind.
Scope	Its scope is narrow.	Its scope is wide.

7. What is off-the-job training? Give four specific examples, where only this type of training will be used. *ISC 2007*

Ans **Meaning of off-the-job training** It is imparted to employees away from the actual work floor. This includes information presentation, information processing and simulation of the work, that helps an employee in gaining the expertise on the job.

Examples Its objective is learning before doing and it finds application in the following cases

(i) In case of factories or environment, where complex and sophisticated machinery is used.

(ii) In banks or other financial institutions, this type of training is provided to brief the employees about the current market and financial positions.

(iii) In big business houses, this training is provided to teach factual information about the ongoing projects.

(iv) These can be taken up by pilots and cabin attendants through off-the-job training methods like vestibule training, simulation and computer modelling techniques.

8. Training is an unavoidable cost. Justify. *ISC 2005*

Ans Employees' better performance is the objective of every organisation.

It is true that when employees are selected, they are admitted only on the behalf of their skills and knowledge but the theoretical aspect is different from the practical one.

The practical part can only be better after providing training as it is a tool that refines, polishes and improve the performance of an employee on the existing job. Thus, for the betterment of an organisation, it is an unavoidable cost that one has to bear.

6/8 Marks Questions

1. Discuss any four types of training that can be given to staff in an organisation. *ISC Specimen 2019*

Or Name and explain any four types of training. *ISC 2014*

Or Explain four types of staff training. *ISC 2011*

Ans Refer to text on page 28 and 29.

2. Differentiate between induction training and job training. *ISC 2016*

Ans Differences between induction training and job training are

Basis	Induction training	Job training
Meaning	It is a kind of training provided to new employees to give them information about the company, its history, activities, performance, objectives, procedures, etc.	It is a kind of training provided while employees are on the job, in order to enhance their skills and abilities for doing a work.
Frequency	An employee is required to undergo this training only once.	An employee can undergo this training several times, depending upon the nature of his work.
Place of training	Training can be conducted outside the workplace or at the workplace.	Training is always conducted at the workplace.
Trainee	The trainee is the new employee of the organisation.	The trainee can either be a new or an old employee of the organisation.
Purpose/ Object	The purpose of this training is to help an employee to adjust as per the needs of organisation.	The purpose of this training is to improve the efficiency of an employee.

3. Define training. Give any four benefits that an employee can get from training. *ISC 2015*

Ans **Meaning of training** It is an important terminology of the Human Resource Management (HRM).

It is described as an attempt to improve the current or future employee performance by increasing an employee's ability to perform through learning.

To succeed in business or in career, it is necessary to provide training, as the work environment is constantly changing.

At every point of time, a new technology is waiting as a challenge and requires new work skills and constant improvement.

According to **Jucius**, "The term 'training' is used to indicate only a process by which the aptitude, skills and abilities of the employees to perform specific jobs are increased."

Importance of training Training is important in an organisation, due to the following reasons

Importance of Training
- Higher productivity
- Reduced supervision
- Better safety
- Higher morale

(i) **Higher productivity** It increases the level of productivity of employees.

(ii) **Reduced supervision** It reduces the burden of continuous and extensive supervision.

(iii) **Better safety** Training makes employees proficient and reduces the chances of accidents.

(iv) **Higher morale** Effective training improves job attitudes and self-confidence of employees.

4. What do you understand by 'remedial training' and 'refresher training'? Explain the importance of each. ISC 2009

Ans **Remedial training** This training is used to upgrade knowledge and skills of a worker to remove mistakes and shortcomings in the work and job performance of employees. Importance of remedial training are

(i) To overcome the shortcomings in the behaviour and performance of old employees.

(ii) By knowing the right way to do job, the productivity and confidence of the employee increases.

Refresher training This training is imparted to the newly hired professionals or in case to acquaint the existing employees with the latest methods of performing their jobs and improve their efficiencies further to avoid personal obsolescence. It is designed to help employees to be trained in the use of new methods and techniques. It is also called 'retraining'. Importance of refresher training are

(i) It helps in relearning the concepts.

(ii) It keeps pace with the technological changes in the field.

5. What is apprenticeship training? Give two advantages and two disadvantages of the same. ISC 2009

Ans **Meaning of apprenticeship training** It is an on-the-job training programme designed for people who want to work in a skilled trade or occupation. It includes learning new skills from skilled persons.

Apprenticeship training provides access to a high level of skill, judgement and creativity. Apprentices are paid while gaining work experience and their wages increase with their level of skills.

Apprenticeships are especially appropriate for jobs requiring technical/production skills.

Advantages of apprenticeship Advantages of apprenticeship training are

(i) **Earn while you learn** It is a training programme which is designed for the employees to enhance their skills and will get certain amount as a wage too.

(ii) **A real job** It provides a real work experience to the employees and thus, they feel that they are doing their normal routine job.

Disadvantages of apprenticeship Disadvantages of apprenticeship training are

(i) **Time consuming** It is a very time consuming process.

(ii) **Traditional approach** It is a traditional style of training. From many years, it is being provided to the employees on the grounds of traditional approach.

Additional Questions

2 Marks Questions

1. Enumerate the features of training.

Ans The following are the features of training

(i) It increases knowledge and skills for doing a job.

(ii) It bridges the gap between 'job requirements' and 'employee skills'.

(iii) It is a job-oriented process.

(iv) It is a continuous and never ending process.

(v) It brings change in attitude of employees.

2. What is meant by training, development and education?

Ans **Training** It is a process by which the aptitudes, skills and abilities of employees to perform specific jobs are increased.

Development It refers to the learning opportunities designed to help employees to grow. It covers not only the activities which improve the performance but also brings change in the personality as a whole.

Education It is a process of increasing the knowledge and understanding of employees in general.

4 Marks Questions

1. What are the advantages and disadvantages of internship training?

Ans Advantages of internship training are

(i) It is usually beneficial to both parties i.e. employers as well as participants.

(ii) Real work experience.

(iii) It increase the market value of applicants.

Disadvantages of internship training are

(i) Low payment.

(ii) Generally, enterprises do not offer job to such applicants.

(iii) Being treated as an assistant i.e. less scope for creativity.

2. Give the merits and demerits of vestibule training?

Ans Merits of vestibule training are

(i) No pressure of work.

(ii) Theory can be related to practice.

(iii) Provided by experienced and expert instructors.

Demerits of vestibule training are

(i) Time consuming process.

(ii) Costly method.

(iii) Difficult to adjust in real work environment.

3. Enumerate merits and demerits of classroom training.

Ans Merits of classroom training are

(i) It improves problem solving skills of employees.
(ii) More useful for technical, professionals and managerial employees.
(iii) Useful for large groups.

Demerits of classroom training are

(i) Expensive method.
(ii) Unsuitable for teaching specific hands-on skills.
(iii) It affects the production schedules of company.

Case Based Questions

Case 1

Mr. Saxena heads the HR department of Paras & Co. Ms. Anu who works in the Accounts department resigned from her job. Since finalisation of account is going on, the vacancy needs to be filled at the earliest with a reliable candidate.

Mr. Saxena has decided to arrange for a short training session so that the new incumbent is able to cope with the work at Paras & Co. As the Company wants the new incumbent to start work at the earliest, they decide to forego the orientation training. *ISC Sem I 2021*

(i) Which source of recruitment is not suitable to replace Ms. Anu?

(a) Casual callers (b) Advertisement
(c) Recommendations by present employees
(d) Placement agencies

Ans (c) Recommendations by present employees

(ii) Which method should Mr. Saxena use to train the new incumbent?

(a) Internship training (b) Remedial training
(c) On-the-job training (d) Classroom training

Ans (c) On-the-job training

(iii) Orientation training is given to .... employees.

(a) new (b) old
(c) inefficient (d) undisciplined

Ans (a) new

(iv) Which type of training should Mr. Saxena arrange for the new incumbent?

(a) Job training
(b) Apprenticeship training
(c) Refresher training
(d) Safely training

Ans (a) Job training

Case 2

SPEED, a reputed automobile company has 100 employees. Sakshi was appointed by the Managing Director as she is his daughter. Rahul, an engineer, was selected by the company directly from his college to work on the shop floor. *ISC Sem I Specimen 2021*

(i) What type of training should be provided to Rahul?

(a) Job training
(b) Refresher training
(c) Promotional training
(d) Remedial training

Ans (a) Job training

(ii) What method of training should be used to provide training to Rahul?

(a) On-the-job training
(b) Vestibule training
(c) Internship training
(d) Classroom training

Ans (c) Internship training

CHAPTER TEST

01 Mark Questions

1. Name the term which describes long term training that include a combination of both on-the-job and in-class training.
2. Which type of training is provided to develop the skill of existing employees to make them fit for undertaking higher job responsibilities?
3. Audo visual aids is an example of which method of staff-training?
4. ………… takes place in the real job environment, where the trainee is exposed to actual work situations.
5. ………… refers to the learning opportunities designed to help employees grow.
6. Which of the following functions in an organisation enhances the skills and capabilities of employees?
   (a) Placement
   (b) Training
   (c) Induction
   (d) Development
7. Under which method, employees learn their job on the equipment they will be using but training is done away from actual workplace?
   (a) Vestibule training
   (b) Internship training
   (c) Classroom training
   (d) Apprenticeship training
8. Which of the following is not a type of staff training?
   (a) Induction
   (b) Internship
   (c) Remedial
   (d) Refresher
9. Vestibule training utilises equipment which closely resemble the actual ones used on the job. State true or false.
10. Off-the job training has practical approach. State true or false.

02 Marks Questions

11. Enumerate any two benefits of classroom training.
12. What is safety training?
13. How do induction training help employees?
14. State any two conditions under which remedial training is provided to the employees.
15. What do you mean by development?

04 Marks Questions

16. Identify and explain the type of training in which trainee learns under the guidance of master worker.
17. Differentiate between training and education on any four basis.

06/08 Marks Questions

18. What is on-the-job training? Give any four examples, how this type of training will be used?
19. What is training programme? Why is it designed in an organisation and what benefits one can avail from such training programmes?
20. Explain any four hindrances and any four benefits in training programme.

Answers

1. Apprenticeship
2. Promotional training
3. Off-the-job training *4.* On-the job training
5. Development
6. (b) Training
7. (a) Vestibule training
8. (b) Internship
9. True
10. False

04

Staff Morale

TREND ANALYSIS 5 YEARS

Average No. of Questions Across all Sets

Topic	Types of Questions	2023	2020	2019	2018	2017
01 Meaning and Factors Affecting Staff Morale	1 Mark	—	—	—	—	—
	2 Marks	—	1	—	—	—
	4 Marks	—	—	—	—	—
	6 Marks	—	—	—	—	—
	8 Marks	—	—	—	1	1
02 Methods of Raising Staff Morale, Morale Productivity Matrix	1 Mark	1	—	—	—	—
	2 Marks	—	—	—	—	—
	4 Marks	—	—	—	—	—
	6 Marks	—	—	—	—	—
	8 Marks	—	—	1	—	—

Meaning and Definitions of Staff Morale

The word 'morale' signifies the enthusiasm, feeling of strength and togetherness among individuals. The term 'staff morale' is used to indicate the mental health of an individual or the group that affects the total environment of the organisation.

According to **Keith Davis**, "Morale represents the attitudes of individuals and groups towards their work environment and towards their voluntary cooperation to the full extent of their ability, in the best interest of the organisation."

According to **University of Michigan**, "Morale is considered as the combination of attitudes towards the company, job and the immediate supervisor."

Characteristics of Staff Morale

Following are the characteristics of staff morale

(i) **State of mind** It is a state of mind of individuals or groups which determines their willingness to co-operate with others in the accomplishment of an organisation's objectives.

(ii) **Contagious phenomenon** It is considered as a contagious phenomenon because employees transmit their attitudes to each other in organisation.

(iii) **Intangible** Staff morale is intangible because it is very difficult to measure the degree of morale accurately.

(iv) **Long-term concept** Staff morale is a long-term concept because it cannot be developed overnight. Companies have to make continuous efforts to create and maintain high morale.

(v) **Positive effect on productivity** Generally, staff morale has a positive effect on productivity. It is considered as a corner stone of the performance of the organisation.

(vi) **Relative term** Staff morale is a relative term. It may be high or low. It depends upon the internal factors of organisation.

Factors Affecting Staff Morale

Various factors affecting staff morale are

(i) **Office environment** Surroundings play an important role in developing attitude of an individual. Employee morale is definitely affected by office environment, so it is important to keep it transparent and clean.

(ii) **Nature of work** The nature of work, an employee is supposed to perform influences his attitude to it. Many jobs of a routine nature create boredom and encourages a feeling of alienation and stress among the employees.

(iii) **Supervision received** The actions of management, their attitude and the leadership exercised influence tremendously the morale of employees.

(iv) **Concept of self** The perception of employees about themselves influence their attitude towards the organisation.

(v) **Employee's age** Studies have reported that people with somewhat higher age have higher morale, because perhaps younger workers are more dissatisfied because of unemployment.

(vi) **Employee's educational and occupational level** There is an inverse relationship between educational level and employee morale. Higher is the educational level, lower is the job satisfaction among individuals.

(vii) **Level of satisfaction** No one likes to work in a vaccum. If an employee is doing well, he needs appreciation for it.

Employees feel happy when they are appreciated or rewarded. This gives a sense of belongingness towards the company and the lack of such benefits, badly affect the employee's morale.

(viii) **Team work** Employees feel happy, if they work in a team. When teams are contributing and working well together, then morale becomes high. If there is the lack of team work, the morale of employees is badly affected.

Morale Stimulants

Various factors stimulating the staff morale are as follows

(i) **Job security** In India, job security creates high morale among the employees about their job and organisation.

(ii) **Leadership** The actions of team leaders (i.e. managers) influence the morale of staff. Fair treatment, good rewards and recognition for good work stimulate the high morale of the employees.

(iii) **Self-concept** High self-concept boosts the level of morale in employees about their work.

Self concept includes

(a) Self-respect (b) Self-confidence
(c) Self-value

(iv) **Personal factors** Young age, higher educational level, experience and high occupational level boost the morale in employees.

Personal factors includes

(a) The employee's age
(b) Educational level (c) Experience
(d) Occupational level

(v) **Nature of work** If employees are assigned to do something interesting and challenging work, it increases the morale of employees.

(vi) **Future prosperity** Expectation of future prosperity boosts the morale of employees.

It includes

(a) Promotion
(b) Increment in remuneration
(c) Recognition of work
(d) Importance in organisation

Morale Depressants

Various factors lowering the staff morale are as follows

(i) **Job insecurity** It lowers employee's morale which adversely affects his/her behaviour, attitude and performance.

(ii) **Nature of work and reward** If there is no excitement and creativity in work (i.e. boring work, monotonous and repetitive work) and there is no possibility of good compensation in near future, employees will be depressed about their work and organisation.

(iii) **Negative managerial style** It creates a feeling of being neglected and uncared among the employees about their work and organisation.

(iv) **Unfavourable work environment** Unfavourable working conditions (i.e. unsafe, inconvenience and dirty working conditions) are morale depressants in the organisation.

(v) **Goals of the organisation** If goals set by management are unrealistic, unacceptable and useless, then employees develop a negative feeling towards job and organisation.

(vi) **Low self-concept** Low self concept decrease the morale of employees about their work.
It includes
(a) Self-respect (b) Self-confidence
(c) Self-value

Methods of Raising Staff Morale

Methods of raising staff morale are mentioned below

(i) **Building responsibility** Everyone wants to feel that his or her work has higher value. One of the key requirement in this phase is to provide a feeling of responsibility to the employees, so that they feel that their work is more important than the other jobs.

(ii) **Offer incentives** It stimulates employees to perform better, while at the same time helping them to feel that they are being appreciated by the organisation. Incentives can be offered in the form of money, appraisal, bonus, parking spaces, free meals, etc.

(iii) **Job enrichment** One of the key ways to increase morality is to make sure, employees understand their chances in upward mobility. It could mean more responsibility, leadership, access to new resources and industry events.
This can help them grow professionally since they are doing new and interesting things, while at the same time, decreases frustration and unhappiness due to boredom of work.

(iv) **Encourage strengths** Organisations should encourage the unique strengths of employees and push them to utilise their skills up to the best advantage of the organisation. This will boost them and help them to make every possible effort to achieve the target.

(v) **Transparency and fairness** Employees need to feel as though they can discuss everything with their bosses, even the negative news. Organisations should be clear and transparent with what they expect from the employees.

(vi) **Regular feedback of performance** By taking sincere feedback, the organisation should approach to bring correct positiveness in the employee's behaviour and performance.

(vii) **Other methods** Some other methods are
(a) Change in work environment
(b) Rotation of jobs
(c) Creation of whole jobs, i.e. satisfying employee's higher needs
(d) Flexible working hours

Indicators/Advantages of High Morale

The various advantages of high morale are

(i) Willingness to do every possible task for the betterment of an organisation.
(ii) Loyalty towards group goals
(iii) Enthusiasm and zeal
(iv) Appreciative enquiry
(v) Greater customer care
(vi) Esprit de corps

Indicators/Disadvantages of Low Morale

The various disadvantages of low morale are

(i) Frustration and apathy among staff members.
(ii) Disobedience of rules and regulations.
(iii) Wastage and spoilage of necessary resources.
(iv) Low productivity of employees.
(v) High rate of strikes and sabotage.
(vi) High rate of accidents and tiredness.
(vii) High rate of labour absenteeism and turnover.

Morale Productivity Matrix

Miller and Form has given four combinations of productivity and morale. This is known as the morale productivity matrix. It is illustrated below

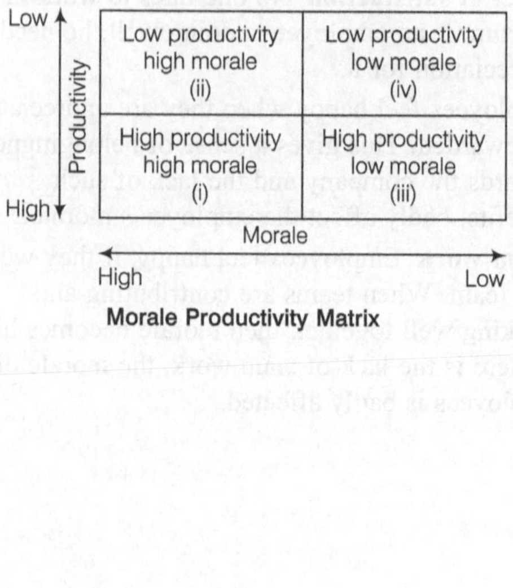

Morale Productivity Matrix

This matrix gives four combinations of morale and productivity

(i) **High productivity-high morale** Generally, high morale leads to higher productivity if it is backed with proper leadership and employees are offered financial and non-financial incentives. Complete identity between organisation's goal and individual's goal leads to this situation.

(ii) **Low productivity-high morale** This situation arises when employees spend their time and energy in fulfilling their individual objectives, totally unrelated with organisational objectives. This situation can also arise due to faulty machinery, lack of training and ineffective supervision.

(iii) **High productivity-low morale** In general, low morale does not lead to high productivity. However, in a short time period, this phenomenon can be observed due to fear of loss of job and good supervision.
Generally, supervisors follow the penalty method to increase the productivity of employees in short period.

(iv) **Low productivity-low morale** This is a common phenomenon as low morale yields low productivity in the long-run, where group goals and individual goals do not get satisfied. So, it can be concluded that there is a complex relationship between morale and productivity.

PYQs Previous Years' Questions

1 Mark Questions

1. Under special circumstances, low morale of employees may lead to high productivity. State true or false. *ISC 2023*

Ans True

2. Sound policies and practices of management are morale depressants. State true or false. *ISC Specimen 2023*

Ans False. Morale depressants are the factors that lower the staff morale. Sound policies and practices of management boost the staff morale. Thus they are morale stimulants.

3. Which one of the following is an indicator of low morale? *ISC Sem I 2021*

(a) Low rate of labour turnover
(b) Group Cohesiveness
(c) Lack of discipline
(d) Infusion of new ideas

Ans (c) Lack of discipline

4. Low morale may lead to high productivity when *ISC Sem I 2021*

(a) there is no supervision
(b) work is machine-paced
(c) employees spend their time and energy in satisfying their personal objectives
(d) there is complete identify between the employees and organisational goals

Ans (b) work is machine-paced

5. The mental conditions or attributes of individuals and groups in an organisation is called .... *ISC Sem I 2021*

(a) staff motivation
(b) staff morale
(c) job specification
(d) job satisfaction

Ans (b) staff morale

6. Which one of the following is an indicator of high morale? *ISC Sem I 2021*

(a) High rate of mistakes made by employees
(b) High quantity and quality of output
(c) High degree of employees grievances
(d) High rate of labour turnover

Ans (b) High quantity and quality of output

7. Which of the following is not a feature of morale? *ISC Sem I 2021*

(a) It is a mental phenomenon
(b) It is contagious
(c) It is a by product of group relationships
(d) It is tangible

Ans (d) It is tangible

8. Staff morale is an indicator of *ISC Sem I Specimen 2021*

(a) motivational level in the organisation.
(b) attitudes of employees towards their job, superior's work environment etc.
(c) the quantity and quality of work done by the employees
(d) organisational objectives.

Ans (a) motivational level in the organisation.

2 Marks Questions

1. Define staff morale. *ISC 2020*

Ans Morale represents the attitudes of individuals and groups towards their work environment and towards their voluntary cooperation to the full extent of their ability, in the best interest of the organisation.

2. Explain how office layout can act as a morale depressant as well as a morale stimulant. *ISC 2016*

Ans Office layout deals with the design and set up of an office. It also takes into account all the equipments, machines and accessories needed in an office.

If the layout of an office coincides with the working needs of the employees, then it acts as a morale booster and increases their productivity.

If, on the other hand, the layout of an office is such that it creates confusion and hinders employee movement, then it acts as a morale depressant and leads to fall in productivity.

Value Points

For getting maximum marks, following points can be included in the answer

- How office layout boost staff morale.
- How office layout lower staff morale.

3. State any two consequences of low morale. *ISC 2014*

Or Mention four indicators of low morale amongst employees of an organisation. *ISC 2010*

Ans Four indicators of low morale are following

(i) High absenteeism and labour turnover

(ii) Disobedience and insubordination

(iii) Wastage and spoilage

(iv) Strikes and sabotage

4. What is the importance of team work in the successful functioning of an organisation? *ISC 2013, 2006*

Ans Team work is essential for the success of an organisation, as it increases the quantity of production by increasing morale of an employee and thereby improving the quality of work.

5. State and explain any one factor that can either act as a morale depressant or a booster, depending on how it is used. *ISC 2012*

Ans Nature of work acts as both, i.e. on one hand it is a morale depressant when the environment of work is not satisfactory or challenging and it acts as a booster when the job or work is satisfactory or challenging in nature.

6. What is the effect of high morale of staff on productivity? *ISC 2011*

Ans Employees morale have a direct effect on company. When employees have high morale, they are more productive and do care for their work. They are committed towards their work, make less mistakes and this will result in completing the project successfully.

7. What do you understand by the term 'morale depressants'? *ISC 2009*

Or What are morale depressants? *ISC 2005*

Ans Morale depressants are factors which result in an unfavourable attitude of an employee towards his work or company. Job insecurity, negative managerial style, unfavourable working conditions, etc are morale depressants.

8. How can a supervisor affect an employee's morale? *ISC 2007*

Ans A supervisor is a person who directly observes the working of a worker.

Thus, he can prioritise the needs and wants of workers and fulfil them. This results in formation of good relationship between workers and supervisors and he can positively mould their behaviour or attitudes.

9. What do you understand by the term 'morale' of employees? *ISC 2004*

Ans Employee morale may be defined as a readiness to co-operate warmly in the tasks and purposes of a given organisation. It is a manifestation of a worker's strength, dependability, pride and confidence in, and devotion to his work.

6/8 Marks Questions

1. Explain any four methods of raising staff morale. *ISC 2019*

Ans Methods of raising staff morale are

(i) **Building responsibility** Everyone wants to feel that his/her work has higher value. If a feeling of responsibility is given to the employee, they feel that their work is more important than the other jobs which helps in increasing their morale.

Methods of Raising Staff Morale

- Building responsibility
- Transparency
- Job enrichment
- Offer incentives

(ii) **Transparency**

Organisations should be clear and transparent with what they expect from employees.

If employees feel the openness to discuss everything with their bosses, their morale is boosted.

(iii) **Job enrichment** Employees enjoy doing jobs which offers them variety and opportunity to show their skills.

Employees are motivated if they are given challenging and interesting job alongwith the autonomy to perform them. This decreases frustration and unhappiness due to boredom of work.

(iv) **Offer incentives** Incentives can be offered in the form of money, bonus, free meals, parking spaces etc. These incentives increase morality and they are motivated to perform better, while at same time helping them to feel that they are being appreciated by organisation.

2. Explain the morale productivity matrix, clearly bringing out the causes of relationship between morale and productivity. ***ISC Specimen 2019***

Or Explain the relationship between morale and productivity. ***ISC 2016***

Or Explain the morale productivity matrix. ***ISC 2012***

Ans An increase in morale may either cause increase or decrease in productivity. A high morale reflects a predisposition to be more productive, if attempts are made to provide effective leadership and coordinate various technical factors.

Miller and Form has given four combinations of productivity and morale. This is known as the morale productivity matrix and is illustrated below. It describes the relationship between morale and productivity.

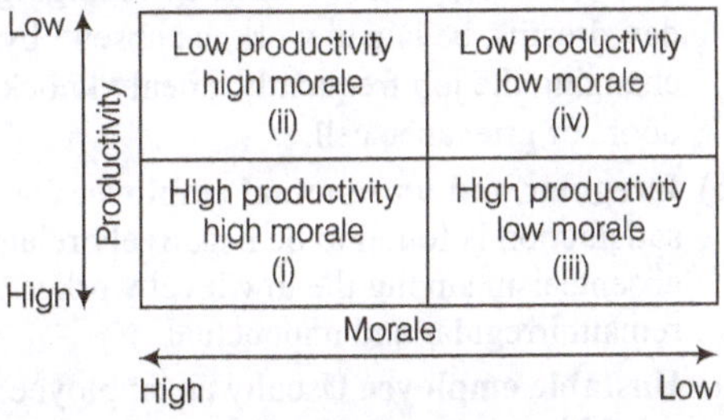

Morale Productivity Matrix

This matrix gives four combinations of morale and productivity

(i) **High productivity-high morale** Generally, high morale leads to higher productivity if it is backed with proper leadership and employees are offered financial and non-financial incentives. Complete identity between organisation's goal and individual's goal leads to this situation.

(ii) **Low productivity-high morale** This situation arises when employees spend their time and energy in fulfilling their individual objectives, totally unrelated with organisational objectives. This situation can also arise due to faulty machinery, lack of training and ineffective supervision.

(iii) **High productivity-low morale** In general, low morale does not lead to high productivity.

However, in a short time period, this phenomenon can be observed due to fear of loss of job and good supervision.

(iv) **Low productivity-low morale** This is a common phenomenon as low morale yields low productivity in the long-run.

So, it can be concluded that there is a complex relationship between morale and productivity.

Value Points

To get maximum marks, following points can be used in answer

- High Productivity–High Morale
- Low Productivity–High Morale
- High Productivity–Low Morale
- Low Productivity–High Morale

3. List any four factors that influence morale. Clearly explain, how they boost or lower the morale. ***ISC 2018***

Ans Following are the factors that influence morale

(i) **Nature of work** If employees are assigned to do interesting and challenging work, it increases the morale of employees. On the other hand, if there is no excitement and creativity in work (i.e. boring, monotonous and repetitive work), employees will be depressed about their work.

(ii) **Self concept** It includes

(a) Self-confidence (b) Self-respect (c) Self-value

High self concept boosts the level of morale in employees, while low self concept will decrease the morale in employees.

(iii) **Goals of the organisation** If goals set by management are realistic, acceptable and useful, then employees develop a positive feeling about their work while if organisation's goals are unrealistic, unacceptable and useless, then employees will be depressed about their work.

(iv) **Work environment** Favourable working conditions (i.e. safety, clean, etc) create high morale among employees while unfavourable working conditions (i.e. unsafe, inconvenience and dirty working conditions) are morale depressants in the organisation.

4. Explain any four factors that influence staff morale. *ISC 2017*

Ans Four factors that influence staff morale are explained below

(i) **Office environment** Surroundings play an important role in developing attitude of an individual. Employee morale is definitely affected by office environment, so it is important to keep it transparent and clean.

(ii) **Nature of work** The nature of work an employee is supposed to perform influences his attitude towards it. Many jobs of a routine nature create boredom and encourages a feeling of alienation and stress among the employees.

(iii) **Appreciation** If an employee is doing well, he needs appreciation for it. Employees feel happy when they are appreciated or rewarded. This gives a sense of belongingness towards the company and in the lack of such benefits, employee's morale is badly affected.

(iv) **Team work** Employees feel happy, if they work in a team. When teams are contributing and working well together, then morale becomes high. If there is lack of teamwork, the morale of employees is adversely affected.

Common Mistake Students get confused among factors that influence /affect staff morale , boost/stimulate staff morale and lower/depress staff morale. Students are advisable to understand the above mentioned points with their meaning to avoid mistakes during exam.

5. Discuss any five methods of raising staff morale in an organisation. *ISC 2010*

Ans Refer to text on page 40.

6. Describe any six measures that may be taken to build high morale among the members of an organisation. *ISC 2007*

Ans Following six measures can be adopted to build high morale

(i) Companies must take a proactive approach, beginning with listening to employees and getting their concerns out into the open.

(ii) Leaders must acknowledge employees' issues and be motivated to make improvements.

(iii) Managers should include as many employees as possible for group discussions or collection of feedback.

(iv) Organisation provides different types of incentives to motivate them to contribute more.

(v) Relationships between the organisation and employees should be clear and transparent.

(vi) Though most employees understand the employee-manager relationship, but it is also important to them that they can sense a feeling of friendship and belongingness in the organisation.

7. What factors will act as morale depressants in your organisation? *ISC 2005*

Ans Following factors act as morale depressants in an organisation

(i) **Unsatisfactory job** Morale tends to be low when the job provides no challenge and satisfaction and job standards are considered very high.

(ii) **Working conditions** When the wages are low, physical work environment is not good, job is not secure and there are no opportunities for promotion, morale of employees tends to be low.

(iii) **Supervision** When supervision is not competent and fair minded, it makes the morale of employees low.

(iv) **Management policies** When management policies are of such kind that exploit the employees, they acts as morale depressant.

(v) **Interpersonal relations** The low confidence of an employee on fellow employees lowers his morale.

(vi) **Employee's educational and occupational level** There is an inverse relationship between educational level and employee morale. Higher is the educational level, lower is the job satisfaction among employees.

8. What are the signs of low morale in the employees? *ISC 2005*

Ans Following are the signs of low morale in employees

(i) **Dissatisfied and restless employee** The employee shows these types of feelings by indulging in day-dreams, be late to work, be absent, by changing the job frequently, openly knocking the doors of grievance cell.

(ii) **Irregular and unpunctual employee** Job satisfaction is found to be negatively related to absenteeism among the low level workers. They remain irregular and unpunctual.

(iii) **Unstable employee** Usually an employee responds to all his grievances, discontentment and unrest by quitting the job.

(iv) **Grieved employee** Low morale is the resultant of grievances. Therefore, organisations have started maintaining separate grievance cell to cure this contagious disease before it takes the shape of huge problem.

(v) **Indisciplined employee** When there is a need to impose discipline by giving threat of punishment etc then, there is low morale prevailing in the organisation.

(vi) **Fatigued employee** The rates of fatigue vary with the intensity of motivation. Highly motivated person will not have fatigue easily as compared to less motivated person.

9. Explain briefly the importance of staff morale. ***ISC 2003***

Ans Following are the points of importance of staff morale

(i) **Accomplishment of a common goal** When morale is boosted, employees feel valued and work with co-operation in the best interests of individuals or groups and the organisation for which they work.

(ii) **Trust and control** High morale helps in creating trust among employees and between employer and employees.

This will also develop a sense of control over their own lives and careers.

(iii) **Leadership and management** High morale creates a sense of leadership in the organisation and the leader controls and manages the employees in a better way.

(iv) **Confidence** It may also develop a sense of confidence as employees are confident and work for the betterment of the company as well as for their individual interests.

(v) **Increased productivity** Employees having a high morale are able to produce better results in terms of productivity, product quantity and quality.

(vi) **Discipline** High morale in employees make them more disciplined and systematic in doing work.

Common Mistake Sometimes, students get confused between staff morale and staff motivation. These two are different terms. So students are advisable to understand both terms clearly to avoid confusion in examination.

10. Discuss briefly the various morale stimulants. ***ISC 2002***

Ans Refer to text on page 39.

Case Based Question

Case 1

Reflections Pvt. Ltd. is a publishing company. Its book on the subject Business Studies for Class 12 is in great demand. As a result, the base level employees are always racing against time and have to work overtime and on holidays to cater to the ever increasing demand.

Managers in the marketing department are under stress as they have to handle dealers pan India. The work stress has led to dissatisfaction among the employees and managers. ***ISC Sem I Specimen 2021***

(i) Name the step of staffing process that has not been performed properly.

(a) Manpower estimation (b) Selection
(c) Recruitment (d) Training

Ans (a) Manpower estimation

(ii) Which of the following is not a characteristic of staff morale?

(a) It is a by product of group relationships
(b) It may be financial or non-financial
(c) It is contagious
(d) It is dynamic in nature

Ans (a) It is a by product of group relationships

(iii) Employees of this publishing company are in which state of morale productivity matrix?

(a) High morale, low productivity
(b) High morale, high productivity
(c) Low morale, low productivity
(d) Low morale, high productivity

Ans (d) Low morale, high productivity

(iv) Which type of need of the base level employees is being satisfied?

(a) Safety
(b) Self-esteem
(c) Esteem of others
(d) Self-actualisation

Ans (d) Self-actualisation

CHAPTER TEST

01 Mark Questions

1. According to Professor Flippo, what is referred as the mental condition or attitude of individuals and groups, that determines their willingness to cooperate?

2. Who has given four combinations of productivity and morale?

3. Name one method of raising staff morale.

4. Job security creates ……… morale among employees about their job.

5. ………… self-concept decrease the morale of employee about their work.

6. Which of these is not a part of an employee's morale?
(a) Satisfaction level (b) Feelings
(c) Attitudes (d) Workload

7. Employee morale relates to
(a) skills (b) empathy
(c) attitude (d) productivity

8. Which of the following is not a morale stimulant?
(a) Leadership (b) Negative managerial style
(c) Job security (d) Future prosperity

9. Increment in remuneration is a moral stimulants. State true or false.

10. High morale always leads to low productivity. State true or false.

02 Marks Questions

11. Give an example that shows high morale of an employee towards an organisation.

12. Give an example that shows low morale of an employee towards an organisation.

13. What is staff morale?

14. State any two depressants that hurts the feeling of employees on work.

15. What do you understand by the term 'high productivity'?

04 Marks Questions

16. State any four characteristics of staff morale.

17. Explain the methods (any two) of raising staff morale.

06/08 Marks Questions

18. What factors are responsible in affecting employee morale?

19. Explain any four morale stimulants and any four morale depressants.

20. Miller and Form has given four combinations of productivity and morale. Explain each of them with an example.

Answers

1. Morale
2. Miller and Form
3. Job enrichment
4. high
5. Low
6. (d) Workload
7. (d) productivity
8. (b) Negative managerial style
9. True
10. False

05

Staff Motivation

TREND ANALYSIS 5 YEARS

Average No. of Questions Across all Sets

	Types of Questions	2023	2020	2019	2018	2017
01 Motivation and Types of Incentives	1 Mark	—	—	—	—	—
	2 Marks	—	—	—	1	—
	4 Marks	—	—	—	—	1
	6 Marks	—	—	—	—	—
	8 Marks	—	—	—	—	—
02 Maslow's Need Theory and Herzberg's Two Factor Theory	1 Mark	1	—	—	—	—
	2 Marks	—	—	1	—	1
	4 Marks	1	—	—	1	—
	6 Marks	—	—	—	—	—
	8 Marks	—	1	—	—	—

Meaning and Definition of Staff Motivation

The term 'motivation' has been derived from the latin word 'movere' which means 'to move'. In general, motivation means incitement or inducement to act in a desired manner to achieve certain goals. Staff motivation means incitement provided to all the employees so that they perform to achieve organisational goals.

According to **Mc Farland**, "Motivation refers to the way in which urges, desires, aspirations, strivings or needs direct, control and explain the behaviour of human beings."

Characteristics of Motivation

Following are the characteristics of motivation

(i) **Motivation is a psychological phenomenon** It is a personal and internal feeling like an urge, drives, desires and aspirations of human being, which influence human behaviour.

(ii) **Goal directed behaviour** Motivation inspires an employee to achieve goals. Thus, it encourages goal directed behaviour.

(iii) **Motivation may be positive or negative** Positive motivation means inspiring people to work better by providing incentives and negative motivation means forcing people to work by threatening or punishment.

(iv) **Motivation is a complex process** As the individuals are heterogeneous in their expectations, perceptions and reactions, therefore different incentives are required to motivate different employees.

(v) **Motivation is a continuous process** Human needs are unlimited. Therefore, motivation is an ongoing process.

Difference between Morale and Motivation

Basis	Morale	Motivation
Meaning	Morale is a composite of attitudes, feeling and sentiments towards works for the accomplishment of organisational goals.	Motivation is the process of stimulating people to action to accomplish desired goals.
Phenomenon	Morale is a group phenomenon.	Motivation is an individual's willingness to work. Thus, it is an individual phenomenon.
Inter-relationship	High morale does not necessarily result in higher motivation.	Higher motivation leads to higher morale.
Productivity	High morale may be associated with low productivity.	High motivation means high productivity.
Concern	Morale is concerned with 'mobilisation of sentiments.'	Motivation is concerned with 'mobilisation of energy.'

Importance of Motivation

Motivation is important for employees as well as employers. Importance of motivation may be summed up as follows

(i) **Improves performance** Motivation helps to improve the performance level of employees. It bridges the gap between the ability to work and willingness to work, resulting in higher level of performance.

(ii) **Builds positive attitude** Motivation helps to change negative attitude of employees to positive attitude, so as to achieve organisational goals, by using incentives such as bonus, praise, punishment and promotion.

(iii) **Reduces employee turnover** Motivation helps to reduce employee turnover and thereby saves the cost of new recruitment and training. When employees' needs are satisfied, they may not think of leaving the organisation. It also helps to retain talented people in the organisation.

(iv) **Introduces changes** Motivation helps the managers to introduce changes and motivate employees, so that they show less resistance in accepting the changes, as they know it is necessary to adapt to changes in order to survive in the competitive world.

(v) **Reduces absenteeism** Motivation helps to reduce absenteeism by providing proper working conditions, adequate rewards and good relations with supervisor.

(vi) **Better industrial relations** Increased labour productivity, in turn, results in higher wages for employees. Motivational schemes create integration of individual interest with organisational objectives. There arises a sense of belonging and mutual cooperation at all levels. Motivation will foster team spirit among workers. This will reduce labour unrest and create better relations between management and workers.

Factors Influencing Motivation

These factors can be categorised into four groups

(i) **Individual factors** It includes

(a) Gender (b) Abilities

(c) Age (d) Experience

(e) Personal life (f) Anxiety

(ii) **Social factors** It includes

(a) Relationship with co-workers

(b) Relationship with leadership

(c) Team spirit

(iii) **Organisational factors** It includes

(a) Working condition/environment

(b) Facilities (c) Work load

(d) Motivational leaders (e) Career development

(f) Salary (g) Reward system

(iv) **Cultural factors or organisational cultures** It includes

(a) Beliefs of organisation

(b) Values of organisation

(c) Ideology of organisation

Types of Incentives to Motivate Employees

Some of the important incentives to motivate employees are listed below

1. Financial Incentives (Monetary)

It refers to those incentives, which are in **monetary** form or measurable in monetary terms and used to motivate employees for better performance.

Some of the important financial incentives are listed below

(i) **Pay and allowances** For every employee, salary is the basic monetary incentive. It includes basic pay, dearness allowance, house rent allowance, etc.

(ii) **Bonus** It is a one time reward for high performance. Bonus may be paid in cash or kind. e.g. Some sales concerns periodically offer prizes and trips to their top sales executives.

(iii) **Profit sharing** It means employees are given a share in the profits of the enterprise. This is in addition to their wages/salaries. It is a group incentive scheme used to improve productivity and profitability.

(iv) **Co-partnership/Stock option** In this system, employees are given a share in both profits and control of the business. They participate in the management of the enterprise in addition to sharing its profit.

(v) **Retirement benefits** Several retirement benefits such as provident fund, pension and gratuity are provided to employees as a financial security after retirement.

(vi) **Productivity linked wages** In this incentive, rewards are given to employees as a percentage of sales/production achieved. Its advantage is that reward is directly related to performance.

(vii) **Perquisites** Apart from basic salary, some companies offer fringe benefits and perquisites to their employees, e.g. Perks like rent free accommodation, education of children, medical allowance, car allowance, etc.

2. Non-financial Incentives (Non-monetary)

All the needs of individuals are not satisfied by money alone. Psychological, social and emotional factors also play an important role in motivating employees.

The incentives which are provided to satisfy these needs, are termed as non-financial or **non-monetary** incentives.

Some of the important non-financial incentives are listed below

(i) **Status** In business terms, status means ranking of positions in the organisation. The authority, responsibility, rewards, recognition, perquisites and prestige of job indicates the status given to a person holding a managerial position. It satisfies psychological and social needs of an individual.

(ii) **Career advancement opportunity** When employees are provided opportunities to grow in status and responsibility, they are satisfied and are committed to organisational goals. Appropriate skill development programmes and sound promotion policy helps employees to achieve this.

(iii) **Job enrichment** It is concerned with designing of jobs that include great variety of work content, require higher level of knowledge and skill. This provides opportunity for growth and development of an employee.

(iv) **Job security** It ensures stability of income, which motivates an individual to work with greater zeal. However, it has one negative aspect i.e. it makes individuals feel that they are not likely to lose their jobs and hence, may become complacent and careless.

(v) **Employee participation** It means involving employees in decision-making regarding the issues related to them, e.g. Encourage participation in joint management committees, work committees, canteen committees, etc.

(vi) **Organisational climate** Better conditions of an organisation like individual autonomy, reward orientation, consideration to employees, risk taking, etc makes an organisation to be different from the other organisations. It can influence employee in a positive/negative way.

(vii) **Employee empowerment** It means giving more autonomy and powers to subordinates. It makes people feel that their jobs are important, as a result of which, they contribute positively to the use of skills and talents in the job performance.

(viii) **Employee recognition** It means acknowledgement of work with a show of appreciation. With such appreciation, employees feel motivated.

Difference between Monetary and Non-monetary Incentives

Basis	Monetary incentive	Non-monetary incentive
Nature	These are measurable in monetary terms.	These are not measurable in monetary terms.
Need satisfaction	They satisfy physiological needs of individuals.	They satisfy social, psychological and esteem needs of individuals.
Instruments	Pay, bonus, profit sharing, stock option, etc.	Status, organisational climate, employee recognition and empowerment, etc.
Suitability	More suitability for workers.	More suitability for managers.
Conflict	Monetary incentives may create conflict among the workers.	Non-monetary incentives do not create any kind of conflict among the employees.

Maslow's Need Hierarchy Theory

Abraham Maslow has given this theory. It is based on human needs thus, it is termed as 'need hierarchy theory'.

According to him, human needs occur in hierarchial order from the lowest to highest level need as follows

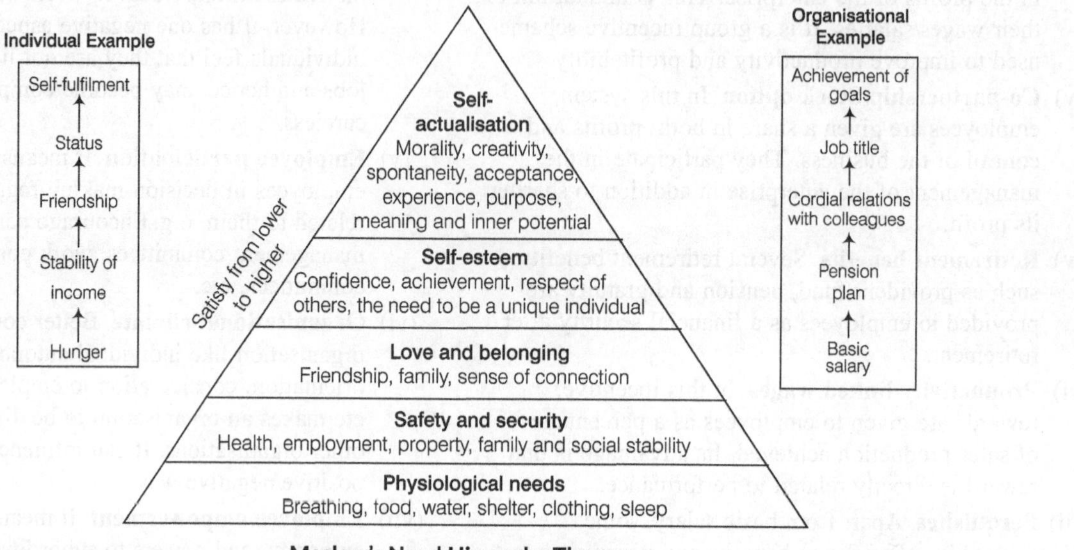

Maslow's Need Hierarchy Theory

(i) **Physiological need** These are biological needs required to preserve human life. Therefore, these needs are also known as survival needs. These include needs for food, clothing, shelter, sleep, etc.
(ii) **Safety/Security need** After the satisfaction of physiological needs, the need for security arises such as physical, emotional and social security needs.
(iii) **Social/Affiliation need** These needs are concerned with affection, sense of belongingness, acceptance and friendship.
(iv) **Esteem need** These include factors such as self-respect, status and recognition. When these needs are fulfilled, it enhances self-confidence and prestige of employees.
(v) **Self-actualisation need** It is the highest level need in the hierarchy. These needs include growth, self-fulfilment and achievement of goals.

Assumptions of Maslow's Theory

The main assumptions of Maslow's need hierarchy theory are

(i) People's behaviour is based on their needs. Satisfaction of such needs influences their behaviour.
(ii) People's needs are hierarchical in order. They start from basic physiological needs and reach to high level needs.
(iii) A satisfied need can no longer motivate a person, only next higher level need can motivate a person.
(iv) A person moves to the next higher level need, only when the lower level need is satisfied.
(v) There are five classification of human needs.

Criticism of Maslow's Theory

Following are the criticism of Maslow's theory

(i) Maslow's theory is almost a non-testable theory (i.e. lack of proper research).
(ii) It may be quite possible that there may be overlapping in need hierarchy.
(iii) Behaviour of employees differ from one to another though need is same.
(iv) It is very difficult for managers to identify the need level for employees.
(v) Classification of needs are somewhat artificial and arbitrary.

Herzberg's Two Factor Theory of Motivation

Another popular need-based approach to motivation is the **dual-structure approach** developed by **Frederick Herzberg**. This is also known as 'Two-factor theory'. There are two groups of factor which motivate to employees. These factors are

(i) **Hygiene factors or maintenance factors** They are required in organisation to avoid dissatisfaction among employees. Hygiene factors do not increase satisfaction among employees but that can increase dis-satisfaction, if they are missing. Hygiene factors include

(a) **Salary** Salary structure should be appropriate and reasonable in the organisation.

(b) **Company policies and administration** Company policies should be fair and clean. Administration should adopt flexible approach for workers.

(c) **Status** It should be familiar and retained.

(d) **Relationship with co-workers** There should not be conflict among co-workers in the organisation.

(e) **Good working conditions** There should be good working environment in organisation.

It include

- Safety
- Cleanliness
- Hygiene

(f) **Job security** There should be job security in organisation for workers.

(g) **Working schedule** Working schedule should be flexible as per the need of employees.

(ii) **Motivational factors or growth factors** They provide job satisfaction to employees with better performance at work.

Motivational factors include

(a) **Responsibility** Employees should be assigned ownership of work with responsibility.

(b) **Growth** There must be scope for growth and advancement opportunities in organisation for talented employees.

(c) **Recognition** Employees should be praised and recognised for good work.

(d) **Interesting work** Work should be interesting, meaningful and challenging for employees.

(e) **Achievement** The employee must have a sense of work achievement.

Relationship between Maslow and Herzberg's Theories

Both theories suggest that human needs have to be satisfied for the motivation of the employees in the organisation. Herzberg's theory is extension of Maslow's theory.

Maslow's theory is more popular in developing countries where there is lack of money while Herzberg's theory is more popular in developed countries where money is less motivating factor.

Both theories are influenced by environmental conditions and workers attitude. The end result is motivation.

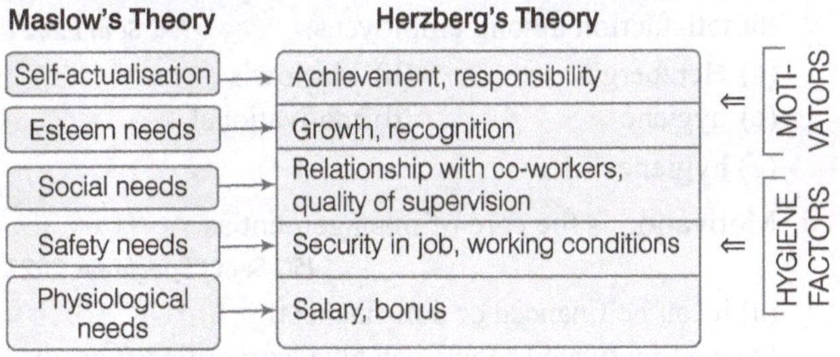

Relationship between these Two Theories

PYQs Previous Years' Questions

1 Mark Questions

1. According to Maslow, one of the human needs deals with the realisation of one's own potential. Name this human need. ***ISC 2023***

Ans Self-actualisation need

2. Name the first need as given in Maslow's hierarchy of human needs. ***ISC Specimen 2023***

Ans Physiological need

3. According to Herzberg's two-factor theory, ... factors are inherent in the job, rather than being present in the surrounding environment. ***ISC Sem I 2021***

(a) dissatisfiers (b) hygiene
(c) maintenance (d) motivational

Ans (d) motivational

4. As stated by Maslow, ... need is also known as the need for self-fulfillment. ***ISC Sem I 2021***

(a) physiological (b) social
(c) self-esteem (d) self-actualisation

Ans (d) self-actualisation

5. Non-financial motivation given to staff includes .... ***ISC Sem I 2021***

(a) allowances (b) fringe benefits
(c) satisfying job (d) promotion

Ans (c) satisfying job

6. Which of the following is not an assumption of Maslow's theory of motivation? ***ISC Sem I 2021***

(a) Human behaviour is not based on needs
(b) A satisfied need no longer influences motivation

(c) Higher level needs remain inactive till the lower-level needs are satisfied
(d) Human needs can be classified into five categories

Ans (a) Human behaviour is not based on needs

7. Which one of the following is a motivational factor according to Herzberg's two-factor theory? ***ISC Sem I 2021***

(a) Status (b) Working conditions
(c) Salary (d) Challenging work

Ans (d) Challenging work

8. Which one of the following is a type of financial incentive given to an employee in an organisation? ***ISC Sem I 2021***

(a) Promotion
(b) Participation in decision-making
(c) Higher authority and responsibility
(d) Recognition and status

Ans (a) Promotion

9. Presence of .... factors is necessary to avoid dissatisfaction among employees. ***ISC Sem I 2021***

(a) Herzberg's (b) Maslow's
(c) hygiene (d) motivational

Ans (c) hygiene

10. Motivation is the core of management as ***ISC Sem I Specimen 2021***

(a) it can be financial or non-financial
(b) well-motivated people can give extraordinary results
(c) money is the biggest motivator
(d) motivation and morale are interrelated

Ans (b) well-motivated people can give extraordinary results

11. Motivation is a very strong tool in the hands of the employer as ***ISC Sem I Specimen 2021***

(a) it helps in recruiting good employees
(b) it gives financial and non-financial incentives
(c) it is a continuous process
(d) it helps in optimum utilisation of human resources

Ans (d) it helps in optimum utilisation of human resources

12. As per Maslow's theory of human needs, how many needs are there? ***ISC Sem I Specimen 2021***

(a) Two (b) Three
(c) Four (d) Five

Ans (d) Five

13. As stated by Maslow, ... include acceptance, affection and association with the social groups. ***ISC Sem I Specimen 2021***

(a) self-actualisation needs (b) esteem needs
(c) social needs (d) safety needs

Ans (c) social needs

14. Esteem needs are of the following two types. ***ISC Sem I Specimen 2021***

(a) Esteem needs and ego needs
(b) Ego needs and satisfaction needs
(c) Self-esteem needs and esteem of others
(d) Self-esteem and self-actualisation needs

Ans (c) Self-esteem needs and esteem of others

15. The satisfiers in Herzberg's theory are also called ***ISC Sem I Specimen 2021***

(a) hygiene factors (b) motivational factors
(c) maintenance factors (d) environmental factors

Ans (b) motivational factors

Concept Enhancer Motivational factors are also called satisfiers because they lead to satisfaction.

16. Which of the following needs are not a part of Maslow's theory of human needs? ***ISC Sem I Specimen 2021***

(a) Psychological needs
(b) Safety needs
(c) Social needs
(d) Esteem needs

Ans (a) Psychological needs

Common Mistake Generally, students misunderstand between psychological and physiological needs. Physiological needs, i.e., breathing, food, shelter, water, clothing, sleep are the part of Maslow's theory of human needs. Students should clear the meaning of both terms to avoid mistakes in examination.

17. Non-financial motivation given to staff does not include ***ISC Sem I Specimen 2021***

(a) status symbol
(b) allowances
(c) appreciation for work
(d) knowledge of results

Ans (b) allowances

2 Marks Questions

1. Briefly explain the two types of esteem needs, as per the human needs stated by Maslow. ***ISC 2019***

Ans Two types of esteem needs are

(i) **Esteem for oneself** This is self-esteem i.e. esteem we have for ourselves. This includes dignity, self-respect, mastery and independence.

(ii) **Esteem of others** This is desire for reputation or respect from others. This includes status and prestige.

2. "Money is the only motivator". Comment? **ISC Specimen 2019**

Or Why is money regarded as the biggest motivator of employees? **ISC 2012**

Ans Money can fulfil every possible need of an individual. It can satisfy almost all the possible wants of an individual. It is the best incentive that is measurable in monetary terms and can motivate employees to perform better.

3. Name any four non-monetary incentives that may be used in an organisation. **ISC 2018**

Or Mention four non-monetary incentives that can be given to motivate an employee. **ISC 2007**

Ans Four non-monetary incentives that way be used in an organisation are as follows

(i) **Job enrichment** It provides opportunity for growth and development.

(ii) **Job security** It motivates the employee to work with greater zeal.

(iii) **Organisational climate** It can influence employee in a positive/negative way.

(iv) **Status** It satisfies psychological and social need of an employee.

4. Enumerate any four human needs according to Maslow's hierarchy. **ISC 2017**

Ans Four human needs according to Maslow's need hierarchy theory are

(i) Physiological needs (ii) Safety and security needs
(iii) Social needs (iv) Self-esteem needs

5. Explain self-actualisation need as given by Maslow. **ISC 2016**

Ans Self-actualisation need is the highest level need in the 'need hierarchy' theory given by Maslow. These needs include needs for growth, self-fulfilment and achievement of goals. These needs represent what an individual wants to achieve after fulfilling the needs of his family and society. An individual strives to fulfil this need when he has been able to fulfil physiological needs, safety and security needs, love and belongingness needs and self-esteem needs.

6. Define motivation. **ISC 2015**

Ans It means incitement or inducement to act in a desired manner to achieve certain goals. According to EFL Brech, "Motivation is a general inspirational process which gets the members of the team to pull their weight effectively to give their loyalty to the group, to carry out properly the tasks that they have accepted, and generally to play an effective part in the job that the group has undertaken."

7. "Money is not the only motivator for staff". Justify this statement. **ISC 2011**

Ans This statement is true in the sense that an individual has certain psychological, emotional and social needs. Money can't satisfy them.

Thus, non-financial incentives such as promotion, job security, recognition, etc are required to satisfy such needs.

8. State two limitations of Maslow's theory of hierarchy of human needs. **ISC 2010**

Ans Limitations of Maslow's theory are

(i) Needs are not the only determinant of behaviour.

(ii) One cannot fix the hierarchy of needs.

9. How does challenging work motivate employees? **ISC 2010**

Ans If jobs are interesting and enriched, they give workers more autonomy and a greater sense of responsibility. This also provides the opportunity for growth and a meaningful work experience. Thus, jobs with great variety of work content, which require higher level of knowledge and skill and provides challenges to an employee, are a source of motivation for them.

10. Safety needs of an employee can be satisfied in either a positive or a negative manner. Explain. **ISC 2008**

Ans Safety needs of an employee are the needs that relate to his physical and economic security.

These can be satisfied in a positive or a negative manner.

(i) **In a positive manner,** through provision of pension, insurance of various kinds, provident fund, etc.

(ii) **In a negative manner,** through fear, by way of demotions, lay-offs, close supervision, etc.

Value Points

To get maximum marks, following point should be included in the answer

- How safety needs of an employee can be satisfied in a positive manner
- How safety needs of an employee can be satisfied in a negative manner

11. How can the safety needs of an employee be satisfied by the employee? *ISC 2004*

Ans Safety and security needs include the desire for physical protection. This can only be possible by providing good working condition, fencing of machinery, economic security in terms of gratuity, provident fund, security of job, etc.

4 Marks Questions

1. Briefly explain the two factors as given by Herzberg, that affect satisfaction and dissatisfaction of employees. *ISC 2023*

Or Briefly explain two factors of Herzberg's theory of motivation. *ISC 2020*

Ans There are two groups of factors which motivate the employees

(i) **Hygiene factors or maintenance factors** They are required in organisation to avoid dis-satisfaction among employees. Hygiene factors include

(a) **Salary** Salary structure should be appropriate and reasonable in the organisation.

(b) **Company policies and administration** Company policies should be fair and clean. Administration should adopt flexible approach for workers.

(c) **Status** It should be familiar and retained.

(d) **Relationship with co-workers** There should not be conflict among co-workers in the organisation.

(e) **Good working conditions** There should be good working environment in organisation. It include

- Safety
- Cleanliness
- Hygiene

(f) **Job security** There should be job security in organisation for workers.

(g) **Working schedule** Working schedule should be flexible as per the need of employees.

Hygiene factors do not increase satisfaction among employees but that can increase dis-satisfaction, if they are missing.

Hygiene Factors
- Salary
- Company policies and administration
- Status
- Relationship with co-workers
- Good working conditions
- Job security
- Working schedule

So, they are known as maintenance factors in organisation. The two factor theory argues that successful manager must reduce job dis-satisfaction by providing employees with hygiene factors.

(ii) **Motivational factors** They provide job satisfaction to employees with better performance at work. These factors are

(a) **Responsibility** Employees should be assigned ownership of work with responsibility.

(b) **Growth** There must be scope for growth and advancement opportunities in organisation for talented employees.

(c) **Recognition** Employees should be praised and recognised for good work.

(d) **Interesting work** Work should be interesting, meaningful and challenging for employees.

(e) **Achievement** The employees must have a sense of work achievement.

Motivational Factors
- Responsibility
- Growth
- Recognition
- Interesting work
- Achievement

2. "Money is not the only motivation for an employee". With reference to the above statement, name and explain any two non-monetary incentives of motivation. *ISC Specimen 2023*

Ans (i) **Status** In business terms, status means ranking of positions in the organisation. The authority, responsibility, rewards, recognition, perquisites and prestige of job indicates the status given to a person holding a managerial position. It satisfies psychological and social needs of an individual.

(ii) **Career advancement opportunity** When employees are provided opportunities to grow in status and responsibility, they are satisfied and are committed to organisational goals.

Appropriate skill development programmes and sound promotion policy helps employees to achieve this.

Concept Enhancer All the needs of individuals are not satisfied by money alone. Psychological, social and emotional factors also play an important role in motivating employees. The incentives which are provided to satisfy these needs are termed as non-monetary incentives.

3. How do motivation factors as given by Herzberg affect motivation of employees? *ISC Specimen 2019*

Ans Refer to Q. No. 1 (4 Marks) on page 54.

4. Explain the first three needs as per the Maslow's hierarchy of human needs. *ISC 2018*

Ans Following are the three needs as per the Maslow's theory

(i) **Basic physiological needs** These are the basic needs, which a person is required to satisfy in order to survive.

Hunger, thirst, shelter and sleep are some of the examples of these needs. In an organisation, basic salary helps to satisfy these needs.

(ii) **Safety/security needs** These needs are concerned with physical, economic and social security, in the form of job security, stability of income, etc.

(iii) **Affiliation/belongingness/social needs** These needs are concerned with affection, sense of belongingness, acceptance and friendship. It is fulfilled when employees have cordial relations with colleagues.

5. Define motivation. Briefly explain any four characteristics of motivation. *ISC 2017*

Ans **Meaning of motivation** It means incitement or inducement to act in a desired manner to achieve certain goals.

According to EFL Brech, "Motivation is a general inspirational process which gets the members of the team to pull their weight effectively to give their loyalty to the group, to carry out properly the tasks that they have accepted, and generally to play an effective part in the job that the group has undertaken."

Characteristics of motivation The four characteristics of motivation are briefly explained below

(i) **Personal and internal feeling** Motivation is a psychological phenomenon which generates within an individual. Motives are the energetic forces within a person that drive him to action.

(ii) **Goal-directed behaviour** Motivation is a behavioural concept that directs human behaviour towards certain goals.

(iii) **Continuous process** Human needs are unlimited. Therefore, motivation is an ongoing process.

(iv) **Complex** Individuals differ in their motivation. Different people seek different things and they work for different reasons.

Human needs and motives are varied and they change from time to time. People satisfy their needs in many different ways. Thus, motivation is complex.

6. Define motivation. Differentiate between monetary and non-monetary factors affecting motivation. *ISC 2013*

Ans **Definition of motivation** It means incitement or inducement to act in a desired manner to achieve certain goals. According to EFL Brech, "Motivation is a general inspirational process which gets the members of the team to pull their weight effectively to give their loyalty to the group, to carry out properly the tasks that they have accepted, and generally to play an effective part in the job that the group has undertaken."

Difference between monetary and non-monetary incentives

Basis	Monetary incentive	Non-monetary incentive
Nature	These are measurable in monetary terms.	These are not measurable in monetary terms.
Need satisfaction	They satisfy physiological needs of individuals.	They satisfy social, psychological and esteem needs of individuals.
Instruments	Pay, bonus, profit sharing, stock option, etc.	Status, organisational climate, employee recognition and empowerment, etc.
Suitability	More suitability for workers.	More suitability for managers.
Conflict	Monetary incentives may create conflict among the workers.	Non-monetary incentives do not create any kind of conflict among the employees.

7. Differentiate between morale and motivation. *ISC 2008*

Ans Difference between morale and motivation is as follows

Basis	Morale	Motivation
Meaning	Morale is a composite of attitudes, feeling and sentiments towards works for the accomplishment of organisational goals.	Motivation is the process of stimulating people to action to accomplish desired goals.
Phenomenon	Morale is a group phenomenon.	Motivation is an individual's willingness to work. Thus, it is an individual phenomenon.
Inter-relationship	High morale does not necessarily result in higher motivation.	Higher motivation leads to higher morale.
Productivity	High morale may be associated with low productivity.	High motivation means high productivity.
Concern	Morale is concerned with 'mobilisation of sentiments.'	Motivation is concerned with 'mobilisation of energy.'

8. Draw Maslow's hierarchy of human needs. *ISC 2005*

Ans

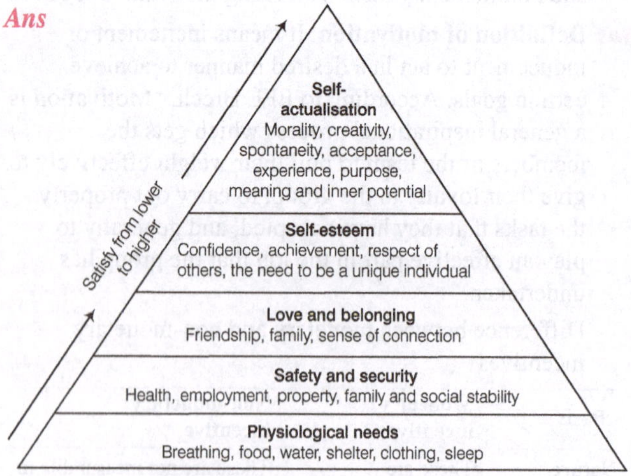

Maslow's Need Hierarchy Theory

9. Money is the biggest, but not the only motivator. Explain. *ISC 2005*

Ans Money can fulfil every possible need of an individual. It can satisfy almost all the possible wants of an individual. It is the best incentive that is measurable in monetary terms and can motivate employees to perform better.

Contrary to this observation, Allen post observes, "Money incentives alone do not bring about desired motivation. Employees in an industry are not 'economic men' so much as they are 'ego men'. What they want above else, is credit for work done, interesting tasks, appreciation, approval and congenial relations with their employers and fellow workers. They want these satisfactions even more than higher wages or job security."

An individual has certain psychological, emotional and social needs. Money can't satisfy them. Thus, non-financial incentives such as promotion, job security, recognition, etc are required to satisfy such needs.

6/8 Marks Questions

1. With the help of a diagram, explain the hierarchy of needs as given by Maslow. *ISC 2015*

Ans Abraham Maslow has given this theory, based on human needs. Thus, it is termed as 'need hierarchy theory'.

According to him, human needs occur in hierarchial order from the lowest to the highest level need as follows

(i) **Physiological need** These are biological needs required to preserve human life. Therefore, these needs are also known as 'survival needs'. These include needs for food, clothing, shelter, sleep, etc.

(ii) **Safety/Security need** After the satisfaction of physiological needs, the need for security arises such as physical, emotional and social security needs.

(iii) **Belongingness/Affiliation need** These needs are concerned with affection, sense of belongingness, acceptance and friendship.

(iv) **Esteem need** These include factors such as self-respect, status and recognition. When these needs are fulfilled, it enhances self-confidence and prestige of employees.

(v) **Self-actualisation need** It is the highest level need in the hierarchy. These needs include growth, self-fulfilment and achievement of goals.

According to Maslow, needs of human beings arise from the lowest level. On satisfaction of one need, he moves on to the next level. Once a need is satisfied, one cannot be motivated by fulfilling the same need.

For diagram Refer to Q. No. 8 on page 56.

2. State and explain any four non-monetary incentives that can be used to motivate employees. *ISC 2014*

Ans Four such non-monetary incentives are

(i) **Status** In business terms, status means ranking of positions in the organisation. The authority, responsibility, rewards, recognition, perquisites and prestige of job indicates the status given to a person holding a managerial position.

It satisfies psychological and social needs of an individual.

(ii) **Career advancement opportunity** When employees are provided opportunities to grow in status and responsibility, they are satisfied and are committed to organisational goals.

Non-monetary Incentives
- Status
- Career advancement opportunity
- Job enrichment
- Job security

Appropriate skill development programmes and sound promotion policy helps employees to achieve this.

(iii) **Job enrichment** Job enrichment is concerned with designing of jobs that include great variety of work content, require higher level of knowledge and skill.

This provides opportunity for growth and development to an employee.

(iv) **Job security** It ensures stability of income, which motivate an individual to work with great zeal. However, it has one negative aspect i.e. it makes individuals feel that they are not likely to loose their jobs and hence may become complacent and careless.

3. Discuss the hierarchy of needs as given by Maslow. ***ISC 2013***

Or State Maslow's need satisfaction theory. Explain the hierarchy of human needs as given by Maslow. ***ISC 2007***

Ans **Maslow's need satisfaction hierarchy theory** Refer to text on page 50.

4. What is motivation? As a manager of growing textile factory, mention any six incentives for your workers. Explain as to how each one of them will help you in motivating the workers. ***ISC 2009***

Ans **Meaning of staff motivation** Refer to text on page 47.

Types of incentives to motivate employees Refer to text on page 48 and 49.

Additional Questions

2/4 Marks Questions

1. Give two points that shows the need of motivation in an organisation.

Ans Motivation is necessary because

(i) It helps in improving the efficiency of employees.

(ii) It creates friendly and supportive environment in an organisation.

2. When we talk about motivation one term also come into the picture i.e. motive. What does this term mean?

Ans A motive is an inner state that energises, activates, moves and directs behaviour towards goals. Motives are the expression of a person's need.

3. Give an example that reveals the negative aspect of motivation in an organisation.

Ans Deduction in salary, when an employee arrives late due to traffic jam.

4. Give an example that reveals the positive aspect of motivation in an organisation.

Ans Rewarding an employee because of his valuable suggestions.

5. Explain the process of motivation.

Ans Motivation is the process of interaction between human needs and incentives. Need is the feeling that something is required. Feeling of needs creates tension and people engage in certain activities to release it. But the satisfaction of one need leads to feeling of a new need and this is a continuing process. When an action is unsuccessful, need satisfaction is blocked. The resultant behaviour may be rational or irrational. Rational behaviour implies search for alternative methods to satisfy needs.

e.g. A salesman who fails to get a promotion may join a diploma course to improve his chance for promotion.

6. "Motivation plays an important role in the life of employees". By stating any four points, prove this statement worthwhile.

Ans Motivation is important because of the following reasons

(i) **Higher efficiency** Motivation is an effective instrument in the hands of management to maximise efficiency of operations. A worker may be very competent but no activity can take place, until the individual is willing to perform that activity. What employees do, depends largely on how much and why they want to do it. Motivated employees give greater performance than demotivated ones.

(ii) **Reduction in labour turnover** High motivation leads to job satisfaction of workers. Opportunities for need satisfaction make employees loyal and committed to the organisation. As a result, labour absenteeism and turnover are low.

(iii) **Better industrial relations** Increased labour productivity in turn results in higher wages for employees. Motivational schemes create integration of individual interests with organisational objectives. There arises a sense of belonging and mutual cooperation at all levels. Motivation will foster team spirit among workers. This will reduce labour unrest and create better relations between management and workers.

(iv) **Facilitates change** High motivation helps to reduce resistance to change. An organisation has to incorporate changes to cope up with environmental changes. Properly motivated employees accept, introduce and implement these changes, keeping the organisation effective.

7. State the assumptions of Maslow's theory.

Ans The main assumptions of Maslow's need hierarchy theory are

(i) People's behaviour is based on their needs. Satisfaction of such needs influences their behaviour.

(ii) People's needs are hierarchical in order. They start from basic physiological needs and reach to high level needs.

(iii) A satisfied need can no longer motivate a person, only next higher level need can motivate a person.

(iv) A person moves to the next higher level need, only when the lower level need is satisfied.

(v) There are five classification of human needs.

8. Anil, after joining Apex Computers found himself in a situation where his boss Aparna does not show any interest in the opinions of her subordinates. Initially, Anil was working for Mahesh, who would reward every attempt and innovative solution. He would also allow mistakes to occur without severe punishment. In the end, Anil loses all of his motivation due to the lack of self-expression.

What is the main reason for Anil's disillusionment? Explain.

Ans The main reason for Anil's disillusionment was his expectation that his new boss would be similar to the previous one. According to Maslow's hierarchy of needs, Mahesh was providing Anil with basic needs, physiological needs and self-fulfillment needs.

The entire pyramid of human motivational requirements was met under the management of Mahesh.

However, Anil under the governance of Aparna, could not satisfy his needs for esteem and self-actualisation. He was highly unmotivated and disinterested due to Aparna's management style.

8 Marks Question

1. Explain the relationship between Maslow's theory of the hierarchy of human wants and Herzberg's two factor theory.

Ans Both theories suggest that human needs have to be satisfied for the motivation of the employees in the organisation. Herzberg's theory is extension of Maslow's theory. Maslow's theory is more popular in developing countries where there is lack of money while Herzberg's theory is more popular in developed countries where money is less motivating factor. Both theories are influenced by environmental conditions and workers attitude. The end result is motivation.

Herzberg's theory may be easily combined with the ideas presented by Maslow.

Maslow's theory argues that fundamental needs must be met first while Herzberg's theory focus on providing hygiene factors to employees. Maslow's higher need i.e. self-esteem and self-actualisation reflected in Herzberg's motivational factors.

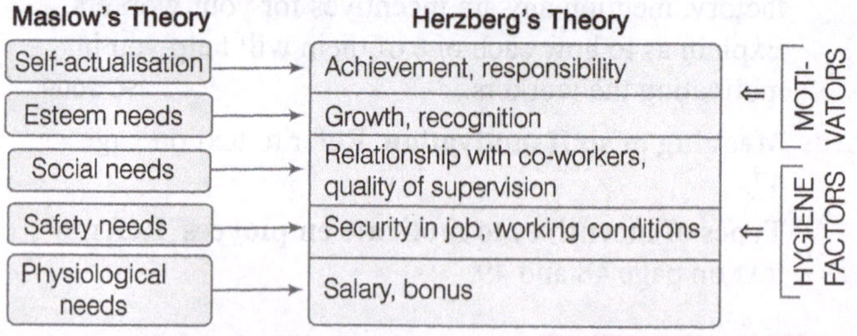

Relationship between these Two Theories

Value Points

To get maximum marks, following points should be included in the answer

- Similarities between Maslow's theory and Herzberg's theory
- Differences beteen Maslow's theory and Herzberg's theory

CHAPTER TEST

01 Mark Questions

1. Who propounded the need's hierarchy theory?

2. The two factor theory is based on which two factors?

3. Bonus helps to motivate employees. Which type of incentive is it?

4. ………… refers to the way in which urges, desires, savings or needs direct and control the behaviour of employees.

5. According to Herzberg's two factor theory, motivation factors and hygiene factors are also known as ………… and ………… .

6. Healthy competition among employees inspires them to work hard and improve their performance. This is a part of
(a) staff motivation (b) staff morale
(c) staff hygiene (d) staff selection

7. According to Maslow's hierarchy of needs, which of the following does not belong to social needs?
(a) Friendship
(b) Exchange of feelings and grievances
(c) Belongingness
(d) Economic security

8. Which of the following is not a motivation factor according to Herzberg's two factor theory?
(a) Achievement (b) Pay and security
(c) Recognition (d) Responsibility

9. According to Maslow's hierarchy of needs, the low level needs can be satisfied by monetary and non-monetary compensations. State true or false.

10. According to Herzberg's two factor theory, recognition is a hygiene factor. State true or false.

02 Marks Questions

11. Under which need an employee desires self-respect, recognition and status?

12. What are non-monetary incentives?

13. What are monetary incentives?

14. What do you understand by the term 'job security'?

04 Marks Questions

15. In an organisation if the work environment is not healthy, how will you motivate others to get the work done?

16. Explain any four incentives used to motivate employees, when they are not motivated by money.

17. State any two assumptions and criticisms of the Maslow's theory of the hierarchy of human needs.

06/08 Marks Questions

18. (i) Explain Herzberg's two factor theory.
(ii) What is the relationship between Maslow's and Herzberg's theories?

19. Define motivation and give in detail the concept of Maslow's need hierarchy theory.

20. Why do you think that motivation is important? Give reasons in support of your answer.

Answers

1. Abraham Maslow
2. Hygiene factors and motivational factors
3. Monetary incentive
4. Motivation
5. satisfiers, dissatisfiers
6. (a) staff motivation
7. (d) Economic security
8. (b) Pay and security
9. True
10. False

06

Staff Remuneration

TREND ANALYSIS 5 YEARS

	Average No. of Questions Across all Sets					
	Types of Questions	2023	2020	2019	2018	2017
01 Remuneration	1 Mark	—	—	—	—	—
	2 Marks	—	—	—	1	1
	4 Marks	—	—	—	—	—
	6 Marks	—	—	—	—	—
	8 Marks	—	—	—	—	—
02 Various Staff Benefits and Types of Leaves	1 Mark	1	—	—	—	—
	2 Marks	—	1	1	—	—
	4 Marks	—	1	—	—	—
	6 Marks	—	—	—	—	—
	8 Marks	—	—	1	—	—

Meaning of Staff Remuneration

It refers to the reward or compensation given to the employees in cash or kind for their work performances. Remuneration provides basic satisfaction to an employee to perform a job efficiently and effectively. Compensation is the total cash and non-cash payment offered by an employer to an employee in return for the services rendered to the organisation, which leads to boost employee morale and satisfaction.

Methods of Wage Payment

There are mainly two methods of wage payment, which are described below

1. Time Rate Method

Under this method, remuneration is directly linked with the time spent or devoted by an employee to the job. The employees are paid a fixed pre-decided amount hourly, daily, weekly or monthly, irrespective of their output.

Following are the **merits** of time rate method

(i) This method leads to quality output.

(ii) This method is very beneficial to new employees, as they can learn their work without any reduction in their salaries.

(iii) This method encourages employees unity too, since there will be no ill-will and jealousy due to same wages received by all.

(iv) This method is easily accepted by trade unions.

(v) Under this method, there is certainty of wages. Employees are certain about their pay and there is no relation between the efficiency and reward.

Following are the **demerits** of time rate method

(i) It requires tight supervision.

(ii) There is indefinite employee cost.

(iii) Lesser efficiency of employees, as there is no distinction made between efficient and inefficient employees.

(iv) Employees generally waste their time in order to earn more wages.

(v) There is no motivation for employees to improve quality of work, leading to limited output.

This method is **suitable** in the following conditions

(i) Where the quality of output is more important than the quantity.

(ii) Where strict supervision is possible.

(iii) When there is frequent disruptions in the flow of work and the disruption is uncontrollable.

(iv) Where work is done in groups and evaluation of indiviual work is difficult.

2. Piece Rate Method

In this method, remuneration is paid on the basis of units or pieces produced by an employee. In this system, emphasis is more on quantity of output rather than quality of output.

Following are the **merits** of piece rate method

(i) There is less supervision required under this method.

(ii) Per unit cost of production is also low due to larger output.

(iii) This system improves the morale of the employees, as the salaries are directly related with their work efforts.

(iv) Machines and equipments are also used optimally to produce goods as employees try to avoid idle time of the machines in a bid to work more to earn more.

(v) Since, workers' wages are directly related with their efforts, each worker will try to produce more.

Main **demerits** of piece rate method are as follows

(i) Its computation is not easy.

(ii) It leads to deterioration in work quality.

(iii) It leads to wastage among resources and mishandling of machinery.

(iv) There is lesser unity among employees.

(v) It is not beneficial for the newcomers.

(vi) It is not easily accepted by trade unions.

This method is **suitable** under the following circumstances

(i) Where the nature of work is repetitive and continuous.

(ii) Where quantity is emphasised more than quality.

(iii) Where work can be measured in standard units.

(iv) Where the output of each employee can be measured independently.

(v) Where strict supervision cannot be exercised.

Difference between Time Rate Method and Piece Rate Method

Basis	Time Rate Method	Piece Rate Method
Basis of payment	Time spent on the job.	Number of units produced.
Nature of payment	Minimum payment to every worker.	No guarantee of minimum payment.
Link with productivity	Wages are not directly linked with productivity.	Wage directly linked with productivity.
Quality of work	High	Low
Cost of maintenance	Low	High
Need for close supervision	High	Low
Attitude of trade unions	Trade unions support it.	Trade unions do not support it.

Wage Records

As per the guidelines of Fair Work Regulations Act, 2009 for most of the employers, it is necessary to keep the employment details. Pay slip and payroll are important in this context.

Pay Slip

A slip of paper given alongwith a person's salary payment that records how much money the person has earned and how much tax or insurance etc., has been deducted is referred to as pay slip. It shows the gross and net salary of an employee. It serves as a conclusive record of the remuneration paid by the employer.

Components of Pay Slip

The following are some of the important components of pay slip

(i) Earnings Under this head, the following are shown

(a) **Basic pay** It is given according to employee's qualification, experience and specialisation. It is full taxable in income tax.

(b) **Dearness allowance** It is provided to employees to compensate for inflation in economy. It is revised according to the consumer price index.

(c) **House rent allowance** It is given to meet the expenses in connection with rent of accommodation.

(d) **Conveyance allowance** It is provided to meet the expenses incurred on conveyance in performance of duties.

(e) **Medical allowance** It is given by employer to employee to meet the medical expenses.

(f) **Special allowance** Such type of allowances are given to specified employee only.

(ii) **Deductions** Under this head, the following are shown

(a) **Professional tax** It is levied by the State Government on the income earned by professional, traders and employees exceed a specific limit.

(b) **Tax deducted at source** It is deducted from salary of employee (if employee's salary exceed prescribed limit) and transferred to government account.

(c) **Employee provident fund** It is a social security scheme under which, an employee has to pay a certain percentage from his salary and equal amount is contributed by the employer.

(iii) **Cost to company** It is cost incurred when company hires an employee.

(iv) **Gross salary** It is the amount of salary prior to deductions. (i.e. TDS, PF, etc).

(v) **Net salary** It is also known as 'take home salary.' It refers to the in-hand amount of salary.

Specimen of Pay Slip

Name of Employee	Department ....
Designation	Month ....
Bank Name	Bank Account No. ....

Earnings (₹)

1. Basic ....
2. Dearness Allowance ....
3. House Rent Allowance ....
4. Conveyance Allowance ....
5. Medical Allowance ....
6. Special Allowance ....

Gross Salary ______

Deductions

1. Professional Tax
2. Tax Deducted at Source
3. Employee Provident Fund

....

Net Salary ______

Dated ....

....

Signature

Payroll

The sum total of all compensation that a business must pay to its employees for a set period of time or on a given date is referred to as payroll. Payroll is usually managed by the accounting department of a business. Small business payrolls may be handled directly by the owner or an associate.

Components of Payroll

The following are the components of payroll

(i) **Employee information** It includes

(a) Name (b) I.D. (c) Date of joining (d) Social security number

(ii) **Days work** It includes total days worked by employee.

(iii) **Salaries** It includes

(a) Basic pay (b) DA (c) Other allowances (d) Overtime

(iv) **Deductions** It is the amount which is subtracted from an employee's total salary. It includes

(a) TDS (b) PF (c) ESI

(v) **Gross and net salary** Gross salary is overall salary without deductions while net salary is in-hand salary, i.e. salary after all deductions.

Specimen of Payroll

Organisation Name .... **Payroll ....**

Month .... **Department ....**

S.No.	Name of the employee	Employee number and date of joining	Total days worked	Basic pay	Over time	D.A.	Other allowances	Total pay	T.D.S.	P.F.	E.S.I.	Total deduction	Net salary	Remarks
Total														

Prepared by ....

Checked by ....

Date ....

Difference between Pay Slip and Payroll

Basis	Pay slip	Payroll
Meaning	Pay slip is a summary of salary. It includes total earnings and total deductions.	It refers to the list of employees that receive compensation from a company.
Scope	Narrow scope.	Wide scope.
Use	Employees can understand what company has paid and why.	Management can understand what company has paid and why.
Phenomenon	Individual.	Group.
Sequence	Pay slip is prepared from payroll (i.e. it is prepared after payroll).	Payroll provides data for preparation of pay slip (i.e. it is prepared before payslip).

Various Staff Benefits

Employee or staff benefits mean benefits that employee receives in addition to the direct remuneration. Following are the main staff benefits

(i) **Employee Provident Fund** It is a retirement benefit applicable to salaried employees. Under this scheme, both the employer and employee contribute fixed amount in EPF account. This fund (i.e. fixed percentage of salary) is pre-set by the government. This fund is managed by Employees Provident Fund Organisation.

(ii) **National Pension System** It was designed only for government employees but all citizens of India are covered in it since 2009. It is managed by the Pension Fund Regulatory and Development Authority (PFRDA). It is considered as an umbrella in old age i.e. social security mechanism.

(iii) **Group insurance** It is an insurance policy where a group of employees is covered by a single insurance policy. Company is responsible for the payment of premium in respect of group insurance policy. There are two types of group insurance, viz. group health insurance and group life insurance.

(iv) **Encashment of leave** As per the service rule of organisation, eligible employees are provided leave for certain number of days. If leave is not utilised by employees, it may be lapsed, encashed or accumulated. Generally, organisation provides leave encashment to employee at the time of retirement or leaving the job.

(v) **Gratuity** Gratuity is the social security scheme which is applicable to every factory, mine, oil field, port, railways, company, shop, establishment or educational institution employing 10 or more employees. All employees are eligible for gratuity irrespective of status of salary but he should have rendered a minimum of 5 years continuous service in the organisation.

Gratuity is payable to employee in the following situations

(a) Retirement of employee

(b) Death of employee

(c) Resignation of employee

(vi) **Leave benefit** In India, leave and holiday privileges are provided to employees and are intended to meet their physical, psychological and social needs.

Types of Leave

The following are the important types of leave

(i) **Casual leave** Casual leaves are granted for certain unforeseen situation. It is known as 'short term period of leave'. For availing casual leave prior approval from employer is required except in case of emergency. Generally, official holidays are not counted when calculating the number of casual leaves.

(ii) **Medical/Sick leave** Medical leave is granted to an employee when he recovers from an injury or illness disabling him or her. Generally, an employee is entitled to sick leave only after a specified period of employment in the organisation. For availing the medical leave, no prior approval is required from employer.

(iii) **Earned leave** Earned leave means leave earned in respect of periods spent in employment. As per the provisions of Factories Act, 1948, any worker covered under the act who has worked for atleast 240 days in a calendar year becomes eligible for earned leave which he can enjoy in the subsequent year. Some organisations pay for earned leave.

(iv) **Privilege leave** Every employee employed in establishment is entitled to privilege leave for a period of not less than 15 days, after every 12 months of continuous job. Generally, privilege leave cannot be availed for more than three times in a calendar year.

(v) **Maternity/Paternity leave** Maternity leave is granted to regulate the employment of women in certain establishments for certain periods before and after child birth and to provide for maternity benefits and certain other benefits.

Every woman shall be entitled to, and her employer shall be liable for the payment of maternity benefit at the rate of average pay. Paternity leave is granted to male employee with less than two surviving children for a period of 15 days to take care of his wife and new born child.

(vi) **Sabbatical/Study leave** In India, sabbatical leave is granted to employees to achieve personal goals (i.e. higher studies, training, etc).

It improves the employee-employer relationship. The end result is increment in productivity. Subbatical leaves may be paid or unpaid.

(vii) **Leave Without Pay** (LWOP) LWOP is granted to a employee for various reasons, including

(a) Educational purposes

(b) Medical ground

(c) Personal issues

Prior approval of LWOP is required from employer. Generally, LWOP is a matter of supervisory discretion and may be limited by company's internal policy.

PYQs Previous Years' Questions

1 Mark Questions

1. .... provides life insurance cover to the employees under a single insurance policy. *ISC 2023*

Ans Group insurance

2. Which system of wage payment is supported by the trade unions? *ISC Specimen 2023*

Ans Time rate system of wage payment is supported by the trade unions.

Concept Enhancer Time rate system of wage payment helps to avoid quarrels among the workers as uniform wages are paid to all.

3. What does the abbreviation HRA stands for? *ISC Specimen 2023*

Ans HRA stands for "House Rent Allowances".

4. .... is a sheet containing full information related to the pay of all the employees working in the organisation. *ISC Specimen 2023*

Ans Pay roll

5. What does the abbreviation NPS stand for? *ISC Sem I 2021*

(a) National Provident Scheme

(b) National Pension Scheme

(c) New Provident Scheme

(d) New Pension Scheme

Ans (b) National Pension Scheme

6. ..... is granted for pursuing higher studies or acquiring specialised training. ***ISC Sem I 2021***
(a) Leave without pay
(b) Earned leave
(c) Sabbatical leave
(d) Privilege leave

Ans (c) Sabbatical leave

7. A pay slip is also known as a .... ***ISC Sem I 2021***
(a) pay slip (b) salary slip
(c) salary sheet (d) wage sheet

Ans (b) salary slip

8. A terminal, one-time monetary benefit given to an employee, when he leaves the organisation is called .... ***ISC Sem I 2021***
(a) wages (b) pension
(c) gratuity (d) public provident fund

Ans (c) gratuity

9. Which of the following is a casual leave? ***ISC Sem I 2021***
(a) Half day leave
(b) Leave to undergo a major operation
(c) Leave to travel abroad for two months
(d) Leave study for a special course.

Ans (a) Half day leave

10. Which one of the following is not a component of a pay slip? ***ISC Sem I 2021***
(a) Status symbol
(b) Tax deducted at source
(c) Provident fund deduction
(d) Basic pay

Ans (a) Status symbol

11. Which one of the following is a limitation of the time-rate system of wage payment? ***ISC Sem I 2021***
(a) It provides a sense of insecurity to the workers.
(b) There is a premium on inefficiency.
(c) Trade unions oppose it.
(d) There are high chances of optimum utilisation of resources.

Ans (b) There is a premium on inefficiency.

12. The employees are entitled to withdraw part of the money from .... during their tenure in the organisation. ***ISC Sem I 2021***
(a) gratuity
(b) group insurance
(c) employee provident fund
(d) pension

Ans (c) employee provident fund

13. Which of the following is false vis-a-vis group insurance? ***ISC Sem I 2021***
(a) Premium is paid by both the employer as well as the employee.
(b) It is provided to all employees without any evidence of insurability.
(c) Premium is paid only by the employer.
(d) In case of the death of an employee, the claim is paid to his nominee.

Ans (a) Premium is paid by both the employer as well as the employee.

14. Quite a few organisations like to follow piece-rate system of wages because ***ISC Sem I Specimen 2021***
(a) quantity of work tends to be high
(b) quality of work tends to be high
(c) there are lesser chances of misuse of machines and material
(d) trade unions support this system

Ans (a) quantity of work tends to be high

15. A male employee is generally granted paternity leave for ***ISC Sem I Specimen 2021***
(a) 8 days (b) 10 days
(c) 15 days (d) 30 days

Ans (c) 15 days

16. Generally how many days of leave are granted as maternity leave? ***ISC Sem I Specimen 2021***
(a) 90 days (b) 120 days
(c) 180 days (d) 210 days

Ans (c) 180 days

17. Identify the odd one out based on the remuneration to be received by the employee for the period of leave. ***ISC Sem I Specimen 2021***
(a) Privilege leave (b) Casual leave
(c) Maternity leave (d) Leave without pay

Ans (d) Leave without pay

18. Group life insurance is a contract between ***ISC Sem I Specimen 2021***
(a) insurance company and the employer
(b) insurance company and an employee
(c) insurance company and a group of employees
(d) the employer and an employee

Ans (a) insurance company and the employer

19. .... is earned in the previous year and is enjoyed in the succeeding year. ***ISC Sem I Specimen 2021***
(a) Privilege leave (b) Sabbatical leave
(c) Extra ordinary leave (d) Special leave

Ans (a) Privilege leave

20. A scheme which provides insurance cover on the lives of several persons under one insurance policy is known as *ISC Sem I Specimen 2021*
(a) Life Insurance
(b) Group Insurance
(c) Government Insurance
(d) National Pension Scheme

Ans (b) Group Insurance

21. For every completed year of service, ... days of earned leave are credited to the employee's leave account. *ISC Sem I Specimen 2021*
(a) 08 (b) 10
(c) 15 (d) 20

Ans (d) 20

22. Which of the following is an advantage of using time rate system of wage payment? *ISC Sem I Specimen 2021*
(a) It provides motivation to workers
(b) Close supervision is not required
(c) Trade unions support it
(d) Inefficient workers are easily identified on the basis of their performance

Ans (c) Trade unions support it

2 Marks Questions

1. Explain the concept of encashment of leave. *ISC 2020*

Ans As per the service rule of organisation, eligible employees are provided leave for certain number of days. If leave is not utilised by employees, it may be lapsed, encashed or accumulated. Leave encashment means that employee will be paid in cash for the leaves that he has not availed.

2. What is meant by gratuity? *ISC 2019*

Ans Gratuity is the social security scheme which is applicable to every factory, mine, port, shop or establishment employing 10 or more employees. All employees are eligible for this, irrespective of salary provided if, they have rendered minimum 5 years of service in an organisation.

Common Mistake Sometimes students misunderstand the term 'gratuity' with 'Pension'. So students are advisable to learn various staff benefits and understand each of them.

3. What is meant by piece rate system of wage payment? *ISC Specimen 2019*

Ans In this system of wage payment, remuneration is paid on the basis of units or pieces produced by an employee.

4. Define remuneration. *2018*

Ans It refers to the reward or compensation given to the employees in cash or kind for their work performances. Remuneration provides basic satisfaction to an employee to perform a job efficiently and effectively.

Common Mistake While giving this answer, students do not mention 'in cash or kind' specifically. It is very important to write this because remuneration includes salary or wages or reward or compensation in cash or kind both.

5. List any two conditions where time rate system of wage payment is most suitable. *ISC 2017*

Or List any two work conditions where time rate system is more suitable than the piece rate system. *ISC 2010*

Or State two conditions under which time rate system is more suitable. *ISC 2007*

Ans Two conditions where time rate system is most suitable are as follows
(i) Where the quality of output is more important than the quantity.
(ii) Where strict supervision is possible.

6. State two conditions where piece rate system is most suitable. *ISC 2015*

Or State two conditions where piece rate system can be used effectively. *ISC 2004*

Ans Two conditions where piece rate system is most suitable are as follows
(i) Where the nature of work is repetitive and continuous.
(ii) Where quantity is emphasised more than quality.

7. What is pay slip? How is it different from a payroll? *ISC 2014*

Or Is a pay slip the same as a payroll? Explain. *ISC 2008*

Ans Pay slip is a slip showing full details of total wages, deduction made and net payment of wages/salary to an individual employee.

Payroll is different from pay slip as pay slip shows the detail of wages of an individual employee whereas, payroll is a sheet showing full information of the pay given to all employees in an organisation.

8. Define remuneration. What is meant by incentives in the context of remuneration? *ISC 2013*

Ans Remuneration refers to the reward or compensation given to the employees in cash or kind for their contribution in work for the betterment of an organisation.

In the context of remuneration, incentives imply certain monetary and non-monetary advantages such as bonus, commission, stock options, perks, allotted parking, etc to an individual in an organisation.

9. What is a time card? State one benefit of a time card to the organisation using it. **ISC 2013**

Ans A time card is used to record the time an employee is working. Time card is also known as a 'punch card'. It is installed at the factory gate. Everytime a worker enters or exits a factory gate, he has to punch the card. This allows the record of in and out time of the workers. The employees punches in and out to mark the time. The time card shows the number of hours, the employees was 'in' and 'out' for the day. It is helpful in computation of the wages of an employee, who is working on time basis. This will help in knowing the ordinary and over timings of different employees.

10. Explain the significance of pay slip. **ISC 2012**

Ans Pay slip shows the details of remuneration paid to the employee. It shows the gross and net salary of an employee. It is important for both the employer and employee. It serves as a conclusive record of the remuneration paid by the employer. The employee can verify his remuneration details, the basic pay, deductions like EPF, ESI, PPF, etc. If any discrepancy is found in calculation, the employee can claim it by showing the pay slip.

11. Why do trade unions oppose piece rate system of remuneration? **ISC 2009**

Ans The piece rate system is not favoured by workers and trade unions. This system encourages rivalry among workers and endangers their solidarity in labour disputes. The workers also resent this, because when the workers start getting higher wages, then the employer decreases the piece rate.

4 Marks Questions

1. With reference to staff benefits provided by an organisation, explain group insurance and employees provident fund. **ISC 2020**

Ans (i) **Group Insurance** It is an insurance policy where a group of employees is covered by a single insurance policy. Company is responsible for the payment of premium in respect of group insurance policy. There are two types of group insurance *viz* group health insurance and group life insurance.

(ii) **Employees Provident Fund** It is a retirement benefit applicable to salaried employees. Under this scheme, both the employer and employee contribute fixed amount in EPF account. This fund is pre-set by the government. This fund is managed by Employees Provident Fund Organisation (EPFO).

Concept Enhancer Staff benefits refer to those benefits that employee receives in addition to the direct remuneration. Examples of various staff benefits are – Employee provident fund, National pension system, Group insurance, Encashment of leave, Gratuity, etc.

2. With reference to remuneration, briefly explain any two benefits given to the staff by the employer. **ISC Specimen 2019**

Ans (i) **Employee Provident Fund** It is a retirement benefit applicable to salaried employees. Under this scheme, both the employer and employee contribute fixed amount in EPF account. This fund (i.e. fixed percentage of salary) is pre-set by the government. This fund is managed by Employees Provident Fund Organisation.

(ii) **National Pension System** It was designed only for government employees but all citizens of India are covered in it since 2009. It is managed by the Pension Fund Regulatory and Development Authority (PFRDA). It is considered as an umbrella in old age i.e. social security mechanism.

6/8 Marks Questions

1. (i) Explain piece rate system of wage payment.

(ii) State any three merits and any three demerits of piece rate system. **ISC 2023**

Or State any three advantages and any three disadvantages of piece rate system of wage payment. **ISC 2016**

Ans (i) In this method, remuneration is paid on the basis of units or pieces produced by an employee. In this system, emphasis is more on quantity of output rather than quality of output.

(ii) Three advantages/merits of piece rate system of wage payment are as follows

(a) There is less supervision required under this method.

(b) Per unit cost of production is also low due to larger output.

(c) This system improves the morale of the employees, as the salaries are directly related with their work efforts.

Three disadvantages/demerits of piece rate system of wage payment are as follows

(a) It is difficult to compute wages under this method of wage payment.

(b) It leads to deterioration in work quality, because to increase the output, the workers might compromise on quality.

(c) It leads to wastage of resources and mishandling of machinery.

2. (i) Define remuneration.

(ii) State any six distinctions between the time rate system and piece rate system. ***ISC Specimen 2023***

Ans (i) Refer to Q. No. 4 (2 Marks) on page 66.

(ii) Distinctions between time rate system and piece rate system are as follows

Basis	Time rate system	Piece rate system
Base of payment	Payment is done on the basis of time spent on the job.	Payment is done on the basis of number of units produced.
Nature of payment	Minimum payment is given to every worker.	There is no guarantee of minimum payment.
Quality of work	In this system, quality of work is high.	In this system, quality of work is low.
Trade union	Trade union support this system.	Trade union oppose this system.
Supervision	Close supervision is required in this method	No need of close supervision in this method.
Link with productivity	Wages are not directly linked with productivity.	Wages are directly linked with productivity.

3. Briefly explain any four types of leave that may be availed by an employee. ***ISC 2019***

Ans Four types of leave that may be availed by an employee are

Types of Leave
- Casual leave
- Medical leave
- Maternity leave
- Earned leave

(i) **Casual leave** These are granted for certain unforeseen situation. It is known as short term period of leave. For availing casual leave, prior approval from employer is required except in case of emergency. Generally, official holidays are not counted when calculating the number of casual leaves.

(ii) **Medical leave** It is granted to an employee when he recovers from an injury or illness disabling him or her. Generally, an employee is entitled to sick leave only after a specified period of employment in the organisation. For availing the medical leave, no prior approval is required from employer.

(iii) **Maternity leave** It is granted to regulate the employment of women in certain establishments for certain periods before and after child birth and to provide for maternity benefits and certain other benefits.

Every woman shall be entitled to, and her employer shall be liable for, the payment of maternity benefit at the rate of average pay.

(iv) **Earned leave** It means leave earned in respect of periods spent in employment. As per the provisions of Factories Act, 1948, any worker covered under the act who has worked for atleast 240 days in a calendar year becomes eligible for earned leave which he can enjoy in the subsequent year. Some organisations pay for earned leave.

4. Explain time rate system of wage payment. State and explain any two advantages and two disadvantages of this system. ***ISC 2014***

Ans **Time rate system of wage payment** Under this method, remuneration is directly linked with the time spent or devoted by an employee on the job. The employees are paid a fixed pre-decided amount hourly, daily, weekly or monthly, irrespective of their output.

It is a very simple and the oldest method of remuneration. It leads to minimum wastage of resources and lesser chances of accidents.

Accordingly, the wages are calculated under this method as,

$$W = T \times R$$

Where, W = Total Wages

T = Time

R = Rate per hour/day

Advantages of time rate system Two advantages of time rate system of wage payment are as follows

(i) This method is simple to understand and easy to calculate. An ordinary worker can also calculate his wage by using this method.

(ii) This method is useful in producing quality output rather than quantity.

Disadvantages of time rate system

Two disadvantages of time rate system of wage payment are as follows

(i) Due to stress on quality, it leads to lesser amount of production in units.

(ii) This method demands continuous supervision. Absence of supervision leads to maximum wastage of resources and time.

Value Points

To get maximum marks in the examination, following points should be included in the answer

- Payment is done on the basis of time spent
- Calculation of wages under time rate system of wage payment

5. What is meant by piece rate system of wage payment? State and justify two distinct situations, where its use is advisable. *ISC 2013*

Or What is piece rate system of remuneration? *ISC 2008*

Or Explain the concept of piece rate system of wage payment. *ISC 2004*

KEY IDEA

Situations where use of piece rate system is advisable, means the conditions where this method is suitable. Students are advisable to understand the difference between suitability and advantage/ significance.

Ans In this method, remuneration is paid on the basis of units or pieces produced by an employee. In this system, emphasis is more on quantity of output rather than quality of output.

Under this system, the determination of employee cost per unit is not difficult because wages differ with output.

This method will prove successful in case the rate of piece is fixed carefully.

If it is not fixed carefully, it may lead to frustration among the workers, who are trying to increase their earnings by producing more.

Accordingly, the wages are calculated under this method as,

$$W = P \times R$$

Where, W = Total wages

P = Number of units produced

R = Piece rate per unit

Its use is advisable in the following conditions

(i) Where the nature of work is repetitive.

(ii) Where quantity is emphasised more than quality.

6. With reference to time rate system of wage payment, answer the following *ISC 2012*

(i) Explain this system of wage payment.

(ii) State two advantages of this system.

(iii) State two disadvantages of this system.

(iv) State two specific conditions when this system can be used effectively.

Ans (i) **Time rate system of wage payment** Refer to Q. No. 4 on page 68.

(ii) **Two advantages of time rate system of wage payment** Refer to Q. No. 4 on page 69.

(iii) **Two disadvantages of time rate system of wage payment** Refer to Q. No. 4 on page 69.

(iv) **Suitability of time rate system of wage payment** Refer to Q. No. 5 on page 66.

7. Explain the advantages and disadvantages of using piece rate system of remuneration. *ISC 2008*

Or Explain the advantages and disadvantages of piece rate system of wage payment. *ISC 2004*

Ans Advantages of using piece rate system of remuneration are as follows

(i) There is less supervision required under this method. Hence, supervision cost is very low.

(ii) Per unit cost of production is also low because of increase in output.

(iii) This system improves the morale of the employees, as the salaries are directly related with their work efforts.

(iv) Since, workers' wages are directly related with their efforts, so each worker will try to produce more. This will improve the work efficiency.

Disadvantages of using piece rate system of remuneration are as follows

(i) As compared to time rate system, it is not easy to compute accurately. It is not liked by trade unions as the piece rate system may not be designed on a scientific basis.

(ii) It leads to deterioration in work quality.

(iii) As supervision is minimum, thus, it leads to wastage of resources.

(iv) Lesser unity of employees, as their individual work is judged.

Additional Questions

2/4 Marks Questions

1. Differentiate between wages and salaries.

Ans Wages are paid to the workers who are engaged in production whereas, salaries are paid to the employees, who are involved in administrative, selling and distribution work.

2. What are incentives?

Ans An incentive or 'reward' can be anything that attracts a worker's attention and stimulates him to work. An incentive plan may consist of both monetary and non-monetary elements.

Examples of monetary rewards are basic salary, performance bonus, profit sharing, etc. Non-monetary rewards may be in form of preferred lunch hours, allotted parking spaces.

3. What is leave without pay?

Ans Leave Without Pay (LWOP) is granted to an employee for various reasons, including

(i) Educational purposes (ii) Medical ground
(iii) Personal issues

Prior approval of LWOP is required from employer. Generally, LWOP is a matter of supervisory discretion and may be limited by company's internal policy.

4. Explain employee provident fund.

Ans It is a retirement benefit applicable to salaried employees. Under this scheme, both the employer and employee contribute a fix amount in Employee Provident Fund (EPF) account.

This amount (i.e. fixed percentage of salary) is pre-set by the government. This fund is managed by Employee Provident Fund Organisation.

5. Explain the two types of group insurance.

Ans **Group insurance** It is an insurance policy, where a group of employees are covered by single policy. There are two types of group insurance

(i) **Group health insurance** It is purchased by employer for the eligible employees. It is helpful in reducing the cost of insurance. It also helps in reducing labour turnover ratio in company.

(ii) **Group life insurance** Under this policy, a single contract covers an entire group of employees. It provides advantages of standardised and very competitive premium rates. Employee cover could cease if he leaves the group (i.e. 'resignation' from job).

6. Explain different types of piece rate method of payment.

Ans Piece rate method are of the following types

(i) **Fixed piece rate method** Under this method, the wages are paid to the workers on the basis of fixed rate of single piece produced.

(ii) **Increasing piece rate method** Under this method, different piece rates are fixed for different levels of production. In case, the level of production increases, a worker will get the revised or increased per piece rate of output.

(iii) **Decreasing piece rate method** Under this method, the piece rate decreases with the increase in the level of production.

7. Give the specimen of payroll in organisation.

Ans **Specimen of Payroll**

Organisation Name .... **Payroll ....**

Month .... **Department ....**

S.N.	Name of the employee	Employee number and date of joining	Total days worked	Basic pay	Over time	D.A.	Other allowances	Total pay	T.D.S	P.F.	E.S.I	Total deduction	Net Salary	Remarks
Total														

Prepared by ....
Checked by ....
Date ....

8. Differentiate between pay slip and payroll.

Ans Difference between pay slip and payroll are

Basis	Pay slip	Payroll
Meaning	Pay slip is a summary of salary. It includes total earnings and total deductions.	It refers to the list of employees that receive compensation from a company.
Scope	Narrow scope.	Wide scope.
Use	Employees can understand what company has paid and why.	Management can understand what company has paid and why.
Phenomenon	Individual.	Group.
Sequence	Pay slip is prepared from payroll (i.e. it is prepared after payroll).	Payroll provides data for preparation of pay slip (i.e. it is prepared before payslip).

9. What are the advantages of group health insurance?

Ans The following are the advantages of group health insurance

(i) It is helpful in reducing the cost of insurance.

(ii) It is helpful in reducing labour turnover ratio in company.

(iii) It is helpful in getting tax benefits to employer.

(iv) It is useful for employee's well being.

6/8 Marks Questions

1. What is pay slip? Explain its components.

Ans **Pay slip** A slip of paper included with a person's salary payment that records how much money, the person has earned and how much tax or insurance etc has been deducted. It shows the gross and net salary of an employee. It is important for both the employer and employee. It serves as a conclusive record of the remuneration paid by the employer. The employee can verify his remuneration details, the basic pay, deductions like EPF, ESI, PPF, etc. If any discrepancy is found in calculation, the employee can claim it by showing the pay slip.

Components of pay slip The following are its components

(i) **Earnings** Under this head, the following points are shown

(a) **Basic pay** It is given according to employee's qualification, experience and specilisation. It is full taxable in income tax.

(b) **Dearness allowance** D.A. is provided to employees to compensate for inflation in economy. It is revised according to the consumer price index.

(c) **House rent allowance** It is given to meet the expenses in connection with rent of accommodation.

(d) **Conveyance allowance** It is provided to meet the expenses incurred on conveyance in performance of duties.

Component of Pay Slip
- Earnings
- Deductions
- Cost to company
- Gross salary
- Net salary

(e) **Medical allowance** It is given by employer to employee to meet the medical expenses.

(f) **Special allowance** Such type allowances are given to specified employee only.

(ii) **Deductions** Under this head, the following are shown

(a) **Professional tax** It is levied by the state government on the income earned by professional, traders and employees exceed a specific limit.

(b) **Tax deducted at source** It is deducted from salary of employee (if employee's salary exceeds prescribed limit) and transferred to government account.

(c) **Employee provident fund** It is a social security scheme under which, an employee has to pay a certain percentage from his salary and equal amount is contributed by the employer.

(iii) **Cost to company** It is cost incurred when company hire an employee.

(iv) **Gross salary** It is the amount of salary includings deductions (i.e. TDS, PF, etc).

(v) **Net salary** It is also known as the 'take home salary.' It refers to the in-hand amount of salary.

2. What is the meaning of employee provident fund? What are its benefits?

Ans **Meaning of employee provident fund** It is a retirement benefit applicable to salaried employees. Under this scheme, both the employer and employee contribute a fix amount in Employee Provident Fund (EPF) account. This amount (i.e. fixed percentage of salary) is pre-set by the government. This fund is managed by Employee Provident Fund Organisation.

Benefits of employee provident fund The following are the benefits of employee provident fund

(i) High interest on balance avilable in EPF account.

(ii) Income tax benefits.

(iii) Withdrawal benefits in event of retirement, death, resignation from job.

(iv) Withdrawal benefits during the service of an employee for various purposes.

(v) Payment of pension in event of death, retirement, etc.

3. Explain the meaning of national pension system and also give its benefits.

Ans **Meaning of national pension system** It was designed only for government employees but all citizens of India are covered in it since 2009. It is managed by the Pension Fund Regulatory and Development Authority (PFRDA). It is considered as an umbrella in old age i.e. social security mechanism.

Benefits of national pension system Following are the benefits of national pension system

(i) Income tax benefits to salaried individuals and self-employed profcssionals.

(ii) NPS is a low cost retirement benefit plan.

(iii) It is managable online i.e. easy access.

(iv) It is well regulated by PFRDA in a transparent mode.

(v) It offers sufficient flexibility to its users.

4. Explain group life insurance and also state its importance.

Ans **Group life insurance** Under this policy, a single contract covers an entire group of employees. It provides advantages of standardised and very competitive premium rates. Employee cover could cease, if he leaves the group (i.e. resignation from job). It gives a sense of security to employees. The end result is increment in productivity of employees. Under this scheme, only one master policy is issued to employer.

Importance of group life insurance These are as follows

(i) It is useful in reducing the cost of insurance.

(ii) It is helpful in determining age proof in services record.

(iii) It is helpful in establishing better industrial relationship.

Case Based Questions

Case 1

Super Dry Fruit Traders has employed Priya to shell almonds to be graded and packed for export. She is paid daily on the basis of the quantity of almonds shelled by her. Her cousin Reema is a supervisor in the firm and is paid on a monthly basis. ***ISC Sem I 2021***

(i) The firm insists on the piece-rate system of wage payment to Priya because

(a) work done by her cannot be measured

(b) it leads to higher overheads

(c) it motivates her to be efficient

(d) il leads to uncertain labour cost

Ans (c) it motivates her to be efficient

(ii) The firm insists on the time-rate system of wage payment to Reema because

(a) work done by her cannot be measured

(b) it leads to higher overheads

(c) it motivates her to be efficient

(d) it leads to uncertain labour cost

Ans (a) work done by her cannot be measured

(iii) Trade unions insist on having the time rate system of wage payment because

(a) it leads to a premium on inefficiency

(b) it reduces wastage

(c) it helps in maintaining solidarity among the workers

(d) it increases the quality of work done

Ans (c) it helps in maintaining solidarity among the workers

(iv) The piece rate system of wage payment is suitable when

(a) the quality of output is more important than the quantity

(b) machines and equipment are delicate and expensive

(c) the output is a direct result of the quantum of effort put in by the workers

(d) it is difficult to accurately measure the contribution of an individual worker

Ans (c) the output is a direct result of the quantum of effort put in by the workers

Case 2

Ram and Shyam Company has two units. The first one headed by Ram manufactures paper bags and the second one headed by Shyam manufactures hand-painted designer envelopes. There is a transparency in their wage payment.

ISC Sem I Specimen 2021

(i) Which method of wage payment should be used by Ram?

(a) Time rate system (b) Piece rate system (c) Cash (d) None of these

Ans (b) Piece rate system

(ii) Which method of wage payment should be used by Shyam?

(a) Time rate system (b) Piece rate system (c) Cash (d) None of these

Ans (a) Time rate system

(iii) Identify one advantage of time rate system of wage payment.

(a) Determination of labour cost
(b) Employee development
(c) Increased supervision
(d) Higher quality of work

Ans (d) Higher quality of work

(iv) Identify one advantage of piece rate system of wage payment.

(a) Optimum use of resources
(b) Labour cost control per unit
(c) Acceptance by trade unions
(d) Sense of security among workers

Ans (b) Labour cost control per unit

CHAPTER TEST

01 Mark Questions

1. Which method of wage payment is suitable when the quality of output is more important than the quantity?
2. What does the abbreviation EPF stands for?
3. Which type of leave is granted to employees to achieve personal goals?
4. In ………… method, remuneration is paid on the basis of units or pieces, produced by an employee.
5. ………… shows the gross and net salary of an employee.
6. Which of the following is not an earning component of pay slip?
   (a) Basic pay (b) Dearness allowance
   (c) Professional tax (d) House rent allowance
7. Wage payment is done on the basis of
   (a) time rate system (b) piece rate system
   (c) Both (a) and (b) (d) None of these
8. ………… leave is granted for certain unforseen situation.
   (a) Medical (b) Casual
   (c) Maternity (d) Sabbatical
9. Remuneration is a reward which is given to employees in cash only. State true or false.
10. Group insurance policy is an insurance policy where a group of employees is covered by a single insurance policy. State true or false.

02 Marks Questions

11. Where can piece wage method be applied suitably?
12. What is the aim of preparing 'pay slip'?
13. 'Time wage system emphasise more on the quality'. Justify.
14. What do you mean by sabbatical leave?

04 Marks Questions

15. Write short notes on
    (i) Gratuity (ii) Employee Provident Fund
16. Explain in brief payroll in organisation.
17. State any two merits and two demerits of piece rate system of wages.

06/08 Marks Questions

18. What are the various methods of payment of wages? Explain their relative advantages and disadvantages.
19. Explain any four types of leaves that an employee gets in an organisation.

Answers

1. Time rate method/system
2. Employees provident fund
3. Sabbatical leave
4. piece rate
5. pay slip
6. (c) Professional tax
7. (c) Both (a) and (b)
8. (b) Casual
9. False
10. True

07

Staff Leadership

TREND ANALYSIS 5 YEARS

Average No. of Questions Across all Sets

	Types of Questions	2023	2020	2019	2018	2017
01 Leadership, Quality of Good Leader	1 Mark	—	—	—	—	—
	2 Marks	—	—	1	1	1
	4 Marks	—	—	—	—	—
	6 Marks	—	—	—	—	—
	8 Marks	—	—	—	—	—
02 Leadership Styles and Situational Leadership	1 Mark	1	—	—	—	—
	2 Marks	—	—	—	—	—
	4 Marks	1	—	1	—	—
	6 Marks	—	—	—	1	—
	8 Marks	—	1	—	—	1

Meaning and Definitions of Leadership/Staff Leadership

Leadership may be defined as the process of influencing the behaviour of people by making them strive voluntarily towards the achievement of goals. It is the ability of maintaining personal relations with followers and motivating them to contribute for achieving goals of the organisation.

According to **George Terry**, ''Leadership is the activity of influencing people to strive willingly for group objectives.''

According to **Harold Koontz** and **Heinz Weihrich**, "Leadership is the art or process of influencing people, so that they will strive willingly and enthusiastically towards the achievement of group goals."

Difference between Leadership and Management

Basis	Leadership	Management
Meaning	Leadership is the process of influencing people to strive willingly for the attainment of objectives.	Management is the process of planning, organising, directing, staffing and controlling.
Necessity	Leadership is not necessary for an organisation.	Management is necessary for an organisation.
Narrow/Wide term	Leadership is a part of managerial function. Its scope is narrow.	Management is a wider term and includes leadership.
Focus	The focus is on achieving satisfaction of followers by fulfilling their expectations and aspirations.	The focus of management is on achieving organisational goals.
Nature of authority	Followers provide authority on their own will.	A manager possesses formal authority over his subordinates, by virtue of his position.

Leadership Styles

It refers to a leader's behaviour. A leadership style is the result of leader's philosophy, personality, experience and value system.

Different leadership styles are discussed below

1. Authoritarian or Autocratic Leadership

An autocratic leader exercises complete control over the subordinates.

He gives orders and expects his subordinates to follow them. It follows one way communication, as the subordinate acts only according to the command given by the manager.

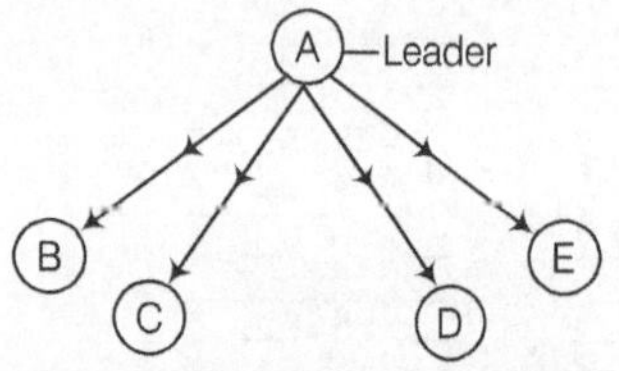

Boss-Centred-Leadership
(A is the leader, who posses around and give orders)

The following are its advantages

(i) This style is suitable in case of emergency like in military and for blue collar employees.
(ii) It is useful in stressful conditions.
(iii) It has a creative competitive environment.
(iv) It helps in the growth of the company.
(v) He uses rewards and holds threat of penalties to train subordinates. Thus, it is helpful in creating responsibility and accountability.

The following are its disadvantages

(i) This style creates frustration, low morale and conflict among subordinates.
(ii) It reduces the creative power of employees.
(iii) It displays tendency of shrink responsibility.
(iv) It is not appropriate when subordinates are educated, skilled and disobedient.
(v) It is unable to realise full utilisation of potential of employees.
(vi) It leads high labour turnover ratio in organisation.

2. Democratic or Participative Leadership

A democratic leader takes decisions after consultation and encourages the participation of subordinates. This leadership style is more common and popular, as it ensures achievement of goals, when they are set with the acceptance of the subordinates themselves.

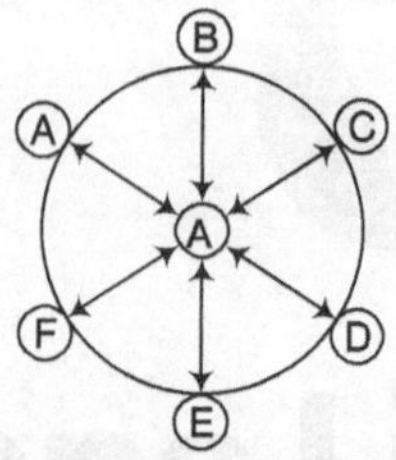

Group-Centred-Leadership
(A is the leader, who consults with the group)

The following are its advantages

(i) This style of leadership creates job satisfaction.
(ii) It fosters a sense of participation, control and autonomy.
(iii) It promotes creativity among employees.
(iv) It creates a healthy working environment.
(v) It gives a chance of decision-making to employees.

The following are its disadvantages

(i) It is a time-consuming process.
(ii) It requires certain skills and educational qualifications.
(iii) It offers an element of continuing uncertainty.
(iv) There is no guarantee for best possible solution for a specific problem.
(v) It creates an environment where no one takes responsibility of failure.

3. Free-rein or Laissez-Faire Leadership

It involves complete delegation of authority, so that subordinates themselves take decisions. The free-rein leader avoids holding power and surrenders the authority to subordinates. He serves as a link who helps in bringing the information and resources needed by the subordinates. This is also known as laissez-faire which means no interference in the affairs of others (In French, laissez means to let/allow and faire means to do).

This style of leadership is appropriate when the subordinates are well trained, knowledgeable, self-motivated and ready to assume responsibility.

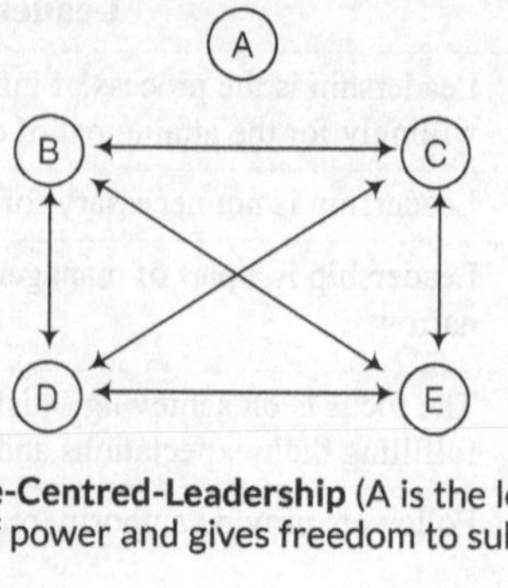

Subordinate-Centred-Leadership (A is the leader, who avoids use of power and gives freedom to subordinates)

The following are its advantages

(i) It provides maximum scope for development of subordinates.
(ii) Full utilisation of the potential of subordinates.
(iii) It reduces the burden of leader.
(iv) It provides high level of motivation to subordinates.
(v) It gives chance to take initiative to the subordinates.

The following are its disadvantages

(i) Subordinates do not get the support of leaders.
(ii) Subordinates move in different directions as there is lack of guidance.
(iii) There is lack of importance of managerial post.
(iv) There is lack of cooperation among employees in the organisation.

Comparison/Difference between Leadership Styles

Basis	Autocratic	Democratic	Laissez-faire
Decision-making	Employees are not involved, only leader takes decision.	Employees and leader collectively takes decision.	Employees are free to take decision, however leader remains responsible for every decision.
Authority	Leaders retain the authority for decision-making.	It is partly delegated to subordinates.	It is completely delegated to suordinates.
Motivation	Negative motivation.	Positive motivation.	Self-motivated to work.
Behaviour orientation	Taste oriented behaviour.	Relationship oriented behaviour.	Relationship oriented behaviour.

We can explain it with the help of following diagram

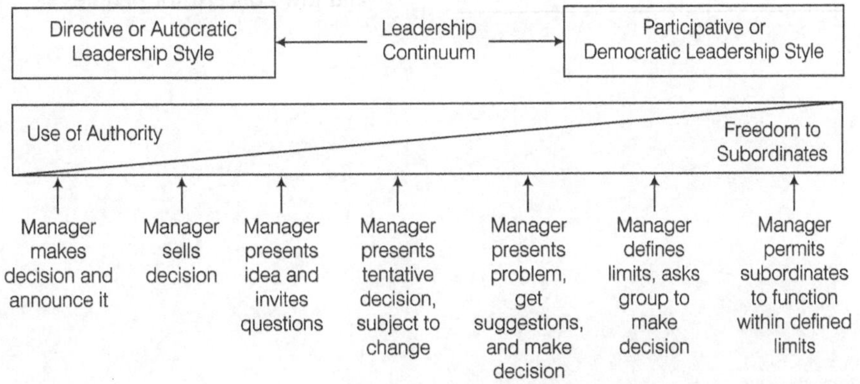

Leadership as a Continuum

Leadership continuum theory was developed by **Tannenbaum and Schmidt** (1958). It represents valuable framework for analysing leadership style (i.e. depicting a broad range of leadership style). Tannenbaum and Schmidt suggested that direction and participation are two essential part of continuum

(i) **Directive leadership** It refers to the situation where leader plays the active role in decision-making and expects group members to be guided by his/her decisions.

(ii) **Participative leadership** It refers to the situation where leader makes group members feel free to participate actively in decision-making process.
It depends upon the following three factors

(a) **Leaders** The behaviour of leaders depend upon the following
- Value system
- Confidence
- Aptitude for leadership

(b) **Followers** The behaviour of the followers is affected by the following
- Morale and motivation
- Knowledge
- Experience
- Willingness to take responsibility

(c) **Situation** The situation is affected by the following
- Organisation norms
- Pressure of time
- Nature of problem
- Effectiveness of followers

Situational Leadership

Situational leadership was developed by **Hersey and Blanchard.** It focuses on leadership in situations. The essence of theory is that different situations demand different kinds of leadership.

In other words, it is required that leaders will match their style with the competence and commitment of the subordinates. Every factor of leadership must be considered in the context of situation. It includes two basic concepts, *viz.* leadership style and follower's maturity level.

1. Leadership Style

There are four styles of leadership

(i) **Directive/Telling approach** Under this style, leaders take decisions and tells subordinates what to do.

(ii) **Coaching/Selling approach** Under this style, leader persuades the followers rather than simply directing them.

(iii) **Participating/Supporting approach** Under this style, leader supports and encourages the followers to act as a team.

(iv) **Delegating** Under this style, leader transfers the decision-making responsibility to his followers.

2. Follower's Maturity Level

There are four levels of follower's maturity

(i) M_1–Low competence and low commitment.

(ii) M_2–Low competence and high commitment.

(iii) M_3–High competence and low commitment/ confidence.

(iv) M_4–High competence and high commitment/ confidence.

Following leadership styles can be used with different maturity level

M_1 = Directive leadership, M_2 = Coaching/Selling leadership
M_3 = Participating leadership, M_4 = Delegating leadership

Managerial Grid

Blake and Mouton (1964) suggested managerial grid theory for effective management. Managerial grid theory is a trademarked and widely recognised theory of leadership style.

It includes two major aspects, *viz.* concern for people and concern for production.

The different styles are depicted in the diagram below

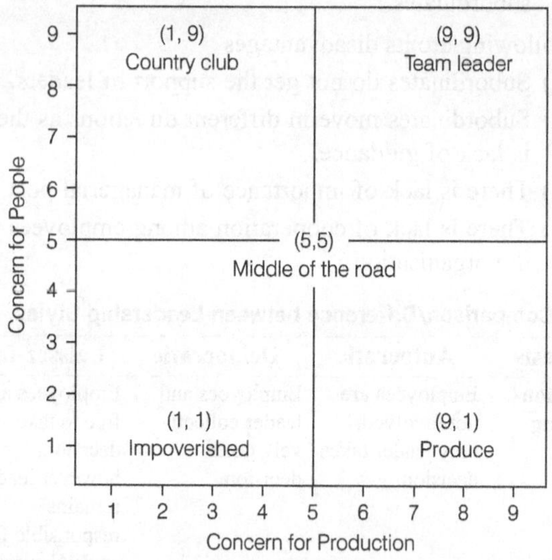

(i) **Country club style** It has a high concern for people and low concern for production.

(ii) **Impoverished style** It has low concern for both people and production.

(iii) **Team leader or management** It has high concern for both people and production.

(iv) **The middle of the road** This style has balance between production and people.

(v) **Produce style** It has high concern for production and low concern for people.

PYQs Previous Years' Questions

1 Mark Questions

1. The ………… style of leadership reduces resistance to change and increases acceptance of new ideas. **ISC 2023**

Ans democratic or participative leadership

> **Concept Enhancer** In democratic/participative leadership style, a leader takes decisions after consultation with subordinates. Thus, it reduces resistance to changes and increases acceptance of new ideas.

2. Under the democratic leadership style, the leader gives complete freedom to his followers. (True/False) **ISC Specimen 2023**

Ans False. In democratic leadership style, a leader takes decisions after consultation and encourages the participation of subordinates.

2 Marks Questions

1. Define leadership. **ISC 2019**

Ans According to **George Terry**, "Leadership is the activity of influencing people to strive willingly for group objectives."

2. Briefly explain any two qualities of good leader. **ISC 2018**

Or State any two qualities of a good leader. **ISC 2016, 2014**

Ans Two qualities of a good leader are

(i) **Courage** The leader must have courage to initiate some action, taking the first step and leading the way in every possible manner.

(ii) **Sense of responsibility** A good leader should be prepared to shoulder the responsibility for the consequences of his decisions and actions. He should always be aware of his duties and obligations.

3. Give any two differences between leadership and management. **ISC 2017**

Ans Refer to text on page 75.

4. Give any two advantages of laissez-faire style of leadership. **ISC 2015**

Ans Two advantages of laissez-faire style of leadership are

(i) Complete freedom to subordinates improves their motivation and morale.

(ii) There is maximum opportunity for the development of subordinates.

5. 'Democratic leadership is ideal for white collar workers'. Justify the statement. **ISC 2012**

Ans Democratic style provides freedom of thinking and listens to suggestions, grievances and opinions of subordinates.

This develops a participative structure in an organisation. Thus, it is ideal for white collar job workers.

6. What is paternalistic leadership? **ISC 2009**

Ans In this style of leadership, a leader is acting like a father and takes care of their subordinates as a parent. In this style, a leader supplies complete concern for his followers or workers. In return, he receives complete trust and loyalty on the part of the subordinates.

7. How is a leader different from a manager? **ISC 2008**

Ans Difference between leader and manager are

Basis	Manager	Leader
Origin	He originates by virtue of his position in the organisation.	He originates by virtue of his personal qualities.
Functions	A manager has to plan organise, staff, direct and control his subordinates.	A leader has to influence, guide and motivate his followers.

8. Explain any one style of leadership. **ISC 2007**

Ans In coercive or autocratic style, the leader's approach is 'Do what I say'. Such style is suitable in case of turn around situation, but in general, if this style is adopted, it kills employees' initiative and adversely affects their pride.

9. Autocratic leadership is ideal for blue collar workers. Explain. **ISC 2005**

Ans The statement is true as an autocratic leader is one who likes to run things by his own way. He takes all decisions without consulting his followers. He gives orders and has complete power to rule upon the workers.

4 Marks Questions

1. Give any four differences between autocratic style of leadership and democratic style of leadership. ***ISC 2023***

Ans Differences between autocratic and democratic style of leadership are as follows

Basis	Autocratic style	Democratic style
Decision-making	In this leadership style, employees are not involved, only leader takes decision.	In this leadership style, employees and leader collectively takes decision.
Authority	Leaders retain the authority for decision-making.	Authority is partly delegated to subordinates.
Motivation	This style does not motivate employees, thus it has negative motivation.	This style motivates employees, thus it has positive motivation.
Behaviour orientation	This style of leadership emphasises task oriented behaviour.	This style of leadership emphasises relationship oriented behaviour.

2. Write a short note on the situational leadership. ***ISC 2019***

Ans Situational leadership refers to the style of leadership in which leaders match their style with competence and commitment of subordinates. It was developed by Hershey and Blanchard which says that different situations demand different kinds of leadership. It has two components

(i) **Leadership style** The leadership can be directive, coaching, participating or delegating.

(ii) **Follower's maturity** Level Depending on competence and commitment, follower's maturity can be M_1, M_2, M_3 and M_4.

Following leadership styles can be used with different maturity level

M_1 = Directive Leadership
M_2 = Coaching Leadership
M_3 = Participating Leadership
M_4 = Delegating Leadership

3. Briefly explain the following

(i) Leadership continuum

(ii) Blake and Mouton managerial grid ***ISC Specimen 2019***

Ans (i) Continuum of leadership behaviour was developed by Tannenbaum and Schmidt and recognise that the chosen leadership style depends on a variety of factors, including leader's personal traits, the perceived qualities of followers. The continuum represents a wide range of action related to

(a) Degree of authority used by leader.

(b) Area of freedom available to followers.

(ii) Blake and Mouton (1964) suggested managerial grid theory for effective management. Managerial grid theory is a trademarked and widely recognised theory of leadership style.

It includes two major aspects

(a) **Concern for people** It includes

- Promoting friendship
- Need of team members
- Helping co-workers
- Working conditions
- Building trust
- Respect their values

(b) **Concern for production** It includes

- Greater output
- Cost effectiveness
- Profit
- Organisational efficiency

6/8 Marks Questions

1. Blake and Mouton have identified five combinations in their graphic model of alternative combinations of leadership styles or behaviours.

With reference to the above statement, explain any four such combinations. ***ISC Specimen 2023***

KEY IDEA

Blake and Mouton proposed a graphic portrayal of leadership style which is known as 'Managerial Grid Theory'.

Ans Blake and Mouton (1964) suggested managerial grid theory for effective management. This grid has two dimensions-concern for people and concern for production.

It classfies leader-managers as having five basic styles. The different styles are depicted in the diagram below

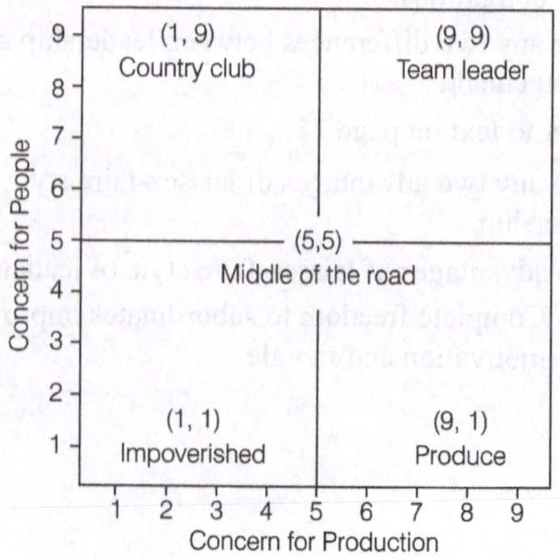

(i) **Country club style** Under this style, the leader has low or no concern for production but high concern for people. He creates a climate in which everyone is relaxed and happy. He concentrates on good human-relations.

(ii) **Impoverished style** This style has low concern for both people and production. The leader has minimum involvement in his job. He only acts as messenger communicating information from superiors to subordinates.

(iii) **Team leader** This style has high concern for both people and production. That leads to high morale and high efficiency. By high consideration, he gets workers committed to the goals of the organisation.

(iv) **Produce/Task style** In this style, the leader is highly concerned with task efficiency or production but low concern for people.

2. With reference to democratic leadership, answer the following

(i) Explain the concept of democratic leadership.

(ii) State any two advantages.

(iii) State any two disadvantages.

(iv) State any two conditions where this style is most effective. **ISC 2020**

Ans (i) A democratic leader encourages the participation of subordinates and take decisions after consulting them. He decentralises authority and allows subordinates to share his power. The leader does, what the group wants and follows the majority opinion. A democratic leader provides freedom of thinking and listens to suggestions, grievances and opinions of the subordinates.

This style is appropriate, where subordinates have accepted the goals of the organisation, the leader trusts the subordinates and wants to share decisions with them.

(ii) Advantages of democratic style of leadership are as follows (any two)

(a) This style of leadership creates job satisfaction.

(b) It fosters a sense of participation, control and autonomy.

(c) It promotes creativity among employees.

(d) It creates a healthy working environment.

(e) It gives a chance of decision to employees.

(iii) Disadvantages of democratic leadership are as follows (any two)

(a) It is a time consuming process.

(b) It reserves certain skills and educational qualifications.

(c) It offers an element of continuing uncertainty.

(d) There is no guarantee for best possible solution for a specific problem.

(iv) Two conditions where this style is effective are

(a) This leadership is effective where group members are skilled and eager to share their knowledge.

(b) It is effective when plenty of time is available to allow people to contribute towards developing a plan for the best course of action.

3. Briefly explain any three leadership styles. **ISC 2018**

Ans Some of the main styles of leadership are as follows

(i) **Authoritative or autocratic leadership** An autocratic leader exercises complete control over the subordinates. He centralises power in himself and takes decisions without consulting the subordinates. He dominates and drives his group through coercion and command.

Autocratic leadership style may be appropriate when subordinates are uneducated, unskilled and submissive.

(ii) **Democratic or participative leadership** Refer to ans 2 (i) on page 81.

(iii) **Free-rein or laissez-faire leadership** It involves complete delegation of authority, so that subordinates themselves take decisions. The free rein leader avoids holding power and surrenders the authority to subordinates. He only serves as a link, who helps in bringing the information and resources needed by the subordinates. This style of leadership is appropriate when the subordinates are well trained, knowledgeable, self-motivated and ready to assume responsibility.

Common Mistake Generally students get confused among different leadership styles. Students are advisable to note that styles based on use of Authority are–Autocratic, Democratic (Participative) and Free-rein (Laissez-faire). So answer accordingly.

4. Write a short note on authoritative leadership. ***ISC 2017***

Ans An authoritative or autocratic leader exercises complete control over the subordinates. This leadership style is very effective in getting productivity in factor situations and facilitates quick decision-making.

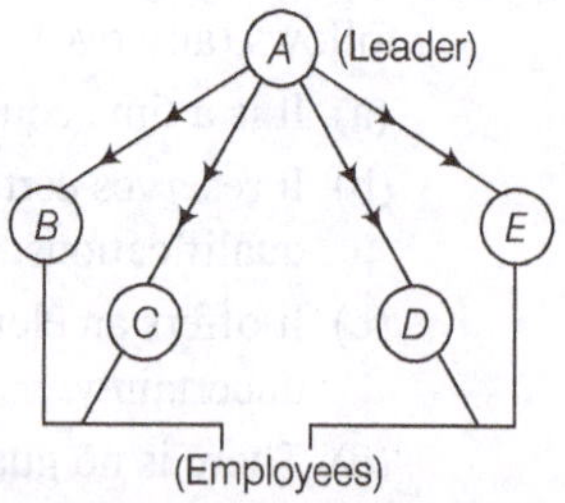

A is the authoritative leader

As shown in the diagram, the decision-making power is centralised in the leader. He centralises power in himself and takes decisions without consulting the subordinates. He dominates and drives his group through coercion and command. Autocratic leadership style may be appropriate when subordinates are uneducated, unskilled and submissive. An autocratic leader gives orders and expects his subordinates to follow them without questions.

Merits of autocratic style of leadership are as follows

(i) This style is suitable in case of emergency like in military and for blue collar employees.

(ii) It is useful in stressful conditions.

(iii) It has a creative competitive environment.

(iv) It helps in the growth of the company.

The following are its demerits

(i) This style creates frustration, low morale and conflict among subordinates.

(ii) It reduces the creative power of employees.

(iii) It displays tendency of shrink responsibility.

(iv) It is not appropriate when subordinates are educated, skilled and disobedient.

(v) It is unable to realise full utilisation of potential of employees.

(vi) It leads high labour turnover ratio in organisation.

Value Points

For getting maximum marks, following value points can be included in the answer

- Meaning of authoritative leadership
- Situation where it is used i.e. suitability
- Merits and demerits of authoritative leadership

5. Define leadership. Explain the importance of autocratic and democratic styles of leadership. ***ISC 2014***

Ans **Meaning of leadership** Leadership may be defined as the process of influencing the behaviour of people by making them strive voluntarily towards the achievement of goals.

It is the ability of maintaining personal relations with followers and motivating them to contribute for achieving goals of the organisation.

In the words of **George Terry,** "Leadership is the activity of influencing people to strive willingly for group objectives."

Importance of autocratic style It plays an important role in the business environment. Business owners often develop a management style to run their organisation and manage employees. An autocratic leadership style relies on one individual to make decisions in a business.

Small businesses often use an autocratic leadership style because the business owner is responsible for all business decisions.

Importance of democratic style It is quite effective for manufacturing and professional organisations. A democratic leader will develop action plans and make decisions in consultation with his subordinates. This kind of leadership is more common now-a-days, since leader also recognises that people perform best when their opinions are valued.

6. Define leadership. Distinguish between leadership and management. ***ISC 2012***

Ans **Definition of leadership** Leadership may be defined as the process of influencing the behaviour of people by making them strive voluntarily towards the achievement of goals.

It is the ability of maintaining personal relations with followers and motivating them to contribute for achieving goals of the organisation.

Difference between leadership and management

Basis	Leadership	Management
Meaning	Leadership is the process of influencing people to strive willingly for the attainment of objectives.	Management is the process of planning organising, directing, staffing and controlling.
Necessity	Leadership is not necessary for an organisation.	Management is necessary for an organisation.
Narrow/ Wide term	Leadership is a part of managerial function. Its scope is narrow.	Management is a wider term and includes leadership.
Focus	The focus is on achieving satisfaction of followers by fulfilling their expectations and aspirations.	The focus of management is on achieving organisational goals.

Basis	Leadership	Management
Nature of authority	Followers provide authority on their own will.	A manager possesses formal authority over his subordinates, by virtue of his position.

Value Points

For getting maximum marks, following point can be included in the answer

- When any 'differences between' is asked in question, then always write differences in tabular form, instead of writing paragraphs on each.

7. Explain laissez-faire leadership. Discuss its advantages and disadvantages. *ISC 2010*

Ans **Meaning of laissez-faire leadership** It involves complete delegation of authority, so that subordinates themselves take decisions. The free-rein leader avoids holding power and surrenders the authority to his subordinates.

He serves as a link, who helps in bringing the information and resources needed by the subordinates. This is also known as 'laissez faire' which means no interference in the affairs of others (In French, laissez means to let/allow and faire means to do).

This style of leadership is appropriate when the subordinates are well trained, knowledgeable, self-motivated and ready to assume responsibility.

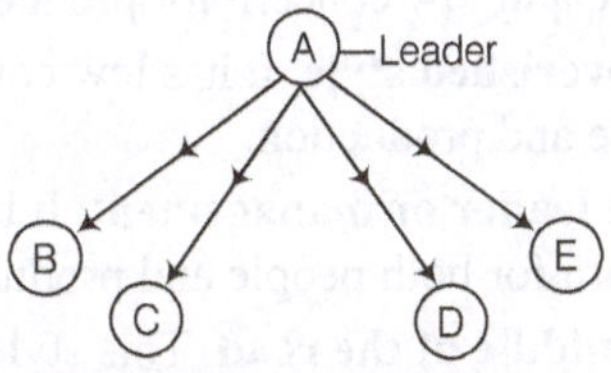

Boss-Centred-Leadership
(A is the leader who bosses around and give orders)

Advantages of laisser-faire leadership Advantages of laissez-faire leadership are as follows

(i) Provides maximum scope for the development of subordinates.

(ii) Full utilisation of potential of subordinates.

(iii) It promotes decisiveness.

Disadvantages of laissez-faire leadership Disadvantages of laissez-faire leadership are as follows

(i) Subordinates do not get the support of leaders.

(ii) Subordinates move in different directions as there is lack of guidance.

(iii) It creates the problem of coordination.

8. Explain four essential qualities of a good leader. *ISC 2009*

Ans Four qualities of a good leader are as follows

(i) **Physical qualities** A good leader must have adequate physical energy and stamina for hard work.

A good physique or attractive personality and charming manners determine success in leadership to some extent.

Qualities of Good Leaders
- Physical qualities
- Self-confidence
- Intelligence
- Sense of responsibility

(ii) **Self-confidence** A good leader must have full confidence in himself. This is necessary to win the confidence of others and to face problems. He should have confidence in himself, whenever he takes any decision or initiates any course of action.

(iii) **Intelligence** A leader should have somewhat higher level of intelligence than average people. He should be able to interpret clearly and concisely the problems faced by groups and its members.

(iv) **Sense of responsibility** A good leader is prepared to shoulder the responsibility for the consequences of his decisions and actions. He is always aware of his duties and obligations.

9. Explain the autocratic and democratic styles of leadership, bringing out clearly the merits of both the styles. *ISC 2006*

Ans **Autocratic style of leadership** Refer to Q. No. 4 on page 82.

Democratic style of leadership In a democratic leadership, leader takes decisions after consultation and encourages the participation of subordinates.

This leadership style is more common and popular, as it ensure achievement of goals, when they are set with the acceptance of subordinates themselves. A democratic leader provides freedom of thinking and listens to suggestions, grievances and opinions of the subordinates.

This improves the attitude of the employees towards their jobs and the organisation, thereby increasing their morale.

This style is of mutual benefit which allows subordinates to become part of team and help leaders (seniors) to make better decisions.

As shown in the figure, the leader involves subordinates in decision-making.

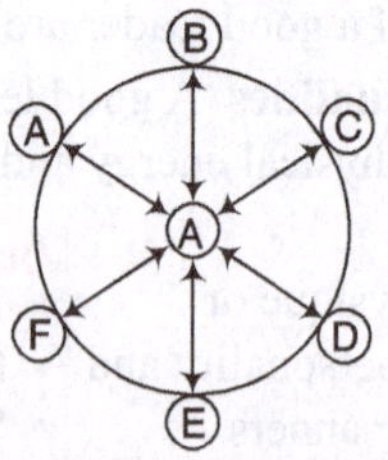

Group-Centred-Leadership
(A is the leader, who consults with the group)

For merits of democratic style of leadership, refer to ans 2 (ii) on page 81.

Additional Questions

2 Marks Questions

1. State any four disadvantages of democratic leadership.

Ans Four disadvantages of democratic style of leadership are as follows

(i) It is a time-consuming process.

(ii) It requires a certain skills and educational qualifications.

(iii) It offers an element of continuing uncertainty.

(iv) There is no guarantee for best possible solution for a specific problem.

2. State the features of leadership.

Ans The following are the main features of leadership

(i) It is the ability of an individual to influence people.

(ii) It tries to bring change in the behaviour of others.

(iii) It is exercised to achieve common goals of the organisation.

(iv) It explains the interpersonal relationship between leaders and followers.

(v) It is a continuous process.

8 Marks Question

1. Explain managerial grid in leadership.

Ans Blake and Mouton (1964) suggested managerial grid theory for effective management. Managerial grid theory is a trademarked and widely recognised theory of leadership style.

It includes two major aspects

(i) **Concern for people** It includes

(a) Promoting friendship
(b) Need of team members
(c) Helping co-workers
(d) Working conditions
(e) Building trust
(f) Respect their values

(ii) **Concern for production** It includes

(a) Greater output
(b) Cost effectiveness
(c) Profit
(d) Organisational efficiency

Managerial grid theory examines how the leader's actions are perceived by others. Concern for people and concern for production are independent aspects. A effective leader always shows high concern for people as well as production. We can use a diagram for explaining different styles of leadership.

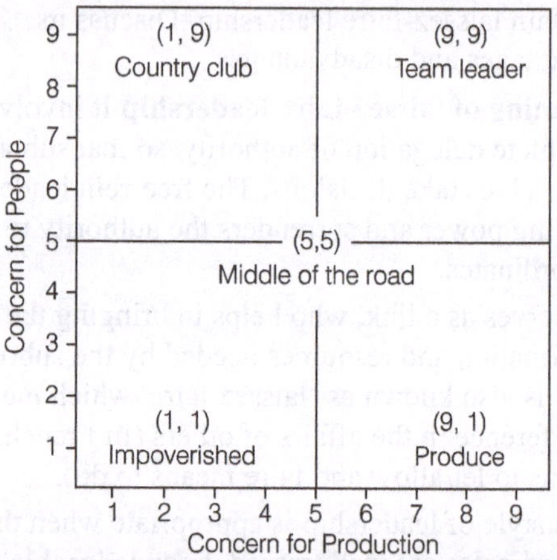

(a) **Country club style** It has a high concern for people and low concern for production.

(b) **Impoverished style** It has low concern for both people and production.

(c) **Team leader or management** It has high concern for both people and production.

(d) **The middle of the road** This style has balance between production and people.

(e) **Produce style** It has high concern for production and low concern for people.

Case Based Question

Case 1

(i) The creator of Microsoft "Bill Gates" recognised the importance of empowering people and discovered that the best approach to surpass market competition is to include competent team members in decision-making.

(i) Which leadership style did Bill Gates follow?

(ii) State two advantages and two disadvantages of the same.

Ans (i) Bill Gates followed democratic or participative leadership style.

(ii) Refer to text on page 76.

CHAPTER TEST

01 Mark Questions

1. In which leadership style, a leader has complete control over subordinates?
2. Who propounded the managerial grid theory?
3. "I need your feedback before I make decision. Please speak out". This is an example of which type of leadership style?
4. .... is the activity of influencing people to strive willingly for group objectives.
5. Situational leadership focuses on leadership in ....
6. Which of the following is a characteristic of a laissez-faire leadership style?
   (a) A leader gives opinion only when asked.
   (b) A leader takes charge.
   (c) Everyone works together and participates together.
   (d) Nobody gives any suggestions or instructions.
7. Which of the following is false regarding participative style of leadership?
   (a) Leader assigns work to the workforce.
   (b) Leader provides guidance during the work-process.
   (c) Leader makes decision based on the conclusions made by the workforce.
   (d) Leader doesn't assign any task to its workforce.
8. As per managerial grid theory, which style has low concern for both people and production?
   (a) Country club style (b) Impoverished style
   (c) Produce style (d) Team leader/Task style
9. Leadership is essential for every organisation. State true or false.
10. Laissez-faire leadership involves complete delegation of authority, so that subordinates themselves take decision. State true or false.

02 Marks Questions

11. Leadership is an integral part of management function of directing. Justify.
12. What is the democratic style of leadership?
13. Being a leader, which style of leadership you would opt and why?
14. State two advantages of free-rein style of leadership.
15. What are the benefits of autocratic style of leadership?

04 Marks Questions

16. Explain in brief, following style of leadership.
    (i) Autocratic
    (ii) Free-rein style
17. Discuss any four qualities of a good leader.
18. Why is democratic style called 'participative leadership style'?
19. Write a short note on
    (i) Situational Leadership
    (ii) Managerial Grid

06/08 Marks Questions

20. Define leadership. Explain leadership continuum.
21. What are the different leadership styles? Explain and compare each for them.

Answers

1. Autocratic
2. Blake and Mouton
3. Democratic *or* participative
4. Leadership
5. situation
6. (a) A leader gives opinion only when asked
7. (d) Leader doesn't assign any task to its workforce
8. (b) Impoverished style
9. False *10.* True

08

Staff Appraisal

TREND ANALYSIS 5 YEARS

Average No. of Questions Across all Sets

	Types of Questions	2023	2020	2019	2018	2017
01 Meaning of Performance and Potential Appraisal	1 Mark	—	—	—	—	—
	2 Marks	1	1	—	—	1
	4 Marks	—	—	—	—	—
	6 Marks	—	—	—	—	—
	8 Marks	—	—	—	1	—
02 Methods of Performance Appraisal	1 Mark	—	—	—	—	—
	2 Marks	1	—	—	—	—
	4 Marks	—	—	—	—	—
	6 Marks	—	—	—	—	—
	8 Marks	—	—	1	—	—

Meaning and Definitions of Performance Appraisal

The word 'performance appraisal' combines two terms, one is 'performance' which refers to 'the degree of accomplishment of the tasks' and the other is 'appraisal' which refers to 'the rating or evaluation of the worth or effectiveness of an employee'.

Thus, it can rightly be said that performance appraisal is the systematic evaluation of performance of the job.

According to **Flippo**, "Performance appraisal is the systematic, periodic and an impartial rating of an employee's excellence in matters pertaining to his present job and of his potentialities for better job."

According to **Scott** and **Spriegal**, ''Performance appraisal is the process of evaluating the employees' performance on the job in terms of the requirement of the job''.

Objectives of Performance Appraisal

The main objectives of performance appraisal are as follows

(i) To evaluate the efficiency of employee's task.

(ii) To identify the shortcomings of an employee, so as to overcome them through systematic guidance and training.

(iii) To find out employee's potential for promotion and advancement.

(iv) To judge the effectiveness of training and placement decisions.

(v) To re-direct the performance and behaviour of the employees in particular direction that will help in achieving the productivity of the company.

(vi) To put psychological pressure on the employees for better performance.

(vii) To take decisions regarding wages and salaries.

Importance of Performance Appraisal

The importance of performance appraisal are as follows

(i) **Helpful in improving job performance** An appraisal system helps the employees to know, how efficiently they have done their tasks, which improves their job performance.

(ii) **Helpful in improving quality of supervision** Performance appraisal leads to an improvement in managerial leadership, as it may help the supervisors to be alert in their duties. This helps to improve the quality of supervision and control.

(iii) **Helpful in career development** The result of performance appraisal provides a picture of the strength and weaknesses of the employees. It guides the employees to modify their present work, so that they can effectively perform their task.

(iv) **Helpful in taking decision** It provides the basis for decisions-making relating to promotion, demotion, transfer and pay rise, etc for the employee.

(v) **Helpful in human resource planning** It helps the management in taking decision for future employment.

(vi) **Helpful in taking lay-off decisions** It is helpful in lay-off. The weakest performers in organisations are the first to be lay-off.

Methods of Performance Appraisal

There are several methods by which an employer judges the effectiveness of an employee, but as per the latest syllabus, we are discussing only three methods

1. Merit Rating/Grading

Merit rating/grading technique has been evolved to know the relative worth of the employee, quantitatively and qualitatively on-the-job, in comparison to the other fellow workers. This process starts at the time of recruitment and continues throughout the life of an employee in an organisation.

It is used for measuring the merit or performance of an employee and comparing it with that of others in the same group. Under this method, rater considers certain features and marks them according to a scale.

The features may be cooperativeness, self-expression, analytical ability, etc. The rating is done on a scale, ranging from A-outstanding, B-very good and so on. As per the description of Dale Yoder, "Performance appraisal refers to all formal procedures used in working organisations to evaluate personalities, contributions and potential of group members''.

Thus, it can rightly be said that merit rating is a systematic evaluation by the supervisor or some qualified person of an individual worker's performance.

Advantages of merit rating are as follows

(i) It increases productivity of employees i.e. encourages employees to more exertion.

(ii) It provides an opportunity to workers to talk about job problem, interest and future.

(iii) It cultivates a spirit of competition among employees.

(iv) It promotes the employee's job satisfaction and morale.

(v) It helps in planning the employee's training.

Disadvantages of merit rating are as follows

(i) Generally, it is based on opinions, it may tend to be unfair.

(ii) There may be biased rating by supervisors.

(iii) Previous rating of employees influence the present rating.

(iv) Workers incentives, which are based on merit rating may not be consider enough.

2. Appraisal by Results

It measures the individual employee's performance on a continuing basis in relation to mutually agreed objectives which are determined at the beginning of the year.

It is based on the management by objectives. It focuses on what must be goals rather than how it is to be accomplished.

It involves

(i) set the organisation's goals.

(ii) set departmental goals.

(iii) discuss departmental goals.

(iv) define expected results.

(iv) performance reviews.

(v) provide feedback.

Advantages of appraisal by results are as follows

(i) It provides continuous performance of each individual staff.

(ii) Employees are judged according to real outcomes.

(iii) It establishes link between organisational and individual performance.

(iv) It measures performance of employees and not personality of employees.

(v) It is easy to implement in organisation.

Disadvantages of appraisal by results are following

(i) It focuses on job completion rather than quality of a job.
(ii) It has negative effect on teamwork in the organisation.
(iii) Setting targets is not a easy work.
(iv) Subordinates in organisation may be represented by this method.
(v) It requires complete support of the top management.
(vi) It is not applicable for all jobs.

3. Appraisal by Superior Staff

It is most common appraisal method which is based on the assumption that manager is the best judge of his employees' performance.

Under this method, employee's responsibilities and actual performance is rated by the superior and often reviewed by a manager of one level higher.

Advantages of appraisal by superior staff are as follows

(i) Appraisal by superior staff reduces time and cost in appraisal procedure in the organisation.
(ii) It provides appropriate appraisal to employees and validate the performance of employees.
(iii) It provides additional information because superiors (i.e. supervisors) have close contact with an employee's work.
(iv) Superiors observe, direct and control the employee's performance. They are accountable for the successful performance of their subordinates.

Disadvantages of appraisal superiors staff are as follows

(i) Generally, under this method, evaluation of performance is one-way.
(ii) Manager may misuse the power of punishment and reward to employees.
(iii) It may be quite possible that manager is unable to give proper feedback on performance of the employee.
(iv) Superiors may emphasise certain aspects of employee performance to neglect the other employee.

4. Self-appraisal

According to **Heery** and **Noon** (2001), "Self-appraisal is the technique of evaluating your own performance and then discussing this with your line manager."

It is useful when supervisors want to increases an employee's involvement in the performance appraisal. The employees who appraise their own performance may become highly motivated.

Advantages of self-appraisal are as follows

(i) It increases the commitment of employee's about their jobs.
(ii) It reduces role conflict in the organisation.
(iii) It provides an opportunity to the employee to express their future career plan.
(iv) It provides to an employee's absolute freedom to look at his strong points as well as his weak points.
(v) As a development tool, self-appraisals are invaluable.

Disadvantages of self-appraisal are as follows

(i) If employee is not self-aware, self-appraisals does not provide adequate feedback and performance validation.
(ii) Self-appraisal is not more acceptable way of appraisal, even mature employees require external feedback and performance validation.
(iii) Self-appraisal may be costly method because it is a continuous process of appraisal.
(iv) Self-appraisal is subject to systematic biases and distortions.

5. 360° Appraisal

360° Appraisal takes information from more than one source. It includes

(i) information from superiors.
(ii) information from subordinates.
(iii) information from peers.
(iv) information from customers.
(v) information from self.

In India, it is used by Crompton Greaves, Wipro, Infosys, Reliance Industries, etc.

Advantages of 360° appraisal are as follows

(i) It leads to improvement in performance of employees because feedback comes from more than one source.
(ii) It provides participative work culture in the organisation. Employees will maintain good relations with all.
(iii) It creates awareness and spirit to compete among the employees.
(iv) It has greater reliability in the feedback i.e. more reliable method of appraisal.
(v) It accomplishes all the purposes of the traditional systems such as reward management, identification of development needs, etc.
(vi) It facilitates focus on internal customer satisfaction.

Disadvantages of 360° appraisal are as follows

(i) It is a time-consuming process.
(ii) It is costly procedure and not suitable for small enterprises.
(iii) It is not a fair method to rate on same parameters to all employees.
(iv) Colleague's responses tend to be biased.
(v) Feedback/information can be useless, if it is not carefully and smartly dealt.

Meaning and Definition of Potential Appraisal

Potential appraisal is a future-oriented appraisal. It is used to measure and judge the potentiality of an employee for future higher positions. Most organisations include potential appraisal as a part of the performance appraisal. Generally, it is done by employee's supervisor on annual basis. It updates training and recruitment activities in the organisation and informs to employees about their future prospects.

According to **K. Ramchandran, Director** and **Senior Vice-President, Philips India Limited,** "People are like icebergs. What you see above the surface (Performance) is only a small part. A large part of the attributes needed to perform excellently in a future job, which I call potential, is not immediately visible. It is hidden below surface."

Distinction between Performance Appraisal and Potential Appraisal

Basis	Performance appraisal	Potential appraisal
Meaning	It is a systematic evaluation of an employee performance for the purpose of making career decisions.	It refers to identification of the hidden talent and skills of an employee for a future role.
Process	It is backward looking process.	It is forward looking process.
Concept	Wide concept, i.e. it includes potential appraisal.	Narrow concept, i.e. it is a part of performance appraisal.
Appraisal	It is a past oriented appraisal.	It is a future oriented appraisal.
Focus	It focuses on employee's present performance in his existing role/job.	It focuses on employee's capability to successfully assume a new role in future.

PYQs Previous Years' Questions

1 Mark Question

1. Which of the following is not a component of the 360° appraisal? *ISC Specimen 2023*
   (a) Self appraisal (b) Industry appraisal
   (c) Peer appraisal (d) Superior appraisal

Ans (b) Industry appraisal

Concept Enhancer 360° Appraisal takes information from more than one source. It includes information from superiors, subordinates, peers, customers and from self.

2/4 Marks Questions

1. (i) State any two objectives of performance appraisal.
   (ii) What is meant by merit grading method of performance appraisal? *ISC 2023*

Ans (i) The objectives of performance appraisal are
(a) To evaluate the efficiency of employee's task.
(b) To find out potential of employees for promotion and advancement.

(ii) It is a method of measuring performance of an employee. Under this method, an employee is graded on certain features, e.g. discipline, reliability, analytical ability, etc. The rating is done on a scale of ranging from excellent (A) to poor (E).
Merit grading/rating technique has been evolved to know the relative worth of the employee, quantitatively and qualitatively on-the-job, in comparison to the other fellow workers.

2. Give any two distinctions between potential appraisal and performance appraisal. *ISC 2020*

Or How is potential appraisal different from performance appraisal? *ISC Specimen 2019*

Or How does performance appraisal differ from potential appraisal? *ISC 2017*

Ans Performance appraisal differ from potential appraisal in the following ways

Basis	Performance appraisal	Potential appraisal
Meaning	Performance appraisal is the process of evaluating the employee's performance on-the-job in terms of the requirements of the job.	Potential appraisal is the appraisal of the qualities of an employee to assess whether he is able to discharge higher responsibilities.
Perspective	It is backward looking.	It is forward looking.

3. Explain two limitations of performance appraisal. **ISC 2011**

Ans Two limitations of performance appraisal are as follows

(i) Performance appraisal is not effective due to unrealistic assumptions on the part of both supervisors and subordinates.

(ii) The effectiveness of appraisal depends upon the psychological characteristics of managers to a great extent.

4. Define staff appraisal. Explain in brief the merit grading method of staff appraisal. **ISC 2008**

> **KEY IDEA**
> Performance appraisal is also known as staff appraisal, employee appraisal, performance review, annual review, etc.

Ans **Staff appraisal** According to **Flippo**, "Performance or staff appraisal is the systematic, periodic and an impartial rating of an employee's excellence in matters pertaining to his present job and of his potentialities for better job."

Performance appraisal is one of the most important functions of personnel management. People differ in their abilities and aptitudes. The personnel management should know these differences in order to develop various development programmes in the organisation and to have an efficient workforce.

Merit grading method Refer to Q. No. 1(ii) (2/4 Marks) on page 89.

5. Define performance appraisal. Mention two methods of performance appraisal. **ISC 2006**

Ans According to **Cummings**, "The overall objective of performance appraisal is to improve the efficiency of an enterprise by attempting to mobilise the best possible efforts from individuals employed in it. Such appraisals achieve four objectives including the salary reviews, the development and training of individuals, planning job rotations and promotions."

Two methods of performance appraisal are as follows

(i) Merit grading

(ii) Interviewing

6. How does performance appraisal help in the training and development of an employee? **ISC 2005**

Ans It diagnoses the strengths and weaknesses of the employees and helps in formulating suitable training and development programmes for overcoming the weaknesses of employee's.

7. Define performance appraisal. **ISC 2004**

Ans According to **Scott** and **Spriegal,** "Performance appraisal is the process of evaluating the employee's performance on the job, in terms of the requirements of the job".

6/8 Marks Questions

1. Explain the components of 360° appraisal used to appraise staff in an organisation. **ISC 2019**

Ans Components of 360° performance appraisal are as follows

(i) **Self appraisal** It gives a chance to the employee to look at his/her strengths and weaknesses, his achievements and judge his own performance. It is also known as self-evaluation or a self-assessment.

> **Components of 360° Appraisal**
> - Self appraisal
> - Superior's appraisal
> - Subordinate's appraisal
> - Peer appraisal

(ii) **Superior's appraisal** It forms the traditional part of the 360° performance appraisal where the employees' responsibilities and actual performance are rated by the superior.

(iii) **Subordinate's appraisal** It gives a chance to judge the employee on the parameters like communication and motivating abilities, superior's ability to delegate the work, leadership qualities etc.

It is also known as internal customers. The correct feedback given by subordinates can help to find employees' abilities to work in a team, cooperation and sensitivity towards others.

(iv) **Peer appraisal** Employee assessments conducted by colleagues in the immediate working environment, i.e. the employee interacts regularly.

Peer appraisal processes exclude superiors and underlyings. This type of appraisal is form of performance appraisal which is designed to monitor and improve job performance.

2. Dicuss any four purposes of performance appraisal. *ISC 2018*

Or Define staff appraisal. Explain in brief, any four objectives of staff appraisal. *ISC 2016*

Or Discuss any four purposes of conducting staff appraisal. *ISC 2013*

Ans Staff appraisal is also referred as 'performance appraisal'.

According to **Flippo**, "Performance or staff appraisal is the systematic, periodic and an impartial rating of an employee's excellence in matters pertaining to his present job and of his potentialities for better job."

Performance appraisal is one of the most important function of personnel management.

Objectives/Purposes of staff appraisal Four objectives of staff appraisal are discussed below

(i) **Improving job performance** An appraisal system helps the employees to know, how efficiently they have done their tasks, which improves their job performance.

(ii) **Helps in career development** The result of performance appraisal provides a picture of the strength and weaknesses of the employees. It guides the employees to modify their present work, so that they can effectively perform their task.

(iii) **Improving quality of supervision** Performance appraisal leads to an improvement in managerial leadership, as it may help the supervisors to be alert in their duties. This helps to improve the quality of supervision and control.

(iv) **Employees related decision** It provides the basis for decision-making relating to promotion, demotion, transfer and pay rise, etc for the employee.

3. Define performance appraisal. Briefly explain the pros and cons of staff appraisal of subordinates by their superiors. *ISC 2015*

Ans **Meaning of performance appraisal** According to **Flippo**, "Performance appraisal is the systematic, periodic and an impartial rating of an employees excellence in matters pertaining to his present job and of his potentialities for better job."

Performance appraisal is one of the most important functions of personnel management. People differ in their abilities and aptitudes. The personnel management should know these differences in order to develop various development programmes in the organisation and to have an efficient workforce.

Generally, the performance of an employee is appraised by his immediate superior.

Pros of staff appraisal Pros of staff appraisal of subordinates by their superiors are as follows

(i) The superior is in direct touch with the subordinate. Therefore, he is in the best position to judge the performance of his subordinate.

(ii) The superior allocates work to his subordinates. He should, therefore, be given the right to assess the performance of the subordinate.

(iii) The superior has the right to supervise and control the work of his subordinates. As the immediate boss, he should evaluate the performance of the subordinate.

(iv) A manager is responsible for the work done by his subordinates. As such, he is entitled to appraise the performance of his subordinates.

Cons of staff appraisal Cons of staff appraisal of subordinates by their superiors are as follows

(i) The superior can be biased in favour of or against a particular subordinate. Therefore, the superior may overrate or underrate the subordinate's performance.

(ii) In case, a subordinate does not flatter his boss or is more loyal to the organisation than to his boss, the boss might get annoyed. He may deliberately under assess the work done by the subordinate.

Appraisal of subordinate staff by superior staff is necessary and used the world over.

However, such appraisal needs to be supplemented. An employee's performance may also be evaluated by his juniors, peers and clients. Such a multidimensional appraisal will help to minimise bias or subjectivity in appraisal.

Common Mistake Students misunderstand such type of questions which are indirect in nature. Students are advisable to read question carefully and understand what questions ask. In this question, pros and cons of staff appraisal of subordinates by their superiors are asked, that means advantages and disadvantages of performance appraisal are to be given as answer.

4. Discuss the importance of performance appraisal. *ISC 2009*

Ans The importance of performance appraisal are as follows

(i) **Helpful in improving job performance** An appraisal system helps the employees to know, how efficiently they have done their tasks, which improves their job performance.

(ii) **Helpful in improving quality of supervision** Performance appraisal leads to an improvement in managerial leadership, as it may help the supervisors to be alert in their duties. This helps to improve the quality of supervision and control.

Importance of Performance Appraisal
- Helpful in improving job performance
- Helpful in improving quality of supervision
- Helps in career development
- Helpful in taking decision
- Helpful in human resource planning
- Helpful in taking lay-off decisions

(iii) **Helps in career development** The result of performance appraisal provides a picture of the strength and weaknesses of the employees. It guides the employees to modify their present work, so that they can effectively perform their task.

(iv) **Helpful in taking decision** It provides the basis for decisions-making relating to promotion, demotion, transfer and pay rise, etc for the employee.

(v) **Helpful in human resource planning** It helps the management in taking decision for future employment.

(vi) **Helpful in taking lay-off decisions** It is helpful in lay-off. The weakest performers in organisation are the first to be lay-off.

5. How does performance appraisal help the employees and the organisation? *ISC 2004*

Ans The word 'performance appraisal' combines two terms, one is 'performance' which refers to 'the degree of accomplishment of the tasks' and the other is 'appraisal' which refers to 'the rating or evaluation of the worth or effectiveness of an employee'. Thus, it can rightly be said that performance appraisal is the systematic evaluation of performance of the job.

According to **Flippo,** "Performance appraisal is the systematic, periodic and an impartial rating of an employee's excellence in matters pertaining to his present job and of his potentialities for better job."

Need for performance appraisal for employees and the organisation are as follows

(i) **Arrange training and development programmes** It diagnoses the strengths and weaknesses of the employees and helps in formulating suitable training and development programmes for overcoming the weaknesses of employees.

(ii) **Proper placement of employees** It facilitates the placement of the right person on the right job. It helps in judging the efficiency of selection and placement procedures.

(iii) **Rational base for determining remuneration** It provides systematic judgements to consider pay-increase, promotion, transfer, demotion, etc. Performance based incentives (or rewards) motivate employees to work hard and give better performance.

(iv) **Accurate evaluation of capabilities of employees** It is a process of assessing the performance of employees in terms of job requirements.

(v) **Attracting competent persons** It offers an opportunity to the employees for making improvements in the pattern of their working behaviour.

(vi) **Enhancing performance of employees** It is helpful in creating and maintaining a satisfactory level of performance by employees. It motivates employees to improve their present level of performance by suggesting changes in their knowledge, behaviour and attitude.

(vii) **Validation of human resource programmes** It helps to judge the effectiveness of recruitment, selection, placement and orientation programmes of the organisation.

It generates data on the promotability and potential of each employee.

(viii) **Unifying the rating procedure** It unifies the rating procedure, so that all employees are rated on the same qualities by the same method of measurement.

(ix) **Legal compliance** It provides a legal basis for making promotions, transfers, rewards and discharge decisions. It helps the organisation to justify its decisions on legal grounds.

6. Performance appraisal of an employee can be conducted by his immediate supervisor. Give three advantages of conducting this type of performance appraisal. *ISC 2001*

Ans Performance appraisal is the process of evaluating the performance and qualifications of the employee in terms of requirements of the job for which he is employed, for purposes of administration, promotions, providing financial rewards, training, etc.

Performance appraisal is generally done by the immediate supervisor.

Three advantages of performance appraisal are as follows

(i) Supervisor is most familiar with his subordinate's work behaviour and actions.

(ii) It is relatively easy and also makes sense because he can make the best assessment for approving or recommending future position for the subordinate in the organisation.

(iii) Hierarchical control can be maintained over the appraisal process.

Value Points

To get maximum marks, following points should be included in the answer

- Meaning of performance appraisal
- Advantages of performance appraisal done by superior staff

Additional Questions

2 Marks Questions

1. Define potential appraisal.

Ans According to **K. Ramchandran, Director** and **Senior Vice–President, Philips India Limited**, "People are like icebergs. What you see above the surface (Performance) is only a small part. A large part of the attributes needed to perform excellently in a future job, which I call potential, is not immediately visible. It is hidden below surface."

2. What do you mean by 360° appraisal?

Ans 360° appraisal takes information from more than one source.

It includes

(i) Information from superiors

(ii) Information from subordinates

(iii) Information from peers

(iv) Information from customers

(v) Information from self

3. State two disadvantages of 360° appraisal.

Ans The main two disadvantages of 360° appraisal are as follows

(i) It is a time-consuming process.

(ii) It is costly procedure and not suitable for small enterprises.

4. Explain the term 'self appraisal'.

Ans According to **Heery** and **Noon** (2001), "Self-appraisal is the technique of evaluating your own performance and then discussing this with your line manager."

It is useful when supervisors want to increase an employee's involvement in the performance appraisal. The employees who appraise their own performance may become highly motivated.

4 Marks Questions

1. Explain the advantages and disadvantages of self-appraisal.

Ans Advantages of self-appraisal are as follows

(i) It increases the commitment of employee's about their jobs.

(ii) It reduces role conflict in the organisation.

(iii) It provides an opportunity to the employees to express their future career plan.

(iv) It provides to an employees absolute freedom to look at his strong points as well as his weak points.

Disadvantages of self-appraisal are as follows

(i) If employee is not self-aware, self appraisals does not provide adequate feedback and performance validation.

(ii) Self-appraisal is not more acceptable way of appraisal, even mature employees require external feedback and performance validation.

(iii) Self-appraisal may be costly method because it is a continuous process of appraisal.

(iv) Self-Appraisal is subject to systematic biases and distortions.

2. Explain the advantages and disadvantages of merit rating/grading system.

Ans Advantages of merit rating/grading system are as follows

(i) It increases productivity of employees i.e. encourages employees to more exertion.

(ii) It provides an opportunity to workers to talk about job problem, interest and future.

(iii) It cultivates a spirit of competition among employees.

(iv) It promotes the employee's job satisfaction and morale.

(v) It helps in planning the employee's training.

Disadvantages of merit rating/grading system are as follows

(i) Generally, evaluation of performance is one-way in this method.

(ii) Manager may misuse the power of punishment and reward to employees.

(iii) It may be quite possible that manager is unable to give proper feedback on performance of the employee.

(iv) Superiors may emphasise certain aspects of employee's performance to neglect the other employees.

Concept Enhancer Merit rating/grading is a method of performance appraisal which is used for measuring the merit or performance of an employee and comparing it with that of others in the same group. This process starts at the time of recruitment and continues throughout the life of an employee in an organisation.

6/8 Marks Questions

1. Differentiate between performance appraisal and potential appraisal. Explain the importance of performance appraisal.

Ans **Distinction between performance appraisal and potential appraisal** Refer to text on page 89.

Importance of performance appraisal Refer to Q. No. 4 on page 92.

2. Explain the appraisal by results. State its advantages and disadvantages.

Ans It measures the individual employee's performance on a continuing basis in relation to mutually agreed objectives which are determined at the beginning of the year.

It is based on the management by objectives. It focusses on what must be goals rather than how it is to be accomplished. It involves

(i) Set the organisation's goals

(ii) Set departmental goals

(iii) Discuss departmental goals

(iv) Define expected results

(v) Performance reviews

(vi) Provide feedback

Advantages of appraisal by results are

(i) It provides continuous performance of each individual staff.

(ii) Employees are judged according to real outcomes.

(iii) It establishes link between organisational and individual performance.

(iv) It measures performance of employees and not personality of employees.

(v) It is easy to implement in organisation.

Disadvantages of appraisal by result are

(i) It focuses on job completion rather than quality of a job.

(ii) It has negative effect on teamwork in the organisation.

(iii) Setting targets is not an easy work.

(iv) Subordinates in organisation may be represented by this method.

(v) It requires complete support of the top management.

(vi) It is not applicable for all jobs.

3. At AIPL, an India-based fast moving consumer goods company, the performance of each and every employee is evaluated by his/her superior, peers and also subordinates.

AIPL believes in the fact that people who are more directly affected by the employee's behaviour and performance can judge the person better. Which type of performance appraisal method is being followed by AIPL? What are the advantages and disadvantages of this method?

Ans AIPL followed the 360° performance appraisal.

Advantages and disadvantages of 360° performance appraisal Refer to text on page 88 and 89.

CHAPTER TEST

01 Mark Questions

1. In which method of staff appraisal, the performance of employees is measured on the basis of merit or grading?

2. Name the future-oriented appraisal that is used to measure and judge the potentiality of an employee.

3. Which performance appaisal method asumes that manager is the best judge of his employee's performance?

4. ………… is the process of evaluating the employee's performance on the job in terms of the requirement of the job.

5. Appraisal by result has ………… effect on teamwork in the organisation.

6. Which of the following is not the method of performance appraisal?
(a) Merit rating (b) Appraisal by result
(c) Potential appraisal (d) 360° appraisal

7. 360° Appraisal takes information from
(a) superiors (b) peers
(c) subordinates (d) All of these

8. Performance Appraisal is helpful in
(a) improving job performance
(b) career development
(c) human resource planning (d) All of these

9. Performance of an employee can not be measured by his/her superiors. State true or false.

10. Performance Appraisal system helps the employees to evaluate the efficiency of their task. State true or false.

02 Marks Questions

11. What is the role of appraisal in the life of an employee?

12. Why is performance evaluated?

13. State any two objectives of appraisal.

14. Why is merit grading important in improving the employer's performance?

04 Marks Questions

15. Differentiate between appraisal by superior staff and self appraisal.

16. State any four limitations of staff appraisal.

17. Define performance appraisal. State its any three importance.

18. State any four differences between performance appraisal and potential appraisal.

06/08 Marks Questions

19. "Multinational companies take 360° feedback about an employee before taking a major decision regarding his/her appraisal." Comment.

20. Write short note on the following
(i) Self-appraisal (ii) Appraisal by results
(iii) Appraisal by superior staff
(iv) Potential appraisal

Answers

1. Merit rating/grading
2. Potential appraisal
3. Appraisal by superior staff
4. Performance appraisal
5. negative
6. (c) Potential appraisal
7. (d) All of these
8. (d) All of these
9. False
10. True

09

Staff Promotion, Transfer and Separation

TREND ANALYSIS 5 YEARS

	Types of Questions	Average No. of Questions Across all Sets 2023	2020	2019	2018	2017
01 Staff Promotion	1 Mark	—	—	—	—	—
	2 Marks	1	—	1	1	—
	4 Marks	—	—	1	—	1
	6 Marks	1	—	—	—	—
	8 Marks	—	1	—	—	1
02 Staff Transfer and Separation	1 Mark	—	—	—	—	—
	2 Marks	—	—	—	1	1
	4 Marks	—	1	1	—	—
	6 Marks	—	—	—	—	—
	8 Marks	—	—	—	—	—

Staff promotion, transfer and separation are the concepts which are continuously considered in human resource management. These are of tremendous importance, as they would help or enable an enterprise to adjust the size of workforce according to changing situation.

Meaning and Definition of Promotion

Promotion is an upward/vertical advancement of an employee in an organisation to another job which gives him better pay, higher status and more opportunities with greater challenge and responsibility.

According to **Edwin B. Flippo**, "A promotion involves a change from one job to another that is better in terms of status and responsibility."

Benefits of Promotion

Following are the points of benefits of promotion

(i) It provides psychological satisfaction to an employee.

(ii) It recognises individual's performance and rewards them accordingly.

(iii) It enhances the morale and loyalty of different members.

(iv) It reduces discontent and unrest among staff members.

(v) It promotes the feeling of job satisfaction among different staff members.

(vi) It provides competent individuals for vacant job positions in an organisation.

(vii) Ultimately, it improves organisational health.

Limitations of Promotion

Following are the limitations of promotion

(i) Often, it is seen that supervisors select employees from their own choices which may be based on bias.

(ii) It is a very difficult task to measure the merit and ability of employees in an objective and impartial way.

(iii) The employees who are working in the organisation often lack a fresh perspective that only an outsider can bring.

(iv) When one employee is promoted, bad feelings can result in the employees left behind. It can lead to dissatisfaction at work and poor work performance.

(v) Promoted employee has to learn new skills, while outsider candidates already possess such skills.

The Open and Closed System of Promotion

Promotion can be classified into two parts

(i) **Open system of promotion** Under this method, all eligible employees of the company are given equal opportunity to be promoted for the higher position. In other words, it is open for all eligible employees and applications are invited from all the eligible employees for promotion.

(ii) **Closed system of promotion** It does not provide equal opportunity of promotion to all eligible employees. It selects the list of employees for promotion which is prepared on the basis of pre-determined promotion policy of the company. Company may reserve certain categories of jobs, especially those at the higher levels of management, and rest categories of job may be reserved for open promotion system.

Distinction between Open and Closed System of Promotion

Basis	Open policy of promotion	Closed policy of promotion
Meaning	Under this policy, all eligible employees of the company are given equal opportunity to be promoted.	It selects the list of employees for promotion which is prepared on the basis of pre-determined promotion policy of the company.
Morale	It provides high morale to employees.	It provides low morale to employees.
Suitability	It is more suitable for low and medium level of managerial jobs.	It is more suitable for high level of managerial jobs.
Opportunity	It provides equal opportunity to all employees for promotion.	It does not provide equal opportunity to all employees for promotion.

Dry Promotion and Upgrading

Dry promotion involves increase in the responsibilities and status of employees without increase in the salary. Under this method of promotion, the employee is moved to the next higher level of job with greater authority, responsibility without any increase in remuneration.

Upgrading involves raise in wages/salary, with a possible change in the designation.

It includes

(i) A horizontal promotion

(ii) Promotions within a grade

(iii) Minor promotion

For example, a promotion of a junior clerk to senior clerk with some rise in pay in the organisation.

Distinction between Dry Promotion and Upgrading

Basis	Upgrading	Dry promotion
Meaning	It involves to raise in salary, with a possible change in the designation.	It is given in lieu of increase in the compensation.
Concept	It is broad concept.	It is narrow concept.
Employee's position	In this method, employee's position remains same but the situation of the job condition gets improved.	In this method, employee's responsibilities and status get increased.

Requirements of a Sound Promotion Policy

The requirements of a sound promotion policy in the organisation can be summarised as follows

(i) **To distribute promotion opportunities** There should be equal ratio between internal promotion and external recruitment at various levels in all the departments.

(ii) **To promote morale among employees** Promotion system should be "open and not closed" so that eligible employees may get promotion at higher position.

(iii) **To establish a well defined system for promotion** There should be some definite system for the selection of employees who are to be promoted within the company. (i.e. criteria for promotion)

(iv) **To evaluate the employees** There must be a true and fair system for evaluation the efficiency and skills of employees for promotion.

(v) **To establish a review system** No promotion policy can be effective without proper review, so there should be suitable system for follow-up councelling and review.

Basis of Promotion

Generally, in an organisation, promotion is done on two basis. One is seniority and the other is ability, which are discussed below

1. Promotion by Seniority

A higher status or position is granted to an employee on the basis of his/her seniority. It keeps the morale of employees high, as they know that their juniors will not supersede them in any case.

To promote the feeling of belongingness in an organisation, management makes a list of prospective candidates and promotes them accordingly.

Advantages of seniority based promotion are as follows

(a) It can essentially guarantee improvement and advancement in a job field.
(b) It promotes the feeling of belongingness towards the organisation.
(c) It promotes the feeling of job secutiry among the employees.
(d) It is economical.
(e) It reduces labour turnover in company.

Disadvantages of seniority based promotion are as follows

(a) It is a slow process and make fast advancement difficult.
(b) Sometimes promotion does not suit the existing position.
(c) It fails to encourage the existing employees for better performance.
(d) It acts as a hurdle in attracting the capable persons.

2. Promotion by Merit

Under this system, employees are promoted for higher post on the basis of qualification, ability and performance. It encourages employee to work hard, so that they may get opportunities for advancement.

Under such system, an employee's meritorious work, achievement and hard work are awarded. It leads to increase in productivity and performance of the organisation.

Advantages of merit based promotion are as follows

(a) It increases the productivity in the organisation.
(b) It motivates the competent employees to work hard.
(c) It helps to retain the capable employees in the organisation.
(d) It encourages employees to increase their efficiencies, skills and knowledge.
(e) It recognises the knowledge and efficiency of employees.

Disadvantages of merit based promotion are as follows

(a) Measurement of merit is a difficult task.
(b) There may be scope for favouritism.
(c) Senior employees may quit the job.
(d) Trade unions distrust the company's integrity in judging the merit of employees.

3. Seniority Cum Merit Promotion

Generally, management wants to adopt merit based promotion system while trade union wants to favour the seniority based promotion system. So, organisation considers both merit and seniority for determining the promotion of an employees. This method is more suitable for middle level technical, supervisory and administrative personnel.

Comparison between Seniority Basis and Merit Basis

Basis	Seniority basis	Merit basis
Meaning	It means length of recognised service in an organisation.	It means ability to work.
Consideration	It considers time from when an employee has joined the company and served for how many years in the company.	It considers employee's skill, knowledge, ability, efficiency and aptitude as measured from educational, training and past record.
Advantage	It promotes the feeling of belongingness towards the organisation.	It motivates the competent employees to work hard.
Disadvantage	It is a slow process and make fast advancement difficult.	It may include favouritism towards particular employee(s).

Meaning and Definitions of Staff Transfer

It is a horizontal or lateral movement of an employee from one department to other or from one place to other. Under transfer, an employee is sent to the other place or department at the same salary, status or responsibility. Such shifting is done without any marked changes in duties and challenges.

Yoder has defined transfer as ''a lateral shift causing movement of individuals from one position to another usually without involving any marked change in duties, responsibilities, skills needed or compensation''.

According to **Arun Monappa** and **Mirza Saiyadain**, "Transfer is a change in assignment in which the employee moves to another job at approximately the same level of responsibility, demanding about the same skill and at about the same level of pay".

Need/Purpose of Transfer

The needs/purposes of a transfer in an organisation are as follows

(i) **To make adjustment in business operation** The need of transfer may arise when production falls and fluctuation in work requirements. To avoid lay-off, organisation transfers the employees from one department to another.

(ii) **To better utilise employee** When employee is not performing well in a particular job. He may be transferred to another job for improving the productivity.

(iii) **To satisfy employee needs** It helps the employees to work according to their convenience.

(iv) **To punish employees** If employees are indulged in undesirable activities, management can transfer such employees to remote and far flung areas.

(v) **To train the employees** It gives training to the employees for their advancement and promotion.

Types of Transfers

Employees transfers may be classified in following types

(i) **Replacement transfers** In replacement transfer, a long serving employee replaces a new employee and thereby giving some relief to the old employee from the heavy work pressure. The main motive of this transfer is to retain the old employees in the organisation when production of all departments are falling.

The **significance** of replacement transfer can be summarised as follows

(a) To recognise the importance of old employees
(b) To avoid lay-off in organisation
(c) To reduce the work pressure of old employees
(d) To reconstruct the organisation
(e) To increase the productivity in the organisation

(ii) **Versatility transfers** To increase the versatility of an employee by shifting him from one job to another so that he may have ample opportunities for gaining a varied and a broader experience of work.

Such transfers are called 'versatility transfers.' This makes it possible for an employee the facility of job enrichment, which in turn, gives the management a more effective and experienced employee for a higher job position.

The **significance** of versatility transfers can be summarised as follows

(a) To help the employees for future promotion
(b) To provide the job enrichment and job enlargement
(c) To increase the versatility of the employees
(d) To create a work force in the organisation

(iii) **Remedial transfers** When an employee is not performing well and satisfactorily and the management feels that he may be more useful or suitable elsewhere and his capacities would be better utilised, the employee is transferred to the other such place/job. Such transfers are called 'remedial transfers.'

The **significance** of remedial transfers can be summarised as follows

(a) To correct the unsatisfactory placement
(b) To increase the productivity in the organisation
(c) To avoid the lay-off in the organisation
(d) To develop the good relationship between employee and employer

(iv) **Production transfers** Production transfer is made to avoid lay-off of efficient and trained employees by providing them with alternative job in the same company.

It helps to stabilise employment in company which reduce the cost of recruitment and selection of fresh employee.

The **significance** of production transfer can be summarised as follows

(a) To transfer surplus employees from one department to another
(b) To avoid lay-off in the organisation
(c) To reduce the cost of recruitment and selection procedure
(d) To stabilise the employment
(e) To retain the efficient and trained employees in the organisation

Staff Separation

Separation is painful to both parties (i.e. employee and employer) so, it should be administered carefully.

Separation means cessation of services of the employees with the organisation.

According to **Yoder**, "Separation is a negative recruitment. It may be in the form of resignation, dismissal or discharge, suspension, retrenchment or lay-off."

Means/Reasons for Separation

The reasons for separation may be

(i) **Retirement** It is a contract with an employee that specifies the age of retirement. Under this, an employee retires from his service on attaining the age of superannuation. At the time of retirement, he receives provident fund amount, gratuity and encashment of earned leaves, etc.

Retirement may be of the following types

(a) **Compulsory retirement** The employee retires automatic after attaining a specific age. The age of retirement set by the government varies from country to country. It generally varies from 50 to 70 year. In India, the retirement age is 60 years.

(b) **Voluntary retirement** Voluntary retirement is yet another type of separation. When organisations give option to its employees to retire even before superannuation, known as voluntary retirement. Under this scheme, an employee receives a lumpsum amount.

(ii) **Lay-off** A lay-off is an indefinite separation of the employee from the payroll. The concerned employee will be called back in future, if there is need for employment.

The purpose of such exercise is to reduce the financial burden of the organisation, when human resources cannot be utilised productively and profitably.

It is a temporary separation which may be take place due to the following reasons

(a) Shortage of power of coal in a factory
(b) Shortage of raw material
(c) Breakdown of machine
(d) Accumulation of stock
(e) For any other reason

(iii) **Retrenchment** It is a permanent termination of an employee's service for economic reasons in a going concern or it is termination due to redundancy of workforce. It creates a sense of insecurity and resentment among the staff.

It occurs due to surplus staff, poor demand for the product, economic slowdown, replacement of labour by machine or closure of department, etc. The Industrial Disputes Act, 1947 makes it obligatory for organisations employing 100 or more employees to give three month's notice to the employees to be retrenched and take prior approval from the government.

Distinction between Lay-off and Retremnchement

Basis	Retrenchment	Lay-off
Meaning	It implies permanent termination of an employees' services for economic reasons.	It is an indefinite separation of the employee from the payroll, to be called back in future, as and when a need arises.
Nature	It is permanent in nature.	It is temporary in nature.
Reason	It usually occurs due to restructuring or cost cutting measures within the company as a whole.	It usually occurs due to lack of work or a downturn in business within a specific division or location.
Reappo-intment	Employees can not be re-appointed as the position was eliminated permanently.	Employees can be re-appointed if the company has new work or projects after the period of lay-off.

(iv) **Resignation** Under resignation, the employee states his inability to work anymore for the organisation. Such resignation may be voluntary on ground of health, better opportunities, marriage or family circumstances, etc.

It may also be compulsory, when the employee is asked to put forward his resignation, if he wants to avoid termination of his service on ground of negligence or misconduct.

(v) **Suspension of employees** It refers to a period of time-off from work as a result of a disciplinary process. A suspension may be for one day or several weeks.

It may be used as a first step disciplinary measure, often with more serious misconduct. It may be paid or unpaid as per the policy of organisation. Suspension may be challenged by employees in unionised organisations.

(vi) **Dismissal** Dismissal is the termination of the services of an employee by an employer, in the case of punishment, for violating disciplinary rules and regulations, prolonged absence from duty, etc. It is a disciplinary step that stops the intolerable offence in an organisation.

If in case, an employee is to be discharged, he must be given the opportunity to explain his conduct and to show the cause, why he should not be dismissed.

Note It follows the principle of natural justice.

Grounds for dismissal

There are numerous reasons due to which an employee can be terminated from his job, some of them are specified below

(a) Inefficiency
(b) Dishonesty
(c) Indiscipline
(d) Insubordination
(e) Misconduct
(f) Physical unfitness
(g) Unauthorised strikes
(h) Drunk while at work
(i) Falsifying records of work
(j) Willful damage to company's property

Steps involved in the **procedure for staff dismissal** are as follows

(a) Charge sheet
(b) Receipt of explanation
(c) Issue of notice of enquiry
(d) Holding of enquiry
(e) The findings
(f) Decision
(g) Communication of the order

Difference between Suspension and Dismissal

Basis	Suspension	Dismissal
Nature	It is temporary separation.	It is permanant separation.
Job	The employee still has a job in this.	The empolyee is terminated from job, i.e., does not have job.
Allowance	Few allowances are paid to employee for suspension period.	No allowancesare paid to employee on dismissal.

Exit Interview

Exit interview is the way of finding out why someone wants to leave the organisation. In other words, it is a meeting with a terminating or leaving employee that is generally arranged by human resource manager to obtain frank and honest feedback.

The main purpose of the exit interview is to gather feedback that can help guide future practices and improve recruiting and selection process.

Importance of Exit Interview

Exit interview is conducted when an employee leaves the organisation. The importance of exit interview can be summarised as follows

(i) **Helpful in finding actual reason for an employee's resignation** It is an effective tool to find out the actual reason for an employee's resignation.

(ii) **Helpful in retaining the talented employees** It helps to retain a talented employee by finding the reason for his dissatisfaction and agreeing on feasible solutions.

(iii) **Helpful in developing good relations with employees** It encourages good relations with the employees because it provides a good opportunity to share the real experiences.

(iv) **Helpful in gathering the trustworthy data** It provides trustworthy data on the problem area, in order to help the management to take remedial actions.

(v) **Helpful in maintaining a positive work culture in organisation** It helps the management to maintain a positive workplace culture because existing employees feel positive about their workplace.

PYQs Previous Years' Questions

1 Mark Questions

1. ……….. means permanent tremination of an employee's services by an organisation due to economic reasons. **ISC Specimen 2023**

Ans Retrenchment

2. A promotion policy which considers only select few employees as potential candidates for promotion is called a/an ……….. policy. **ISC Specimen 2023**

(a) open (b) closed
(c) confidential (d) secured

Ans (b) closed

3. ……….. transfer is done to correct the mistakes made at the time of placement. **ISC Sem I 2021**

(a) Replacement (b) Remedial
(c) Refresher (d) Regulatory

Ans (b) Remedial

4. …….. transfer is used to relieve an employee of heavy stress of workload. **ISC Sem I 2021**

(a) Replacement (b) Production
(c) Promotion (d) Shift

Ans (a) Replacement

5. Which one of the following does not involve increase in pay benefits? **ISC Sem I 2021**

(a) Upgradation (b) Dry promotion
(c) Open promotion
(d) Closed promotion

Ans (b) Dry promotion

6. Some organisations prefer seniority-based promotion to merit-based promotion because **ISC Sem I 2021**

(a) it stimulates the employees to improve their performance
(b) it eliminates bias and nepotism
(c) it rewards the ability of the employees
(d) it brings in fresh ideas

Ans (b) it eliminates bias and nepotism

7. Under …….. promotion, job vacancies are not announced and the management chooses the candidate from a group of select few. **ISC Sem I 2021**

(a) seniority-based (b) merit-based
(c) open (d) closed

Ans (d) closed

8. A transfer is not always a punishment as **ISC Sem I 2021**

(a) it involves a raise in the salary
(b) it may be done to allow outsiders to bring in fresh ideas
(c) it may be done to increase labour turnover
(d) it may be done to make the employees more versatile

Ans (d) it may be done to make the employees more versatile

9. ……….. transfer helps in stabilising employment and prevents loss of job by shifting the employee to an understaffed branch. **ISC Sem I 2021**

(a) Versatility (b) Production
(c) Replacement (d) Remedial

Ans (b) Production

10. An employee is moved from one job to another, carrying higher salary, greater status and more responsibilities. This is known as **ISC Sem I Specimen 2021**

(a) promotion (b) transfer
(c) upgradation (d) dry promotion

Ans (a) promotion

11. The transfer that involves employees to be transferred from the overstaffed unit to that unit where vacancies are to be filled up is called **ISC Sem I Specimen 2021**

(a) promotional transfer
(b) production transfer
(c) replacement transfer
(d) remedial transfer

Ans (b) production transfer

12. Trade unions do not favour merit based promotion as **ISC Sem I Specimen 2021**

(a) it is a costly method
(b) it leads to less salary for workers
(c) it leads to more work for workers
(d) it involves discrimination between the workers

Ans (d) it involves discrimination between the workers

13. In case of ……….. the status and responsibilities of an employee remain same, but there is an increase in salary. **ISC Sem I Specimen 2021**

(a) promotion (b) transfer
(c) upgradation (d) dry promotion

Ans (c) upgradation

14. Seniority based promotion is better than merit based promotion because *ISC Sem I Specimen 2021*

(a) it stimulates the employees to improve their performance.
(b) it reduces labour turnover.
(c) it rewards the ability of the employees.
(d) it brings in fresh ideas.

Ans (a) it stimulates the employees to improve their performance.

15. Seniority cum merit-based promotion is very popular because *ISC Sem I Specimen 2021*

(a) it is able to counter the limitations of both the approaches-seniority basis and merit basis.
(b) it is easier for the organisation to follow it.
(c) trade unions prefer it.
(d) it is very cheap and fast.

Ans (a) it is able to counter the limitations of both the approaches-seniority basis and merit basis.

16. ……….. includes employees being shifted from one job to another to widen their job knowledge. *ISC Sem I Specimen 2021*

(a) Shift transfer
(b) Remedial transfer
(c) Replacement tranfer
(d) Versatility transfer

Ans (d) Versatility transfer

2 Marks Questions

1. Define promotion. *ISC 2023, 2016*

Ans Promotion is an upward/vertical advancement of an employee in an organisation to another job which gives him better pay, higher status and more opportunities with greater challenge and responsibility.

According to **Scott** and **Spreigal**, "A promotion is the transfer of an employee to a job that pays more money or that enjoys some preferred status."

2. State any two limitations of promotion of employees in an organisation. *ISC 2019*

Ans Limitations of promotion are as follows

(i) It is very difficult task to measure the merit and ability of employees in an objective and impartial way.
(ii) The employees who are working in the organisation often lack a fresh perspective that only an outsider can bring.

3. Differentiate between upgrading and dry promotion. *ISC 2018*

Ans Difference between upgrading and dry promotion are

Basis	Upgrading	Dry promotion
Meaning	It involves to raise in salary, with a possible change in the designation.	It is given in lieu of increase in the compensation.
Concept	It is broad concept.	It is narrow concept.

4. Give one benefit each of voluntary retirement scheme to the employee and to the employer. *ISC 2018*

Ans One benefit of voluntary retirement scheme to the employee as follows

(i) Voluntary retirement scheme provides lumpsum amount to the employees.

One benefit of voluntary retirement scheme to the employer as follows

(i) Voluntary retirement scheme provides reduction in the surplus staff.

5. Explain any one distinction between suspension and termination with reference to staff dismissal. *ISC 2017*

Ans One distinction between suspension and termination is that suspension is temporary in nature but termination is permanent in nature.

6. What is meant by production transfer? *ISC 2016*

Ans Production transfers are made when more personnel are needed in one branch or process and there is surplus staff in the other branch or process. So, employees are transferred to under-staffed unit from over-staffed unit. This form of transfer helps to prevent lay-offs and offers stability to employees.

7. Explain the significance of remedial transfer. *ISC 2015*

Ans These transfers are made to rectify errors in selection and placement of employees. For example, if an employee is by mistake given a job for which he is not fit, he may be transferred to the right job. This will help to improve the performance and job satisfaction of employees. Remedial transfers also permit better use of human resources in the organisation.

8. What is meant by dry promotion? *ISC 2015*

Ans It refers to upgradation of an employee to a higher scale without changing the job. It involves increase in the responsibilities and status of employees without increase in the salary. Under this method of promotion, the employee is moved to the next higher level of job with greater authority.

9. Why lay-off is considered to be a softer version of retrenchment? *ISC 2015, 2009*

Ans Retrenchment means permanent termination of an employee's services due to economic reasons such as closing of business.

Whereas lay-off is temporary removal of an employee from the payroll due to circumstances beyond the control of the employer. Under it, the employer-employee relationship does not come to an end. The services of the employee are not terminated and he is expected to be called for work in future. Therefore, it is considered to be a softer version of retrenchment.

10. How can transfer be used as punishment by the employee? *ISC 2014*

Ans Offering transfers as a penalty is a wonderful strategy of the organisations. In case of misconduct or wrong doing of an employee, he/she is awarded transfers in some remote town areas, where they feel awkward and punished.

11. State any two essential requirements of a fair staff dismissal procedure. *ISC 2013*

Ans The two essential requirements of a fair staff dismissal procedure are as follows

(i) An enquiry should be conducted before dismissing a person.

(ii) The concerned employee should be informed of the charges against him.

12. Give two points of distinction between retrenchment and lay-off. *ISC 2011*

Ans Difference between retrenchment and lay-off

Basis	Retrenchment	Lay-off
Meaning	It implies permanent termination of an employees' services for economic reasons.	It is an indefinite separation of the employee from the payroll, to be called back in future, as and when a need arises.
Nature	It is permanent in nature.	It is temporary in nature.

13. 'Transfer is a mild form of punishment.' Explain. *ISC 2010*

Ans Yes, the statement is true in the sense that severe punishments are not given to an employee in case of several misconducts, in order to maintain harmony within the organisation.

Therefore, in such circumstances punitive transfers are being given to them, which may act as a punishment and secondly, it does not give any financial or physical harm. Thus, it is considered as a mild form of punishment.

14. Explain the significance of versatility transfer. *ISC 2009*

Ans Such transfers are made to provide an employee job enrichment and to prepare him as an experienced and excellent employee for higher posts.

15. Explain the term 'retrenchment'. *ISC 2008*

Ans Retrenchment implies permanent termination of an employee's services for economic reasons in a going concern. It creates a sense of insecurity and resentment among the staff members.

16. What is meant by closed system of promotion? *ISC 2008*

Ans Under this method, candidates are restricted and the opportunity of promotion is not disclosed to all the candidates.

17. State two advantages of merit based promotion. *ISC 2008, 2007*

Ans Two advantages of merit based promotion are

(i) The worth of an individual is appreciated and given due recognition.

(ii) It encourages an employee to work hard, so that he may get an opportunity for advancement in the organisation.

18. What is meant by staff promotion? *ISC 2007*

Ans A promotion may be defined as an upward advancement of an employee in an organisation to another job, which commands better pay/wages, better status/prestige and higher opportunities/challenges, responsibility and authority, better working conditions, hours of work, facilities and a higher rank.

19. Mention two grounds for dismissal of an employee. *ISC 2007*

Ans Grounds for dismissal of an employee can be

(i) Inefficiency of an employee

(ii) Misconduct by an employee

20. When are workers in an organisation retrenched? *ISC 2006*

Ans Retrenchment can be given due to redundancy of workforce.

21. List any two differences between promotion and transfer. *ISC 2006*

Ans Difference between promotion and transfer are

Basis	Promotion	Transfer
Type of movement	It is an upward movement of employees in an organisation structure.	It is a horizontal movement of employees in an organisation structure.
Morale	It boosts up the morale of an employee.	It sometimes decreases the morale of employees.

22. What is versatility transfer? *ISC 2005*

Ans Such transfers are done in order to increase the versatility of the employee by shifting him at different places and to provide him ample opportunities for gaining varied and versatile experience of work.

23. What is meant by staff dismissal? *ISC 2005*

Ans Staff dismissal means termination of an employee by an employer in the case of punishment, for violating disciplinary rules and regulations, etc.

24. Name four types of transfer. *ISC 2004*

Ans Four types of transfer are as follows

(i) Organisational transfers/Production transfer
(ii) Remedial transfer (iii) Versatility transfer
(iv) Personal transfer

4 Marks Questions

1. State any four merits of seniority based promotion. *ISC Specimen 2023*

Ans Advantages of seniority based promotion are as follows

(i) An advantage of such promotion is that it can essentially guarantee improvement and advancement in a job field.
(ii) It promotes the feeling of belongingness towards the organisation.
(iii) It promotes the feeling of job security among the employees.
(iv) It is economical.

Common Mistake Students get confused between promotion and basis of promotion and give merits of promotion here. So students are advisable to understand the difference between promotion and basis of promotion as merits and demerits of every type of promotion are different in nature.

2. Briefly explain the two types of retirement. *ISC Specimen 2023*

Or What is meant by retirement? Explain the two types of retirement. *ISC 2019*

Ans Retirement is the contract under which the employee retires from his service, on attaining the age of superannuation. Types of retirement are

(i) **Compulsory retirement** The employee retires automatically after attaining a specific age. The age of retirement set by the government varies from country to country.
(ii) **Voluntary retirement** When organisation gives option to its employees to retire even before superannuation, known as voluntary retirement. Under this scheme, an employee receives a lump-sum amount.

3. What is the meant by staff separation? List any four means of the same. *ISC 2020*

Ans **Staff separation** Separation is painful to both parties i.e. employer and employee. So, it should be administered carefully. Separation means cessation of services of the emplyees with the organisation.

Means of staff separation are

(i) **Retrenchment** It is a permanent termination of an employee's service for economic reasons in a going concern.
(ii) **Resignation** Under resignation, the employee states his inability to work anymore for the organisation.

Means of Separation
- Retrenchment
- Resignation
- Dismissal
- Retirement

(iii) **Dismissal** It is the termination of the services of an employee, in the case of punishment, for violating disciplinary rules and regulations etc.
(iv) **Retirement** It is a contract with an employee that specifies the age of retirement. Under it, an employee retires from his service, on attaining the age of superannuation.

4. Explain any two types of transfer. *ISC 2007*

Ans Two main types of transfer are as follows

(i) **Organisational transfer** Such transfers are being done in an organisation to meet the current needs of organisation, arising due to changes in technology, quantum of work, etc.
(ii) **Remedial transfer** Such transfers are being done in an organisation to utilise the services of the employee in better way, as the management feels that the concerned employee can do better at some other place/department.

5. Seniority should not be the sole criterion for promoting an employee. *ISC 2005*

Ans Promotion by seniority means promotion is given on the basis of length of service in the company or at a particular position. This system of promotion is preferred by employees and employers because it is easy to administer and satisfies the personal aspirations of the employees.

However, this system suffers from certain drawbacks like

(i) The internal sources may be inadequate to meet the requirement of higher jobs.

(ii) The worth of an individual is not appreciated.

(iii) It causes dissatisfaction and frustration among good employees and they may leave the organisation.

Value Points

To get maximum marks in the examination, following points should be included in the answer

- Meaning of seniority based promotion
- State its limitations

6/8 Marks Questions

1. State any three advantages and three disadvantages of merit based promotion. *ISC 2023, 2015*

Or State any two advantages and any two disadvantages of merit based promotion. *ISC 2019*

Ans Advantages of merit based promotion are as follows

(i) Merit based promotion stimulates the employees to improve their performance. The young and ambitious employees have incentive to improve their skills and efficiency.

(ii) In order to judge the merit of employees, appraisal of their performance is done. Such appraisal reveals the deficiencies which can be removed through further training.

(iii) Only competent employees can make an organisation successful. Under merit-based promotion, the job satisfaction and motivation of employees are higher, thus, creating a successful organisation.

Disadvantages of merit based promotion are as follows

(i) There is no foolproof formula to measure an individual's merit. Therefore, promotions based on merit may involve favouritism.

(ii) Merit-based promotions may demoralise and frustrate senior employees when their juniors are promoted.

(iii) Trade unions do not favour merit-based promotion as it involves discrimination between their members and affects their solidarity.

2. Explain any four advantages and any four limitations of seniority based promotion. *ISC 2020*

Or Define promotion. Explain three advantages and three disadvantages of seniority based promotion. *ISC 2014, 2010*

Or Write a detailed note on seniority based promotions. *ISC 2008*

Ans **Promotion** It is an upward/vertical advancement of an employee in an organisation to another job which gives him better pay, higher status and more opportunities with greater challenges and responsibilities.

It basically means a change from a lower level job to a higher level job.

Advantages of seniority based promotion Refer to Q. No. 1 (4 Marks) on page 105.

Disadvantages of seniority based promotion

Disadvantages of seniority based promotion are as follows

(i) It is a slow process and makes fast advancement difficult.

(ii) Sometimes promotion does not suit the existing position.

(iii) It fails to encourage the existing employees for better performance.

(iv) It acts as a hurdle in attracting the capable persons.

3. What is meant by staff attrition? Briefly explain any three means of staff attrition. *ISC Specimen 2019*

Ans Staff Attrition is the departure of employees from the organisation, either voluntary resigning a laid off by company. It is a gradual reduction in employee numbers.

Type of attrition are as follows

(i) **Retirement** Refer to Q. No. 2 (4 Marks) on page 105.

(ii) **Voluntary attrition** (Resignation) Refer to text on page 100.

(iii) **Involuntary attrition** When an employee is terminated from his job due to some reasons, it is called involuntary attrition. This can be through a position elimination, for example due to lay off, poor performance or termination etc.

Concept Enhancer There are four means of attrition i.e. voluntary, involuntary, compulsory (retirement) and natural attrition. Natural attrition takes place due to the causes and factors that are beyond the control of the individual and organisation as well, like end of life, insanity, etc.

4. Explain the meaning and relevance of the four types of transfers. *ISC Specimen 2019*

Ans Refer to text on page 99.

5. (i) Define promotion.

(ii) With regard to promotion, explain the following

(a) Upgrading (b) Open promotion

(c) Closed promotion *ISC 2017*

Ans (i) **Promotion** It is an upward/vertical advancement of an employee in an organisation to another job which gives him better pay, higher status and more opportunities with greater challenges and responsibilities. It basically means a change from a lower level job to a higher level job.

(ii) (a) **Upgrading** It means that an employee's salary has been increased without improvement in status and responsibility. It simply means that the employee is drawing higher salary for his current job. It is also referred to as 'dry promotion.'

(b) **Open promotion** Under this system of promotion, the company announces the vacancies at higher level internally and considers all the current employees as potential candidates for promotion. This system of promotion is generally used for lower and middle level management.

(c) **Closed promotion** Under this system of promotion, the company does not announce the vacancies internally and only certain specific employees are considered for promotion. This system of promotion is generally used for higher level management.

6. Explain the procedure of staff dismissal that a large organisation should follow. **ISC 2016**

Or Explain the procedure for dismissal of an employee. **ISC 2007**

Ans Procedure for dismissal of an employee is discussed below

(i) **Charge sheet** The first step in the procedure is to frame and issue a written charge sheet. The charge sheet should be based on a written complaint against the employee. It should contain details of the offence with which the employee is charged and the allegations of misconduct made against him. The charge sheet should indicate the time limit, in which a reply to the charge sheet should be submitted to the concerned authority.

Procedure for Dismissal of an Employee

- Charge sheet
- Receipt of explanation
- Issue of notice of enquiry
- Holding of enquiry
- The findings
- Decision
- Communication of the order

(ii) **Receipt of explanation** The employee may submit his explanation within the prescribed period of time or he may ask for an extension of time for its submission. In the latter case, the request should be considered in good faith, in accordance with the rule of natural justice.

(iii) **Issue of notice of enquiry** In the case, the explanation received from the employee is found to be unsatisfactory, a notice of enquiry should be issued to him.

The notice should mention the time, date and place of enquiry and the name of the officer, who would conduct the enquiry.

The employee is required to be present at the specified time and place alongwith his witness, if he has any.

(iv) **Holding of enquiry** On the specified day, time and place, the enquiry office will hold the enquiry in the presence of the employee.

The contents of the charge sheet and an explanation of the procedure to be followed during the enquiry are communicated to the employee.

If the employee pleads his innocence, the enquiry proceeds. But if he pleads guilty, unconditionally and in writing , the enquiry is dropped.

(v) **The findings** Once the enquiry is over, the enquiry officer has to give his findings. His report must contain the procedure, the statements recorded, the document produced and examined, the charges made, the explanations given and the evidence produced.

The officer should, then record his own findings on each of the charges and the grounds on which he has reached to a particular conclusion.

He should specifically mention which charges have been proved and which have not been proved. The officer then submits his findings to the authority entitled to dismiss the employee.

(vi) **Decision** On receiving the report from the enquiry officers, the concerned authority may take a decision for dismissal of the employee.

(vii) **Communication of the order** A copy of the dismissal order is then handed over to the concerned employee.

7. State and explain any four ways in which an employee's association with his organisation may come to an end. **ISC 2012**

Ans Four ways in which an employee's association with his organisation may come to an end are as follows

(i) **Retrenchment** It is a permanent termination of an employee's service for economic reasons in a going concern or it is termination due to redundancy of workforce.

It creates a sense of insecurity and resentment among the staff.

(ii) **Dismissal** Dismissal or discharge refers to terminating the services of an employee by way of punishment for misconduct or unsatisfactory performance. Unsatisfactory performance implies persistent failure of the employee to perform his job upto the specified standards. Dismissal is a drastic step and should, therefore, be resorted with great care.

(iii) **Retirement** It is a contract with an employee that specifies the age of retirement. Under it, an employee retires from his service, on attaining the age of superannuation. At the time of retirement, he receives his provident fund amount, gratuity and encashment of earned leaves, etc.

(iv) **Resignation** It means an employee takes or is made to take the initiative to leave the job. It may be voluntary or involuntary.

8. What is meant by staff transfer in an organisation? Explain any three types of staff transfer. *ISC 2011*

Ans **Meaning of staff transfer** A transfer is a horizontal or lateral movement of an employee from one job, section, department, shift, place or position to another at the same or another place where his salary, status and responsibility remains the same.

Types of staff trasfers Three types of staff transfers are as follows

(i) **Remedial transfers** When an employee is not performing well and satisfactorily and the management feels that he may be more useful or suitable elsewhere and his capacities would be better utilised, the employee is transferred to the other such place/job. Such transfers are called 'remedial transfers.'

(ii) **Versatility transfers** To increase the versatility of an employee by shifting him from one job to another so that he may have ample opportunities for gaining a varied and a broader experience of work. Such transfers are called 'versatility transfers.' This makes it possible for an employee the facility of job enrichment, which in turn, gives the management a more effective and experienced employee for a higher job position.

(iii) **Replacement transfers** In replacement transfer, a long serving employee replaces a new employee and thereby giving some relief to the old employee from the heavy work pressure. The main motive of this transfer is to retain the old employees in the organisation, when production of all departments are falling.

Additional Questions

2 Marks Questions

1. What is open system of promotion?

Ans Under this method, all eligible employees of the company are given equal opportunity to be promoted for the higher position. In other words, it is open for all eligible employees and applications are invited from all the eligible employees for the promotion.

2. Explain seniority-cum-merit basis of promotion.

Ans Generally, management wants to adopt merit based promotion system while trade union wants to favour the seniority based promotion system.

So, organisation considers both merit and seniority for determining the promotion of an employees. This method is more suitable for middle level technical, supervisory and administrative personnels.

3. Define transfer.

Ans **Yoder** has defined transfer as "a lateral shift causing movement of individuals from one position to another usually without involving any marked change in duties, responsibilities, skills needed or compensation".

4 Marks Questions

1. What are the purposes of staff transfer in the organisation?

Ans The needs/purposes of a transfer in an organisation are as follows

(i) **To make adjustment in business operation** The need of transfer may arise when production falls and fluctuation in work requirements. To avoid lay-off, organisation transfers the employees from one department to another.

(ii) **To better utilise employee** When employee is not performing well in a particular job. He may be transfered to another job for improving the productivity.

(iii) **To satisfy employee needs** It helps the employees to work according to their convenience.

(iv) **To punish employees** If employees are indulged in undesirable activities, management can transfer such employees to remote and far flung areas.

2. What is exit interview? Explain three points of importance of exit interview.

Ans **Exit interview** It is the way of finding out why someone wants to leave the organisation. In other words, it is a meeting with a terminating or leaving employee that is generally arranged by human resource manager to obtain frank and honest feedback.

The main purpose of the exit interview is to gather feedback that can help guide future practices and improve recruiting and selection process.

Importance of exit interview Exit interview is conducted when an employee leaves the organisation.

The importance of exit interview can be summarised as follows

(i) **Helpful in finding actual reason for an employee's resignation** It is an effective tool to find out the actual reason for an employee's resignation.

(ii) **Helpful in retaining the talented employees** It helps to retain a talented employee by finding the reason for his dissatisfaction and agreeing on feasible solutions.

(iii) **Helpful in maintaining a positive work culture in organisation** It helps the management to maintain a positive work place culture because existing employees feel positive about their workplace.

3. Differentiate between open system of promotion and close system of promotion.

Ans Difference between open policy of promotion and closed policy of promotion

Basis	Open policy of promotion	Closed policy of promotion
Meaning	Under this policy, all eligible employees of the company are given equal opportunity to be promoted.	It selects the list of employees for promotion which is prepared on the basis of pre-determined promotion policy of the company.
Morale	It provides high morale to employees.	It provides low morale to employees.
Suitability	It is more suitable for low and medium level of managerial jobs.	It is more suitable for high level of managerial jobs.
Opportunity	It provides equal opportunity to all employees for promotion.	It does not provide equal opportunity to all employees for promotion.

4. Explain the requirement of a sound promotion policy.

Ans The requirements of a sound promotion policy can be summarised as follows

(i) **To distribute promotion opportunities** There should be equal ratio between internal promotion and external recruitment at various levels in all the departments.

(ii) **To promote morale among employees** Promotion system should be 'open' and not 'closed' so that eligible employees may get promotion at higher position.

(iii) **To establish a well defined system for promotion** There should be some definite system for the selection of employees who are to be promoted within the company. (i.e criteria for promotion)

(iv) **To evaluate the employees** These must be a true and fair system for evaluation the efficiency and skills of employees for promotion.

(v) **To establish a review system** No promotion policy can be effective without proper review, so there should be suitable system for follow-up, councelling and review.

5. Define promotion. Explain the limitations of promotion.

Ans **Promotion** If is an upward/vertical advancement of an employee in an organisation to another job which gives him better pay, higher status and more opportunities with greater challenge and responsibility.

According to **Scott** and **Spreigel**, "A promotion is the transfer of an employee to a job that pays more money or that enjoys some preferred status."

Limitations of promotion The limitations of promotion can be summarised as follows

(i) **Managers may reward their favourities rather than the best employees** Often, it is seen that supervisors select employees from their own choices which may be based on bias.

(ii) **Merit and ability are difficult to measure** It is a very difficult task to measure the merit and ability of employee in an objective and impartial way.

(iii) **Lack of fresh ideas** The employees who are working in the organisation often lack a fresh perspective that only an outsider can bring.

(iv) **Dissatisfaction at work** When one employee is promoted, bad feelings can result in the employees left behind. It can lead to dissatisfaction at work and poor work performance.

(v) **More efforts** Promoted employee has to learn new skills, while outside candidates already possess such skills.

Case Based Questions

Case 1

Reva, Anup, Parth and Neha are working in different departments of the same organisation at its Delhi branch. Reva has got an increase in salary but her status and responsibility remain the same. Neha has been shifted to Chandigarh with increase in salary, status and responsibility.

Anup has also been transferred to Chandigarh because of a sudden increase in work at the Chandigarh branch. Parth has good leadership qualities, so before promoting him, the organisation wants him to understand the various types of jobs that he will be coordinating. Therefore, he has been transferred from the finance department to the sales department. ***ISC Sem I 2021***

(i) The organisation has .... Reva.
(a) upgraded (b) dry promoted
(c) promoted (d) transferred

Ans (a) upgraded

(ii) The organisation has .... Neha.
(a) upgraded (b) dry promoted
(c) promoted (d) transferred

Ans (c) promoted

(iii) The organisation has given .... transfer to Anup.
(a) production
(b) remedial
(c) versatility
(d) replacement

Ans (a) production

(iv) The organisation has given .... transfer to Parth.
(a) production
(b) remedial
(c) versatility
(d) replacement

Ans (c) versatility

Case 2

Siddharth has done MBA in finance and has a job experience of 3 years in the organisation. He has received a rating of 2 on merit scale which is 'excellent' Another employes Kapil has a tenure of 7 years. He also has a rating of 2 on the merit scale.

Sanjay has a tening of 8 years and has received a rating of 3 on the merit scale which is 'Very good' Amol has a tenure of 3 years and his rating is I on the merit scale which is 'outstanding'. ***ISC Sem I Specimen 2021***

(i) If sniority based promotion is adopted by the organisation, who should be promoted?
(a) Siddharth (b) Kapil
(c) Sanjay (d) Amol

Ans (c) Sanjay

(ii) It merit based promotion is adopted by the organisation, who should be promoted?
(a) Siddharth (b) Kapil
(c) Sanjay (d) Amol

Ans (d) Amol

(iii) Identify one advantage of seniority based promotion.
(a) Nepolism and favouritism is eliminated
(b) Employees solidarity is affected
(c) It stimulates the employees to imporve their efficiency
(d) Gray hair is a sure sign of maturity and wisdom

Ans (c) It stimulates the employees to improve their efficiency

(iv) Identify one advantage of merit based promotion.
(a) It increases loyalty and commitment of employees towards the organisation
(b) Trade unions support it
(c) It is easy to measure merit of employees
(d) It increases productivity and profits of the organisation.

Ans (d) It increases productivity and profits of the organisation

CHAPTER TEST

01 Mark Questions

1. In which kind of promotion, all eligible employees of the company are given equal opportunity to be promoted for the higher position?

2. Which method of promotion is best for management as well as trade union?

3. What is the way of finding out why an employee wants to leave the organisation?

4. .... involves raise in wages or salary with a possible change in the designation.

5. Retrenchment is the .... termination of an emplyee's service for economic reasons.

6. What is meant by dry promotion?
(a) When responsibilities are increased but not the status
(b) When responsibilities and salary are increased
(c) When responsibilities and status are inceased but not the benefits and pay
(d) Promotion is effective from next year

7. Shifting of an employee from one job to another,one department to another or from one shift to another is called
(a) transfer (b) promotion
(c) separation (d) attrition

8. Which of the following must be considered by promotion policy?
(a) Merit of employees (b) Potential of employees
(c) Seniority of employees (d) All of these

9. Separation may be voluntary or involuntary. State true or false.

10. Exit interview is helpful in finding actual reason for an employee's resignation. State true or false.

02 Marks Questions

11. What is promotion by seniority?

12. How an employee is promoted in an organisation on the basis of ability?

13. State two benefits of promotion.

14. What is staff separation?

04 Marks Questions

15. What are the merits of promotion?

16. Why is transfer of an employee done in the organisation?

17. Explain any two reasons for separation.

06/08 Marks Questions

18. Write a short note on the following
(i) Exit interview
(ii) Seniority-cum merit promotion
(iii) Promotion by merit
(iv) Promotion by seniority

19. What is promotion? Why is there a need of promotion policy in the organisations?

20. Define transfer. Explain the following transfers
(i) Replacement (ii) Versatility
(iii) Remedial (iv) Production

Answers

1. Open system of promotion
2. Seniority-cum-merit promotion
3. Exit interview
4. Upgrading
5. permanent
6. (c) When responsibilities and status are increased but not the benefits and pay
7. (a) transfer
8. (d) All of these
9. True
10. True

10

Emerging Trends in Human Resources

TREND ANALYSIS 5 YEARS

01 Emerging Trends in HR

Types of Questions	2023	2020	2019	2018	2017
1 Mark	—	—	—	—	—
2 Marks	—	—	—	—	—
4 Marks	1	1	—	—	—
6 Marks	—	—	—	—	—
8 Marks	—	—	—	—	—

Average No. of Questions Across all Sets

The Human Resources (HR) sector is changing dramatically due to the process of complete transformation. HR trends keep changing, so it is essential for the organisation to stay up to date on the current trends. For the last 10 years, the attention of HR has been on employee satisfaction.

Important Emerging Trends in HR

Following are the important emerging trends in human resources

(i) **Flexible hours/Flexitime** A flexible hours schedule is an alternative to the traditional work schedule, e.g. 9 am to 5 pm work schedule. It allows employees to alter their workday start and finish times, e.g. an employee can opt to work from 8 am to 4 pm or from 11 am to 7 pm.

Typically, it involves 'core time' of the day during which all employees are required to be at work, e.g. Between 12 am to 4 pm. The working day outside of 'core time' is called as 'flexible hours time'.

(ii) **Permanent part time** A permanent part time employee is an employee who works on a regular basis, but for fewer hours a week than a full time working employee.

An employee is to be considered as a permanent part time employee, if

(a) He/She works less than 38 hours in a week.

(b) He/She usually works regular hours each week.

(c) He/She is entitled to same benefits as a full time employee, but on a proportional basis.

(d) He/She is a permanent employee or on a fixed term contract.

(iii) **Work from home** Work from home agreement is a concept where the employee can do his or her job from home. It gives a flexible working hours to the employees as well as the job for the employer is done with ease.

It is helpful in providing work life balance to the employees. There is a lot of savings with respect to cost of office infrastructure life space, electricity bills and travelling.

(iv) **Retainership** Under retainership, a retainer is a professional (consultant, freelancer, lawyer, etc), who is retained by a firm or a company for giving expert advice on some complex matters such as intellectual property issue, legal issue, tax issues, labour laws, etc. A retainer would charge a retainership fee for his services. He does not have fixed working hours and is not required to put in daily attendance.

Retainership contract is one in which employees are hired on retainership basis. They are also not covered under PF, ESIC, Bonus or Gratuity.

(v) **Virtual teams** A virtual team is a group of employees who reside at different geographical areas but they are working together as a team through use of internet technology (e.g. E-mail, fax, video and audio conferencing, etc). Members of a virtual team communicate electronically and may never meet face-to-face. They are required to achieve common goals of the organisation.

(vi) **Self Managing Teams** (SMTs) A self managing team is a group of employees working together, who are accountable and responsible for most or all aspects of their tasks. The team is self-regulating and operates with few external control. Self managing teams are common in manufacturing, service industry, professional services and virtual environment.

PYQs Previous Years' Questions

1 Mark Questions

1. A team consisting of employees working in different locations bill connected through internet is called a/an .... team. *ISC Sem I 2021*

(a) offline (b) cooperative
(c) virtual (d) official

Ans (c) virtual

2. Flexible work hours are not completely flexible since *ISC Sem I Specimen 2021*

(a) all employees are expected to be present during core period.
(b) the management may withdraw the choice anytime.
(c) the employees are supposed to be in the office at the same time every day.
(d) the employee has to work a fixed number of hours per day/week as decided by the management.

Ans (a) all employees are expected to be present during core period.

3. Self-management teams can be successful *ISC Sem I Specimen 2021*

(a) in any organisation
(b) only in IT sector
(c) only when the members of the organisation are very competent, motivated and committed
(d) only if flexible work hours are allowed

Ans (a) in any organisation

4. Freedom to come to work for the prescribed number of hours in a week or month as per the employee's convenience and choice is called *ISC Sem I Specimen 2021*

(a) permanent part time
(b) flexi time
(c) work from home (d) temporary appointment

Ans (a) permanent part time

5. When an outside expert is hired by an organisation to do a specialised work, it is called *ISC Sem I Specimen 2021*

(a) retainership
(b) virtual team
(c) self management teams
(d) permanent part time

Ans (a) retainership

6. Telecommuting is the use of personal computers, networks and other communication devices to work without attending office in person. It is also known as *ISC Sem I Specimen 2021*

(a) work from home
(b) flexible hours
(c) retainership
(d) outsourcing

Ans (a) work from home

Concept Enhancer Telecommuting is the ability for an employee to complete work assignment from outside the traditional workplace by using telecommunications tools such as email, phone, chat and video app. It is also called telework, remote work, etc.

4 Marks Questions

1. In the recent past, new trends have emerged at workplace. With reference to this statement, explain any two emerging trends in humna resources. *ISC 2023*

Or Explain any four emerging trends in HRM.

Ans The business environment is dynamic as a result. HR trends keep changing, so it is essential for the organisation to stay up to date on the current trends for last 10 years, the attention of HR has been on employee satisfaction.

Following are the emerging trends in HRM (any two)

(i) **Flexible hours** A flexible hours schedule allows employees to alter their workday start and finish times, e.g. An employee can opt to work from 8 am to 4 pm or from 11 am to 7 pm.

(ii) **Permanent part time** A permanent part time employee is an employee who works on a regular basis, but for fewer hours a week than a full time working employee. The employee is entitled to same benefits as a full time employee, but on a proportional basis.

(iii) **Work from home** It is a concept where the employee can do his or her job from home. It gives a flexible working hours and work life balance to the employee.

(iv) **Self-managing team** It is a group of employee working together, who are accountable and responsible for most or all aspects of their works. The team is self-regulating and operates with few external controls.

2. Explain the concepts of virtual teams and retainership. *ISC 2020*

Ans **Virtual team** A virtual team is a group of employees who reside at different geographical locations but they are working together as a team through use of internet technology e.g. E-mail, fax, video and audio conferencing, etc.

Retainership Under retainership, a retainer is a professional who is retained by a firm for giving expert advice on some complex matters and charges retainership fee. He does not have fixed working hours.

3. Briefly explain flexible hours and work from home, giving their meaning and significance. *ISC Specimen 2019*

Ans **Flexible hours/Flexitime** A flexible hours schedule is an alternative to the traditional work schedule, e.g. 9 am to 5 pm work schedule. It allows employees to alter their workday start and finish times, e.g. An employee can opt to work from 8 am to 4 pm or from 11 am to 7 pm.

Typically, it involves 'core time' of the day during which all employees are required to be at work, e.g. Between 12 am to 4 pm. The working day outside of 'core time' is called as 'flexible hours time'.

Significance of flexible hours is as follows

(i) Improves productivity
(ii) Increases employees' job satisfaction
(iii) Reduces stress and fatigue
(iv) Better business growth and profitability
(v) Improves diversity and retention

Work from Home Work from home is a concept where the employee can do his or her job from home. It gives a flexible working hours to the employees.

Benefits of work from home to the employer are as follows

(i) There is a lot of saving with respect to cost of infrastructure like space, electricity, furniture, etc.
(ii) Employees feel motivated as they get a good work life balance and become more productive.
(iii) Job for the employer is done with the ease.
(iv) It reduces absenteeism and tardiness.

Additional Questions

2/4 Marks Questions

1. What do you mean by emerging trends in HR?

Ans Emerging trends in HR refers to the changes in the HR field, due to dynamic environment, HR trends keep changing, so it is essential for the organisation to stay up to date on the current trends. For the last 10 years, the attention of HR has been on employees' satisfaction.

2. Write any four emerging trends in HR.

Ans Emerging trends in HR are as follows

(i) Flexible hours (ii) Work from home
(iii) Retainership (iv) Permanent part time

3. What do you mean by 'core time' in flexible hours?

Ans Under flexible hours schedule, 'core time' refers to the time of the working day during which all employees are required to be at work, e.g. Between 12 pm to 4 pm.

4. Who is called a 'permanent part time worker/employee'?

Ans A permanent part time employee is an employee who works on a regular basis, but for fewer hours a week than a full time working employee. An employee is to be considered as a permanent part time employee, if

(i) He/She works less than 38 hours in a week.
(ii) He/She usually works on regular hours each week.
(iii) He/She is entitled to same benefits as a full time employee, but on a proportional basis.
(iv) He/She is a permanent employee or on a fixed term contract.

5. Who is a retainer?

Ans A retainer is a professional (consultant, freelancer, lawyer, etc), who is retained by a firm or a company for giving expert advice on some complex matters such as intellectual property issue, legal issue, tax issue, labour laws, etc.

A retainer would charge a retainership fee for his services. He does not have fixed working hours. He is also not covered under PF, ESIC, Bonus or Gratuity. He is not required to put in daily attendance.

Retainership contract is one in which employees are hired on retainership basis.

6. How does a virtual team work together?

Ans A virtual team is a group of employees who reside at different-geographical areas but they are working together as a team through use of internet technology, e-mail, fax, video and audio conferencing, etc.

Members of a virtual team communicate electronically and may never meet face-to-face. They are required to achieve common goals of the organisation.

Value Points

For getting maximum marks, following value points can be included in the answer

- Meaning of virtual term
- Use keyword 'internet' while answering how a virtual team work together

7. Explain self-managing team as a new emerging trend in HR.

Ans A self-managing team is a group of employees working together who are accountable and responsible for most or all aspects of their tasks. The team is self-regulating and operates with few external control.

Self-managing teams are common in manufacturing, service industry, professional services and virtual environment.

A self-directed team defines its own goals. Team members determine schedules, procedures and the need to make adjustments.

Case Based Question

Case 1

Smita, Kanti, Anil and Uttam are working for Himtech Ltd. Smita, goes in the slums to teach underprivileged children every morning. She would be happy if her office started late so that she could reach on time.

Kanti's husband has met with a serious accident and has been advised bed rest for two months. There is 110 one except Kanti to take care of him. Anil wants to start a catering business from his home, to supplement his income. He is not sure of his success in this business and is therefore not willing to resign from the job.

Uttam stays far away from office and so by the time be reaches office, he is already exhausted and unable to work efficiently. They are all good employees otherwise. Since the company wants to retain them, they want to offer a solution to each of them. ***ISC Sem I 2021***

(i) The company can offer .... to Smita to solve her problem.

(a) flexible hours (b) permanent part time
(c) work from home (d) retainership

Ans (a) flexible hours

(ii) The company can offer .... to Kanti to solve her problem.

(a) flexible hours
(b) permanent part time
(c) work from home
(d) retainership

Ans (c) work from home

(iii) The company can offer .... to Anil to solve his problem.

(a) flexible hours
(b) permanent part time
(c) work from home
(d) retainership

Ans (b) permanent part time

(iv) The company can offer .... to Uttam to solve his problem.

(a) flexible hours
(b) permanent part time
(c) work from home
(d) retainership

Ans (c) work from home

CHAPTER TEST

01 Mark Questions

1. Name the concept where the employee can do his/her job from home.

2. Expand SMTs.

3. ………… is the time during which all employees are required to be at work.

4. ………… gives expert advice on complex matters to firm.

5. Which of the following is/are emerging trend(s) in HR?
(a) Flexitime
(b) Retainership
(c) Virtual teams
(d) All of the above

6. An employee is to be considered as a permanent part time employee, if he/she
(a) works less than 38 hours in a week
(b) work for atleast 8 hours per day
(c) works more than 45 hours in a week
(d) works on Saturday and Sunday

7. Human resources trends keep changing over the time. State true of false.

8. Virtual teams work together in an office-area.

02 Marks Questions

9. What do you mean by flexible hours schedule?

10. Explain the concept of work from home.

11. What is retainership?

04 Marks Questions

12. Distinguish between permanent part time employee and permanent full time employee.

13. Distinguish between virtual teams and self managing teams.

08 Marks Question

14. Explain any four new emerging trends in HR field.

Answers

1. Work from home *2.* Self Managing Teams
3. Core time *4.* Retainers
5. (d) All of the above
6. (a) work less than 38 hours in a week
7. True *8.* False

11

Business Communication : Concept, Methods and Types

TREND ANALYSIS 5 YEARS

	Types of Questions	Average No. of Questions Across all Sets 2023	2020	2019	2018	2017
01 Communication	1 Mark	1	—	—	—	—
	2 Marks	—	1	—	—	1
	4 Marks	—	—	—	—	—
	6 Marks	—	—	—	—	1
	8 Marks	—	—	1	—	—
02 Types and Barriers of Communication	1 Mark	2	—	—	—	—
	2 Marks	—	—	—	2	1
	4 Marks	—	—	—	—	—
	6 Marks	—	1	—	—	—
	8 Marks	—	—	—	—	—

Meaning and Definitions of Communication

Communication is as a process of exchange of ideas, facts, feelings, views, etc between two or more people to create common understanding. It involves a systematic and continuous cycle of listening and understanding.

According to **Rogers**, "Communication is a process by which people create and share information with one another in order to reach common understanding."

According to **Louis Allen**, "Communication is the sum of all things, one person does when he wants to create understanding in the mind of another. It involves systematic and continuous process of telling, listening and understanding."

Elements of Communication Process

The elements involved in the communication process are

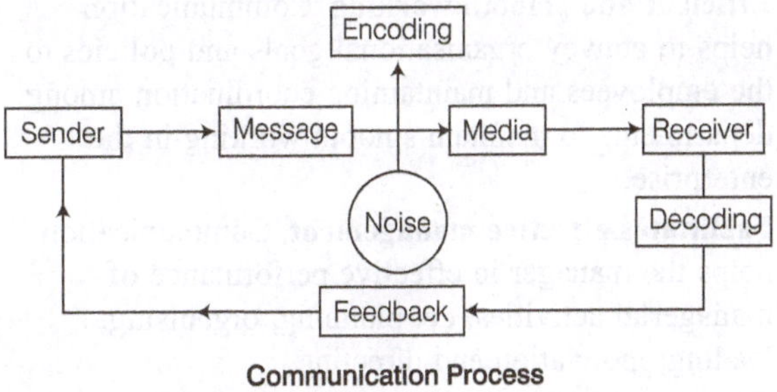

Communication Process

(i) **Sender** The person who conveys the message, is known as the 'sender' or 'communicator'. He may be a speaker, a writer or an actor. He initiates the process of communication. He is the source of communication.

(ii) **Message** It is the subject matter of communication. It may consist of facts, information, ideas, opinions, etc. It exists in the mind of the sender.

(iii) **Encoding** The sender translates the message into words, gestures or other symbols, which he feels will make the receiver understand the message. This is known as 'encoding of message'.

(iv) **Channel or Media** The encoded message is transmitted through some medium, which is known as the 'communication channel', e.g. Speaking, writing, phone call, internet, etc.

(v) **Receiver** The person, who receives the message, is called the receiver. The receiver may be a listener, reader or viewer.

(vi) **Decoding** It means process of conversion of symbols into the message by the receiver.

(vii) **Feedback** The receiver sends his response to the sender of the message. Such response is known as feedback. When the feedback is received by the sender, the process of communication is complete.

(viii) **Noise** It means an obstruction or hindrance in the communication process. Some examples of noise are

(a) Ambiguous symbols

(b) Poor telephone connection

(c) Gestures and postures that may distort the message

(d) An inattentive listener

Importance of Communication

The following points bring forth the importance of communication

(i) **Efficient and smooth working** Communication helps to convey organisational goals and policies to the employees and maintaining coordination among departments to maintain smooth working in the enterprise.

(ii) **Facilitates effective management** Communication helps the manager in effective performance of managerial activities, i.e. planning, organising, leading, motivation and directing.

(iii) **Better relations** Through communication, superiors and subordinates sort out their mutual differences and reduce conflicts, thereby, leading to better relations and congenial atmosphere.

(iv) **Total quality management** Communication becomes indispensible in total quality organisations, in order to reach at a common consensus related to products and quality of work.

(v) **Better marketing** Communication helps enterprises to know consumer preferences on one hand and provide information about products and services to them, on the other. This results in effective marketing.

(vi) **Job satisfaction** Communication reduces misunderstanding among employees, enhancing cooperation and achievement of goals. This leads to job satisfaction and motivation of the employees.

Methods of Communication

Information can be transmitted in several ways. Following are the important methods of communication in the business organisation

1. Oral or Verbal Communication

It may take place face to face or through mechanical devices. In any organisations, oral communication is very common medium of communication and a considerable amount of information is communicated orally.

The main **advantages** of oral/verbal communication are as follows

(i) It is time saving communication.

(ii) It creates healthy climate in the organisation.

(iii) It is very economical. It saves money spent on stationery in an organisation.

(iv) It provides immediate feedback to the participants.

(v) It is an effective tool of persuasion.

(vi) It is very much flexible and effective.

Oral communication suffers from the following **disadvantages**

(i) Generally oral communication is not found in record so it is impossible to preserve the message for future.

(ii) It has no legal validity.

(iii) In oral communication, meaningless and unorganised speech/thought can mislead the main objective of communication.

(iv) Under this method, it is difficult to fix the adjunct responsibility.

(v) It is not suitable for lengthy messages.

(vi) In oral communication, secret information may be disclosed.

2. Written Communication

It means the exchange of ideas and opinions in writing. It is transmitted by written words in the form of letters, memos circulars, bulletins, reports, instruction card, manuals, magazine, handbooks etc. Written messages are authentic and based upon formal authority responsibility relationship.

The main **advantages** of written communication are as follows

(i) It is found in record so the documents of written communication are easy to preserve.
(ii) It has legal validity and build up the legal defene of the organisation.
(iii) It is permanent in nature.
(iv) It helps to make communication effective in the organisation.
(v) Responsibility can be easily assigned.
(vi) It reduces the possibility of misunderstanding between superiors and subordinates.

Written communication suffers from the following **disadvantages**

(i) It is a time consuming method of communication.
(ii) It is costly in terms of money and manhours.
(iii) It is not suitable for illiterate person.
(iv) Written communication has lack of flexibility.
(v) Prompt feedback is not possible.

3. Gestural Communication

Communication through gestures or postures is often used as a mean to supplement verbal communication. The important gestures may be waving of hand, pouting of lips, movement of eyes, shaking hands and patting on back.

It there is a face to face conversation between two persons, they can better understand the feelings, attitudes and emotions of each other.

The main **advantages** of gestural communication are as follows

(i) It enhances and supplements the understanding of a verbal message between sender and receiver.
(ii) Information can be easily presented in gestural communication.
(iii) It provides quick expression of message.
(iv) It reduces wastage of time of the communicator.
(v) It helps illiterate people in the organisation.
(vi) It may be substituted for verbal communication.
(vii) It is more usable for handicapped people (i.e. deaf people).

Gestural communication suffers from the following **disadvantages**

(i) If gestures are not evaluated correctly, they may be misleading and misguiding to the listeners.
(ii) It is not considered as a credible method of communication.
(iii) In some cases gestural communication involves huge cost.
(iv) It does not follow any rules, regulations and formalities or structures like other methods of communication.
(v) It is not suitable for long conversations.
(vi) There is no break in communication so everybody does not prefer to communicate through gestural communication.

4. Visual Communication

It is a process of sending and receiving information through visual images. It is about conveying a message by visual means and visual aids i.e. photography, multimedia, illustration etc and can help to simplify complex ideas and lead to more audience involvement.

The purpose of visual communication is to inform, persuade and engage the audience for a pre-determined organisational goal. It is also very useful reaching out to an illiterate target group.

The main **advantages** of visual communication are as follows

(i) Easy to understand the information.
(ii) Equal use for both educated audience and illiterate audience.
(iii) Colourful paintings, interesting photographs, graphs, charts etc, make communication interesting.
(iv) It provides prompt response of audience.
(v) It is an effective way of advertising.
(vi) It is very popular mode of communication.

Visual communication suffers from the following **disadvantages**

(i) As compared to other methods of communication, it is more costly.
(ii) It is a time consuming process of communication.
(iii) All the topics cannot be represented through visual communication.
(iv) In many cases, visual messages are difficult to understand. The receivers are unable to assess the correct meaning of message.
(v) Visual communication creates negative/adverse effect, if it is designed poorly.

Difference between Oral Communication and Written Communication

Basis	Oral communication	Written communication
Meaning	It means exchange of ideas and opinions through the word spoken.	It means exchange of ideas and opinions in writing.

Basis	Oral communication	Written communication
Requirement of literacy	Not required for oral communication.	Necessary for written communication.
Legal validity	It has no legal validity.	It has legal validity.
Feedback of receivers	Receivers give immediate feedback for message.	Receivers do not give immediate feedback for message.
Understanding of message	Easy to understand the message.	Difficult to understand the message.
Transmission of message	Fast.	Slow.

Types of Communication

I. On the Basis of Area of Operation

There are of two types *viz* internal and external communication

1. Internal Communication

It refers to the exchange of ideas, opinions within the organisation. It is the life blood of any organisation and refers to the way in which everyone gets the information one needs.

This type of communication takes place within the organisation. It takes place in two ways, one is formal communication and the other is informal communication.

Advantages of internal communication are as follows

(i) It establishes coordination among employees to achieve the organisational goals.
(ii) It helps in establishing good relationship between superiors and subordinates.
(iii) It facilitates the decision making process in the organisation.
(iv) It is helpful in promoting transparency in the organisation.
(v) It is helpful in enhancing employee morale in the organisation.
(vi) It is helpful in developing managerial efficiency in the organisation.
(vii) It is necessary for smooth running of the organisation.

Disadvantages of internal communication are as follows

(i) It may create conflict among employees.
(ii) It is a time consuming process of communication.
(iii) Often it spreads misinformation among employees.
(iv) Generally, employees take wrong decision due to this type of communication.
(v) It is not more suitable for performance reviews of employees.

2. External Communication

This type of communication takes place between the organisation and another person or entity, that are present in the external environment. Example of these people and entities include actual customers, potential customers, suppliers, investors, shareholders and society at large.

The main **advantages** of external communication are as follows

(i) It helps in maintaining favourable relationships with outsiders.
(ii) It increases the prestige of organisation among its investors, customers, suppliers and the general public.
(iii) It exchanges valuable information which is vital for improvement in business activities.
(iv) It is helpful in achieving organisational's goals and mission.
(v) It provides information about products and services to the customers in an effective manner.
(vi) It protects the organisation during any crisis.

External communication suffers from the following **drawbacks**

(i) Generally, it is found in formal communication which is not always appropriate for some specific cases.
(ii) There may exist significant distance between sender and receiver of information.
(iii) It does not enjoy the benefits of flexibility in communication process.
(iv) It is a time consuming process.
(v) Prompt feedback may not be received in several cases.

Difference between Internal Communication and External Communication

Basis	Internal communication	External communication
Meaning	It is the communication between the members of organisation. (i.e. employees, managers etc)	It is the communication between the organisation and outsiders. (i.e. customers, creditors, debtors etc).
Frequency	High.	Low.
Purpose	To exchange information within the organisation.	To maintain relationship with outsiders.

Basis	Internal communication	External communication
Form of communication	It may be formal or informal communication.	Generally, it is formal communication.
Distance	Less distance between sender and receiver of information.	More distance between sender and receiver of information.
Examples	Communication between employees and management.	Communication between account manager and creditors.

II. On the Basis of Relationship

On the basis of relationship, communication can be of the following types

1. Formal Communication

It refers to the communication that takes place through official channels in an organisation. Such type of communication takes place between managers or employees within the organisation. It may be oral or written, but the complete records of such type of communication is maintained in an organisation.

The main **advantages** of formal communication are as follows

(i) It increases the efficiency of the organisation.
(ii) It is an easy communication method.
(iii) It ensures timely communication of messages in the organisation.
(iv) It reduces the chance of misunderstanding among employees.
(v) Under this method, offenders in the communication process are easily identifiable.
(vi) There is less chances of distortion of messages.

Formal communication suffers from the following **drawbacks**

(i) Generally, it is difficult to be implemented in the organisation.
(ii) It is a time consuming process of communication.
(iii) It is not suitable in case of emergency.
(iv) It is not suitable for confidential messages.
(v) The cost of formal communication system is high than other systems.

2. Informal Communication

It takes place in an organisation without following the formal lines of communication. Such type of communication usually takes place among the workers to exchange their views and to satisfy their social needs.

The network of communication followed in the informal communication is referred to as 'grapevine network'.

Some of the popular type of this network are listed below

(i) Single strand (ii) Gossip
(iii) Probability (iv) Cluster

The main **advantages** of informal communication are as follows

(i) It promotes personal relations which is essential for successful public relations.
(ii) It exchanges the information speedily. (i.e. fast and effective communication)
(iii) It brings together employees in matters of common interest.
(iv) It helps to solve of difficult problems in organisation.
(v) It is helpful in interpreting the formal messages/ information.
(vi) It gives the employees a better opportunity to raise their complaint and grievances.

Informal communication suffers from the following **drawbacks**

(i) Often it spreads wrong or distorted information which may be harmful for the organisation.
(ii) Any secret information is likely to be flashed without any hesitation.
(iii) Organisation has no proper mechanism to control the informal communication.
(iv) It is a difficult task to determine the responsibility in informal communication.
(v) Generally most of the informations which are exchanged under informal communication are undetectable.

Difference between Formal and Informal Communication

Basis	Formal communication	Informal communication
Mutual relationship among members	Based on formal superior-subordinate relationship.	Based on interpersonal contacts
Nature	Systematic and orderly.	Unsystematic and erratic.
Speed of communication	It is slow and time consuming.	It is fast and time saving.
Authenticity	Official and well planned messages are authentic.	Unofficial and unplanned messages may not be authentic.
Contents or subject matter	Work related matters, e.g. orders and instructions are communicated.	Personal matters are discussed.
Objectives	To achieve organisational objectives.	To meet personal needs and interests.

III. On the Basis of Direction

On the basis of direction, the following are the different types of formal communication

1. Vertical Communication

It is also called as 'two-way communication' because in this communication, the management can give directives and send information downward and in addition receive periodic information from subordinates about the effectiveness of their directives and the progress of the organisation.

Types of vertical communication are

(i) **Downward Communication** It flows form individuals at higher levels of the hierarchy to those at lower levels. It is from the superior to the subordinate.

(ii) **Upward Communication** It flows from subordinates to superiors and continues upwards in organisational hierarchy.

The main **advantages** of vertical communication are as follows

(i) Under this system, good relations can be developed between superiors and subordinates.

(ii) It develops the sense of discipline among the employees in the organisation.

(iii) It secures effective decision making in the organisation.

(iv) There is no scope of ambiguity in the communication system.

(v) It helps in finding out whether every thing in the organisation is going according to plan or not.

(vi) It helps in informing organisational goals, plan, policies, etc to the subordinates in the organisation.

(vii) Superiors can motivate their subordinates through vertical communication.

Vertical communication suffers from the following **disadvantages**

(i) There may be delay in vertical communication because it maintains long chain of command in the organisation.

(ii) Often superior staff neglects to send message to their subordinates.

(iii) Information may lose its originality due to lengthy channel of communication.

(iv) Lower level employees may feel neglected because flow of orders is from top level to bottom level of employees in the organisation.

(v) There is no scope of informal communication.

(vi) It is a time-consuming process.

(vii) It is not more suitable for quick decision making.

(viii) It is less flexible.

2. Horizontal Communication

It is the flow of information across departmental boundaries, on the organisational level.

It is communication between co-worker with different areas of responsibility. In other words, it is the exchange of information between employees belonging to the same hierarchical level either in the same department or in different department.

The main **advantages** of horizontal communication are as follows

(i) It ensures better understanding between employees which boosts the morale of the employees.

(ii) It ensures quick feedback in the communication process.

(iii) It is helpful in creating a sense of team work in the organisation.

(iv) It helps in increasing the productivity and coordination in the organisation.

(v) It is useful in establishing inter-departmental and intra-departmental difference without the intervention of the superior staff.

(vi) It is generally a very effective way of communication.

The main **disadvantages** of horizontal communications are as follows

(i) It minimises the role of top level management so top level management discourage the horizontal communication.

(ii) It is not much effective due to inter-departmental conflict.

(iii) There may be jealousy among employees who have equal rank.

(iv) There is more possibility that employees will waste their time in gossiping.

(v) It does not follow strict rules so there may be lack of discipline.

Difference between Vertical Communication and Horizontal Communication

Basis	Vertical communication	Horizontal communication
Meaning	When information flows from higher authorities to subordinates and from subordinates to higher authorities, it is called 'vertical communication'.	When employees of the same level (i.e. same rank) share information with each other, it is called 'horizontal communication.'

Basis	Vertical communication	Horizontal communication
Degree of formality	It is more formal than horizontal communication.	It enjoys a greater degree of informality.
Method of communication	Generally written communication is used.	Generally, oral communication is used.
Time	It takes more time to exchange the information.	It takes less time to exchange the information.
Secrecy of information	Secrecy can be maintained.	It is difficult to maintain secrecy.
Example	Communication between sales manager and sales executive.	Communication between sales and purchase manager.

3. Diagonal Communication

When the flow of information is among persons at different levels who have no direct reporting relationship, it is called diagonal communication.

The main **advantages** of diagonal communication are as follows

(i) It maintains efficiency and speed in working.
(ii) It expedites action and prevent others being used merely as conduits between sender and receiver.
(iii) It allows workers to get information faster.
(iv) It improves team-work.

The main **disadvantages** of diagonal communication are as follows

(i) It departs from the normal chain of command.
(ii) It increases competitiveness.
(iii) The internal disorder can occur in the organisation.
(iv) It has a bad effect on formal relations.

Barriers to Communication

There are certain barriers that may interrupt the flow of communication process. These are as follows

1. Semantic Barriers

These are concerned with the meaning of words and symbols. Semantic barriers arise in the process of encoding and decoding of message. These barriers are as follows

(i) **Badly expressed message** Use of wrong words, omission of necessary words and inadequate vocabulary results in badly expressed messages. The intended meaning is not conveyed in such messages.
(ii) **Technical jargon** Specialists often use technical language, which common man does not understand, e.g. Patients often do not understand many words used by doctors.
(iii) **Unclarified assumptions** A message may be misunderstood, when the sender does not clarify the assumptions behind it, e.g. The sales manager may instruct his staff, 'Make every effort to achieve the sales target.' He may mean that sales are to be increased, but without increasing the rate of discount. But the staff may interpret that every effort means discount can be allowed at a higher rate.
(iv) **Faulty translations** When the translator is not proficient in both the languages involved in translation, the meaning of the message may get distorted.

2. Socio-psychological Barriers

The state of mind of both sender and receiver affect the process of communication, e.g. A worried or angry person cannot communicate effectively.

Some of the socio-psychological barriers are given below

(i) **Lack of attention** When the receivers' mind is preoccupied, he fails to listen to what is being said, e.g. A worker explains some problems to his supervisor. The supervisor is preoccupied with a telephone call and does not grasp the message.
(ii) **Premature evaluation** Communication is likely to fail if the receiver evaluates the meaning of message before the sender completes the message. Such premature evaluation may occur due to pre-conceived notions or prejudice against the communicator.
(iii) **Poor retention** The receiver, who cannot retain the information for a long time, may fail to understand it. Poor retention may be due to lack of interest.
(iv) **Distrust** When the sender and the receiver do not believe each other, the message may not be understood in its original sense.

3. Organisational Barriers

Some of the organisational barriers are as follows

(i) **Organisational policy** Communication is hampered, if the policy of an organisation does not support the free flow of communication, e.g. In a highly centralised organisation, people are discouraged to communicate freely.

(ii) **Complex organisation structure** When there are several managerial levels, communication gets delayed and distorted. There is loss of information as the message is transmitted again and again before it reaches the receiver.

(iii) **Rules and regulations** Rigid rules and cumbersome procedures act as a barrier to effective communication. Communication through the prescribed channels may result in delays.

(iv) **Status** The status of a conscious manager may not allow his subordinates to express their feelings freely. Subordinates at lower levels may hesitate to speak freely to high level managers.

4. Physical and Mechanical Barriers

They are the environmental, natural conditions and defects in mechanical devices i.e. fax, phone, internet etc, which act as barrier in the communication process. They include

(i) **Noise** Noise interferes with the transmission of signal, (i.e. unwanted sound during the communication process).

(ii) **Time** It may be known as 'communication gap' between sender and receiver of the information.

(iii) **Distance** The distance between sender of information and receiver of information can be a strong barrier in the effective communication.

(iv) **Work place design** It is also a important barrier in the process of communication. It includes

(a) Seating arrangement (b) Distance

(c) Physical structure of rooms

(v) **Defects in the mechanical devices** It is caused due to minor or major problem in mechanical devices, i.e. microphone, fax, phone, internet, etc.

Measures to Overcome Barriers to Communication

Important measures to overcome the barriers of communication

(i) **Clarify the ideas before communicating** The message to be conveyed should be clear in all aspects. It should be analysed in depth and stated in precise and simple words.

(ii) **Know and understand the receiver** The communicator should know the level of understanding of the receiver. The content, language and tone of the message should be adjusted to suit the education and intelligence of the receiver. The language used in the message should not offend the sentiments of the receiver.

(iii) **Consult others before communication** It is better to involve others in developing the message to be transmitted. Involvement and participation of subordinates will help to get their acceptance and commitment.

(iv) **Convey helpful and valuable things** The message will evoke the desired response if it contains something useful for the receiver. Therefore, message should be designed according to the needs and interests of people with whom you are communicating.

(v) **Be a good listener** Attentive and patient listening on the part of the management will encourage employees to communicate freely.

(vi) **Ensure proper feedback** The communicator may ensure the success of communication by asking questions regarding the message conveyed. Such feedback makes the process more responsive.

PYQs Previous Years' Questions

1 Mark Questions

1. Which barrier of communication can be overcome by using words familiar to the receiver? *ISC 2023*

Ans Semantic barrier of communication can be overcome by using words familiar to the receiver.

2. With reference to the types of business communication, identify the odd one out. *ISC 2023*

(a) Formal communication (b) Internal communication
(c) Diagonal communication
(d) Oral communication

Ans (d) Oral communication

Concept Enhancer Formal communication, internal communication and diagonal communication are types of communication while oral communication is a method of communication.

3. ………… refers to that part of the communication process, where the sender puts his/her ideas or facts into words, symbols, pictures or gestures that can be understood by the receiver. *ISC Sem II 2022*

Ans Encoding

4. ………… method of communication involves the use of graphs, charts and diagrams. *ISC Sem II Specimen 2022*

Ans Visual communication

5. Which of the following types of barrier arises due to problem in language? *ISC Sem II Specimen 2022*

(a) Physical barrier
(b) Semantic barrier
(c) Status barrier
(d) Socio-psychological barrier

Ans (b) Semantic barrier

2 Marks Questions

1. With reference to communication, explain feedback. State any one relevance of feedback in the process of communication. *ISC Sem II 2022*

Or Explain the term 'feedback' in the process of communication. *ISC 2004*

Ans The receiver sends his response to the sender of the message. Such response is known as feedback. When the feedback is received by the sender, the process of communication is complete.

Relevance It would help in evaluating the effectiveness of the sender's message.

2. Define communication. *ISC Sem II Specimen 2022, 2019*

Ans According to Rogers, "Communication is a process by which people create and share information with one another in order to reach common understanding."

3. Briefly explain grapevine vis a vis communication. *ISC Sem II Specimen 2022*

> **KEY IDEA**
> Informal communication is referred as grapevine.

Ans This type of communication takes place among the workers to exchange their views and to satisfy their social needs. It does not follow the formal channels established by management. It spreads throughout the company in all directions. Thus, it is called grapevine.

4. List any four socio-pschological barriers to communication. *ISC Specimen 2019*

Ans The socio-phychological barriers to communication are

(i) Lack of attention
(ii) Premature evaluation
(iii) Poor retention
(iv) Distrust

5. Explain the meaning of internal communication. Name its two types. *ISC 2018*

Ans Internal communication refers to the exchange of ideas, opinions within the organisation. It is easy to use during difficult situations. i.e. conflicts, crisis etc. It motivates the employees of an organisation to increase their productivity. It takes place into two ways

(i) Vertical communication
(ii) Horizontal communication

> **Common Mistake** Students generally get confused among different types of communication and do mistakes, so students are advisable to make flow chart while learning and understand different types of communication as per their basis.

6. Bring out the significance of using grapevine as a channel of communication in an organisation. *ISC 2018*

Ans Grapevine is the informal communication system in the organisation.

The significance of using grapevine as a channel of communication can be summarised as follows

(i) Grapevine communication fulfills is the psychological need of employees because it is arises due to personal interest and needs that are not fulfilled by formal communication.
(ii) Grapevine communication is helpful in building team work, motivate employees, and create corporate identity.

7. List the components of a communication process. *ISC 2017*

Ans The components of a communication process are listed below

(i) Sender (ii) Encoding
(iii) Channel and medium (iv) Receiver
(v) Decoding (vi) Feedback

> **Common Mistake** Sometimes students write unwanted explanation in the answer which is not required. In this question, listing the components of communication process is asked that means only name of components should be written. So students are advisable to write precise answers.

8. Explain the two types of external communication. *ISC 2017*

Ans Two types of external communication are

(i) **Outward communication** All the messages that go out of an organisation are referred to as outward communication. Messages can be sent through telephone calls, circulars, speeches, etc. Outward communication affects the public image of the organisation.

(ii) **Inward communication** All the messages that are received by an organisation are referred to as inward communication. Messages can be received through telephone calls, letters, reports, etc. Inward communication provides important information to the organisation.

9. What is decoding, with reference to communication process? **ISC 2016**

Ans Decoding means the process of conversion of symbols into the message by the receiver. Through this element the receiver tries to understand and assess the message.

10. Give any two limitations of visual communication. **ISC 2016**

Ans Two limitations of visual communications are

(i) Visual communication provides limited amount of information.

(ii) They do not provide qualitative facts.

11. Differentiate between horizontal communication and vertical communication. **ISC 2015**

Ans Difference between horizontal communication and vertical communication are

Basis	Horizontal communication	Vertical communication
Meaning	Communication that takes place between individuals working at the same level is referred to as horizontal communication.	Communication taking place between two levels in an organisation is called 'vertical communication.' It may be upward or downward.
Example	Production manager contacts marketing Manager to discuss about production schedule.	Application for grant of leave by supervisor to the General Manager.

12. Explain the two types of vertical communication. **ISC 2015**

Ans Two types of vertical communication are

(i) **Upward communication** It refers to flow of communication from subordinate to superior, e.g. Application for grant of leave, submission of progress report, request for grants etc.

(ii) **Downward communication** It indicates communication from a superior to subordinate, e.g. Sending notice to employees to attend a meeting, passing on guidelines framed by top management to the subordinates etc.

13. What is the importance of feedback in communication process? **ISC 2014**

Or Discuss the importance of feedback in communication. **ISC 2010**

Ans Communication is the exchange and flow of information and ideas from one person to another. It involves a sender transmitting an idea, information or feeling to a receiver. Effective communication occurs only if the receiver understands the exact information or idea that the sender intended to transmit and this is possible only with feedback, as it would help in evaluating the effectiveness of our message. It makes communication meaningful.

14. Why is communication called a two-way process? **ISC 2011**

Ans Communication is considered as a two-way process because it involves two parties sending and receiving their informations in a cyclic form which means that one person or group expresses an idea which is received and understood by the other. After understanding it, the receiver gives the feedback to the sender that the message has been understood.

15. Why should a communicator be precise and brief while communicating? **ISC 2009**

Ans A communicator should be precise and brief while communicating because complexity and longevity of the communication process kills the essence and effectiveness of the message. Message needs to be simple, straight and accurate.

16. What is vertical communication? **ISC 2007**

Ans Vertical communication is also called as 'two-way communication' because in this communication, the management can give directives and send information downward and in addition receive periodic information from subordinates about the effectiveness of their directives and the progress of the organisation.

17. What is horizontal communication? **ISC 2006**

Ans Horizontal communication is the flow of information across departmental boundaries, either laterally or diagonally. The aim of such communication is to solve specific problem, task coordination, information sharing, conflict resolution, etc.

18. Explain the term 'encoding' in the process of communication. **ISC 2005**

Ans The sender translates the message into words, symbols, gestures or actions, which he feels will make the receiver understand the message. This is known as 'encoding of message'.

19. What do you understand by gestural communication? What are the ways in which you can indulge in it? **ISC 2004**

Ans It is communication that uses body movements, voice patterns, time, touch, etc, to communicate the message. One can indulge in it by waving of hands, pointing of lips, movement of eyes, shaking hands, patting on back, etc.

4 Marks Questions

1. Oral communication is often considered a non-reliable medium that has no legal proof. However, it remains the most popular method of communication in organisations.

Give any four reasons to support the above statements. *ISC Specimen 2023*

Or In spite of oral communication having no legal validity, it is the most common method of communication. Give four reasons to justify the above statement. *ISC Sem II Specimen 2022*

Or Oral communication is an unreliable yet popular method of communication. Discuss. *ISC 2013*

Or The most unreliable and the most pupular method of communication is verbal. Comment. *ISC 2004*

Ans Oral communication is the powerful means of exchange of idea because the receiver not only hears the message but also observes the physical gestures of the speakers. It is the face to face communication between individuals.

The reasons of being the most popular method of communication are as follows

(i) It is time saving communication.
(ii) It creates healthy climate in the organisation.
(iii) It is very economical. It saves money spent on stationery in an organisation.
(iv) It provides immediate feedback to the participants.
(v) It is an effective tool of persuasion.
(vi) It is very much flexible and effective.

Value Points

For getting maximum marks, following value points can be included in the answer

- Meaning of oral communication
- Advantages of oral communication

2. Although gestural communication aids oral communication in conveying the message, it has certain limitations. State any two advantages and any two disadvantages of gestural communication. *ISC Sem II 2022*

Ans For advantages and disadvantages of gestural communication, refer to text on page 119.

3. Discuss the types of communication on the basis of area of operation. *ISC Sem II 2022*

Ans On the basis of area of operation, communication can be classified as

(i) **Internal communication** Refer to text on page 120.
(ii) **External communication** Refer to text on page 120.

4. Manohar is a supervisor at the manufacturing unit of an automobile company. Most of his subordinates are not well educated. Manohar often finds that they are unable to understand his instructions.
Identify the barrier to communication in the given context. Suggest any three ways to overcome this barrier. *ISC Sem II 2022*

Ans The type of barrier discussed in the case is semantic barrier.

Ways to overcome this barrier Refer to text on page 124.

5. Distinguish between

(i) Internal communication and external communication.
(ii) Formal communication and informal communciation *ISC Specimen 2019*

Ans (i) Difference between internal communication and external communication are (any two)

Basis	Internal communication	External communication
Meaning	It is the communication between the members of organisations.	It is the communication between the organisation and outsiders.
Example	Communication between employees and management.	Communication between account manager and creditors.
Purpose	To exchange the information within the organisation.	To maintain relationship with outsiders.
Form of communic-ation	It may be formal or informal communication.	Generally, it is formal communication.

(ii) Refer text on page 121.

6. Written communication is the most common method of communication in a business organisation. Give reasons. *ISC 2008*

Ans Because of the following points, this method is very common in business

(i) Written communication has the advantage of being stored for future reference or legal document.
(ii) Written communication is easier to understand than speech, as it allows ample time to the reader to read at his leisure, analyse and think about the message.
(iii) Written communication can be composed in advance before it is delivered.
(iv) Written communication is less prone to errors, as they are organised more carefully than the spoken messages.

7. Explain the importance of communication in a commercial organisation. *ISC 2006*

Ans Importance of communication are

(i) **Efficient and smooth working** Communication helps to convey organisational goals and policies to the employees and maintaining coordination among departments to maintain smooth working in the enterprise.

(ii) **Facilitates effective management** Communication helps the manager in effective performance of managerial activities, i.e. planning, organising, leading, motivation and directing.

(iii) **Better relations** Through communication, superiors and subordinates sort out their mutual differences and reduce conflicts, thereby, leading to better relations and congenial atmosphere.

(iv) **Total quality management** Communication becomes indispensible in total quality organisations, in order to reach at a common consensus related to products and quality of work.

6/8 Marks Questions

1. Define communication. State any six differences between formal communication and informal communication. *ISC 2020*

Ans According to **Rogers**, "Communication is a process by which people create and share information with one another in order to reach common understanding."

For differences between formal and informal communication, refer to text on page 121.

2. Give any eight distinctions between oral communication and written communication. *ISC 2019*

Ans Difference between oral and written communication are

Basis	Oral communication	Written communication
Meaning	It means exchange of ideas and opinions through words spoken.	It means exchange of ideas and opinions in writing.
Literacy	Not required for oral communication.	Necessary for written communication.
Legal validity	It has no legal validity.	It has legal validity.
Feedback	Receivers give immediate feedback for message.	Receivers do not give immediate feedback for message.
Speed	There is fast transmission of message.	There is slow transmission of message.
Understanding of message	Easy to understand the message.	Difficult to understand the message.
Non-verbal cues	Non-verbal cues can be used in oral communication.	Non-verbal cues cannot be used in written communication.
Formality	It maintains informal relationship communication.	It maintains formal relationship communication.

Value Points

For getting maximum marks, following value points can be included in the answer

- Do not write differences in one word but explain in a sentence.
- Use basis of differences and ensure that differences under both heads match with basis.

3. Briefly explain any six reasons for the rising need for efficient communication. *ISC 2017*

Ans Reasons for the rising need for efficient communication are briefly explained below

(i) **Efficient and smooth working** Communication helps to convey organisational goals and policies to the employees and maintaining coordination among departments to maintain smooth working in the enterprise.

(ii) **Facilitates effective management** Communication helps the manager in effective performance of managerial activities, i.e. planning, organising, leading, motivation and directing.

(iii) **Better relations** Through communication, superiors and subordinates sort out their mutual differences and reduce conflicts, thereby, leading to better relations and congenial atmosphere.

(iv) **Total quality management** Communication becomes indispensable in total quality organisations, in order to reach at a common consensus related to products and quality of work.

Rising Need for Efficient Communication

- Efficient and smooth working
- Facilitates effective management
- Better relations
- Total quality management
- Better marketing
- Job satisfaction

(v) **Better marketing** Communication helps enterprises to know consumer preferences on one hand, and provide information about products and services to them, on the other. This results in effective marketing.

(vi) **Job satisfaction** Communication reduces misunderstanding among employees, enhancing cooperation and achievement of goals. This leads to job satisfaction and motivation of the employees.

4. Discuss any three barriers to effective communication. **ISC 2016**

Ans Three barriers to effective communication are discussed below

(i) **Semantic barriers** These are concerned with the meaning of words and symbols. Semantic barriers arise in the process of encoding and decoding of message. These barriers can take the form of badly expressed message, technical jargon, unclassified assumptions and faulty translations.

(ii) **Psychological barriers** The state of mind of both sender and receiver affect the process of communication, e.g. a worried or angry person cannot communicate effectively. These barriers can be in the form of lack of attention, premature evaluation, poor retention and distrust.

(iii) **Organisational barriers** Sometimes factors related to organisation structure, authority, rules and regulations etc. act as barriers to communication. These barriers can be in the form of organisational policy, rules and regulations, complexity in organisation structure, organisational facilities and status of a superior.

5. Explain the various elements of the communication process. **ISC 2015**

Or Explain the components of the communication process. **ISC 2009**

KEY IDEA

The communication process refers to a series of actions or steps taken in order to successfully communicate. These actions or steps are known as elements or components.

Ans Refer to text on page 117 and 118.

6. Discuss any four advantages and limitations of face-to-face communication. **ISC 2015**

Ans Face-to-face communication implies a direct personal talk between two individuals.

Following are the advantages of face-to-face communication

(i) **Control over reader's attention** Face-to-face communication provides the advantages of exercising control over listener's attention. The speaker can effectively capture the listener's attention by making his message clear and interesting.

(ii) **Effect of facial expressions** Another advantage of face-to-face communication is that the speaker can make his communication more vivid and forceful, by conveying through facial expressions, tone and pitch of the voice.

(iii) **Suitable for discussions** Face-to-face communication is most suitable for discussion where instantaneous feedback is imperative. Even communication on telephone or teleconferencing is not as effective, as it is in case of face-to-face situation, when a lot of discussion for negotiation, brainstorming or persuasion has to be done.

(iv) **Immediate feedback** Face-to-face communication facilitate immediate feedback and clarification of doubts, arising in the mind of the receiver.

Limitations of face-to-face communication are as follows

(i) **Inattentive listening** For effective communication, the ability of the communicator matters, but the listening skill of the listener also plays an important role. Most of the persons seem listening, but do not listen because of wandering of mind to other matters, selective perceptions, egoism, etc. As a result, the communication does not take place because of inattentive listening.

(ii) **Difficulty in arranging personal contacts** Face-to-face communication suffers from the limitation of arranging personal contacts. If the various departments and persons are working at different places, especially noticed in big organisations, it is very frustrating and difficult to arrange their personal contacts. Moreover, it is not easy and economical, rather expensive and time consuming process.

(iii) **Unproductive in unhealthy relations** Face-to-face communication sometimes proves counter productive, when the relations between the parties are unhealthy. It may lead to further conflict and confrontation.

(iv) **Large audience** When the number of listeners is very large, face-to-face communication becomes difficult and proves ineffective.

7. Discuss the advantages of written communication. **ISC 2014, 2011**

Or

State three advantages and three disadvantages of written communication. **ISC 2006**

Ans Advantages of written communication are

(i) **Permanent records** Written communication has the advantage of being stored for future reference or legal document.

(ii) **Easier to understand** Written communication is easier to understand than speech as it allows ample time to the reader to read at his leisure, analyse and think about the message. He can take a break.

(iii) **Composing in advance** Written communication can be composed in advance before it is delivered. The sender can ponder over the words and their effect on the receiver and accordingly, can change his message.

Disadvantages of written communication are

(i) **Time consuming process** Written communication involves a considerable time in writing, rewriting, printing or proof reading the message to be communicated.

(ii) **Not suitable for illiterate** Written communication is not suitable for illiterate people as they cannot read or write.

(iii) **Formalism** Written communication is more formal and rigid than oral communication. As a result, it leads to defensive behaviour among employees and red-tapism in the organisations.

8. Write a short note on internal communication in an organisation. *ISC 2013*

Ans It is the transmission of information between organisational members or parts of the organisation. It takes place across all levels and organisational units of an organisation.

In its simplest terms, internal communication is communication within an organisation. It encompasses both 'official' communication such as memos, guidelines, policies and procedures, etc and the 'unofficial' communication that goes on among and between the staff members of all organisations namely, the exchange of ideas and opinions, the development of personal relationships and the proverbial conversation around the water cooler.

It goes in all directions among line staff (those who do the specific work of the organisation and work directly with the target population), administrators, supervisors, clerical and support staff, volunteers and even the Board of Directors.

Internal communication is a lot more than people talking to one another. However, it is the life blood of any organisation, the way in which everyone gets the information one needs.

It means that anyone can easily get his question answered, as well as that no one gets left out when there's a birthday celebration for a staff member.

Good internal communication ensures the following

(i) Provide people the information they need, to do their jobs effectively.

(ii) Make sure they know about everything that concerns them.

(iii) Provide people with clear standards and expectations for their work.

(iv) Give feedback on their performance.

(v) Provide them emotional support for difficult work.

(vi) Suggest new ideas about both, their work and their lives.

(vii) Allow them to take the pulse of the organisation and understand its overall situation.

(viii) Help them maintain a shared vision and a sense of ownership in the organisation.

9. Define communication. Discuss the significance of feedback in a sound communication process. *ISC 2012*

Ans **Definition of Communication** In the words of **Rogers**, "Communication is a process by which people create and share information with one another in order to reach common understanding."

Significance of feedback Feedback is essential in communication so as to know whether the recipient has understood the message in the same terms as intended by the sender and whether he agrees to that message or not.

There are a lot of ways in which company takes feedback from their employees, such as employee surveys, memos, emails, open-door policies, company's news letter, etc. Employees are not always willing to provide feedback. The organisation has to work a lot to get the accurate feedback.

The managers encourage feedback by asking specific questions, allowing their employees to express general views, etc. The organisation should be receptive to the employee's feedback.

10. What is meant by semantic barriers? Explain any three semantic barriers to communication. *ISC 2012*

Ans Semantic barriers are concerned with the meaning of words and symbols. Semantic barriers arise in the process of encoding and decoding of message.

These barriers are as follows

(i) **Badly expressed message** Use of wrong words, omission of necessary words and inadequate vocabulary results in badly expressed messages. The intended meaning is not conveyed in such messages.

(ii) **Unclarified assumptions** A message may be misunderstood, when the sender does not clarify the assumptions behind it, e.g. the sales manager may instruct his staff, "Make every effort to achieve the sales target." He may mean that sales are to be increased, but without increasing the rate of discount. But the staff may interpret that every effort means a discount can be offered at higher rates.

(iii) **Faulty translations** When the translator is not proficient in both the languages involved in translation, the meaning of the message may get distorted.

Additional Questions

2 Marks Questions

1. Mention two limitations of oral communication.

Ans Two limitations of oral communication are

(i) **Physical distance** When there is a long physical distance between two individuals, oral communication may not be possible.

(ii) **Misunderstanding** Oral communications are likely to be misunderstood due to poor vocal expression and noise. The speaker may not be able to make himself quite clear or the listener may be inattentive.

2. Differentiate between oral communication and written communication.

Ans Difference between oral communication and written communication are

Basis	Oral communication	Written communication
Meaning	It means exchange of ideas and opinions through the words spoken.	It means exchange of ideas and opinions in writing.
Legal validity	It has no legal validity.	It has legal validity.

3. State two advantages and disadvantages of formal communication.

Ans Advantages of formal communication are as follows

(i) It reduces the chance of misunderstanding among employees.

(ii) It increases the efficiency of the organisation.

Disadvantages of formal communication are as follows

(i) It is a time consuming process of communication.

(ii) It is not suitable in case of emergency.

4. Explain any two advantages of external communication.

Ans Advantages of external communication are as follows

(i) It provides information about products and services to the customers in a effective manner.

(ii) It helps in maintaining favourable relationship with outsiders which protect the organisation during crisis.

CHAPTER TEST

01 Mark Questions

1. In the process of communication, who conveys the message?

2. Name the method of communication in which postures and gestures are used to communicate.

3. Which communication barrier arises when there is faulty translation that results in distorted meaning to the message?

4. .... communication means exchange of ideas and opinions in writing.

5. On the basis of area of operation, there are two types of communication *viz* .... and .... communiction.

6. In the internal communication network, a message flows in a
(a) downward, upward, lateral or informal manner
(b) distorted, upward, lateral or informal manner
(c) downward, lateral, horizontal or informal manner
(d) downward, upward, lateral or formal manner

7. The 'grapevine' is a source of information, it is a form of
(a) lateral communication
(b) informal communication
(c) downward communication
(d) None of the above

8. A written communication is better than an oral one if
(a) immediate feedback is required
(b) the decoder is reluctant to receive the message
(c) the decoder is likely to misunderstand the message
(d) the message is supposed to have detailed accuracy

9. Noise refers to an obstruction or hindrance in the communication process. State true or false.

10. Oral communication has legal validity. State true or false.

02 Marks Questions

11. What do you mean by communication?

12. Two heads of different departments are communicating with each other. In this case, which channel of communication are they following?

13. Name the element of communication process, which represents reaction or response to a message?

14. Why is informal communication referred to as grapevine?

04 Marks Questions

15. Distinguish between formal and informal communication.

16. State the two merits and two demerits of gestural communication.

06/08 Marks Questions

17. Discuss in brief all the methods of communication.

18. Explain, how an organisation can overcome the barriers of communication?

Answers

1. Sender
2. Gestural communication
3. Semantic barrier
4. Written
5. internal, external
6. (a) downward, upward, lateral or informal manner
7. (b) informal communication
8. (d) the message is supposed to have detailed accuracy
9. True
10. False

12

Business Correspondence (Business Letters & Reports) and Current Trends

TREND ANALYSIS 5 YEARS

	Types of Questions	2023	2020	2019	2018	2017
		Average No. of Questions Across all Sets				
01 Business Correspondence and Letter	1 Mark	—	—	—	—	—
	2 Marks	—	1	—	1	—
	4 Marks	—	—	—	—	—
	6 Marks	—	—	—	—	—
	8 Marks	1	1	1	1	—
02 Business Reports and Current Trends in Business Communication	1 Mark	1	—	—	—	—
	2 Marks	—	—	—	—	1
	4 Marks	—	1	—	1	1
	6 Marks	—	—	—	—	—
	8 Marks	—	—	1	—	1

Meaning of Business Correspondence

Business correspondence is the exchange of information in written format for the purpose of business activities. Business correspondence in written form can take place between organisations, within an organisation or between customers and organisations. It is generally in form of letters, e-mails, memos, reports, etc.

Need of Business Correspondence

The following points bring forth the need of business correspondence

(i) **Clarity of idea** There is clarity in written message because both sender and receiver can read the message several times which is not possible in oral communication.

(ii) **Valuable record for both parties** Business correspondence acts as a record for both parties which is not possible in oral communication.

(iii) **Legal document** Business correspondence is used as a legal evidence in case of any dispute between two parties.

(iv) **Useful for future reference** Any business correspondence kept in record can be referred to any time for knowing the past dealings.

(v) **To build mutual understanding** Business correspondence are exchanged between sender and receiver for carrying out a business activity. It builds mutual understanding between two parties.

Functions of Business Correspondence

The main functions of business correspondence can be summarised as follows

(i) **The function of providing contacts** Business correspondence provides contact between two parties (i.e. seller and buyer) without any physical meeting.

(ii) **Legal function** Business correspondence forms a very important reference base and used as a legal evidence in case of any dispute.

(iii) **Promotional functions** Companies launch new products and services in market. Business correspondence helps them in making direct sales to the small targeted customers and regular dealers.

(iv) **Goodwill functions** Business correspondence promote goodwill among parties which are connected with the organisation in a systematic manner.

(v) **Informational functions** Business correspondence acts as a record of valuable information about previous policies strategies and other activities of the organisation.

Business Letter

A business letter is usually a letter from one company to another or between such organisations and their customers, clients and other external parties. The overall style of letter depends on the relationship between the parties concerned.

Main Elements/ Contents of a Business Letter

The main elements of a business letter are as follows

1. Sender's Address

According to the latest format, sender's address is written at the top alongwith pin code. Do not write sender's name with the address.

K-127, Ashok Nagar
New Delhi-110092

or

House no. 373, Sector 14
Gurgaon-122001

While writing the address, one must not use 'comma' at the end of each line. If the address is not provided in the question, then you may create a fictitious address, but writing an address is mandatory.

2. Date

It appears directly below the sender's address, after leaving one line space. It is advisable to always write the full date, e.g. 25th December, 2015.

3. Salutation

This consists of words of greeting and is written on the left hand side of the page just below the date after leaving one line space. The form of greeting depends upon your relation to the person to whom the letter is being written.

For Example, To near relatives → My Dear Dad, Dearest Friend, Dear Sister

To acquaintances → Dear Mr Sharma, Dear Miss Goyal

To unknown persons → Dear Sir/Madam, Respected Sir/Madam, Sir/Madam

4. Subject

Subject is generally used in writing a formal letter. It can be written after the receiver's address or even after the salutation. It should be short and to the point. For example, **Subject** Application for the post of content writer.

5. The Body

The body is the main part of any letter. This is written in response to the topic given, in simple and direct language.

The body includes three main parts

(i) Introductory paragraph/sentence → States the purpose of writing.

(ii) Informative paragraphs → Details about the subject of the letter.

(iii) Concluding paragraph/sentence → The closure of the letter/conclusion stating hope, request or comment.

6. Complimentary Close

It is a courteous way of ending the letter. The expression used must match the salutation.

For example,

(i) Yours affectionately/yours/with love for family and friends.

(ii) Yours sincerely/yours faithfully for principal, boss or for any other official purposes.

7. Name/Signature

It is written just below the 'complimentary close' and includes the sender's name, designation (if applicable) and signature/name.

For example,

Yours truly/sincerely
Ankita Chakravarti
Editor

Format of a Business Letter

Sender's Address
Date
Receiver's Name/Rank and Address
Subject (Indicate the theme of the letter)
Salutation (Dear Sir/ Ma'am)
Introduction to be given in Ist paragraph describing the purpose of writing.
The IInd paragraph will contain the required information.
The conclusion will be given in the last paragraph, which will contain hope/comment or request.

Complimentary close

[Name and designation of the sender]

Types of Letter

There are of several types of business letter, but as per the syllabus, following are important that are to be recalled

1. Solicited Letters of Application for a Job

Solicited letter of application is sent in response to an announced job opening. Candidates know what qualifications the organisation is seeking.

In other words, if the organisation announced an opening, the application for job is considered solicited because it was asked for. The main purpose of a solicited application is to obtain an interview for a specific job position which the applicant mentions in his application.

Format of Solicited Letters

Sender Address
Date
Receiver's name/rank
Subject Application for the post of.....
Dear Sir/Ma'am,
In response to your advertisement in.................I would like to apply for the same. [Ist Paragraph]
Give your introduction and other relevant information. [IInd Paragraph]

Complimentary close

Format of Bio-data

Name –
Home Address –
Mobile –
E-mail –
Educational Qualification –
Extra –
Age –
Personal Details –
Hobbies –
References –

2. Unsolicited Letters of Application for a Job

Unsolicited application for job is sent to an organisation that has not announced an opening of a new job opportunity. The main purpose of such application is to inform the organisation that the applicant is interested in working with the organisation, if any suitable position exists in near future.

Format of Unsolicited Letter of Application

Format is same as in case of solicited application. Only the opening paragraph will differ.

It should start with, From reliable sources I have come to know that there is a vacancy for......

Bio-Data

Name –
Father's Name –
Address –
Contact Mob. No. –
E-mail –
Date of Birth –

Educational Qualifications

Name of Exam	College/Board/ University	Year	Percentage

Work Experience –
Languages Known –
References –

3. Interview Letter

After evaluations of written tests, deserving candidates are called for interview. The interview letter states the time and date, when the interview shall take place and the authority before whom the candidate is supposed to appear.

While drafting interview letters, following points must be considered

(i) Be precise and specific.
(ii) Use direct approach with clear message.
(iii) Mention the time, date and place of interview.
(iv) Name the office and authority before whom the candidate is supposed to appear.
(v) State clearly that the candidate is required to submit his/her certificates and testimonials in original at the time of the interview.
(vi) Inform the candidate whether he/she is entitled to any TA or DA.

Format of Interview Letter

Logo of Company

Dear (Name of applicant)

Date

Post (Name of the Post)

Sir,

With reference to your application to the above post, please come on (date of interview) at (venue of interview), telephone number .... at (time) for an interview.

The interview is scheduled to last approximately (state duration) and will take the form of (short description of format of interview).

Please bring the following while coming for the interview.

(List of documents)

Thanking you

Yours truly/sincerely,

For (Name of company)

Name of officer with sign

Post

4. Job Offer Letter

If a candidate successfully clears all rounds of interviews and satisfies the criteria determined for a potential candidate, then he is regarded as a suitable candidate for the company. Now, as he has cleared all the necessary rounds and proved his suitability, the company officially provides him a letter and this letter is known as the offer letter.

Format of Job Offer Letter

Name & Address of employer

Date

Name (applicant)

Address (applicant)

Offer letter for (Job title)

Dear Mr/Mrs (Name of applicant)

Following our recent discussions, we are delighted to offer you the position of (Position title) with our organisation. As a member of our organisation, we would ask for your commitment to deliver outstanding quality and results that exceed client expectations. The following points outline the terms and conditions, we are proposing.

Title (Position Title)

Job description	—	(Brief summary of job)
Start date	—	Date
Salary	—	Amount per month/year
Probation period	—	(Months/years)
Working hours	—	(In hours) per day
Reporting	—	(Name of the reporting officer)
Vacation	—	Months/days
Termination	—	(Brief explanation of conditions)

Sincerely

Name (HR Person's and Sign)

Title (Position in department)

Organisation (Name)

With the signature below, I accept this offer for employment.

Name & Sign (Date)

(applicant)

5. Resignation Letter

A resignation letter is an official letter given by an employee to his/her employer stating his/her intention to leave his/her current position at the company. It includes the details about the last day of work and outlines any next step for transition.

Format for Resignation Letter

Employee's Name

Employee's address

Employee's City, State, Zip Code

Employee's Phone number

Employee's E-mail

Date

Name of Manager

Title or Position

Organisation Name

Address

City, State, Zip Code

Dear Sir/Madam

Body of Letter

Your Sincerely,

Employee's Signature

Employee's Name

6. Enquiry Letter

An enquiry letter is written by a potential customer, on the look out for a product or with a desire to avail the service offered by a seller or an organisation. An enquiry letter is neither a contract, not does it entail any contractual obligation between the two. It is actually a preliminary exercise that may lead to a contract.

Format for Enquiry Letter

Address (sender)

Date

Name and address of addressee with designation

Subject ....

Sir,

Body of letter

(a) Reference of inquiry

(b) Summary of inquiry

(c) Request for sending information

Yours sincerely

Name of sender

7. Quotation Letter

A letter of quotation is a formal statement of promise that is submitted usually in response to a request for quotation by potential buyer to supply the goods or services required by a buyer, at specified prices and within a specified period.

Format for Quotation Letter

Address (sender)

Date

Name

Address (receiver)

Subject..........

Dear Sir,

We understand that you deal in (name of business). Kindly send us the prices and services terms for the following item.

S.N.	Name of item	Quantity	Total
....	....	....	....
....	....	....	....
....	....	....	....
....	....		....

Expecting a prompt reply.

Name and designation of sender

8. Order Letter

It is a confirmed request, by one party to another to buy, sell, deliver or receive goods or services under specified terms and conditions.

When accepted by the receiving party, an order becomes a legally binding contract. The letter which is written by a potential buyer to the seller requesting him to deliver goods is known as order letter or purchase order.

Format of Order Letter

Sender's Address

Date

Receiver's Name/Rank and Address

Subject Order for...........

Dear Sir/Ma'am,

Details about the order (Ist Paragraph)

Delivery and mode of payment (IInd Paragraph)

Complimentary Close

9. Complaint Letter

A complaint letter is a letter written by a customer of a service/product commenting on poor service/product. It usually outlines the fault (s) with the service and highlights customer dissatisfaction with the particular service/product.

Format of Complaint Letter

Sender's Address

Date ....

Receiver's Name/Rank and Address

Subject Complaint against...........

Dear Sir/Ma'am,

Details of Complaint (Ist Paragraph)

Mode of Redressal (IInd Paragraph)

Complimentary Close

10. Reply to Complaint Letter

The reply to complaint letter is used by a company to respond to customer who has lodged a formal complaint about company's defected products and services.

For example, Write a letter from a business firm to a customer in reply to his complaint that the goods sent were received in damaged condition.

Reply to Complaint Letter

Sender's Address

Date ....

Receiver's Address

Subject Complaint received

Dear Sir/Ma'am

Express your regret (Ist Paragraph)

Relief offered (IInd Paragraph)

Complimentary Close

Meaning and Definitions of Business Reports

Business reports play a very singnificant role in the modern business (i.e. backbone of modern communication).

A report is written for a clear purpose and to a particular audience. Specific information and evidence are presented, analysed and applied to a particular problem or issue. The information is presented in a clearly structured format, making use of sections and headings, so that the information is easy to locate and follow.

According to **Lesikar** and **Flatley**, "A business report is an orderly and objective communication of factual information that serves a business purpose."

According to **J. Stanley Jones**, "A report is a special form of narrative which aims chiefly at conveying information, based upon facts."

Types of Reports

Business reports can be classified into several categories

(i) **Statutory reports** The reports which are prepared according to the form and procedure laid down by law, for example, Companies Act are called statutory report.

Generally, statutory report is drafted by the directors of the company (Private Limited) to forward to shareholders atleast 21 days before the date of annual general meeting.

Examples of statutory report are as follows

(a) Director's report to the annual general meeting

(b) Annual return

(c) Auditor's report

(ii) **Non-statutory reports** Business reports which are drafted to help the management in formulating policies and in taking important decisions in company are known as 'non-statutory reports.' These reports do not require any legal compliance.

Generally, non-statutory reports are prepared for the following purposes

(a) Effective functioning of company

(b) Expansion of business

(c) Starting a new venture

(d) Entering into joint venture

(e) Developing new technology

Difference between Statutory Report and Non-statutory Report

Basis	Statutory report	Non-statutory report
Meaning	The report which is prepared according to the form and procedure laid down by law.	The report which is prepared to help the management in formulating policies and in taking important decisions.
Compulsory/ Optional	It is compulsory.	It is optional.
Purpose	The main purpose is the comply with the law.	The main purpose is to increase the quality of the managerial decisions.
Example	Auditor's report. Director's report to the annual general meeting.	Reports for administrative purposes. Reports for policy formulation.

(iii) **Private reports** Private reports are those reports which are prepared by selected individual for a specific purpose and not shared publically. For example, director of company may depute the human resource manager to prepare a private report about the conduct of employees. These reports will not be shared publically.

(iv) **Public reports** Public reports are those reports which are prepared by management of companies or corporations, for a specific purpose and shared publically. Such type reports spread awareness among public.

In India, government also publish the public report for spreading awareness among public.

Examples of public report are as follows

(a) RBI's report on inflation

(b) Reports of health institutions

Difference between Private Reports and Public Reports

Basis	Private reports	Public reports
Meaning	Private reports are those reports which are prepared by selected individual for a specific purpose and not shared publically.	Public reports are those reports which are prepared by companies, corporations and government for a specific purpose and shared publically.

Basis	Private reports	Public reports
Purpose	To take administrative and managerial decisions.	To spread awareness among public.
Significance	Significance for an individual organisation.	Significance for entire community.
Example	Individual employee's conduct report.	Government report on inflation.

(v) **Informational reports** Informational reports are intended mainly explain something or to educate readers. They present the factual information without analysis. Such reports bring information to the attention of management or other stakeholders (i.e. shareholders, debtor, creditor, government, etc), so that proper action/decision may be taken.

Examples of informational reports are as follows

(a) Monthly sales report

(b) The annual report prepared by the company secretary

(vi) **Interpretative reports** Interpretative reports analyse the facts and provide conclusion to readers. These reports are drafted only after deep investigation and study of the given subject.

In other words, we can say that interpretative reports and those reports which analysis the data, draw conclusions and makes recommendations for users.

Examples of interpretative reports are as follows

(a) Survey/feasibility reports

(b) Technical reports (c) Market research reports

Difference between Informational Reports and Interpretative Reports

Basis	Informational reports	Interpretative reports
Meaning	Informational reports are those reports which try to explain something or educate readers	Interpretative reports analyse the facts and provide conclusions to the readers.
Purpose	To provide the explanation about any issue or problem.	To provide the solution or recommendation about any problem or issue.
Nature	Generally such reports are of routine nature.	Generally, such reports are special reports.
Example	Monthly sales reports. Monthly debtors report.	Market research reports. Feasibility reports.

(vii) **Routine/Periodic reports** Routine reports contain mere statement of facts in detail without any opinion or recommendation for readers. These reports may be submitted either daily, weekly, monthly, quarterly or annually. Routine reports are usually prepared on a prescribed performa.

Examples of Routine reports are as follows

(a) Inspection reports (b) Production reports

(c) Sales reports

(viii) **Special reports** Special reports are drafted to convey special information related to a particular problem or issue. These reports contain opinions or recommendations for readers which are based on facts and arguments.

Special reports play significant role in decision-making process. Generally, these reports and related to a single occasion or situation.

For example, an employee died in the factory due to fire and management demands a detail report from supervisor, such report is known as special report.

Difference between Routine Reports and Special Reports

Basis	Routine reports	Special reports
Meaning	Routine reports are those reports which contain mere statement of facts in detail without any opinion or recommendation.	Special reports are drafted to convey special information related to a particular problem or issue.
Scientific report	They are not scientific reports because such reports are not based on cause and effect relationship.	They are considered as scientific reports because these are based on cause and effect relationship.
Purpose	To provide routine information to users in detail or in summary.	To provide solution to the specific problem.
Example	Inspection reports. Sales reports.	Reports on the desirability of opening a new branch. Report on fire accident in company.

Format of Report

A business report can generally be structured as follows

(i) **A covering letter or memo** Covering letter introduces the report to outsiders while memorandum is appropriate for insiders.

(ii) **Title page** It includes
   (a) Date of completion/Submission
   (b) The author(s)
   (c) Organisation/Association of author(s)

(iii) **Table of contents** Table of contents states the pages for various sections.

(iv) **Executive summary** It helps the reader quickly grasp the report's purpose, conclusions and recommendations.

(v) **Introduction** It will explain the problem/issue. It includes
   (a) Briefly describe the context
   (b) Outline the scope of report
   (c) Preview the report structure
   (d) Assumptions, if any made

(vi) **Finding and discussion** The discussion is the main part of the report. It gives enough information analysis and evidence to support of recommendations.

(vii) **Conclusions/recommendations** A business report usually needs both conclusions and recommendation. Conclusions relate to past or present while recommendation is related to the future situation.

(viii) **References** When informations from other sources are used in report, reference must be given in text and in a list of references.

(ix) **Appendices** The appendices are the supplementary material that enhance the understanding of readers.

Current Trends in Business Communication

Current trends in business communication include e-mail and video conferencing which are disscussed ahead

E-mail or Electronic Mail

E-mail is the modern and widely used business communication system that is supported by information technologies. People across the world use e-mail as an instant means of communication because it can reach anyone anywhere within minutes, even seconds, of being send. For someone connected to the internet, its cost is very little to send and receive mail.

Uses of E-mail

The main uses of e-mail can be summarised as the follows

(i) **Speedy communication** E-mail is considered as the fastest mode of communication. It sends the messages in few seconds or minutes.

(ii) **Record of communication** It keeps the record of sending and receiving messages which can be used in future for reference.

(iii) **Transmitting documents** It can send all types of documents (i.e. text, images, audio, video, etc).

(iv) **Reduces geographical barriers** E-mail reduces geographic and time zone barriers for businesses.

(v) **Useful in marketing and market research** Companies send commercial mails to target group of customers. E-mail is a highly effective market research tool for several reasons.

Video Conferencing

It is an audio-visual communication between two or more people residing in separate locations for the purpose of communication. It is a live mode of communication. It provides transmission of static images and text between two locations.

Many countries are using this technology for conducting distance education due to its high speed. In India, many companies are also using it for their internal training programmes.

Uses of Video Conferencing

Following are the uses of video conferencing

(i) **Helps in distance learning** It plays a very important role in modern field of education and training.

(ii) **Develops relationship** Video conferencing is a substitute for face-to-face communication which develops personal and business relationship.

(iii) **E-meeting** Now-a-days, big organisations or companies conduct meeting through video conferencing because it saves time and money.

(iv) **E-recruitment** Video conferencing plays a very important role in e-recruitment process.

(v) **Enhances business opportunities** It enhances the business opportunities through effective customer services. It provides competitive advantages.

(vi) **Increases productivity and efficiency** Video conferencing increases the efficiency and productivity of organisation due to the following reasons.

These are
   (a) Reduced unproductive travel time
   (b) Larger participation
   (c) Immediate information exchange
   (d) Faster response and quicker decisions

PYQs Previous Years Questions

1 Mark Questions

1. A report may have an attachment containing statistical data, tables, graphs, etc. What is this attachent know as? **ISC 2023**

Ans This attachment is known as appendixes.

2. …… should be enclosed alongwith job application. **ISC Sem II 2022**

Ans Bio-data

2 Marks Questions

1. List any two situations where a complain letter may be written by the buyer. **ISC Sem II Sepecimen 2022**

Ans A complaint letter may be written by the buyer when

(i) defective or wrong goods have been sent to the him/her.

(ii) there is delay in the execution of an order.

Concept Enhancer A complaint letter is written by a customer commenting on poor service/product. It usually outlines the fault(s) with the service and highlights customer dissatisfaction with the particular service/product.

2. What is a quotation letter? **ISC 2020**

Or

What is a letter of quotation? **ISC 2014**

Ans A letter of quotation is a formal statement of promise that is submitted usually in response to a request for quotation by potential buyer to supply the goods or services required by a buyer at specified prices and within a specified period.

3. Briefly explain what is meant by letter of enquiry? Which letter is written in response to it? **ISC 2018**

Or What is letter of enquiry? Give the name of the letter that is received in its response. **ISC 2011**

Or What is letter of enquiry? **ISC 2007**

Ans An enquiry letter is written by a potential customer, on the look out for a product or with a desire to avail the service offered by a seller or an organisation.

An enquiry letter is neither a contract nor does it entail any contractual obligation between the two. It is actually, a preliminary exercise that may lead to a contract.

Quotation is received in its response.

4. What are routine reports? Give any two examples of the same. **ISC 2017**

Ans Routine reports are prepared at regular intervals in the routine course of business. Such reports contain factual information without any suggestion. Such reports provide a regular means of communication and have a standard layout.

Two examples of routine reports are as follows

(i) Production reports (ii) Sales reports

5. What is the role of an appendix in a report? **ISC 2016, 2005**

Or Give two advantages of having an appendix in a report.

KEY IDEA
Appendix is a section at the end of report which include extra information that doesn't fit into the main text.

Ans Advantages/Role of an 'Appendix' in a report are as follows

(i) It contains the information that is not essential to explain the findings, but that supports the analysis.

(ii) It includes figures/tables/chart/graphs/ questionnaires, which are directly related to the research problem or purpose.

6. Differentiate between a statutory report and a non-statutory report. **ISC 2015**

Ans Difference between statutory report and non-statutory report are

Basis	Statutory report	Non-statutory report
Meaning	These are meant to be made under the law which are mandatory to publish.	These reports are usually made by a professional governing body for the purpose of company's internal affairs.
Preparation	Statutory reports are prepared and submitted in the prescribed form.	Non-statutory report is prepared and submitted to the management to facilitate planning and controlling.

7. Explain informational report. **ISC 2014**

Ans An informational report is a factual text that provides a summary analysing, interpreting and making recommendations. Examples of such reports are sales reports and progress reports.

8. Define report. *ISC 2013*

Ans According to **J. Stanley Jones**, "A report is a special frorm of narrative which aims chiefly at conveying information, based upon facts."

9. What is meant by cross reference in a report? State its importance in a good report. *ISC 2012*

Ans It is an instance within a document which refers to related information elsewhere in the same document. Cross reference is important because they form a network structure of relations existing between different parts of data internally as well as externally.

10. List the steps involved in report writing. *ISC 2010*

Ans Steps involved in reporting are collection of facts, plan the report, organise the information, write the report and review it.

11. Explain clarity in a good business letter. *ISC 2007*

Ans Clarity means arranging the words and sentences in such a manner, so as to convey the exact meaning and nothing else. You should therefore, be choosy in words and avoid all ambiguity.

12. What is a complaint letter? *ISC 2005*

Ans A complaint letter is a letter written by a customer of a service/product commenting on poor service/product. It usually outlines the fault(s) with the service and highlights customer dissatisfaction with the particular service/product.

4 Marks Questions

1. Name and explain any two types of reports. *ISC Specimen 2023*

Ans Two types of reports are

(i) **Statutory reports** The reports which are prepared according to the form and procedure laid down by law, for example, Companies Act are called statutory report. Generally, statutory report is drafted by the directors of the company (Private Limited) to forward to shareholders atleast 21 days before the date of annual general meeting.

Examples of statutory report are as follows

(a) Director's report to the annual general meeting
(b) Annual return
(c) Auditor's report

(ii) **Non-statutory reports** Business reports which are drafted to help the management in formulating policies and in taking important decisions in company are known as 'non-statutory reports.' These reports do not require any legal compliance.

Generally, non-statutory reports are prepared for the following purposes

(a) Effective functioning of company
(b) Expansion of business
(c) Starting a new venture
(d) Entering into joint venture
(e) Developing new technology

2. List any two uses of e-mail. *ISC Sem II 2022*

Or Briefly explain any four advantages of e-mail. *ISC 2017*

Ans Following are the advantages of an e-mail

(i) **Easy to use** It is very easy to send and receive e-mails.

(ii) **Global search** E-mails can be sent to anyone-anywhere in the world, provided he/she has an e-mail id.

(iii) **Easy reference** E-mails sent and received are stored in outbox and inbox respectively. These can be viewed for reference as and when needed.

(iv) **Speed** E-mail is the fastest form of communication. It is delivered within seconds.

3. State any two differences between *ISC 2020*

(i) Informative report and Interpretative report
(ii) Routine report and Special report

Ans (i)

Basis	Informational reports	Interpretative reports
Purpose	To provide the explanation about any issue or problem.	To provide the solution or recommendation about any problem or issue.
Nature	Generally such reports are of routine nature.	Generally, such reports are special reports.

(ii)

Basis	Routine reports	Special reports
Purpose	To provide routine information to users in detail or in summary.	To provide solution to the specific problem.
Scientific report	These are not scientific reports because they are not based on cause and effect relationship.	These are scientific reports because these are based on cause and effect relationship.

4. Explain the process of report writing. *ISC 2018*

Ans The following are the sequential steps in report writting process

(i) **The subject-matter should be analysed logically** It is the first step in report writting. Under this step, problem is analysed in a scientific and logical manner.

(ii) **The final outcome is assessed** The final outcome of problem is assessed so that an appropriate solution may be drawn for the problem.

(iii) **A rough draft for the final outcome is prepared** It provides a rough idea to the report writer which may be changed as per the requirement of the report.

(iv) **Re-writting and polishing the rough draft** If rough draft of report does not disclose some important facts or information, there may be requirement of re-writing of facts and polishing the information in a systematic manner.

(v) **Final bibliography is prepared** Finally the bibliography is prepared. A bibliography is a list of books, articles, speeches, websites, laws etc which are used in researching the topic and writing a report. It validates the report.

(vi) **Writing the final draft** It is the last step of report writing. Now report is presented to its readers. (i.e. management, government, general public and shareholders, etc)

Value Points

For getting maximum marks, following value points can be included in the answer
- Process/Steps should be written sequence-wise
- For each step in description, write brief sentence of each major part i.e. heading

5. Explain any four functions of a business letter. *ISC 2016*

Or Explain the functions of business letter. *ISC 2014*

Ans Functions of business letter are as follows

(i) **Promotional functions** Business organisations have to grow and enlarge, improving the quality of their products, by producing new products and providing better services. The customers have to be kept informed through letters regarding these developments.

(ii) **Informational functions** Business letters provide valuable data about earlier policies, transactions and the activities that are important for the organisation.

Functions of Business Letter
- Promotional functions
- Informational functions
- Legal functions
- Goodwill functions

(iii) **Legal functions** Business letters can provide evidence in legal disputes, if any, that occur in a transaction. They are useful as legal documents in quotations and offers.

(iv) **Goodwill functions** Business letters promote goodwill among parties transacting business. They build a good rapport between parties in a business transaction.

6. Briefly explain any three essentials of a good report. *ISC 2016*

Ans The three essentials of a good report are

(i) **Accurate** A good report should be accurate. It should be to the point and also cover relevant facts and figures. The information contained must be accurate and unbiased to facilitate correct decisions.

(ii) **Simplicity** A good report should be written in a simple and lucid language which is easy to understand.

Use of words with double meaning or ambigous meaning should be avoided. It should be such that offers easy understandability to its readers.

(iii) **Complete** A good report should be complete in all aspects and should contain all the necessary information needed.

It should start with specifying the purpose of writing such a report, the facts unhearthed and the conclusions drawn and the recommendations made.

7. Describe four essential qualities of a good reporter. *ISC 2006*

Ans Qualities of a good reporter are as follows

(i) **Qualification** A reporter must be qualified because drafting of report is a complex and specialised task.

(ii) **Experience and efficiency** A person who is experienced must be efficient also. A reporter endowed with two such qualities can perform his reporting with quality and standard.

(iii) **Knowledge of subject-matter and time** A reporter must know details regarding the subject-matter to be addressed and he must report on that topic in due time, otherwise, the objective of a report would go in vain.

So, knowledge and timeliness are also essential qualities of a good reporter.

(iv) **Faithfulness and neutrality** Report must be free from biased information. The information provided in the report must be reliable and valid. False, invalid and biased information are supposed to hamper the decision and would result in wrong decision.

8. What are the essentials of a good business letter? *ISC 2006*

Ans Essentials of good business letter are as follows

(i) **Clarity of thought** Arrange the words and sentences in such a manner, as to convey the exact meaning and nothing else. You should therefore, be choosy in words and avoid all ambiguity.

(ii) **Forcefulness** Forcefulness is important. In ordinary routine correspondence, it is not necessary, but in a business letter, it makes a difference between securing a client and losing him.
A forceful and convincing statement makes an appeal to the emotions of the reader who makes more than a usual attempt to develop understanding with the correspondent.

Essentials of Good Business Letter
- Clarity of thought
- Forcefulness
- Relevant information
- Brevity
- Language

(iii) **Relevant information** The letter should provide the relevant details forming part of the message. Facts, figures, illustrations and other such information, which are accurate and reliable, as well as relevant to the context of the communication, should be incorporated in the letter.

(iv) **Brevity** Any good communication, oral or written, should necessarily incorporate this essential feature. Brevity is a very important attribute for any business letter. For everyone connected with business, time is of essence.
The time that one can allot for reading business letters is certainly limited. Thus, it states that message should be short but clear and understandable to the reader in short time.

(v) **Language** It is an extremely important facet of business communication. First and foremost, it is necessary to ensure that the language used is appropriate, i.e. the language with which the reader is at ease.
Apart from English and Hindi, various regional languages are in common use in businesses in different parts of the country. Public sector organisations such as banks follow the three languages formula.

6/8 Marks Questions

1. You are employed as the Head of the Department of Mathematics in a school. You have decided to quit the job to pursue higher studies. Draft a resignation letter addressed to the principal of the school. *ISC 2023*

Ans Ramcharan Singh
15/302, Lajpat Marg
Delhi-502001
15th March, 2023
K.P. Vyas
Principal
Ryan International School
Laxmi, Nagar,
Delhi-502019
Subject Resigning from post of HoD of Mathematics
Dear Sir,
Kindly accept this as a formal resignation letter as I am resigning from the post of Head of the Department of Mathematics at Ryan International school, effective from 1st May, 2023.
After a brief consideration, I have decided to pursue my higher studies I truly enjoyed the eight years, spent in this school and it has been a pleasure working under your guidance. My students have given me a memorable experience and the administration has been supportive throughout my tenure.
Sincerely,
Ram Charan Singh

Common Mistake Generally students do number of mistakes while drafting an application like they forget to write subject but it should be written in formal letter, students write yours faithfully/obediently as complimentary close but it has to be 'yours sincerely/truly'.

2. Draft an interview-letter for the post of Operations Manager in an MNC. *ISC Specimen 2023*

Ans XYZ Ltd.
100, Yamuna Vihar
New Delhi-110001
25th March, 2023
Manoj Sharma
15, Daryaganj
New Delhi-110007
Subject Call for Interview
Dear Sir,
Thank you for your application dated 10th March, 2023, for the post of Operation Manager in our company. I appreciate your interest in joining our company.
Your are requested to come over to our office for interview with me at 10:00 am, on March 28th, 2023 with your original testimonial and certificates.
Yours truly
XYZ Ltd.
B.K. Agarwal
HR Manager

3. Draft an application letter for the post of a sales executive in a reputed Multinational Company, in response to an advertisement published in the newspaper. *ISC 2020*

Ans 80, Raja Ram Marg

New Delhi

15th December, 2021

The Personnel Manager,

Line Ltd.

Gwalior

Subject Application for the post of sales executive

Dear Sir

This is with reference to your advertisement in 'Times of India' dated 4th June, 2021. I request you to consider my qualifications and experience for the post of a 'Sales executive'.

Particulars of My Qualifications and Personal Details are

Name	Mr. Rohan Mehra
Address	Raja Ram Marg, New Delhi
Age	30 Years
Education	B.Com UoR 78%
	M.Com UoR 70%
	MBA (Marketing) DU 82%

Work experience –Worked as a sales executive with JIO Ltd. Lucknow for 5 Years.

Language–Hindi, English, German

I hope to receive a positive response from your company.

Yours truly

Mr. Rohan Mehra

Encls : Two

4th June, 2021

4. Briefly explain any four types of reports. *ISC 2019*

Ans Types of reports are

(i) **Routine reports** These reports are prepared at regular intervals in routine course of business. These reports contain factual information without any suggestion. Routine reports are usually prepared on a prescribed performa. e.g. inspection reports, sales reports.

(ii) **Informational reports** These reports presents data collected or facts observed in an organised form without any recommendation or analysis. These are meant to educate readers. e.g. monthly and annual report of company prepared by company secretary.

(iii) **Private reports** These reports are prepared for a specific purpose and not shared publically. These are prepared by selected individuals. e.g. HR manager may prepare private report about conduct of employees.

(iv) **Statutory reports** These reports are prepared according to form and procedure laid down by law. These are drafted by directors in a private limited company to forward to shareholders atleast 21 days before date of annual general meeting. e.g. Director's report to annual general meeting, annual return, auditor's report.

Types of Reports

- Routine reports
- Informational reports
- Private reports
- Statutory reports

5. Draft a letter of appointment for a school teacher, offering him/her a job of a History teacher in a secondary school. *ISC 2019*

Or Draft a letter of appointment for a school teacher, offering her a job of an English teacher in a secondary school. *ISC 2016*

Or Draft a letter of appointment for a school teacher offering her the job of an English teacher in a primary school. *ISC 2011*

Ans Arya School,

30-A-Nagla Road

Manipur

15th July, 2014

Ref Number CB/2/2012

Mr A Gupta

40, Durga Nagar

Delhi

Dear Sir/Ma'am,

With reference to your application for the post of an History/English teacher and the subsequent interview, I am glad to inform you that you have been selected. Your basic salary will be ₹10,000/- in the scale of ₹ 5,500 and DA, HRA and CCA as per the UGC norms.

The appointment is on probation period for one year and will be confirmed after satisfactory appraisal. Please inform your acceptance immediately and report to the Principal of our school on 25th July, 2016 at 10:00 am.

Yours truly

Madhav Saran

Headmaster

6. In response to an advertisement in the newspaper, draft an application letter for the post of an accountant in a medium sized organisation.

ISC Specimen 2019

Ans 100, Lajpat Nagar
New Delhi-500001
20th March, 2023
The Personnel Manager
XYZ Pvt. Ltd.
New Delhi

Subject Application for the post of Accountant

Dear Sir,

This is with reference to your advertisement in 'Times of India' dated March 20, 2023. I request you to consider my qualifications and experience for the post of an 'Accountant'.

Particulars of my qualifications and personal detail are

Name	Rajesh Sharma
Address	Lajpat Nagar, New Delhi
Age	30 Years
Education	B.Com UoR 78% M.Com Uor 72%
Work experience	Worked as an accountant with ABC Pvt. Ltd. for 3 years
Language known	Hindi, English

I hope to receive a postive response from your company.

Your truly
Rajesh Sharma
Ends: Two
20th March, 2023

7. Draft an application letter for the post of an Assitant Manager (Sales) at a reputed retail firm in response to a newspaper advertisement. An appropriate bio-data of the applicant should be prepared and enclosed with the application.

ISC 2018

Ans 2, Court Road
Moradabad-244001
12th August, 20XX
The Personnel Manager
Alpha Tech (Private) Limited
7, Mall Road
Moradabad-244004

Subject Application for the Post of Assistant Manager (Sales)

Respected Sir,

In response to your advertisement in 'The Indian Express', I wish to be considered for the post of Assistant Manager. I feel my qualifications and experiences are suitable for the post mentioned above. I am enclosing my bio-data, a testimonial and attested copies of my certificates.

I hope to receive a positive response from your company.

Yours truly
Niraj Bhardwaj

Enclosed : Bio-data, testimonial, attested copies of certificates

Bio-data

Name	Niraj Bhardwaj
Father's Name	Nishant Bhardwaj
Address	2, Court Road, Moradabad-244001
Contact Telephone no.	0591-246839X
E-mail	nirajb1987@gmail.com
Date of Birth	2nd October, 1987
Health Status	Medically fit
Marital Status	Unmarried

Educational Qualifications

Name of Exam	College/Board/ University	Year	Percentage
High School	CBSE	2004	75%
SSCE	CBSE	2006	72%
BA (Honours)	DCP College, Delhi	2009	62%
MBA (Marketing)	College of Business Management, Kolkata	2011	68%

Work Experience	Working as Senior Sales Executive with Tri-Tech since July, 2011
Languages Known	English, Hindi, French
Strengths	Good time management
References	(i) Dr S Kumar (998764321X) HOD Economics DCP College, New Delhi (ii) Mr BS Yadav (964389273X) General Manager Rico Private Limited, Moradabad
Testimonial from	Mr Karim Khan, Director, College of Business Management, Kolkata

Common Mistake When question asks to enclose a bio-data, then generally students include it in the application letter, but it should be given as a covering letter, i.e, at last.

8. What are reports? Explain cross-referencing and appendix with regard to reports. ***ISC 2017***

Ans **Reports** Reports are written for a clear purpose and to a particular audience. Specific information and evidence are presented, analysed and applied to a particular problem or issue. The information is presented in a clearly structured format, making use of sections and headings, so that the information is easy to locate and follow.

Cross referencing A good report must contain cross references. Cross referencing means that in a report a mention is made about a point which is dealt with at another part of a report. Cross referencing is used in a report as it helps to save time and space and also helps the users of the report.

For example, in the summary of the report, against every point, the page number in which that point has been explained in detail, should be mentioned.

Appendix Appendix is added to a report and generally contains statistical data related to the facts reported, which are presented through tables and graphs. Appendix is added to explain the contents of the report and to validate the conclusion of the report.

9. As the manager of a company, write a letter of complaint to XYZ Furniture Ltd for having delivered some chairs in a broken condition and asking them for replacement of the broken chairs. ***ISC 2016***

Ans Telephone: 0ll-4426×× ...... Company

6-A Industrial Area

Telegram:...... Okhla, Delhi

Reference No:213/2016 9th August, 2016

XYZ Furniture Ltd.

29, Laxmi Nagar, Delhi

Subject Complaint about broken chairs

Dear Sir,

On 13th July, 2016 we have placed an order of 25 chairs of Finex Company, model number F-26. The order number was A-125. We received the chairs on 8th August, 2016 through Batra Transport Company. On inspection, we found that 7 chairs are broken.

The chairs were ordered for our new showroom which is due for opening on 20th August, 2016.

So, please replace the defective chairs at the earliest and not later than 16th August, 2016.

Thanking You,

Manager

------------- Company.

10. Draft an application in response to an advertisement for the post of a Physics teacher for teaching classes XI and XII. An appropriate bio-data of the applicant should be prepared and enclosed with the application. ***ISC 2015***

Ans Goyal Bhawan

D2/16 Sector 18

Faridabad

20th February, 2015

To

The Principal

Faridabad Public School

Sector 15-A, Faridabad

Subject Application for the post of Physics teacher.

Sir,

I am very glad to state that I possess the required qualification and experience for the post of Physics PGT, as per your advertisement in the Hindustan Times of 12th February, 2015.

I did my masters in Science (Physics) from Delhi University in 1999. I have been teaching classes XI and XII, and taking competitive classes for the last 15 years. I have a reputed and appreciable job background and assure you that if given a chance, I would discharge my duties with utmost dedication and sincerity. My bio-data and other necessary details are attached herewith.

Looking forward and waiting for a positive reply soon.

Yours truly

Vinesh Gupta

Encls : One

Bio-data

Name of the candidate	Vinesh Gupta
Name of the post applied	Postgraduate Physics teacher
Job related skills/software	Taking XI and XII C.B.S.E. classes and competitive classes, Evaluate and grade students' class work, laboratory work, assignments, and papers, Prepare and deliver lectures to undergraduate and/or graduate students on topics such as quantum mechanics, particle Physics and optics.
Category	Teaching lecturer faculty
Sub category	Teacher
Years of experience	18 years
State	Uttar Pradesh
Gender	Female

Salary expected per month (₹)	Negotiable
Highest qualification attained	M.Sc./MSc : Master of Science
Major/Specialisation	Physics
Email Id	[Private]

11. A consignment of 1000 bed sheets received by your organisation has the following defects

(i) 200 bed sheets are of the colour not ordered.

(ii) 60 bed sheets have defective weaving.

In the light of these defects, write a letter of complaint to the supplier, M/s ABC Ltd. *ISC 2013*

Ans M/s ABC Ltd 12, New Arya Complex

Telephone : 2760672 Agra

Ref Number : 150/2500 23rd June, 2014

Parvati Handlooms Ltd

120, Tilak Nagar

Delhi

Subject Supply of defective bed sheets Vide Order Number 150/2500

Dear Sir,

On 18th June, we placed our order number 25 with you for 1000 bed sheets. On 22nd June, we received the consignment. On opening it, we found that 60 bed sheets had defective weaving and 200 bed sheets were of the colour for which order was not placed.

All the bed sheets ordered are required by our customers.

Please replace the defective goods immediately, so that we could receive them before 30th of June, 2014.

Yours truly

XYZ

Manager

12. Draft a letter of order with the following details

(i) 100 units of 60 watts tubelights @ ₹ 40 per unit.

(ii) 150 units of 100 watts bulbs @ ₹ 15 per unit.

(iii) 250 units of 40 watts CFL bulbs @ ₹ 70 per unit. *ISC 2012*

Ans Rajaram & Sons

Lalganj, Miraganj Road, Amritsar

Telephone........ Fax...

6th August, 2010

To,

XYZ Ltd

12, Arya Nagar

Amritsar (Punjab)

Dear Sir,

We thank you for your quotation for tubelights dated 2nd August, 2010. The prices are satisfactory, thus we are pleased to place a order with you for the following items at the prices and terms quoted.

Description	Quantity	Unit Price	Total
Tubelights of 60 Watts	100	40	4,000
100 Watts Bulbs	150	15	2,250
40 Watts CFL Bulbs	250	70	17,500
			₹ 23,750

Terms of payment, $2\frac{1}{2}$% one month, 5% 7 days.

Signed ....

Purchasing Officer

XYZ Ltd

13. Explain the following with the help of examples.

(i) Routine and special reports *ISC 2011*

(ii) Informational and interpretative reports

Ans (i) **Routine reports** These reports are prepared at regular intervals in the routine course of business. Such reports contain factual information without any suggestion. Such reports provide a regular means of communication. Such reports have a standard layout.

Special reports These reports are specially prepared and presented to cover significant events. These are prepared after through investigation. Such reports are prepared to facilitate managerial decision on important matters, e.g. performance appraisal report.

(ii) **Informational report** An informational report presents the data collected or facts observed in an organised form. It does not contain recommendations. It describes the situation, as it is and not as it should be, e.g. Marketing research report.

Interpretative report Such a report not only contains facts but also conclusions, e.g. audit report.

14. On behalf of a multinational corporation, draft an interview letter for the post of management trainee. *ISC 2010, 2008*

Ans XYZ Ltd

100, Yamuna Bank

New Delhi-110001

7th July, 2014

Mrs Aarti Sharma

2, Daryaganj

Delhi-110007

Subject Call for interview.

Dear Madam,

Thank you for your application dated the 1st July, 2014, for the post of a management trainee in our company. I appreciate your interest in joining our company.

You are requested to come over to our office for interview with me at 10:00 a.m, on 10th July, 2014 with your original testimonials and certificates.

Yours truly

XYZ Ltd

RK Verma

Manager

15. Draft an application in response to an advertisement inviting applications for the post of an assistant manager in a multinational company. Prepare and enclose a bio-data for the same. *ISC 2009*

Ans 6, Lajpat Nagar

Delhi

20th January, 20xx

The Personnel Manager,

Saranath Ltd

Lucknow

Subject Application for the post of assistant manager

Dear Sir,

This is with reference to your advertisement in 'The Times of India' dated 7th July, 2014. I request you to consider my qualifications and experience for the post of an 'Assistant Manager'.

I am enclosing my bio-data and attested copies of my certificates.

I hope to receive a positive response from your company.

Yours truly

Ms Akansha Sharma

Encls : Bio, data, attested copies of certificates

7th July, 2014

Bio-Data

Name : Ms Akansha Sharma

Address : Daryaganj, Delhi

Age : 30 years

Marital status : Married

Education : Name of the examination passed and ranks

- ICSE with 82%
- B.Com—Delhi University with first rank in the university in year 2002.
- M.Com—Delhi University with third rank in the university in year 2006.
- MBA—IGNOU with first division in finance management.

Extra-curricular : Member of the College Planning Forum

- Worked as an assistant in a firm of Auditors, M/S Mehra and Co, Dehradun.

Language : Hindi, English, French

16. Explain any three types of reports used in commercial organisation. *ISC 2008*

Ans Three types of reports used in a commercial organisation are as follows

(i) **Routine report** Refer to Q. No 13 (i) on page 148.

(ii) **Special report** Refer to Q. No 13 (i) on page 148.

(iii) **Private report** These reports are confidential in nature and is meant for a particular individual. Its contents are not disclosed or made public.

17. Describe four types of letters used for quick communication. *ISC 2006*

Ans Four types of letter used for quick communication are as follows

(i) **Offer letter** If a candidate successfully clears all rounds of interviews and satisfies the criteria determined for a potential candidate, then he is regarded as a suitable candidate for the company. Now, as he has cleared all the necessary rounds and proved his suitability, the company officially provides him a letter and this letter is known as the offer letter.

Types of Letters
- Offer letter
- Enquiry letter
- Complaint letter
- Quotation letter

(ii) **Enquiry letter** An enquiry letter is written by a potential customer, on the look out for a product or with a desire to avail the service offered by a seller or an organisation. An enquiry letter is neither a contract, nor does it entail any contractual obligation between the two. It is actually a preliminary exercise that may lead to contract.

(iii) **Complaint letter** A complaint letter is a letter written by a customer of a service/product commenting on poor service/product. It usually outlines the fault (s) with the service and highlights customer dissatisfaction with the particular service/product.

(iv) **Quotation letter** A letter of quotation is a formal statement of promise that is submitted usually in response to a request for quotation by potential buyer to supply the goods or service required by a buyer at specified price and within a specified period.

Case Based Question

Case 1

Mulberry Bags, Ltd. is a leading manufacture of designer handbags, and there is a continuous demand for their products. Bags and More, a retail frim is interested in buying Mulberry Bags Ltd. They send any enquiry letter to mulberry Bag Ltd. for the same. In due course, Bags and more receive its consignment from Mulberry Bags Ltd. They realise that the order was for 100 black tote bags and 200 blue hobo bags. However, they have received 100 blue tote bags and 150 black hobo bags.

Name and explain in brief the two letters that were exchanged between the two companies after the enquiry letter was sent and before the consignment was received.

ISC Sem II Specimen 2022

Ans (i) The first after the enquiry letter was sent is quotation letter.

A letter of quotation is a formal statement of promise that is submitted usually in response to a request for quotation by potential buyer to supply the goods or services required by a buyer, at specified prices and within a specified period.

(ii) After quotation letter, order letter was sent to Mulberry Bags Ltd.

It is a confirmed request, by one party to another to buy, sell, deliver or receive goods or services under specified terms and conditions. When accepted by the receiving party, an order becomes a legally binding contract. The letter which is written by a potential buyer to the seller requesting him to deliver goods is known as order letter or purchase order.

CHAPTER TEST

01 Mark Questions

1. Which letter is given by an employee if he/she leaves the job?

2. Name the report which is prepared according to the form and procedure laid down by law.

3. Name the means of audio-visual communication between two or more people residing in different locations.

4. …… is the exchange of information in written format for the purpose of business activities.

5. …… letter of application is sent in response to an announced job opening.

6. The annual report prepared by the company secretary is

(a) public report (b) private report
(c) informational report (d) routine report

7. The main part of a letter is

(a) name (b) subject
(c) body (d) signature

8. It is a confirmed request by one party to another to buy, sell, deliver or receive goods or services.

What is that letter?

(a) Quotation letter (b) Order letter
(c) Complaint letter (d) Confirmation letter

9. Statutory reports are optional. State true or false.

10. E-mail is considered as the fastest mode of communication. State true or false.

02 Marks Questions

11. What is business correspondence?

12. In which form, report can be presented?

13. What are the uses of video conferencing?

14. Differentiate between private report and public report.

15. Explain the meaning of E-mail.

04 Marks Questions

16. Explain the format of report writing in business.

17. What are the purposes of business correspondence?

18. Differentiate between solicited letter of application and unsolicited letter of application for job.

06/08 Marks Questions

19. You are interesting in doing a short-term course in computer graphics during your holidays. Write a letter to the director, easy computers, enquiring about their short term courses and asking for all the necessary details. You are Naresh/Nandini.

20. You are Prem/Parul of 16, TT Nagar Bhopal. You would like to apply for the post manager (finance) in a reputed firm in Mumbai. Write a letter to the Public Relations Officer, Chantac Enterprises, Mumbai, applying for the job. Write the letter giving your Bio-data.

Answers

1. Resignation letter
2. Statutory report
3. Video conferencing
4. Business correspondence
5. Solicited
6. (c) informational report
7. (c) body
8. (b) Order letter
9. False
10. True

13

Business Size and Finance

TREND ANALYSIS 5 YEARS

	Types of Questions	Average No. of Questions Across all Sets				
		2023	2020	2019	2018	2017
01 Various Business Entities	1 Mark	—	—	—	—	—
	2 Marks	—	1	—	—	—
	4 Marks	1	—	—	—	—
	6 Marks	—	—	—	—	—
	8 Marks	—	—	—	—	—
02 Sources of Business Finance	1 Mark	—	—	—	—	—
	2 Marks	—	—	—	—	—
	4 Marks	—	1	—	—	—
	6 Marks	—	—	—	—	—
	8 Marks	1	—	1	—	—

TOPIC 1

Various Business Entities

The most important decision that a businessman has to take while starting a new venture is the form and size of business organisation that he should choose. For deciding the form of business organisation, the merits and demerits of each type of organisation should be carefully analysed and the most appropriate form of business should be chosen.

Various forms of business entities/organisations are sole proprietorship, partnership, private limited company and public limited company.

Sole Proprietorship

A business which is owned, managed and controlled by a single individual, who is the recipient of all profits and bearer of all risks, is known as 'sole proprietorship'.

The term 'sole proprietorship' defines itself evidently, as sole means only and proprietor refers to owner. Thus, a sole proprietor is one and only owner of this type of business organisation. It is a popular form of business organisation.

According to **J.L. Hansen**, "Sole trade is a type of business unit where a person is solely responsible for providing the capital, for bearing the risk of the enterprise and for the management of business."

According to **L.H. Haney**, "The individual proprietorship is the form of business organisation at the head of which stands an individual as one who is responsible, who directs its operations and who alone runs the risk of failure."

Partnership

A partnership is a form of organisation in which two or more persons agree to cooperate to advance their mutual interests in a business venture. This form of organisation is an improvement over sole proprietorship as it ensures greater capital investment, varied professional and managerial skills and sharing of risks.

According to **L.H. Haney**, "Partnership is the relation between persons competent to make contracts who have agreed to carry on a lawful business in common with a view to private gain."

According to **The Indian Partnership Act, 1932** (Section 4), "Partnership is the relation between persons who have agreed to share the profits of a business carried on by all or any of them acting for all."

Distinction between Sole Proprietorship and Partnership

Basis	Sole proprietorship	Partnership
Number of members	In a sole proprietorship, there is only one member/owner.	In a partnership, there can be minimum two members and maximum fifty members.
Agreement	In a sole proprietorship, there is no agreement as there is only one member.	A partnership is based on agreement between/ among members.
Sharing of profits	A sole proprietor is the recipient of all the profits.	Partners have to share profit amongst them in an agreed ratio.
Decision-making	In sole proprietorship, the decision-making power rests with the sole proprietor.	In partnership, all the partners can participate in decision-making.

Private Limited Company

According to **the Companies (Amendment) Act, 2013,** a private company means a company which (features)

(i) restricts the right of its members to transfer shares.
(ii) has minimum two members and maximum two hundred members, excluding present and past employees. A One Person Company (OPC) can be formed with only one member.
(iii) does not invite public to subscribe to its share capital.
(iv) have a minimum paid-up capital as may be prescribed.*

It is necessary for a private company to use the words 'private limited' after its name.

Note As per Section 2 (62) of the Companies Act, 2013, One Person Company (OPC) means a company which has only one person as its member. It is a special form of private company. Only Indian citizen can incorporate an OPC. If the paid-up share capital of OPC exceed ₹ 50 lakh or if its annual turnover exceeds ₹ 2 crore, then it will seize to be an OPC.

Public Limited Company

According to **the Companies (Amendment) Act, 2013**, a public company means a company which (features)

(i) has a minimum of seven members and there is no limit on the maximum number of members.
(ii) does not restrict the right of its members to transfer its shares.
(iii) is not prohibited from inviting the general public to subscribe to its shares, debentures or public deposits.
(iv) has a minimum paid-up capital as may be prescribed.*

A private company which is subsidiary of a public company is also treated as a public company.

Note *The Companies Act, 2013 has not yet prescribed minimum capital with respect to private and public

Distinction between Public and Private Limited Company

Basis	Public company	Private company
Minimum number of members	Seven	Two
Maximum number of members	No limit	Two hundred (excluding past and present employees)
Minimum number of directors	Three	Two
Public invitation of capital	It is free to invite the public to buy its shares and debentures.	It cannot invite the public to buy its shares and debentures.
Commencement of business	It cannot commence business after incorporation unless certificate of commencement of business is obtained.	It can commence business immediately after incorporation.
Transfer of shares	No restriction	Restriction on transfer

PYQs Previous Years' Questions

1 Mark Questions

1. A public limited company should have a minimum number of two members. State true or false. **ISC Specimen 2023**

Ans False. As per Companies Act, a public company should have a minimum seven members.

2. What is the minimum and maximum number of partners in a partnership firm? **ISC Sem II 2022**

Ans Minimum number of partners – 2

Maximum number of partners – 50

3. As per the Companies Act, what is the minimum and maximum number of members in a public limited company? **ISC Sem II Specimen 2022**

Ans As per Companies Act, there should be a minimum of seven members in a public limited company and there is no limit on the maximum number of members.

2 Marks Questions

1. State any two differences between private limited company and public limited company. **ISC Sem II 2022**

Ans Differences between private and public companies are

Basis	Private company	Public company
Minimum number of members	Two	Seven
Maximum number of members	Two hundred (excluding past and present employees)	No limit

2. Define sole proprietorship. **ISC Sem II Specimen 2022**

Ans According to **J. L. Hansen,** "Sole trade is a type of business unit where a person is solely responsible for providing the capital, for bearing the risk of the enterprise and for the management of business."

3. Define partnership. **ISC 2020**

Ans According to the Indian Partnership Act, 1932, "Partnership is the relation between persons who have agreed to share the profits of a business carried on by all or any of them acting for all."

4 Marks Question

1. Define the following business entities
   (i) Sole proprietorship
   (ii) Partnership **ISC 2023**

Ans (i) Refer to Q. No. 2 (2 Marks) on Page 154.

(ii) **Partnership** According to Section 4 of **The Indian Partnership Act, 1932,** "Partnership is the relation between persons who have agreed to share the profits of a business carried on by all or any of them acting for all."

Additional Questions

2/4 Marks Questions

1. Write the factors that determine the choice of formation of an organisation.

Ans It is important to choose an appropriate form of organisation as each form has certain advantages as well as limitations. Depending upon the convenience and resources available, an entrepreneur has to choose the right form.

The important factors determining the choice of organisation are cost and ease in setting up the organisation, liability, continuity, capital, management ability, nature of business and degree of control.

2. Give two examples each of private company and public company.

Ans Examples of **Private company** Aamir Khan Productions Private Limited, 3C Consultant Private Limited, etc.

Examples of **Public company** Dunlop India Limited, Indian Oil Corporation Ltd.

3. State any four important privileges available to a private company.

Ans The important privileges available to a private limited company are as follows

(i) The minimum number of members required to form a private company is only two, while atleast seven members are needed to form a public company.

(ii) A private company does not need to issue a prospectus.

(iii) Allotment of shares can be done without receiving the minimum subscription.

(iv) A private company can start business as soon as it receives the certificate of incorporation and does not have to wait for the receipt of certificate of commencement of business.

4. Give the differences between sole proprietorship and partnership.

Ans Differences between sole proprietorship and partnership are

Basis	Sole proprietorship	Partnership
Number of members	In a sole proprietorship, there is only one member/owner.	In a partnership, there can be minimum two members and maximum fifty members.
Agreement	In a sole proprietorship, there is no agreement as there is only one member.	A partnership is based on agreement between/ among members.
Sharing of profits	A sole proprietor is the recipient of all the profits.	Partners have to share profit amongst them in an agreed ratio.
Decision-making	In sole proprietorship, the decision-making power rests with the sole proprietor.	In partnership, all the partners can participate in decision-making.

5. Explain briefly the features of sole proprietorship.

Ans Following are the features of sole proprietorship (any four)

(i) **Formation and closure** Hardly any legal formality is required to start a sole proprietary business. Closure of the business can also be done easily.

(ii) **Unlimited liability** In case of losses and repayment of debt, personal property of the owner can also be used if the assets of firm are insufficient.

(iii) **Sole risk bearer and profit recipient** In sole proprietorship firm, whole risk is borne by a single individual and he is the sole receiver of profits.

(iv) **Control** The sole proprietorship firm is owned, managed and controlled by a single individual. All the decisions are taken by him solely.

(v) **No separate entity** A sole proprietorship firm has no legal identity apart from that of its owner.

Features of Sole Proprietorship
- Formation and closure
- Unlimited liability
- Sole risk bearer and profit recipient
- Control
- No separate entity

6. Explain the features of partnership.

Ans Features of partnership are as follows (any four)

(i) **Formation** As per Indian Partnership Act, 1932, a partnership firm can be formed on the basis of an agreement between the partners.

(ii) **Liability** The liability of all the members of a partnership firm is unlimited.

(iii) **Risk bearing** The partners bear the risks (loss) involved in the business jointly.

(iv) **Decision-making and control** Each partner has a right to participate in management and decision-making of the organisation.

(v) **Lack of continuity** Existence of firm is affected by death, retirement, lunacy, madness and insolvency (bankruptcy) of any of its partner.

6/8 Marks Questions

1. What do you understand by a sole proprietorship firm? Explain its merits and limitations.

Ans **Meaning of sole proprietorship** It is the form of business which is owned, managed and controlled by an individual. It is the simplest form of business, established with the limited resources, ability and capital of the individual, known as 'sole trader'.

Merits of a sole proprietorship A sole proprietorship enjoys the following merits

(i) The establishment of a sole tradership concern is easier as compared to other forms of organisation.

(ii) The sole trader is free to change the nature and scope of his business operation, whenever the situation demands so.

(iii) Sole tradership facilitates quick decision-making and prompt action as the sole trader has exclusive control over his business.

Demerits of sole proprietorship A sole proprietorship has following demerits

(i) The financial resources which a sole trader can raise are limited.

(ii) The sole proprietor has to take all the decisions and he may not be an expert in all the matters of business.

(iii) In the eyes of law, owner and business are considered one and the same. Therefore, illness, death or insolvency of the owner affects the business and can lead to its closure.

2. Explain the merits and limitations of partnership.

Ans Partnership firm enjoys the following merits

(i) A partnership firm can be formed with minimal legal formalities by an agreement between the prospective partners, whereby they agree to carry out the business of the firm and share risks. Registration of the firm is also not compulsory. Closure of the firm can also be done easily.

(ii) The partners can look after different functions according to their areas of expertise. This reduces the burden of work on individual partners and leads to more effective decisions.

(iii) All the partners share the risks involved in running a partnership firm. This reduces the anxiety, burden and stress on individual partners.

(iv) A partnership firm is not legally required to publish its accounts and submit reports. Hence, it can maintain confidentiality of information relating to its operations.

A partnership firm suffers from the following limitations

(i) All partners of a firm have unlimited liability. Personal assets of the partners may be used for repaying debts, if the business assets are insufficient.

(ii) Partnership firms usually do not operate on a large scale as there is a restriction on the number of partners and hence, contribution in terms of capital investment remains insufficient for business expansion beyond a point.

(iii) Decision-making authority in a partnership is shared by all the partners. Difference in opinion may lead to conflicts between partners.

(iv) Partnership comes to an end with the death, retirement, insolvency or lunacy of any partner. It may result in lack of continuity, if the remaining partners do not enter into a fresh agreement to continue the business.

3. Give the differences between public company and private company.

Ans Differences between public and private companies are

Basis	Public company	Private company
Minimum number of members	Seven	Two
Maximum number of members	No limit	Two hundred (excluding past and present employees)
Minimum number of directors	Three	Two
Public invitation of capital	It is free to invite the public to buy its shares and debentures.	It cannot invite the public to buy its shares and debentures.
Commencement of business	It cannot commence business after incorporation unless certificate of commencement of business is obtained.	It can commence business immediately after incorporation.
Transfer of shares	No restriction	Restriction on transfer

TOPIC 2

Source of Business Finance

Meaning of Business Finance

Business is concerned with the production and distribution of goods and services for the satisfaction of needs of society. In order to produce and distribute goods and services, business needs money. Therefore, finance is called 'the soul of any business'. The requirements of funds by business to carry out its various activities is called 'business finance'.

Classification of Sources of Finance

Sources of funds can be classified on the basis of period, ownership and source of generation. It is illustrated in the chart below

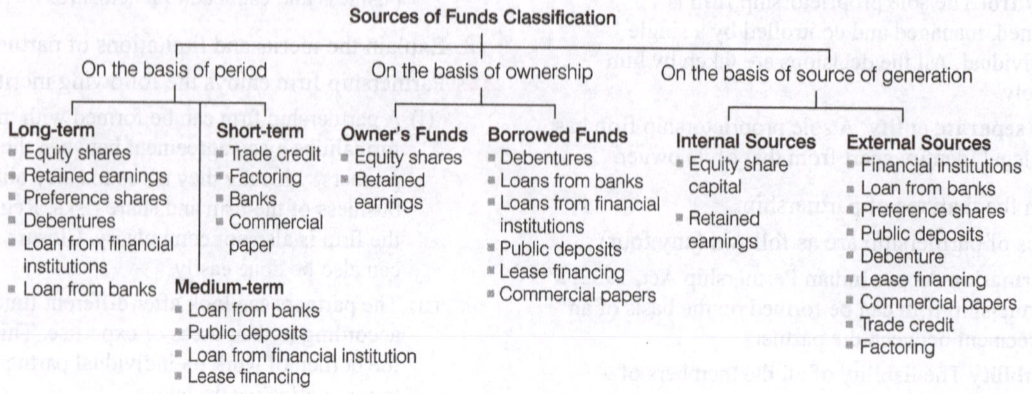

Sources of Finance

A brief description of various sources (as per syllabus) is given below

1. Equity Shares

The capital obtained by issue of equity shares is known as 'equity share capital'. It is considered as a permanent source of capital for a company, as it is not required to be returned during the life of the company. The return on equity shares is paid in the form of dividend.

The company pays dividend only in case of profits. The rate of dividend is not fixed and depends upon the surplus profit left after paying dividend to preference shareholders.

Because of these features, the equity shareholders are known as the 'residual owners' of the business. They are original risk bearers. Voting rights are conferred upon them, to enable them to participate in the affairs of the business.

2. Preference Shares

The capital raised by issue of preference shares is called 'preference share capital'. Preference shares confer following two preferential rights to its holders

(i) Preferential right to receive dividend at a pre-determined rate, before dividend is paid to equity shareholders.

(ii) Preferential right to receive repayment of capital at the time of dissolution of the company. This right authorises them to receive payment against capital before any amount is paid to equity shareholders.

3. Debentures and Bonds

Debenture is an important instrument for raising long-term debt capital. Debenture is basically a written acknowledgement of the company, under its seal, that it has borrowed certain amount of money. In general, it refers to long-term loan to the company by the debentureholders on which they receive a fixed rate of interest.

Bonds are also loan instruments and resemble debentures in all aspects except one. No pre-determined rate of interest is announced at the time of issuing bonds, but a specific rate of interest is announced while issuing debentures.

4. Retained Earnings/Profits

It means that part of trading profits which are not distributed in the form of dividends, but retained by directors for future expansion of the company. This is also referred to as 'ploughing back of profits'. In other words, these are sacrifice made by equity shareholders. Therefore, referred to as internal equity.

It is calculated as

$$\boxed{\text{Retained Earnings (RE)} = \text{Net Income} - \text{Dividends}}$$

5. Public Deposits

It refers to the deposits that are raised by business organisations directly from the public. Under it, a company directly raises loans from the public, in the form of deposits for a fixed period of time at a fixed rate of interest. This rate is generally higher than that offered on bank deposits.

Companies generally invite public deposits for a period upto three years. Its acceptance is regulated by the Reserve Bank of India. Any person who is interested in depositing money with a company can do so by filing a prescribed form. The company issues a deposit receipt as acknowledgement of debt.

6. Loans from Commercial Banks

Commercial banks such as State Bank of India (SBI), Canara Bank, etc, advance money to the business firms for different purposes and different time periods. Banks extend in many ways like, cash credits, overdrafts, discounting of bills of exchange and issue of letter of credit.

The repayment is made by the borrower in instalments as per the agreement between the bank and the borrower. Interest charged by banks depends upon a number of factors, such as nature of advance, period for which the loan is taken, etc.

Loan is generally offered by banks on the basis of security of assets.The loan can be repaid either in instalments or in lumpsum.

7. Trade Credit

It is an agreement in which credit is extended by one trader to another for purchase of goods and services. It facilitates the purchase of supplies without immediate payment. It is a short-term (Say, 30 days to 90 days) source of finance.

8. Discounting of Bills of Exchange

It is a process under which a holder of the bill exchange it from the bank before its maturity date. The bank takes the bill and deducts a small percentage as interest (discount) and advances the balance amount.

9. Global Depository Receipt (GDR)

Depository receipts are issued by a depository bank, when local currency shares of a company are delivered to it. Such depository receipts in terms of US dollars are called GDRs.

In the Indian context, a GDR is an instrument issued abroad by an Indian company to raise funds in some foreign currency and is listed and traded on a foreign stock exchange.

10. Angel Investors

The term 'angel' originally comes from broadway, where it was used to describe wealthy individual who provide money for theatrical productions.

An angel investor or angel, also known as a business angel or informal investor is an affluent individual who provides capital for a business start-up, usually in exchnage for convertible debt or ownership equity.

Angel investors generally provide capital for a business start-up and early stage companies having a high-risk, high-return matrix.

11. Venture Capitalists

These are private investors and venture capital firms who provide capital to start up ventures or supports small companies that wish to expand but do not have access to equity markets. Venture capitalists are willing to invest in such companies because they can earn a massive return on their investments. Venture capital firm raise fund from different investors.

12. Crowdfunding

It is a method of funding a project or venture by raising small amounts of money from a large number of people, typically using the internet. Crowdfunding has the potential to increase entrepreneurship by expanding the pool of investors.

13. Peer to Peer Lending (Funding)

It is a method of debt financing used to raise loans for people who need to borrow from people who want to invest. It enables individuals to borrow and lend money without any financial institution as an intermediary.

14. Factoring

Factoring is a type of finance in which a business would sell its accounts receivable (invoices) to a third party to meet its short-term liquidity needs.

Under the transaction between both the parties, the factor would pay the amount due on the invoices less its commission or fees.

PYQs Previous Years' Questions

1 Mark Questions

1. Briefly explain peer to peer funding. *ISC Sem II 2022*

Ans It is a method of debt financing used to raise loans for people who need to borrow from people who want to invest. It enables individuals to borrow and lend money without any financial institution as an intermediary.

2. Ploughing back of profit is an ………… source of financing. *ISC Sem II Specimen 2022*

Ans Owner's fund

Concept Enhancer Owner's fund means funds that are provided by the owners of an enterprise, which may be a sole trader or partners or shareholders of a company.

2 Marks Questions

1. Briefly explain the concept of retained profits. *ISC Sem II 2022*

Ans It means that part of trading profits which are not distributed in the form of dividends, but retained by directors for future expansion of the company. This is also referred to as 'ploughing back of profits'.

It is calculated as

Retained Earnings (RE) = Net Income − Dividends

Value Points

For getting maximum marks, following value points can be included in the answer

- Meaning of retained profit
- How it is calculated?

2. Why are preference shares called hybrid securities? *ISC Sem II 2022*

Ans Preference shares are called hybrid securities because they carry the characteristic of both debt and equity.

Like debt, they carry a fixed rate of dividend.

Like equuity, they receive dividend only if anything is left after paying the debt interest.

3. Briefly explain crowdfunding. *ISC Sem II Specimen 2022*

Ans It is a method of funding a project or venture by raising small amounts of money from a large number of people, typically using the internet. Crowdfunding has the potential to increase entrepreneurship by expanding the pool of investors.

4 Marks Questions

1. State any four differences between angel investors and venture capitalists. ***ISC Specimen 2023***

Ans Differences between angel investors and venture capitalists are

Basis	Angel investors	Venture capitalists
Meaning	They can be described as an investor who offer promising start up businesses funding by offering a share of the company.	They can be described as an investor in private equity who lends capital to companies with high growth potential in exchange for equity stakes.
Investment	An investment is made in the pre-revenue business	An investment is made in the pre-profitability business.
Size of investment	Their investment size is comparatively less.	Their investment size is larger than angel investors.
Funds	They are individual investors who invest their own funds.	They are professionally managed firm who pools money from funds companies, etc. to invest.

2. Briefly explain the process of financing a business through retained profits and crowdfunding. ***ISC Specimen 2023***

Ans **Retained profits** Refer to Q.No. 1 (2 Marks) on page 158.

Crowdfunding Refer to Q.No. 3 (2 Marks) on page 158.

3. Akshay is planning to start manufacturing of educational toys for children. He has some savings and has also borrowed some money from his friends and relatives to invest in this business. However, he needs more money to start the business.
Name and explain any two sources of business finance available to him. ***ISC Sem II 2022***

Ans Any two sources of business finance available to him are

(i) **Loan from commercial banks** Refer to text on page 157.

(ii) **Trade credit** Refer to text on page 157.

4. Explain angel investors and crowdfunding as sources of finance for a business venture. ***ISC 2020***

Ans **Angle investors** The term 'angel' originally comes from broadway, where it was used to describe wealthy individual who provide money for theatrical productions. An angel investor or angel, also known as a business angel or informal investor is an affluent individual who provides capital for a business start-up, usually in exchnage for convertible debt or ownership equity. Angel investors generally provide capital for a business start-up and early stage companies having a high-risk, high-term matrix.

Crowdfunding Refer to Q. No. 3 (2 Marks) on page 158.

8 Marks Question

1. With reference to business finance, explain the following ***ISC 2019***

(i) Preference shares
(ii) Debentures
(iii) Retained earnings
(iv) Public deposits

Or Explain any four sources of finance available to an organisation. ***ISC Specimen 2019***

Ans (i) **Preference shares** Preference shares are those long-term source of funds which confer following two preferential rights to its holders

(a) Preferential right to receive dividend at a predetermined rate, before dividend is paid to equity shareholders.

(b) Preferential right to receive repayment of capital at time of dissolution of company before any amount is paid to equity shareholders.

(ii) **Debentures** Debenture is a written acknowledgement of company, under its seal, that it has borrowed certain amount of money. In general, it refers to long-term loan to company by debenture-holders on which they receive a fixed rate of interest.

(iii) **Retained earnings** Refer to Q. No. 1 (2 Marks) on page 158.
This practice is referred as 'Ploughing back of profits'.

(iv) **Public deposits** It refers to loan raised from public in form of deposits for a fixed period of time at a fixed rate of interest.
The rate of interest is generally higher than that offered on bank deposits. Its acceptance is regulated by RBI.

Common Mistake Students get confused between interest and dividend. Dividend is received on shares while interest is received on debentures. Students are advisable to understand the concept in respect of interest and dividend received as returns.

Additional Questions

2/4 Marks Questions

1. What is business finance? Why does business need funds? Explain.

Ans Requirements of funds by business to carry out its various activities is called business finance. Finance is the life blood of the business. Funds are required to commence and carry on business. All business activities such as planning, organising, managing, controlling, purchasing, selling, directing, marketing, etc cannot take place without finance.

Business needs funds for purchasing fixed and current assets for day-to-day operations, purchase of raw material, to pay salaries, etc.

2. List sources of raising long-term and short-term finance.

Ans Sources of long-term finance are as follows

(i) Equity shares (ii) Retained earnings

(iii) Preference shares

(iv) Debentures

(v) Loans from banks and other financial institutions

Sources of short-term finance are as follows

(i) Trade credit

(ii) Factoring

(iii) Commercial papers

(iv) Short-term loans from banks

3. Discuss the features of equity shares as a source of finance.

Ans Features of equity shares are as follows

(i) The equity shareholders are the primary risk bearers as they provide fixed capital to the business.

(ii) The equity share capital is not redeemable during the lifetime of the company.

(iii) Returns are uncertain as the rate of dividend is not fixed.

(iv) Equity shareholders can participate in the company's decisions and management.

4. What preferential rights are enjoyed by preference shareholders? Explain.

Ans The following preferential rights are enjoyed by preference shareholders

(i) Receiving a fixed rate of dividend, out of the net profits of the company, before any dividend is declared for equity shareholders.

(ii) Preference over equity shareholders in receiving their capital after the claims of the company's creditors have been settled but before any amount is paid to equity shareholders at the time of liquidation.

5. Define and write the features of preference shares.

Ans Preference shares are those which carry a preference both regarding dividend and the return of the capital over equity shareholders.

Following features will be revealed

(i) Offer fixed rate of dividend.

(ii) Preferential payment of dividend.

(iii) Preferential right in redemption of capital, in case of winding up of a company.

(iv) Investors who want steady income without undertaking much risk, can prefer these shares.

6. Differentiate between equity shares and preference shares.

Ans The differences between equity shares and preference shares are

Basis	Equity shares	Preference shares
Participation in management	Full right to participate.	No right to participate.
Sequence of dividend	Dividend is paid at last.	Preference is given in payment of dividend.
Sequence of refund of capital	On winding up of the company, capital is refunded after preference shares.	Preference is given in refunding the capital.
Refund of capital for lifetime	Not possible at all.	Capital can be refunded in case of redeemable preference shares.
Permanency of dividend	Dividend is uncertain as it fluctuates with the amount of divisible profits decision of board of directors.	Dividend is certain and fixed.

7. What are GDRs? Explain its advantages.

Ans **Meaning of GDRs** Depository receipts are issued by a depository bank, when local currency shares of a company are delivered to it. Such depository receipts in terms of US dollars are called GDRs.

The various advantages of raising finance through issue of GDRs is the reason why companies are using this source of finance.

Advantages of GDRs Some of the advantages of issuing GDRs are as follows

(i) Companies can raise finance from the global market.

(ii) The control of the company is not diluted as the holders of GDR do not enjoy voting rights.

(iii) GDRs are not subject to strict disclosure requirements, as in the case of ADRs.

(iv) The cost of maintaining GDRs is less as compared to ADRs.

8. As a financial consultant, state the various factors which are required to be considered before finalising the source of finance.

Ans Various factors to be considered before finalising the source of finance are as follows

(i) Cost of finance

(ii) Financial strength

(iii) Form of organisational structure

(iv) Control

(v) Degree of risk

(vi) Tax benefits

9. Explain the nature of business finance.

Ans The nature of business finance can be summed up with the help of the given points

(i) The concept of business finance is very wide and is used in every type of business house whether it is small or large.

(ii) It includes all types of funds and capital that are needed to start, run, expand and diversify the business.

(iii) The primary goal of business finance is to increase the corporate value.

10. Explain the features of debentures.

Ans The following are the features of debentures

(i) Debentures are basically borrowed funds. Because of this feature, the debentureholders are deemed to be the creditors of the company.

(ii) Generally, companies pay half yearly interest, to the debentureholders at a specified rate.

(iii) Public issue of debentures requires that the issue be rated by a credit rating agency like CRISIL (Credit Rating and Information Services of India Ltd.) on aspects like track record of company, its profitability, debt servicing capacity, credit worthiness and the perceived risk of lending.

6/8 Marks Questions

1. Give the difference between shares and debentures.

Ans The differences between shares and debentures are

Basis	Shares	Debentures
Nature of finance	Shares are a part of owner's fund.	Debentures are a part of debt fund.
Nature and rate of return	Dividend is the return on shares. The rate of dividend is not fixed and is dependent on the profits of the company and the decision of the management.	Interest is the return on debentures. The rate of interest is fixed and is required to be paid even if the company incurs losses.
Status of holders	Shareholders are deemed to be the owners of the company.	Debentureholders are deemed to be the creditors of the company.
Degree of control	Shareholders can exercise reasonable degree of control on the affairs of the business by exercising their right to vote.	Debentureholders are not in the position to control the affairs of the business as they do not have the right to vote.
Security offered	No security is required to be offered at the time of issue of shares.	Security is required to be offered, either by creating a charge on assets or by mortgaging the assets, at the time of issue of debentures.
Level of risk	Shareholders assume a high level of risk.	Risk is comparatively lower for debenture holders.
Period of redemption	Shares are not generally redeemable during the life of the company, except in case of redeemable preference shares.	Debentures are generally redeemable during the life of the company, except in case of perpetual debentures.
Effect on borrowing capacity	Issue of shares does not affects the borrowing capacity of the company.	Issue of debentures affects the borrowing capacity of the company.

2. State the merits and demerits of public deposits and retained earnings as methods of business finance.

Ans Merits of public deposits are as follows

(i) The procedure of obtaining deposits is simple and does not contain restrictive conditions as in case of a loan agreement.

(ii) Cost of public deposits is generally lower than the cost of borrowings from banks and financial institutions.

(iii) Public deposits do not usually create any charge on the assets of the company and hence the assets can be used as security for raising loans from other sources.

(iv) The control of the company is not diluted as the depositors do not have voting rights.

Demerits of public deposits are as follows

(i) New companies generally find it difficult to raise funds through public deposits due to lack of goodwill.

(ii) It is an unreliable source of finance as the public may not always respond when the company needs money.

(iii) Collection of public deposits may prove difficult, particularly when the size of deposits required is large.

Merits of retained earnings are as follows

(i) Retained earnings are a permanent source of funds for an organisation.

(ii) Retained earnings do not involve any explicit cost in the form of interest, dividend or floatation cost.

(iii) This source offers a greater degree of operational freedom and flexibility.

(iv) It enhances the capacity of business to absorb unexpected losses.

(v) It might lead to increase in the market price of equity shares issued by the company.

Demerits of retained earnings are as follows

(i) Excessive ploughing back may cause dissatisfaction amongst the shareholders as they would get lower dividends.

(ii) As the profits of business are fluctuating, it is an uncertain source of fund.

3. Which type of source of finance facilitates the purchase of supplies without immediate payments? State its merits and demerits also.

Ans **Trade credit** It facilitates the purchase of supplies without immediate payment. Such credit appears in the records of the buyer as sundry creditors or accounts payable.

It is commonly used by business organisation as a source of short-term financing. It is granted to those customers who have reasonable amount of financial standing and goodwill.

Merits of trade credit are as follows

(i) Trade credit is a convenient and continuous source of funds.

(ii) It may be readily available in case the credit worthiness of the customers is known to the seller.

(iii) It helps to promote the sale of an organisation.

(iv) It does not create any charge on the assets of the firm.

Demerits of trade credit are as follows

(i) This may motivate a firm to overtrade.

(ii) Only limited amount of funds can be raised through this source.

(iii) It is generally a costly source of fund as compared to others, as sellers charge more for goods sold on credit.

4. Explain the merits and demerits of raising funds through equity shares.

Ans Merits of equity shares are as follows

(i) Equity shares are suitable for those investors who are willing to assume risk for higher returns.

(ii) Payment of dividend to the equity shareholders is not compulsory. Therefore, there is no burden on the company.

(iii) It is considered as a good source of long-term finance. A company is not required to payback the equity capital during its lifetime. It is repaid only at the time of liquidation of company.

(iv) Equity capital provides credit worthiness to the company and confidence to prospective loan providers.

(v) Funds can be raised through equity shares without creating any charge on the assets of the company. These assets can be mortgaged to raise finance from other sources.

(vi) Democratic control in the management of the company is assured due to the voting rights of equity shareholders.

Demerits of equity shares are as follows

(i) Investors who want steady income may not prefer equity shares due to fluctuating returns.

(ii) The cost of equity shares is more, as compared to other sources of funds.

(iii) Every successive issue of equity shares dilutes the voting power and earnings of existing equity shareholders.

(iv) Many formalities and procedural delays are involved while raising funds through equity.

5. Explain the merits and demerits of raising funds through preference shares.

Ans Merits of preference shares are as follows

(i) The dividends to be paid to the preference share-holders are fixed. This ensures the investors the security of fixed returns.

(ii) These shares are suitable for those investors who want fixed income with comparatively low risk.

(iii) It does not affect the control of equity shareholders. As these shares do not carry voting rights.

(iv) Payment of fixed dividends to preference shareholders enable a company to declare higher dividends for equity shareholders.

(v) The holders of these shares have a preferential right of repayment over equity shareholders, when the company liquidates.

(vi) Assets are not required to be mortgaged for raising preference share capital. Thus, the assets of the company are free from any charge and can be used to raise debt capital.

Demerits of preference shares are as follows

(i) Preference shares are not suitable for those investors who are willing to take risk and are interested in higher returns.

(ii) These shares dilute the claim of equity shareholders over the assets of the company.

(iii) The company has to pay higher rates of dividends to the preference shareholders as compared to interest on debentures.

(iv) The dividend on these shares is to be paid only when the company earns profit. Thus, the returns are not assured and they are unable to attract the investors.

(v) The dividend paid on preference shares is not deductible from profits as expense. Thus, there is no tax savings, as in the case of interest on loans.

6. Explain merits and demerits of discounting of bills of exchange.

Ans Merits of discounting of bills of exchange are as follow

(i) It provides cash immediately to drawer (saler).

(ii) Bank earns commission on bill.

(iii) There is no need of collateral, i.e. no extra security is to be offered.

Demerits of discounting of bills of exchange are as follows

(i) It is a short-term source of finance.

(ii) Bill may be dishonoured, i.e. it becomes addition burden.

(iii) It is a indirect loss to company.

7. What are angel investors? Explain merits and demerits of angel investors.

Ans **Meaning of angel investors** Refer to Q. No. 4 (4 Marks) on page 159.

Merits of angel investors are as follows

(i) They are free to make investment decisions quickly.

(ii) No need for collateral assets.

Demerits of angel investors are as follows

(i) It takes longer time to find a suitable angel investor.

(ii) Giving up shares of the business to angel investor.

8. Define and explain the merits and demerits of the following

(i) Venture capitalists

(ii) Crowdfunding

(iii) Peer-to-Peer lending (Funding)

Ans (i) **Venture capitalists** These are private investors and venture capital firms who provide capital to start up ventures or supports small companies that wish to expand but do not have access to equity markets. Venture capitalists are willing to invest in such companies because they can earn a massive return on their investments. Venture capital firm raise fund from different investors.

Merits of venture capitalists are as follows

(a) Venture capitalists are generally invest in innovative projects which offer high profitability in long-run.

(b) In addition to capital, venture capitalist provides valuable information, resources, technical assistance, etc to make a business successful.

Demerits of venture capitalists are as follows

(a) Uncertain form of financing.

(b) Benefit from venture capital can be realised in long-run only.

(ii) **Crowdfunding** It is a method of funding a project or venture by raising small amounts of money from a large number of people, typically using the internet. Crowdfunding has the potential to increase entrepreneurship by expanding the pool of investors.

Merits of crowdfunding are as follows

(a) It is easy and fast way to raise finance.

(b) Launching a project or business through crowdfunding can be a valuable form of marketing.

(c) Crowdfunding investors can often become the most loyal customers through financing process.

Demerits of crowdfunding are as follows

(a) If the target amount of crowdfunding is not reached, potential investors get their money back.

(b) Failed projects risk damage the reputation of the business.

(c) A strong, established existing network of people is vital to the success of a project.

(iii) **Peer-to-peer lending** (Funding) It is a method of debt financing used to raise loans for people who need to borrow from people who want to invest. It enables individuals to borrow and lend money without any financial institution as an intermediary.

Merits of peer-to-peer lending are as follows

(a) Peer-to-Peer lending can potentially give access to significantly higher returns.

(b) Peer-to-Peer lending spread capital across multiple loans. This enables better management of risk.

Demerit of peer-to-peer lending is as follows

Under Peer-to-peer lending, potential high return is offered because people are investing in small businesses with a very high risk.

9. Give the merits and demerits of raising finance through debentures.

Ans Merits of raising finance through debentures are as follows

(i) It is preferred by those investors, who want fixed income at lesser risk.

(ii) Debentures are fixed charge funds and do not participate in the profits of the company.

(iii) The issue of debentures is suitable in the situation when the sales and earnings are relatively stable.

(iv) Debentures do not carry voting rights. Therefore, financing through debentures does not dilute the control of equity shareholders on management.

(v) The interest paid on debentures is admissible as an expense according to the provisions of income tax. This helps a company to reduce its tax liability. Because of this, it is also economical for a company to raise finance through this source.

Demerits of raising finance through debentures are as follows

(i) Debentures put a permanent burden on the earnings of a company. There is a greater risk when earnings of the company fluctuate.

(ii) In case of redeemable debentures, the company has to make provisions for repayment on the specified date, even during periods of financial difficulty.

(iii) Each company has certain borrowing capacity. With the issue of debentures, the capacity of a company to further borrow funds reduces.

10. Briefly explain the merits and demerits of raising finance from commercial banks.

Ans Merits of raising finance from commercial banks are as follows

(i) Banks provide timely assistance to business by providing funds as and when needed.

(ii) Secrecy of business can be maintained as the information supplied to the bank by the borrowers is kept confidential.

(iii) Formalities such as issue of prospectus and underwriting are not required for raising loans from a bank. This, therefore, is an easier source of funds.

(iv) Loan from a bank is a flexible source of finance as the loan amount can be increased according to business needs and can be repaid in advance when funds are not needed.

Demerits of raising finance from commercial banks are as follows

(i) Funds are generally available for short periods and its extension or renewal is uncertain and difficult.

(ii) Banks make detailed investigation of the company's affairs, financial structure, etc. This makes the procedure of obtaining funds slightly difficult.

(iii) In some cases, difficult terms and conditions are imposed by banks for the grant of loan.

11. Explain trade credit and bank credit (loan) as sources of short-term finance for business enterprises.

Ans **Trade credit** It is the credit extended by one trader to another for the purchase of goods and services. It facilitates the purchase of supplies without immediate payment and is commonly used by business organisations as a source of short-term financing.

Trade credit appears in the records of the buyer as 'sundry creditors' or 'accounts payable'. It is granted prudently to those customers who have reasonable amount of financial standing and goodwill.

The volume and period of credit extended depends on factors such as reputation of the purchasing firm, financial position of the seller, volume of purchases, past record of payment and degree of competition in the market.

Terms of trade credit may vary from industry to industry and from person to person. As we know, trade is the purchase and sale of goods for profit motive. So, trade credit strictly refers to the routine business activity.

Bank credit Commercial banks provide funds for different purposes and for different time periods to firms of all sizes by way of cash credits, overdrafts, term loans, purchase/discounting of bills and issue of letter of credit. The rate of interest charged by banks depends on various factors such as the characteristics of the firm and the level of interest rates in the economy.

The loan is repaid either in lumpsum or in instalments. Bank credit is not a permanent source of funds and is generally used for medium to short periods. The borrower is required to provide some security or create a charge on the assets of the firm before a loan is sanctioned by a commercial bank.

Case Based Questions

Case I

ABC Ltd is a hardware manufacturing company listed on National Stock Exchange. The company operates only in Delhi-NCR. The management plans to expand their area of operation across the country. They require funds for their expansion plans.

Briefly explain each source of finance given below. State whether these sources can be used by ABC Ltd or not for raising funds. Give a reason to support your answer.

(i) Angel Investors
(ii) Factoring
(iii) Global Depository Receipts
(iv) Loans from Financial Institutions *ISC 2023*

Ans (i) **Angel Investors** This source can be used for raising fund because angel investors generally provide capital for a business start-up and early stage companies who want to expand their business.

(ii) **Factoring** This source can not be used for raising fund because factoring is a type of finance in which business would sell its account receivable to third party to meet its short-term liquidity needs.

(iii) **Global Depository Receipts** This source can not be used for raising fund because GDR is an instrument issued abroad by an Indian company to raise fund in foreign currency and listed and traded on foreign stock exchange.

(iv) **Loans from Financial Institutions** This source can be used for raising fund because financial institutions provide loans at a fixed rate of interest to business entities for their businesses. It is a good source of raising funds for their expansion plans.

Case 2

Glory, a well-established company is listed on the stock exchange. Ramesh and Suresh want to invest in the company. While Ramesh decides to buy equity shares, Suresh wants to buy preference shares in the company.

Justify the decisions made by Ramesh and Suresh. *ISC Specimen 2022*

Ans Preference shareholders have priority over equity owners in the payment of capital, dividends and profits. Thus, Suresh's decision can be justified.

Ramesh decision can be justified as from an equity investment, there is possibility to increase the value of the principal amount of investment. It is a permanent capital with higher returns. Equity shareholders have right to vote and participate in company's affair.

Conclusion Both Ramesh and Suresh's decisions are justified. Investors with a low-risk profile can invest in preference shares. Investors with a high risk appetite can invest in equity shares.

CHAPTER TEST

01 Mark Questions

1. Which business entity is owned, managed and controlled by single individual?
2. What is the limit of minimum number of members in a public company?
3. Deposits that are raised by business organisations directly from the public are known as ....
4. .... shareholders have voting rights in a company.
5. .... enables individuals to borrow and lend money without any intermediary.
6. Which of the following is not a business entity?
   (a) Partnership (b) Sole trade
   (c) Crowdfunding (d) Public limited company
7. Which of the following is a long-term source of fund?
   (a) Factoring (b) Debentures
   (c) Trade credit (d) Commercial paper
8. An instrument issued abroad by an Indian company to raise funds in foreign currency is known as
   (a) public deposits (b) global depository receipt
   (c) factoring (d) venture capitalist
9. Minimum two persons are required to form a partnership firm. State true or false.
10. Preference shareholders gets their money afterequity shareholders'. State true or false.

02 Marks Questions

11. Write any two benefits of sole proprietorship.
12. Define private company.
13. Define public company.
14. Write the nature of business finance.
15. Define GDR.

04 Marks Questions

16. Write the two merits and two demerits of sole proprietorship.
17. Define partnership. Write its features.
18. Distinguish between bonds and debentures.
19. Distinguish between crowdfunding and peer-to-peer lending.

06/08 Marks Questions

20. Write the features of private and public company.
21. Explain various forms of business entities.
22. Explain the various sources of business finance.

Answers

1. Sole proprietorship
2. Seven
3. public deposits
4. Equity
5. Peer-to-Peer lending (Funding)
6. (c) Crowdfunding
7. (b) Debentures
8. (b) global depository receipt
9. True
10. False

14

Globalisation and Recent Trends in Business

TREND ANALYSIS 5 YEARS

	Average No. of Questions Across all Sets					
	Types of Questions	2023	2020	2019	2018	2017
01 Globalisation	1 Mark	1	—	—	—	—
	2 Marks	—	1	—	—	—
	4 Marks	—	—	1	—	—
	6/8 Marks	—	—	—	—	—
02 E-business	1 Mark	—	—	—	—	—
	2 Marks	—	—	1	—	—
	4 Marks	1	—	1	—	—
	6/8 Marks	—	1	—	—	—
03 Outsourcing	1 Mark	1	—	—	—	—
	2 Marks	—	—	2	—	—
	4 Marks	1	—	—	—	—
	6/8 Marks	—	1	—	—	—

TOPIC 1

Globalisation

The three strongest trends that are shaping the modern business are

(i) E-business or digitisation (ii) Outsourcing
(iii) Internationalisation and globalisation

Meaning of Globalisation

It is the process of integration of the economy of a country with the world economy. It includes free flow of goods and services, knowledge, technology, capital and people across all boundaries.

Nature of Globalisation

Following points explain the nature of globalisation

(i) **Complements liberalisation** Liberalisation means freedom of entrepreneurs to establish any business, industry or trade either in their own countries or abroad. Globalisation complements liberalisation.

(ii) **Free trade between countries** It means absence of excessive government control over trade.

(iii) **Globalisation of economic activities** Economic activities are governed by domestic market and world market.

(iv) **Flows** Inflows and outflows of goods, services, technology, capital, finance and people between the countries.

(v) **International cooperation** The increase in multinational corporations, global and regional organisations makes international community.

(vi) **Connectivity** Nations of the world being connected with each other through international transmission of knowledge, literature, technology, culture and information.

Opportunities of Globalisation for Business

Following are the opportunities/advantages of globalisation for business

(i) Enhanced economic growth has led to high per capita income.

(ii) Free movement of labour between countries.

(iii) Gains from transfer of advanced technology across national borders.

(iv) Encourages producers and consumers to benefit from economies of scale and division of labour.

(v) Competitive markets reduce monopoly and provide incentives for cost reduction.

(vi) Borrowing and lending of money through opening up of capital markets.

(vii) Improved governance and better labour protection.

Threats of Globalisation for Business

Following are the threats/disadvantages of globalisation for business

(i) **Inequality Globalisation** Leads to rising inequalities in income and wealth due to rural-urban divide in countries.

(ii) **Inflation** Rising demand for food and energy has caused a steep rise in commodity prices at world level.

(iii) **Threats to natural environment** Globalisation causes irreversible damage to eco-systems, land degradation, deforestation, loss of biodiversity and shortage of water.

(iv) **Trade imbalance** Generally, developing and underdeveloped countries are facing the problem of trade deficit.

(v) **Tax heavens** Citizens part their illicit or unaccounted money in tax heavens and avoid taxation from their home countries.

(vi) **Trade war** Due to continuous trade deficit, trading partner countries started to increase tariff rates on imports.

PYQs Previous Years' Questions

1 Mark Questions

1. Globalisation hars increased competition among companies. State true or false. ***ISC 2023***

Ans True

2. State any one feature of globalisation. ***ISC Sem II Specimen 2022***

Ans Globalisation has increased the inflows and outflows of goods, services, technology, capital, finance and people between the countries.

2 Marks Questions

1. What is meant by globalisation in business? ***ISC Sem II 2022***

Ans Globalisation is the process of interaction and integration of the economy of a country with the world economy. It includes free flow of a goods, services, knowledge, technology, capital and people across the national boundaries.

2. List any two opportunities that globalisation has brought in. ***ISC 2020***

Ans Following are the opportunities/advantages of globalisation for business (any two)

(i) Enhanced economic growth has led to high per capita income.

(ii) Free movement of labour between countries.

(iii) Gains from transfer of advanced technology across national borders.

(iv) Encourages producers and consumers to benefit from economies of scale and division of labour.

3. State any two threats caused to business by globalisation. ***ISC Specimen 2019***

Ans Threats caused to business by globalisation are

(i) Globalisation leads to rising inequalities in income and wealth due to rural urban divide in countries.

(ii) Due to continuous trade deficit, trading partner countries started to increase tariff rates on imports.

4 Marks Questions

1. Discuss any two problems that may arise due to globalisation. *ISC Sem II Specimen 2022*

Ans Problems that may arise due to globalisation are

(i) Globalisation causes irreversible damage to eco-system, land-degradation, deforestation, loss of biodiversity and shortage of water.

(ii) Due to globalisation, rising demand for food and energy has caused a steep rise in commodity prices at world level.

2. Discuss any four ways in which globalisation has transformed the manner in which business is conducted. *ISC 2019*

Ans Ways in which business is transformed due to globalisation are

(i) Producers now can reap more benefit from economies of scale and division of labour.

(ii) Competitive markets reduce monopoly and provide incentives for cost reduction.

(iii) Globalisation facilitates free flow of goods, services, knowledge, technology, capital and people across national boundaries which led to higher productivity.

(iv) Improved governance and capital markets also helps in transformation of business.

Additional Questions

2/4 Marks Questions

1. Write any four advantages of globalisation.

Ans Advantages of globalisation are as follows

(i) **Free movement** Globalisation includes free flow of a goods, services, knowledge, technology, capital and people across national boundaries.

(ii) **Economic growth** Globalisation has led to world economic growth and high per capita income.

(iii) **Technology transfer** Gains from transfer of technology across national borders.

(iv) **Reduce monopoly** Competitive global markets reduce monopoly and provide incentives for cost reduction.

2. How different countries are connected with each other?

Ans Nations of the world being connected with each other through international transmission of knowledge, literature, technology, culture and information.

3. What is the reason behind the trade war between countries?

Ans The main reason of trade war between countries is continuous trade deficit and increased tariff rates on imports by countries.

6/8 Marks Questions

1. Explain the nature of globalisation.

Ans Following points explain the nature of globalisation

(i) **Complements liberalisation** Liberalisation means freedom of entrepreneurs to establish any business, industry or trade in abroad globalisation complements liberalisation.

(ii) **Free-trade between countries** It means absence of excessive government control over trade.

(iii) **Globalisation of economic activities** These activities are governed by domestic market.

(iv) **Flows** Inflows and outflows of goods, services, technology, capital, finance and people between countries.

(v) **International cooperation** The increase in multinational cooperations' global and regional organisations makes international community.

(vi) **Connectivity** Nations of the world being connected with each other through international transmission of knowledge, literature, technology, culture and information.

Nature of Globalisation
- Complements liberalisation
- Free-trade between countries
- Globalisation of economic activities
- Flows
- International cooperation
- Connectivity

2. Explain the threats of globalisation for business.

Ans Refer to text on page 168.

TOPIC 2

E-business

Meaning of E-business

Electronic business or e-business refers to the conduct of industry and commerce using a computer network such as the internet.

Nature of E-business

Following are the nature of a e-business

(i) It is very easy to set up e-business.
(ii) There are no geographical boundaries to conduct business.
(iii) There is no personal touch.
(iv) There are flexible business hours.
(v) Anyone can buy anything from anywhere at anytime.
(vi) The transaction risk is higher than traditional business.
(vii) Technical knowledge is required to do a e-business transaction.

Importance/Benefits of E-business

To the Buyer

(i) It provides a wide range of products to consumers to choose from.
(ii) It provides convenience to buy goods or services without causing any physical constraints to the consumers.
(iii) It is time saving.
(iv) Internet is used as a main vehicle to conduct transactions in e-business.
It allows customers to search for adequate information regarding product before committing purchase.

To the Seller

(i) e-Business is relatively easy to start. The benefits of internet technology are received by big or small business on a regular basis.
(ii) It offers the convenience of doing business 24 hours × 7 days a week.
(iii) It is one of the most speedy modes of doing business.
(iv) Internet has a wide reach which allows the seller an access to the global market.
(v) Use of internet has reduced the dependence on paperwork.

Online Means of Conducting Business

It is a transaction technology of e-commerce. It facilitates trading in goods and services or transferring money from one person to other through internet. Online transaction is an efficient and faster mode of transaction than the traditional one. It is also known as 'PIN- debit' transaction. It is password-protected payment method that authorises transfer of funds.

Scope/Types of E-business

Following are the scope/types of e-business

1. Business to Consumer (B2C)

As the name implies, B2C (business-to-customers) transactions have business firms at one end and their customers on the other end. This category is related to electronic retailing. This variant of e-business enables a business to be in touch with its customers 24 hours a day.

2. Consumer to Consumer (C2C)

C2C transactions originate from the consumer and they end on the consumer. This type of commerce is best suited for dealing in goods for which there is no established market mechanism.

C2C transactions also involves the formation of consumer's groups and forum, which helps consumers to get solutions to their problems and grievances. e.g. selling used books, clothes, electronics on cash or barter (www.olx.com).

3. Business to Business (B2B)

B2B transactions take place between two business firms. Hence, the name is B2B (business-to-business). A business interacts with a number of other business firms which may be suppliers or vendors of diverse inputs. Also they may be a part of the channel through which a firm distributes its products to the consumers.

4. **Intra Business** (Intra B)

Here, parties involved in the electronic transactions are from within a given business firm only. It enables the smooth flow of transaction within the different departments of a specific firm.

In other words, it can be said that a computer-based interaction among the different departments makes it possible for the firm to reap advantages of efficient inventory and cash management, greater utilisation of plant and machinery, effective handling of customers' orders, effective human resource management, etc.

5. **Business to Government** (B2G)

B2G refers to business transactions between private business firms and government. It covers contracts of all sorts–for goods, services and information between business of all sizes and government at all levels (state, local and central).

6. **Government to Business** (G2B)

G2B focuses on transactions between government and various business organisation, including contract bids, data collection and grants, sale of government services and goods alongwith procurement facilities.

PYQs Previous Years' Questions

1 Mark Questions

1. The ministry of corporate affairs has sent the certificate of incorporation to ABC Ltd. via an email. which online means of business has been used by the ministry? *ISC Specimen 2023*

Ans Government to Business (G2B)

2. Explain the consumer to consumer mode of conducting online business. *ISC Sem II 2022*

Ans Consumer to Consumer (C2C) includes transactions which have consumers on both the ends. It also includes formation of consumer's groups and forum, which helps consumers to get solutions to their problems and grievances. e.g. Selling old books, electronics through WWW.olx. com.

3. Expand the following

(i) P 2 P (ii) B 2 B *ISC Specimen 2019*

Ans (i) P 2 P ⇒ Peer-to-Peer

(ii) B 2 B ⇒ Business-to-Business

2 Marks Questions

1. State any two benefits of e-business to the buyers. *ISC 2019*

Ans Benefits of e-business to the buyers are

(i) **Convenience** It offers the convenience of doing business 24 hours × 7 days a week.

(ii) **Speed** It is one of the most speedy modes of doing business. One can avail anything, anytime, anywhere at the click of a mouse.

4 Marks Questions

1. State any four points highlighting the importance of e-business to the buyer. *ISC 2023*

Ans Following are the importance/benefits of e-business to the buyer are

(i) It provides a wide range of products to consumers to choose from.

(ii) It provides convenience to buy goods or services without causing any physical constraints to the consumers.

(iii) It is time saving.

(iv) Internet is used as a main vehicle to conduct transactions in e-business.

It allows customers to search for adequate information regarding product before committing purchase.

2. What is the meaning of e-business? State any three features of e-business. *ISC Specimen 2023*

Ans **E-business** Electronic business or e-business refers to the conduct of industry and commerce using a computer network such as the internet.

Features of E-business Refer to text 'Nature of e-business' on page 170.

3. Explain B2C and C2C as online means of conducting business. *ISC 2019*

Or

Briefly explain any two online means of conducting business.

Ans (i) **B2C** Business to Customers (B2C) is related to electronic retailing. This includes transactions that have business firms at one end and customers at other end.

The advantage of this is that business can remain in touch with customers 24 hours a day.

(ii) **C2C** Refer to Q. No. 2 (1 Mark) page 171.

8 Marks Question

1. Aamir runs a grocery shop started by his grandfather. As online business is becoming popular, Aamir's son Imran wants to stop physical sale of groceries and go for online sale.

State any four benefits to the business if Imran stops physical sale and starts online sale of groceries.

ISC Sem II 2022

Or What is meant by e-business? Briefly explain any seven benefits of e-business. *ISC 2020*

Ans Electronic business or e-business refers to the conduct of industry and commerce using a computer network such as the internet.

Benefits of E-business Refer to text point (i) to (v) on page 170.

(vi) **Less investment** Business firms can get quick supplies from the vendors. They need not maintain huge inventories, therefore less capital is blocked in inventory.

(vii) **Customer satisfaction** E-commerce allows quick response and redressal to customer complaints. This helps to increase customer satisfaction.

Additional Questions

6/8 Marks Questions

1. Explain business to consumer transactions.

Ans As the name implies, B2C (business-to-customers) transactions have business firms at one end and their customers on the other end. This category is related to electronic retailing. This variant of e-business enables a business to be in touch with its customers 24 hours a day.

B2C transactions may include

(i) Selling and distribution of goods

(ii) Conducting consumer surveys

(iii) After sales service

(iv) Promotional activities

(v) Delivery of products

The most common and visible B2C transaction is the use of ATM machines for withdrawing cash. Here, the bank is the business firm and the person withdrawing cash is the customer.

Value Points

For getting maximum marks, following value points can be included in the answer

- Give meaning of business-to-consumer transaction
- Mention what does it include.
- Example of B2C transaction

2. Write the importance of e-business.

Ans Refer to text on page 170.

3. Explain the various types of e-business.

Ans Following are the various types of e-business

(i) **Business to Consumer** (B2C) B2C transactions have business firms at one end and their customers on the other end. This category is related to electronic retailing. It offers convenience of doing business 24 hours × 7 days a week, e.g. ATM.

(ii) **Consumer to Consumer** (C2C) C2C transactions originate from the consumer and they end on the consumer. It is best suited for dealing in goods for which there is no established market mechanism. e.g. www.olx.com.

(iii) **Business to Business** (B2B) B2B transactions take place between two business firms. A business interacts with a number of other business firms which may be suppliers or vendors of diverse inputs.

(iv) **Intra Business** (Intra B) Here, parties involved in the electronic transactions are from within a given business firm only. It enables the smooth flow of transaction within the different departments (production, HR, accounts, marketing) of a specific firm.

(v) **Business to Government** (B2G) It refers to business transactions between private business firms and government. It covers contracts of all sorts–for goods, services and information.

(vi) **Government to Business** (G2B) G2B focuses on transactions between government and various business organisation, including contract bids, data collection and grants, sales of government services and goods along with procurement facilities.

Types of e-business

- Business to Consumer
- Consumer to Consumer
- Business to Business
- Intra Business
- Business to Government
- Government to Business

TOPIC 3

Outsourcing

Meaning of Outsourcing

The term 'outsourcing' means having an external vendor, who provides such services on regular basis that would normally be performed within the organisation. It involves delegation of one or more business processes to an external service provider, who then manages the selected business process based on defined measures of performance.

Features of Outsourcing

Outsourcing possesses the following distinct features

(i) **Outsourcing involves contracting out** Outsourcing means sourcing from outside or entrusting outside agencies to perform activities on contract, which were previously done in house. e.g. School can give contract to outside agency for running canteen.

(ii) **Generally, non-core business activities are outsourced** Initially, the business firms prefer to outsource non-core business activities as these are not crucial and does not affect the performance of the business. Once the firms begin to realise the benefits of outsourcing, then they might outsource core activities as well.

(iii) **Processes may be outsourced to captive units or to a third party** A business firm may outsource its activities to either a captive unit or to a third party. A captive unit is basically a unit of the business firm itself.
The chart given below illustrates the various outsourcing service providers

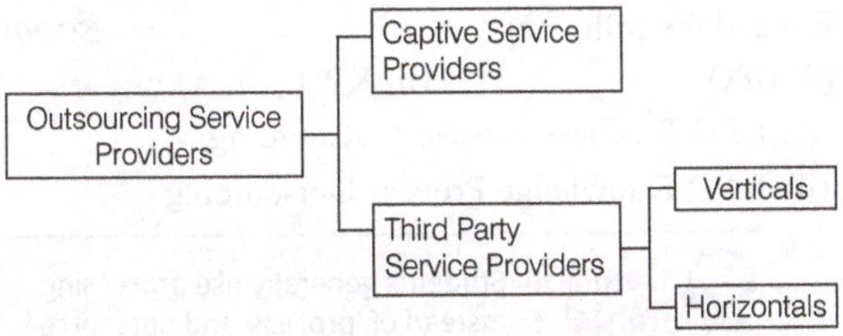

Types of Outsourcing Service Providers

Parties Involved in Outsourcing

1. Outsourcer

A business firm/organisation which provides goods or services by contract from outside a particular organisation.

The following advantages accrue to the outsourcer

(i) **More profits** Generally, outsourcer has expertise in his work and he can earn more profits.

(ii) **Quality services** Outsourcers provide personalised quality services to their clients.

(iii) **Accountability** Outsourcer is accountable for providing better services.

(iv) **Employment generation** BPO and KPO sectors generating more and more employment for the youth.

The outsourcer faces the following disadvantages

(i) **High risk** The outsourcer faces high risk due to accountability of performing the required task.

(ii) **Sharing losses** In case of losses incurred by client, the outsourcer has to share the losses.

(iii) **Competition** Outsourcer has to face very tough competition from other firms.

2. The Outsourced (Outsourcee)

The firm which hires the services of a outside party for the tasks that were traditionally performed by in house staff.

The following advantages accrue to the outsourced

(i) **More focus** Outsourcing of non-core activities helps the firm to put more focus on core functions of the business.

(ii) **Reduce costs** Outsourcing helps in reducing overhead and labour costs substantially.

(iii) **Increase productivity** Focus on core activities and specialised services of outsourcer help the business firm to increase productivity and efficiency.

The outsourced faces the following disadvantages

(i) **Hidden costs** Although outsourcing work is considered economical, but there may be hidden costs involved in signing a contract.

(ii) **Lack of secrecy** Personal data and information of the firm may be at risk.

(iii) **Lack of flexibility** Generally, outsourcing contracts could prove too rigid to accommodate change.

3. Service Provider

A business firm outsources its activities to a service provider (third party), who operates independently and provides services.

The following are the advantages of service provider

(i) **Control over work** Service provider has better knowledge and control over his tasks.

(ii) **Sharing risk** Risk of the project failure is to be shared by all parties involved in outsourcing.

(iii) **Personalised services** Service provider provides customer specific services.

The following are the disadvantages of service provider

(i) **Poor management** Service provider has to fulfil needs of multiple organisations at a time. It may lead to poor management.

(ii) **Low quality of services** Service provider saves his costs by reducing quality of services.

Types of Outsourcing

Outsourcing can take the form of BPO, KPO and LPO

(i) **BPO** (Business Process Outsourcing) It is a subset of outsourcing that involves contracting of the operations and responsibilities of specific business functions or processes to a third party service provider, with a view to benefit from their experience, expertise and efficiency. This allows companies to focus on their core processes.

e.g. Customer care services can be given to a BPO by an electronic goods manufacturer. Genpact, Wipro, Infosys BPO, etc are some of the BPO companies operating in India.

(ii) **KPO** (Knowledge Process Outsourcing) It is a form of outsourcing, in which knowledge-related work is carried out by experts in a different company or by a subsidiary of the same organisation. This may be in the same country or in an offshore location to save cost.

Unlike BPO, this typically involves high-value work carried out by highly skilled staff. In KPO, the companies look for individuals who are homogeneous mixes of specialised knowledge, work experience, English speaking, etc.

(iii) **LPO** (Legal Process Outsourcing) It refers to the practice of a law firm or corporation obtaining legal support services from an outside law firm or legal support services company (LPO Provider).

e.g. Mindcrest, Pangea 3 and Lawscribe.

PYQs Previous Years' Questions

1 Mark Questions

1. Which of the following can not be completely outsourced by an organisation? *ISC 2023*

(a) Recruitment of clerical staff
(b) Tabulation of wages
(c) Training of data entry personnel
(d) Promotion of employees

Ans. (d) Promotion of employees

2. .... means getting high end knowledge work done from an outside agency to improve the efficiency and quality of business. *ISC Specimen 2023*

Ans KPO (Knowledge Process Outsourcing)

3. .... is a type of outsourcing used to get the high-end knowledge work done. *ISC Sem II 2022*

(a) BPO
(b) IPO
(c) LPO
(d) KPO

Ans (d) KPO

2 Marks Questions

1. Briefly explain LPO. *ISC Sem II Specimen 2022*

Ans LPO (Legal Process Outsourcing) refers to the practice of a law firm or corporation obtaining legal support services from an outside law firm or legal support services company.

2. What is meant by outsourcing? *ISC 2019*

Ans Outsourcing means having an external vendor, who provides such services on regular basis that would normally be performed within the organisation.

3. Expand the following *ISC 2019*

(i) BPO (ii) KPO

Ans (i) **BPO** Business Process Outsourcing

(ii) **KPO** Knowledge Process Outsourcing

Common Mistake Students generally use processing instead of 'process' and outsource/outsourced, etc instead of 'Outsourcing', so students are advisable to understand the full form of key-terms as they are very important from exam point of view.

4 Marks Questions

1. What is meant by outsourcing? Name and explain any two parties involved in outsourcing. ***ISC Specimen 2023***

Ans **Outsourcing** Refer to Q. No. (2 Marks) on page 174.

Parties involved in outsourcing Following are the parties involved in outsourcing

(i) **Outsourcer** A business firm which provides goods or services by contract from outside a particular organisation.

(ii) **The outsourced** (Outsourcee) The firm which hires the services of a outside party for the tasks that were traditionally performed by in house staff.

(iii) **Service provider** A business firm outsources its activities to a service provider (third party), who operates independently and provides services.

8 Marks Question

1. Discuss any two advantages and any two disadvantages each to the 'Outsourcer' and to the 'Outsourced', in the process of outsourcing. ***ISC 2020***

Ans (i) **Outsourcer** Advantages accrue to the outsourcer are

(a) **More profits** Generally, outsourcer has expertise in his work and he can earn more profits.

(b) **Quality services** Outsourcers provide personalised quality services to their clients.

Disadvantages faced by the outsourcer are

(a) **High risk** The outsourcer faces high risk due to accountability of performing the required task.

(b) **Sharing losses** In case of losses incurred by client, the outsourcer has to share the losses.

(ii) **The outsourced** (outsourcee) Advantages accrue to the outsourced (outsourcee) are

(a) **More focus** Outsourcing of non-core activities helps the firm to put more focus on core functions of the business.

(b) **Reduce costs** Outsourcing helps in reducing overhead and labour costs substantially.

Disadvantages faced by the outsourced (outsourcee) are

(a) **Hidden costs** There may be hidden costs involved in singing a contract.

(b) **Lack of secrecy** Personal data and information of the firm may be at risk.

Additional Questions

2/4 Marks Questions

1. Write three features of outsourcing.

Ans Features of outsourcing are as follows

(i) Outsourcing involves contracting out from outside agencies to perform activities, which were previously done in house.

(ii) Generally non-core business activities are outsourced.

(iii) Processes may be outsourced to captive units (own business units) or to a third party (outsider).

2. Distinguish between BPO and KPO.

Ans The differences between BPO and KPO are as follows

Basis	BPO	KPO
Activities	BPOs usually deal with fringe business activities such as customer care, finance, HR, etc.	KPOs deal in specialised and knowledge based services.
Focus	BPO's main focus is on reduction of cost or being cost effective.	KPOs stress more on specialised solutions rather than cost reduction.
Qualification	Basic education is enough, in case you want a job in BPO sector.	KPO requires competent and highly skilled professionals.
Involvement with clients	Generally in BPO, there is a less involvement with clients.	In KPOs, there is greater involvement with clients.

3. Explain the different categories of BPO.

Ans Generally, BPOs can be IT based or non-IT based. IT based BPOs are called 'ITES-BPO', where ITES stands for Information Technology Enabled Services. IT and Non-IT based BPOs can further be categorised as

(i) **Backend** In this, internal business functions like research and development, HR and administration, etc are outsourced.

(ii) **Customer facing or front office outsourcing** It is related to customer related services like marketing, grievance, handling, etc.

6/8 Marks Questions

1. Explain the concept, scope and advantages of BPO.

Ans **Concept of BPO** BPO (Business Process Outsourcing) is a subset of outsourcing that involves contracting of the operations and responsibilities of specific business functions or processes to a third party service provider, with a view to benefit from their experience, expertise and efficiency.

This allows companies to focus on their core processes. e.g. Customer care services can be given to a BPO by an electronic goods manufacturer. Genpact, Wipro, Infosys BPO, etc are some of the BPO companies operating in India.

Scope of BPO A business can outsource the following services to a BPO

(i) Telemarketing Services
(ii) Accounting Services
(iii) Customer Support Services
(iv) Customers Relation Management and Human Resource Management

Advantages/Needs of BPOs for the business BPOs help in optimising the performance of the business. The following advantages accrue to a business which outsources its services to a BPO

(i) Outsourcing helps a business to focus on its core activities and excel in them.
(ii) Outsourcing to a BPO is cost effective.
(iii) Outsourcing ensures specialised and expert services.
(iv) It ensures a business to conduct its operations smoothly.
(v) Outsourcing to a BPO helps a business to deal with labour problems.

2. Explain the concept, scope and advantages of KPO.

Ans **Concept of KPO** KPO (Knowledge Process Outsourcing) is a form of outsourcing, in which knowledge-related work is carried out by experts in a different company or by a subsidiary of the same organisation. This may be in the same country or in an offshore location to save cost.

Unlike BPO, this typically involves high-value work carried out by highly skilled staff. In KPO, the companies look for individuals who are homogeneous mixes of specialised knowledge, work experience, English speaking, etc.

Scope of KPO Scope of KPO in business firm follows

(i) Investment research services.
(ii) Legal process outsourcing
(iii) Data analytics
(iv) Animation and design
(v) Medical services
(vi) Writing and content development, etc.

Advantages/Needs of KPO for the business
KPOs offer the following advantages to a business firm

(i) KPO firms provide cost-effective expert services to the business firms.
(ii) They provide effective IT based solutions for the various problems faced by business firms.
(iii) They increase the effectiveness and efficiency of the outsourced activity.
(iv) They help the business firm to concentrate upon its core activity.

3. Explain the concept, scope and advantages of LPO.

Ans **Concept of LPO** LPO (Legal Process Outsourcing) refers to the practice of a law firm or corporation obtaining legal support services from an outside law firm or legal support services company (LPO Provider). e.g. Mindcrest, Pangea 3 and Lawscribe.

Scope of LPO Scope of LPO in business firm are as follows

(i) Agency work
(ii) Document review
(iii) Legal research and writing
(iv) Drafting of pleadings and briefs
(v) Patent services.

Advantages/Needs of LPO for the business
LPOs offers the following advantages to a business firm

(i) Most firms and corporation outsource primarily for cost saving measures:
(ii) Outsourcing legal services provides firms to get access high level legal talent and expertise.
(iii) By using the services of external personnel, the firms can expand their internal team and reduce the turnaround time for critical legal projects.

Case Based Question

Case 1

1. Apple outsources the production of its I-phones to hundereds of separate firms including Foxconn that manufatures the final phone. As part of the supply Chain, Apple outsources multiple components from Samsung such as the flash drive and the mobile DRAM.

With reference to this, answer the following questions.

(i) Who is the outsourcer here? State two advantages and two disadvantages of outsourcer.

(ii) Who is the outsourced here? State two advantages and two disadvantages of outsourced.

Ans (i) Foxconn and Samsung.

Advantages and Disadvantages of Outsourcer Refer to text on page 173.

(ii) Apple

Advantages and Disadvantages of Outsourced Refer to text on page 173.

CHAPTER TEST

01 Marks Questions

1. Expand the following
(i) B2 B (ii) B2 G

2. Name the party or Firm which provides goods or services by contract from outside a particular organisation.

3. What is known as process of integration of the economy of a country with the world economy?

4. .... refers to the conduct of industry and commerce using internet.

5. LPO stands for .... Process Outsourcing.

6. What is/are the threats of globalisation?
(a) Inflation (b) Tax heavens
(c) Trade imbalance (d) All of these

7. Transactions take place between two business firms known as
(a) B2C (b) C2C
(c) B2B (d) B2G

8. A business firm which hires the services of a outside party for the tasks, is known as
(a) outsourced firm (b) outsourcer firm
(c) outsourcing firm (d) service provider firm

9. Technical knowledge is required to do e-business. State true false.

10. Olx is B2B based platform. State true or false.

02 Marks Questions

11. What is globalisation?

12. What do you mean by free trade between companies?

13. What do you mean by online means of conducting business?

14. What is outsourcer?

15. Explain LPO.

04 Marks Questions

16. What are the benefits of e-business to the consumers?

17. Distinguish between B2B and Intra B.

18. Distinguish between outsourcer and outsourcee.

19. What are the benefits of service provider?

06/08 Marks Questions

20. Explain the advantages and disadvantages of globalisation.

21. What do you understand by e-business? State briefly varous types of e-business.

Answers

1. (i) Business to Business
(ii) Business to Government

2. Outsourcer

3. Globalisation

4. E-business

5. Legal

6. (d) All of these

7. (c) B2B

8. (a) Outsourced firm

9. True

10. False

15

Business Regulators and Intermediaries

TREND ANALYSIS 5 YEARS

		Average No. of Questions Across all Sets				
	Types of Questions	2023	2020	2019	2018	2017
01 Business Regulators	1 Mark	1	1	—	—	—
	2 Marks	—	—	1	—	—
	4 Marks	1	—	—	—	—
	6 Marks	—	—	—	—	—
	8 Marks	—	—	—	—	—
02 Business Intermediaries	1 Mark	—	1	—	—	—
	2 Marks	—	—	—	—	—
	4 Marks	—	—	—	—	—
	6 Marks	—	—	—	—	—
	8 Marks	—	—	—	—	—

Meaning of Business Regulators

The business regulators are organisations or government agencies which are established to regulate the business activities such as financing, investing, etc. In India, business activities are regulated with the help of independent regulators (i.e. SEBI).

On the other hand, the Indian Government is also known for playing a significant role in regulating the business activities.

Important Business Regulators in India

Some important business regulators in India are the following

1. Reserve Bank of India (RBI)

RBI is the Central Bank of our country which regulates the monetary policy of the Indian Government.

It was established on 1st April, 1935 in accordance with the Provisions of the Reserve Bank of India Act, 1934.

The Preamble of the RBI describes the basic functions of RBI as, "To regulate the issue of bank notes and keeping of reserves with a view to securing monetary stability in India and generally to operate the currency and credit system of the country to its advantages, to have a modern monetary policy framework to meet the challenge of an increasingly complex economy, to maintain price stability, while keeping in mind the objective of growth".

Thus, we can say that RBI is the apex institution of our country's monetary system.

The role of RBI can be summarised as follows

(i) **RBI regulates the issue of bank notes** The issue of paper money is the most important function of RBI. It regulates the credit and currency according to the economic situation of the economy.

It brings stability in the economy and creates confidence among the public.

(ii) **RBI regulates banking system to ensure and liquidity** RBI regulates the proper ratio between liquidity (i.e. bank's ability to pay short-term obligations) and solvency (i.e. bank's capacity to meet its long-term financial obligations).

(iii) **Licencing** In India, the approval for new banks are provided by RBI. It regulates the number of banks required in the country for business activities.

(iv) **RBI regulates foreign exchange** It regulates the stability of the external value of rupee and maintain desired level of foreign exchange reserve in the country.

(v) **Regulator for government securities** It protects and regulates the market for government securities. It channelises credit in desired directions as per the requirement of economy.

(vi) **RBI regulate inflation** It keeps inflationary trends under control. It tries to control inflation by raising the policy rates (i.e. repo rate, CRR and SLR). It leads to rise in the lending rate and fall in the inflation rate in the economy.

(vii) **RBI regulates the priority sector lending** RBI has prescribed that a portion of bank lending should be for development of specific sectors (i.e. agriculture, education, export and social infrastructure, etc).

(viii) **Economic stability** RBI is responsible for the maintenance of economic stability and assisting the economic growth of the country.

2. Securities and Exchange Board of India (SEBI)

SEBI was established on 12th April, 1992 in accordance with the provisions of the Securities and Exchange Board of India Act, 1992. The Preamble of SEBI describes the basic functions of SEBI as, "To protect the interests of investors in securities and to promote the development of and to regulate the securities market and for matter connected therewith or incidental thereto".

Thus, we can say that SEBI was set-up for the purpose of keeping a check on malpractices and protect the interest of investors.

The role of SEBI can be summarised as follows

(i) **SEBI regulates securities market** In India, SEBI is responsible for successfully creating a credible regulatory structure of stock market, which is essential for investor protection and capital market development.

(ii) **SEBI regulates price rigging** SEBI regulates price rigging in the stock market. Price rigging means manipulation of price of securities in the stock market.

(iii) **SEBI regulates the affairs of securities market** It regulates affairs of the securities market such as stock market. It registers and regulates the functions of intermediaries (i.e. stock brokers, sub-brokers, underwriters and merchant bankers, etc).

(iv) **SEBI regulates educational and training schemes** SEBI conducts educational and training seminars. It also conducts research to develop the securities markets. It has a website which delivers investor education.

(v) **SEBI regulates the merger and acquisition of the companies** SEBI sees whether the merger or acquisition of big companies are for development of business or to harm the capital market. It regulates such practices in the market.

(vi) **Stopping fraud in capital market** It has many powers for stopping fraud in the securities market.

(vii) **SEBI regulates the public issue in India** SEBI validates the IPO (Initial Public Offering) prospectus and makes sure that all the information in this document are correct, so that investor may take appropriate decision.

(viii) **SEBI regulates insider trading** SEBI keeps a stringent check whether insiders (i.e. directors, promoters, etc) are buying securities of the company for making profit.

(ix) **Auditing performance of the stock market** SEBI works to bring transparency and ethical values in the performance of the stock market in the economy.

3. Insurance Regulatory and Development Authority of India (IRDAI)

The IRDAI is an autonomous, statutory body tasked with regulating and promoting the insurance and re-insurance industries in India. It was constituted by the Insurance Regulatory and Development Act, 1999.

It is a 10-member body including the chairman, five full-time and four part-time members who are appointed by the government.

It basically regulates the work of the following

(i) **Insurance companies** It is a corporate organisation that provides coverage, in the form of compensation resulting from loss, damages, injury, treatment, etc in exchange for premium payments. e.g. LIC, GIC etc.

(ii) **Insurance agents and brokers** These are persons who sell insurance policies. An agent who sells the policies of a particular insurance company only is referred to as 'captive agent'. An agent who sells policies of different insurance companies is referred to as independent agent'.

Its role is summarised below

(i) Issuing, renewing, modifying, withdrawing, suspending or cancelling registrations

(ii) Protecting the interest of policy holders

(iii) Specifying the qualifications, code of conduct for agents

(iv) Promoting efficiency

(v) Levying fees and other charges

4. Food Safety and Standard Authority of India (FSSAI)

It is an autonomous body established under the Ministry of Health and Family Welfare, Government of India. It was established under the Food Safety and Standards Act, 2006 which aims at regulating and ensuring food safety. It mainly oversees the work of the following

(i) **Food processors** These are entities who transform agricultural products into food. It includes many forms of processing foods, from grinding grain to make flour to complete industrial methods to make convenience foods.

(ii) **Food packers** Persons who package food to provide protection and safety to them and also preserves their nutrition are referred to as food packers.

It plays the following role in ensuring food safety

(i) Laysdown science-based standards for food articles.

(ii) Regulates the manufacture, storage, distribution, sale and import of food.

5. Bureau of Indian Standards (BIS)

BIS is the National Standard Body of India. It is responsible for the harmonious development of the activities of standardisation, marking and quality certification of goods and for matters connected therewith or incidental thereto. It is establised by the Bureau of Indian Standards Act, 2016 which came into effect on 12th October, 2017.

Indian Standard Institute (ISI)

ISI mark is a certification mark for industrial products in India. The mark certifies that a product confirms to the Indian Standards as developed by the Bureau of Indian Standards. It is by far the most recognised standard certification mark in India.

It generally certifies the following categories of goods

(i) **Industrial goods** These goods are made up of machinery, manufacturing plants and materials, and any other goods or component used by other industries or firms.

(ii) **Consumer electrical goods** These refer to machines or devices that are in our homes and are used for washing, cooling, heating etc. e.g. Washing machines, fridge, heaters, etc.

(iii) **Goods made by steel manufacturers** Industries which are engaged in manufacturing goods out of steel such as utensils, machinery parts etc. fall under this category.

Its role is summarised below

(i) It ensures good quality of products.

(ii) It prevents inferior and sub-standard products from reaching market.

(iii) It ensures the safety of consumers.

Meaning of Business Intermediaries

The business intermediary refers to an institution, firm or individual who performs as middlemen between lenders and borrowers. They take money from the lenders and loan it directly or indirectly to the borrowers. In other words, the institutions which cannel funds from saver to borrowers are called business/financial intermediaries.

Important Business Intermediaries in India

Following are the important business intermediaries in India

1. Indian Banks/Commercial Banks

Banks are oldest and most important financial intermediaries in India. Banks accept deposits from the general public and extend loans to the households, firms and the government. They play a very important role in the mobilisation of savings.

The role of banks can be summarised as follows

(i) **Encouragement of saving and capital formation** Banks provide different kinds of deposit schemes to its customers. It enables to create banking habits and encourage savings in the economy.

(ii) **Mobilisation of savings** Banks mobilise saving into productive investments. They act as a middlemen between savers (i.e. depositors) and borrowers (i.e. business firms) for productive and investment purposes.

(iii) **Development of agriculture** The commercial banks help the agriculture sector in a number of ways. In India, the commercial banks are moving fast towards the attainment of agricultural development goal.

(iv) **Development of industry** Banks finance the industrial sector in many ways. They provide short-term, medium-term and long-term loan to industry.

(v) **Development of foreign trade** Banks provide foreign facilities to exporters and importers.

(vi) **Banks provide stability in the economy** Banks provide loan to investors and consumers that tend to stimulate the growth in both the aggregate demand and aggregate supply for goods and services. They raise the living standard of the people and reduce the recession in the economy.

(vii) **Banks provide range of services to the whole community** Commercial banks are backbone of the whole community as they provide services such as loans and advances, guarantee facilities, etc.

(viii) **Credit creation** In India, banks are called the factories of credit. Generally, commercial banks provide loan more than they accept deposit from people, known as credit creation process. Credit creation is the basic condition of economic growth and development in the economy.

2. Foreign Banks

Foreign banks are those banks which are incorporated outside India and operate through branches in India. The Narasimham committee on financial sector reform recommended the opening up of the Indian financial system to the entry of foreign banks. Foreign banks are allowed to operate in India through branches and representative offices.

A new foreign bank desirous of opening a branch in India is required to apply to RBI giving relevant information about its shareholders, financial position and the dealings with Indian parties. The request is examined keeping in view the financial soundness of the bank.

Role of foreign banks in Indian economy can be summarised as follows

(i) **Helpful in developing innovation and achieve expertise** Generally, foreign banks try to innovate new products (i.e. new schemes, services, etc). They provide quality service to industry. In other words, they lead the other domestic banks, in the various fields.

(ii) **Foreign banks create healthy competition** They provide a healthy competition in domestic market on general efficiency level in the banking system.

(iii) **Foreign banks encourage foreign investment in country** They have much influence on foreign investment in the country. Countries, on opening their doors to foreign banks, expect them to aid in the development of trade and foreign direct investment.

(iv) **Role in foreign exchange and money market** Generally, foreign banks in India participate in foreign exchange and money market contribute for deepening of the financial system.

(v) **Foreign banks play important role in financial products** Foreign banks provide the type of financial products that exporters needs, such as letter of credit and derivatives to hedge currency risk. They also have a higher proportion of foreign exchange and derivatives business.

3. Non-Banking Financial Companies (NBFCs)

NBFCs are essentially banks, since they perform the basic twin functions of attracting deposit from the public and giving loans. However, unlike commercial banks, they are not incorporated as a bank and are not governed by the provisions of the Banking Regulation Act, 1949. NBFCs encompass an extremely hetrogeneous group of intermediaries. They are regulated by the RBI.

Role of NBFCs can be summarised as follows

(i) **NBFCs act as intermediaries** NBFCs like banks and other financial institutions act as middlemen between the savers and borrowers.

(ii) **Economic development** NBFCs transfer unproductive financial assets (i.e. savings of surplus units) into productive assets (i.e. deficit units who take loan). They contribute to the country's economic growth and development.

(iii) **Infrastructure lending** Generally, NBFCs provide lending more to infrastructure than to banks. Infrastructure projects require large amount of funds and they are riskier projects.

(iv) **To finance economically weaker section** NBFCs cover all the areas or sections which are being untouched by RBI and other commercial banks.

(v) **Serve as competition for commercial banks** NBFCs provide competition to commercial banks in the provision of financial services. They target particular groups and particular sectors.

(vi) **NBFCs provide wealth management** NBFCs provide wealth management such as discounting services, managing portfolio of shares and advice on merger and acquisition of companies.

4. Stock Exchanges

According to **Section 2(i)** of the **SCRA**, "Stock exchange means anybody of individuals whether incorporated or not, constituted for the purpose of assisting, regulating or controlling the business of buying, selling or dealing in securities."

In other words, we can say that the institution were buying and selling of shares essentially takes place in the stock exchange. The first organised stock exchange in India was set up in 1877 at Bombay. It is known as Bombay Stock Exchange (BSE).

Role of stock exchanges in Indian economy can be summarised as follows

(i) **Mobilisation of saving** It provides a platform for an individual as well as institutional investors. It regulates the trading transaction with proper rules and regulations.

(ii) **Barometer of economy** It is considered as a barometer of the economy. Each economy is identified by its most significant stock exchange.

(iii) **Fund for development** It mobilises the fund for development purposes. It enables the government to raise the fund for developmental activities like power project, railways, roads, constructions, etc.

(iv) **Liquidity of investment** It provides liquidity of investment to investors (i.e. securities can sell out at anytime during trading hours of stock exchange).

(v) **Facilitating company expansion** Stock exchange helps companies to spread out and grow by acquisitions or mergers.

(vi) **Evaluation of securities** It determines the price of securities through the demand and supply forces.

5. Stock Brokers

The most important financial intermediaries are the stock brokers. They play an important role in stock exchange. The member of stock exchange is known as stock broker. Stock broker buys and sells the securities on the behalf of his clients.

SEBI regulates the stock brokers through rules and regulations. Stock brokers play the role of agent and charge commission for transaction in the stock exchange.

Role of stock brokers in stock market can be summarised as follows

(i) **Role in new issue market** Stock brokers perform the function of underwriting and marketing of new issues through a networks of sub-brokers.

(ii) **Role in stock market** Stock brokers operate as a jobber (i.e. wholesaler) offering bid and offer rate for making his profit.

(iii) **To maintain a register of transaction** In stock market, every broker has to maintain a register of transaction, such as client's ledger, cash book, etc.

(iv) **To work in welfare of stock market** Stock brokers are expected to maintain standard of integrity, promptness and fairness. Stock brokers act with due skill, care and diligence in the conduct of all business transactions. In short, they work for the welfare of stock market.

(v) **Research and advice** Stock brokers have research team that prepare the report card of companies and analyse the macro-economic scenario. They have technical analysts who provide market trends and advice to clients.

(vi) **Disclosure** Stock brokers disclose all material information related to an investment recommendation.

6. Merchant Bankers

According to **SEBI**, "Any person who is engaged in the business of issue management either by making arrangements regarding selling, buying or subscribing to the securities as manager, consultant, advisor in relation to such an issue management is a merchant banker."

In other words, merchant bankers are firms or banking corporation act as an intermediaries for raising capital for companies and duly authorised by SEBI.

Role of merchant bankers can be summarised as follows

(i) **Helpful in deciding the composition of capital mixture for the client** Merchant bankers help the client on two fronts

(a) What type of security (whether or equity or both) should be issued by client?

(b) At what price securities should be debt bought or sold?

(ii) **Underwriting the issue of the client** A company can allow the merchant banker to act as an underwriter for securities.

(iii) **Helpful in arranging foreign collaborations** Merchant bankers provide assistence to their client when they enter into any foreign merger, joint venture, etc.

(iv) **Global custody** Merchant bankers provide the services of global custody to local fund managers for cross-boarder settlement and administration.

(v) **Drafting** Helpful in drafting and finalising of the prospectus of companies and obtaining clearance from the various agencies concerned.

7. Depositories

Depositories are the organisations which hold securities (i.e. share, debenture, bonds, etc) of shareholders in an electronic form and facilitates the transfer of ownership as per the requirement.

According to **Section 2(c)** of the **Depositories Act, 1996,** "Depository means a company formed and registered under the Company Act, 1956 and which has been granted a certificate of registration under Section 12(1A) of the SEBI Act, 1992."

There are two depositories registered with SEBI, namely

(i) National Securities Depository Limited (NSDL)

(ii) Central Depository Service Limited (CDSL)

Role of depositories in stock market can be summarised as under

(i) **Depositories minimise the movement of physical securities** Depositories provide de-materialisation of securities (i.e. process of converting physical form of securities into electronic form).

(ii) **Pledge and hypothecation** Depositories allow the securities to be used as collateral to secure loan and other credits.

(iii) **Transfer the ownership of securities** Depositories enable easy transfer of ownership between two parties and take certain legal actions like endorsement and payment of stamp duty.

(iv) **To enhance liquidity in stock markets** The seller of securities get immediate cash payment for their transaction. Such practices enhance the liquidity in stock market.

(v) **Option of re-materialisation** Shareholders have the option of converting their electronic holding shares for a re-materialisation.

(vi) **Transparency** Blanks transfer are avoided and holding of shares in *benami* names is also prevented in a systematic manner.

8. Mutual Funds

A mutual fund is a professionally managed investment fund to pool money from investors, with a promise that the money would be invested in a particular manner. In India, SEBI regulates the mutual funds.

Mutual funds take the services of professionally who are expert in the investment world and who predict the market for the use of best interests of the investors.

In other words, we can say that mutual funds are financial intermediaries which pool the savings of large numbers of investors and then re-invest in best funds for earning profits and then distribute the dividends among the investors.

Their role is summarised as below

(i) **Helpful in creating awareness among middle investors** Mutual funds create awareness among middle class about the benefits of investment in stock market.

(ii) **Mutual funds attract foreign capital** Mutual funds attract foreign capital from foreign investors due to their expert professional advice and secure profitable avenues abroad for domestic savings.

(iii) **Portfolio diversification** Mutual funds enable the investors to hold a diversified investment even with a small amount of investment (i.e. ₹ 500).

(iv) **Transparency** Mutual funds provide regular information to its investors on the value investment in addition to disclosure of portfolio held by their schemes.

(v) **Beat inflation** Mutual funds prove as an ideal investment option. Generally, return an investment in mutual funds exceed the rate of inflation.

(vi) **Taking advantages of growing economy** Mutual funds are linked to the stock market. Investors in mutual funds have a chance to take advantage of growth in the economy.

9. Credit Rating Agencies

The credit rating agencies are the companies that assess the ability and willingness of debtors to pay back their interest and loan amount on time.

The debtors or assessed entities may be companies, NGOs, government and even countries. Credit rating agencies does not take any guarantee for the repayment of the debt. They provide grade only to the debts instruments which is given after conducting a detail analysis by experts. Credit rating is very useful to investors, banks, financial institutions and companies.

Following credit rating agencies are engaged in credit rating in India

(i) Credit Rating Information Services of India Ltd. (CRISIL).

(ii) Investment Information of Credit Rating Agency of India Ltd (IICRA).

(iii) Credit Analysis and Research Ltd (CARE).

(iv) Onida Individual Credit Rating Agency Ltd (ONICRA).

Role of credit rating agencies in Indian economy can be summarised as follows

(i) **Helpful for investors** Credit rating agencies provide rating to any instruments or entity which may be strong base for evaluation of investment.

(ii) **Helpful for issuers** Issuers seek rating for a number of reasons, such as marketability, pricing, satisfaction of investors, satisfaction of lenders etc.

(iii) **Regulatory use** Credit ratings are used for regulatory purposes around the world.

(iv) **Management evaluation** Evaluation of management of companies is one of the important functions of the credit rating agencies.

(v) **Helpful in establishing business relationship** Credit rating is also a valuable input in establishing business relationship of various types.

(vi) **Helpful in formulating public policy** Credit rating agencies provide rating on the opinion of professionals which may become valuable input in formulating the public policy guidelines.

PYQs Previous Years' Questions

1 Mark Questions

1. Expand FSSAI. *ISC 2023*

Ans Food Safety and Standards Authority of India.

2. With reference to regulators, identify the odd one out of the following *ISC Specimen 2023*

(a) RBI (b) LIC
(c) IRDAI (d) FSSAI

Ans (b) LIC

3. Name any two types of banks that are intermediaries of RBI. *ISC Sem II 2022*

Ans Two types of banks that are intermediaries of RBI are

(i) Indian banks
(ii) Foreign banks

4. ………… is also known as mercantile credit. *ISC Sem II Specimen 2022*

Ans Trade credit

5. What is meant by intermediary? *ISC Sem II Specimen 2022*

Ans Intermediary refers to an institution, firm or individual who performs as middlemen between lenders and borrowers.

2 Marks Questions

1. Briefly explain the role of stock brokers as an intermediary. *ISC Sem II 2022*

Ans Role of stock brokers may be summarised as follows

(i) Role in new issue market
(ii) Role in stock market
(iii) Research and advice
(iv) Disclosure the material information

2. Expand the following *ISC Sem II 2022, 2020*

(i) NBFC (ii) FSSAI

Ans (i) **NBFC** Non-Banking Financial Companies.

(ii) **FSSAI** Food Safety and Standard Authority of India

3. State any two functions of FSSAI. *ISC 2019*

Ans Functions of FSSAI are

(i) It lays down science-based standards for food articles.

(ii) It regulates manufacture, storage, distribution, sale and import of food.

Common Mistake Students get confused between FSSAI and intermediaries of FSSAI and write the functions of food processors and food packers instead of FSSAI functions. So students are advisable to learn the concept of regulations and their intermediaries distinctively.

4. What is the role of RBI as a regulator in the Indian banking system? *ISC Specimen 2019*

Ans Role of RBI as a regulator is as follows

(i) Regulates the issue of bank notes.
(ii) Regulates banking system to ensure liquidity.
(iii) Regulates foreign exchange, inflation and economic stability.
(iv) Licencing banks.

5. Expand the following *ISC Specimen 2019*

(i) POS (ii) IRDAI

Ans (i) POS - Point of Sale

(ii) IRDAI - Insurance Regulatory and Development Authority of India

4 Marks Questions

1. Briefly explain any two business regulators. *ISC 2023*

Ans Two business regulators are as follows

(i) **Securities and Exchange Board of India** SEBI was established on 12th April, 1992 in accordance with the provisions of the Securities and Exchange Board of India Act, 1992.

The Preamble of SEBI describes the basic functions of SEBI as, "To protect the interests of investors in securities and to promote the development of and to regulate the securities market and for matter connected therewith or incidental thereto".

Thus, we can say that SEBI was set-up for the purpose of keeping a check on malpractices and protect the interest of investors.

(ii) **Insurance Regulatory and Development Authority of India** (IRDAI) The IRDAI is an autonomous, statutory body tasked with regulating and promoting the insurance and re-insurance industries in India. It was constituted by the Insurance Regulatory and Development Act, 1999. It is a 10-member body including the chairman, five full-time and four part-time members who are appointed by the government.

2. Briefly explain any two intermediaries of SEBI. *ISC Specimen 2023*

Ans (i) **Stock Exchange** According to Section 2(i) of the SCRA, "Stock exchange means anybody of individuals whether incorporated or not, constituted for the purpose of assisting, regulating or controlling the business of buying, selling or dealing in securities."

In other words, we can say that the institution were buying and selling of shares essentially takes place in the stock exchange. The first organised stock exchange in India was set up in 1877 at Bombay.

It is known as Bombay Stock Exchange (BSE).

(ii) **Stock Brokers** The most important financial intermediaries are the stock brokers. They play an important role in stock exchange. The member of stock exchange is known as stock broker. Stock broker buys and sells the securities on the behalf of his clients.

SEBI regulates the stock brokers through rules and regulations. Stock brokers play the role of agent and charge commission for transaction in the stock exchange.

3. Which institution regulates insurance agents and insurance companies? Explain these two intermediaries. *ISC Sem II 2022*

Ans Insurance Regulatory Development Authority of India (IRDAI) regulates insurance agents and insurance companies.

For their explanation, refer to text on page 180 and 181.

Value Points

For getting maximum marks, following value points can be included in the answer

- Who is IRDAI?
- Intermediaries of IRDAI.
- Role of IRDAI as a regulator of insurance companies and insurance agents and brokers.

4. Explain any four roles that RBI plays as a regulator? *ISC Sem II Specimen 2022*

Ans The role of RBI can be summarised as follows

(i) **RBI regulates the issue of bank notes** The issue of paper money is the most important function of RBI. It regulates the credit and currency according to the economic situation of the economy. It brings stability in the economy and creates confidence among the public.

> **Role of RBI**
> - RBI regulates the issue of bank notes
> - RBI regulates banking system to ensure and liquidity
> - Licencing
> - RBI regulates foreign exchange

(ii) **RBI regulates banking system to ensure and liquidity** RBI regulates the proper ratio between liquidity (i.e. bank's ability to pay short-term obligations) and solvency (i.e. bank's capacity to meet its long-term financial obligations).

(iii) **Licencing** In India, the approval for new banks are provided by RBI. It regulates the number of banks required in the country for business activities.

(iv) **RBI regulates foreign exchange** It regulates the stability of the external value of rupee and maintain desired level of foreign exchange reserve in the country.

5. What is meant by the terms regulator and intermediaries? *ISC Specimen 2019*

Ans **Regulator** The business regulators are organisations or government agencies which are established to regulate the business activities such as financing, investing, etc.

In India, business activities are regulated with the help of independent regulators (i.e. SEBI). On the other hand, the Indian Government is also known for playing a significant role in regulating the business activities.

Intermediaries The business intermediary refers to an institution, firm or individual who performs as middlemen between lenders and borrowers. They take money from the lenders and loan it directly or indirectly to the borrowers. In other words, the institutions which cannel funds from saver to borrowers are called business/financial intermediaries.

Additional Questions

2 Marks Questions

1. Who are the business regulators?

Ans The business regulators are organisations or government agencies which are established to regulate the business activities such as financing, investing, etc.

The major regulators in India are as under

(i) Reserve Bank of India (RBI)

(ii) Securities and Exchange Board of India (SEBI)

(iii) Ministry of Finance

2. State two examples of non-banking financial companies in India.

Ans Two examples of non-banking financial companies in India are as follows

(i) Bajaj Finance Limited

(ii) Muthoot Finance Limited

Concept Enhancer Non-banking financial companies are entities that provide financial services similar to bank, but do not hold a banking license and are unregulated.

3. Differentiate between central bank and commercial bank.

Ans The following difference found between central bank and commercial bank are

Basis	Central bank	Commercial bank
Meaning	The bank which regulates the monetary system of the country known as 'central bank'.	The banks which do banking business to earn the profit are known as 'commercial banks'.
Objective	Public welfare and economic growth and development through monetary policy.	Earning profits from banking services.

4. Explain the role of SEBI in Indian economy.

Ans The role of SEBI can be summarised as follows

(i) **SEBI regulates securities market** In India, SEBI is responsible for successfully creating a credible regulatory structure of stock market.

(ii) **SEBI regulates the merger and acquisition the companies** SEBI sees whether the merger or acquisitions of big companies are for development of business or to harm the capital market. It regulates such practices in the market.

5. Which facilities are provided by banks to exporters and importer?

Ans The following facilities are provided

(i) Adequate pre-shipment packing credit for export

(ii) Cash credit

(iii) Overdraft facilities

(iv) Discounting of export bills

(v) Bank guarantee

6. Enumerate the services provided by banks.

Ans The following services are provided by banks

(i) Deposits (ii) Loan and advances

(iii) Demand draft

(iv) Sale and purchase of foreign exchange

(v) Locker facilities (vi) Guarantee facilities

(vii) Traveller's cheque

(viii) Trusty and executor services

7. Name any four foreign banks in India.

Ans ABN-AMRO Bank, Citi Bank, HSBC, Standard Chartered Bank.

8. Enumerate some of the activities of non-banking financial institutions.

Ans The following are the activities of non-banking financial institutions

(i) Business of loan and advances

(ii) Hire-purchase (iii) Bonds

(iv) Acquisition of shares

(v) Chit fund

(vi) Investment

(vii) Leasing

4 Marks Questions

1. Write an explanatory note on 'commercial bank'.

Ans A commercial bank is an institution that operates for profits. Banks accept the deposits from the general public and extend loans to the households, firms and the government. They play a very important role in the mobilisation of saving scattered all over the country.

The essential characteristics of banking business as defined in Section 5 (b) of the Banking Regulation Act, 1949 are as follows

(i) Acceptance of deposit from the general public.
(ii) Investment or lending.
(iii) Repayable on demand.
(iv) Withdrawable by means of any instrument whether a cheque or otherwise.

2. Explain the role of foreign bank in Indian economy.

Ans Foreign banks are those banks which are incorporated outside India and operate through branches in India. The role of foreign banks can be summarised as follows

(i) **Helpful in developing innovation and achieve expertise** Generally, foreign banks try to innovate new products and services. They provide quality service to industry.
(ii) **To create healthy competition** They provide a healthy competition in the domestic market on general efficiency level in the banking system.
(iii) **To encourage foreign investment in the country** They have much influence on foreign investment in the domestic country.
(iv) **Role in foreign exchange and money market** Generally, foreign banks in India participate in the foreign exchange and money market contribute for deepening of the financial system.

3. SEBI is the watchdog of security market. Do you agree? Give four reasons in support of your answer.

Ans Yes, I agree as SEBI regulates and protects the interest of investors. As a watchdog, SEBI regulates the market and protect the investors from manipulative activities.

There are the following protective functions of SEBI

(i) To promote code of conduct relating to the stock market.
(ii) To check inside-trading in the market.
(iii) To check unfair practices in the market.
(iv) To regulate the functioning of stock exchange and the securities market.

6/8 Marks Questions

1. Define depositories and explain the role of depositories in Indian stock market.

Ans According to Section 2(c) of the Depositories Act, 1996, "Depository means a company formed and registered under the Company Act, 1956 and which has been granted a certificate of registration under Section 12 (1A) of the SEBI Act 1992."

In simple words, depositories are the organisations which hold securities of shareholders in an electronic form and facilities the transfer of ownership as per the requirement.

Role of depositories in stock market The role of depositories can be summarised as follows

(i) **Depositories minimise the movement of physical securities** Depositories provide de-materialisation of securities (i.e. process of converting physical form of securities into electronic form).
(ii) **Transfer the ownership of securities** Depositories enable easy transfer of ownership between two parties and take certain legal actions like endorsement and payment of stamp duty.
(iii) **Transparency** Blanks transfers are avoided and holding of shares in *benami* names is also presented in a systematic manner.
(iv) **Option of re-materialisation** Shareholders have the option of converting their electronic holding shares for a re-materialisation.
(v) **To enhance liquidity in stock market** The seller of securities get immediate cash payment for their transaction. Such practices enhance the liquidity in stock market.
(vi) **Eliminate the risk of theft, loss, fraud, damage and delay in deliveries** It secures the safety of securities. It reduces the time and cost of transaction in stock market.

2. Write short notes on
(i) Mutual funds (ii) Credit rating agencies

Ans (i) **Mutual funds** A mutual fund is a professionally managed investment fund to pool money from investors, with a promise that the money would be invested in a particular manner.

In India, SEBI regulates the mutual funds. Mutual funds take the services of professionals who are expert in the investment world who predict the market for the use of best interests of the investors. In simple words, we can say that mutual funds are financial intermediaries which pool the savings of large numbers of investors and then re-invest in best funds for earning profits and then distribute the dividends among the investors.

Role of mutual fund in Indian economy

(a) Mutual funds are helpful in creating awareness among middle investors.
(b) Mutual funds attract foreign capital.
(c) Mutual funds enable the investors to hold a diversified investment.
(d) Mutual fund provides transparency in transaction.
(e) Mutual funds are helpful in facing the inflation.

(ii) **Credit rating agencies** The credit rating agencies are the companies that assess the ability and willingness of debtors to pay back their interest and loan amount on time.

The debtors or assessed entities may be companies, NGOs, Government and even countries. Credit rating agencies does not take any guarantee for the repayment of the debt.

They provide grade only to the debts instruments which is given after conducting a detail analysis by experts.

Credit rating is very useful to investors, banks, financial institutions and companies.

Following credit agencies are engaged in credit rating in India

(a) Credit Rating Information Services of India Ltd (CRISIL).
(b) Investment Information of Credit Rating Agency of India Ltd (ICRA).
(c) Credit Analysis and Research Ltd (CARE).
(d) Onida Individual Credit Rating Agency Ltd (ONICRA).

Role of credit rating agencies are as follows

(a) Helpful for issuers
(b) Helpful for investors
(c) Regulatory use
(d) Helpful in formulating public policy
(e) Establish a link between risk and return

Value Points

For getting maximum marks, following value points can be included in the answer

- Meaning of mutual funds and credit rating agencies.
- Role of mutual funds and credit rating agencies in Indian economy.

3. Mahesh is a government employee who acts upon his knowledge about a new regulation to be passed which will benefit a sugar exporting firm and buys its shares before the regulation becomes public knowledge. Mahesh has done insider trading for making profit.

Who is the regulator for insider trading? Explain.

Ans Securities and Exchange Board of India (SEBI) is the regulator for insider trading.

Refer text on page 180 for 'SEBI'.

CHAPTER TEST

01 Mark Questions

1. Who regulates the issue of bank notes in India?

2. Expand BIS.

3. Name the organisation which hold securities of shareholders in electronic form and facilitates the transfer of ownership as required.

4. .... regulates security market in India.

5. CRISIL is a ....

6. .... is a certification mark for industrial products in India.
(a) Bureau of Indian Standards (BIS)
(b) Indian Standards Institute (ISI)
(c) Non-Banking Financial Companies (NBFCs)
(d) Mutual fund

7. The role of RBI as business regulator is
(a) issue bank notes (b) regulate security market
(c) regulate insider trading
(d) All of the above

8. Which of the following is a business intermediary?
(a) SEBI (b) NBFC
(c) RBI (d) FSSAI

9. Foreign banks are those banks which are incorporated outside India and operate through branches in India. State true or false

10. Mutual fund is an intermediary of Reserve Bank of India. State true or false

02 Marks Questions

11. Name any two credit rating agencies in India.

12. What is the use of business intermediaries in securities market?

13. Differentiate between banks and non-banking financial companies.

14. Explain any one relevance of SEBI in the stock market.

04 Marks Questions

15. Differentiate between merchant bankers and commercial banks.

16. Explain the importance of credit rating to the small investors.

17. Explain role of mutual fund as financial intermediary.

06/08 Marks Questions

18. State any two business regulators that work in India. Explain their role in brief.

19. Explain the following terms
(i) Banks
(ii) Merchant bankers
(iii) Stock exchange
(iv) SEBI

20. State various business regulators of India.

Answers

1. Reserve Bank of India
2. Bureau of Indian Standards
3. Depository
4. SEBI
5. Credit rating agency
6. (b) Indian Standard Institute (ISI)
7. (a) issue bank notes
8. (b) NBFC
9. True
10. False

Assertion/Reasoning Based MCQs

Chapter 1 Introduction to HRM & Job and Manpower Planning

Direction (Q. No. 1 to 5) *There are two statements marked as Assertion (A) and Reason (R). Read the statements and choose the appropriate option from the options given below*

(a) Both Assertion (A) and Reason (R) are true and Reason (R) is the correct explanation for Assertion (A)

(b) Both Assertion (A) and Reason (R) are true, but Reason (R) is not the correct explanation for Assertion (A)

(c) Assertion (A) is true, but Reason (R) is false

(d) Both Assertion (A) and Reason (R) are false

1. **Assertion** (A) Human resource management refers to the part of management which manages the people at work.

   Reason (R) It is people oriented and covers all types of people at all levels in the organisation.

Ans (a) Both Assertion (A) and Reason (R) are true and Reason (R) is the correct explanation for Assertion (A)

2. **Assertion** (A) Job enrichment is the designing of a job to provide a worker with great responsibility.

   Reason (R) It brings boredom and monotony.

Ans (b) Job enrichment brings more challenge to the workers.

3. **Assertion** (A) Human resource management is a goal-oriented process.

   Reason (R) An organisation has a set of basis goals which are the basic reasons for its existence.

Ans (a) Both Assertion (A) and Reason (R) are true and Reason (R) is the correct explanation for Assertion (A)

4. **Assertion** (A) Job and manpower planning is a continuous process of identifying human resource requirements for an organisation in terms of quality and quantity.

   Reason (R) This planning helps in selecting right employee and in right number.

Ans (a) Both Assertion (A) and Reason (R) are true and Reason (R) is the correct explanation for Assertion (A)

5. **Assertion** (A) Job enlargement is the designing of a job to increase the total number of tasks that workers perform.

   Reason (R) Job enlargement requires less supervision of employees as compared to job enrichment.

Ans (c) Job enlargement requires more supervision of employees as compared to job enrichment.

Chapter 2 Staff Recruitment and Selection

Direction (Q. No. 1 to 5) *There are two statements marked as Assertion (A) and Reason (R). Read the statements and choose the appropriate option from the options given below*

(a) Both Assertion (A) and Reason (R) are true and Reason (R) is the correct explanation for Assertion (A)

(b) Both Assertion (A) and Reason (R) are true, but Reason (R) is not the correct explanation for Assertion (A)

(c) Assertion (A) is true, but Reason (R) is false

(d) Both Assertion (A) and Reason (R) are false

1. **Assertion** (A) E-recruitment is the process of stimulating people to apply through web based resources for a vacant job position in the organisation.

   Reason (R) E-recruitment lacks a personal touch between employers and job seekers.

Ans (a) Both Assertion (A) and Reason (R) are true and Reason (R) is the correct explanation for Assertion (A)

2. **Assertion** (A) An intranet is a private network available only to those with the company.

   Reason (R) Low maintenance cost is involved in intranet.

Ans (c) High maintenance cost is required in intranet.

3. **Assertion** (A) Selection is the process of selecting the best candidate from those who have applied for the job.

   Reason (R) It is a negative process as it involves rejection of candidates at every stage of it.

Ans (a) Both Assertion (A) and Reason (R) are true and Reason (R) is the correct explanation for Assertion (A)

4. **Assertion** (A) Aptitude tests are commonly used in staff selection to assess candidates' cognitive abilities.

   Reason (R) Aptitude tests provide objective and standardised measures of candidates' abilities and potential job performance.

Ans (a) Both Assertion (A) and Reason (R) are true and Reason (R) is the correct explanation for Assertion (A)

5. Assertion (A) Internal recruitment can improve employee morale and loyalty.

Reason (R) Internal recruitment gives existing employees opportunities for career growth and advancement within the organisation.

Ans (a) Both Assertion (A) and Reason (R) are true, and Reason (R) is the correct explanation for Assertion (A)

Chapter 3 Staff Training

Direction (Q. No. 1 to 5) *There are two statements marked as Assertion (A) and Reason (R). Read the statements and choose the appropriate option from the options given below*

(a) Both Assertion (A) and Reason (R) are true and Reason (R) is the correct explanation for Assertion (A)
(b) Both Assertion (A) and Reason (R) are true, but Reason (R) is not the correct explanation for Assertion (A)
(c) Assertion (A) is true, but Reason (R) is false
(d) Both Assertion (A) and Reason (R) are false

1. Assertion (A) Staff training is essential for maintaining a competent and efficient workforce.

Reason (R) Regular training programs help employees acquire new skills and knowledge, thus enhancing their job performance.

Ans (a) Both Assertion (A) and Reason (R) are true and Reason (R) is the correct explanation for Assertion (A)

2. Assertion (A) Staff training leads to higher employee satisfaction and retention.

Reason (R) Training demonstrates an organisation's investment in employees' professional development, leading to increased job satisfaction and loyalty.

Ans (a) Both Asssertion (A) and Reason (R) are true and Reason (R) is the correct explanation for Assertion (A)

3. Assertion (A) Training that is imparted away from the actual work floor, to enhance the capabilities of employees is referred to as "off-the-job training".

Reason (R) Off-the-job training involves learning while doing and is inexpensive in nature.

Ans (c) Off-the-job training is based on principle "learning before doing and is expensive in nature."

4. Assertion (A) Job training is provided to employee to handle a specific job and the employee can undergo this training several times, depending upon the nature of his work.

Reason (R) The objective of job training is to improve the efficiency of an employee.

Ans (a) Both Assertion (A) and Reason (R) are true and Reason (R) is the correct explanation for Assertion (A)

5. Assertion (A) On-the-job training is a source of human capital formation.

Reason (R) After on-the-job training of employees, firm insist that the workers should work for a specific period of time.

Ans (b) Both Assertion (A) and Reason (R) are true, but Reason (R) is not the correct explanation for Assertion (A)

Chapter 4 Staff Morale

Direction (Q. No. 1 to 5) *There are two statements marked as Assertion (A) and Reason (R). Read the statements and choose the appropriate option from the options given below*

(a) Both Assertion (A) and Reason (R) are true and Reason (R) is the correct explanation for Assertion (A)
(b) Both Assertion (A) and Reason (R) are true, but Reason (R) is not the correct explanation for Assertion (A)
(c) Assertion (A) is true, but Reason (R) is false
(d) Both Assertion (A) and Reason (R) are false

1. Assertion (A) Staff morale is an indicator of motivational level in the organisation.

Reason (R) It is a state of mind of individuals which determine their willingness to co-operate with others in the accomplishment of organisation's objectives.

Ans (a) Both Assertion (A) and Reason (R) are true and Reason (R) is the correct explanation for Assertion (A)

2. Assertion (A) Regular feedback and performance evaluations impact staff morale.

Reason (R) Providing constructive feedback and conducting fair performance evaluations help employees understand their strengths and area of improvement, by positively influencing their morale.

Ans (a) Both Assertion (A) and Reason (R) are true and Reason (R) is the correct explanation for Assertion (A)

3. Assertion (A) Staff morale is influenced by the quality of workplace relationships.

Reason (R) Positive relationships among colleagues and supervisors contribute to a supportive and enjoyable work environment.

Ans (a) Both Assertion (A) and Reason (R) are true and Reason (R) is the correct explanation for Assertion (A)

4. **Assertion** (A) Morale depressants are factors which result in an unfavourable attitude of an employee towards his company or work.

Reason (R) If goals set by management are unrealistic, unacceptable and useless, then employees develop a negative feeling towards job and organisation.

Ans (a) Both Assertion (A) and Reason (R) are true and Reason (R) is the correct explanation for Assertion (A)

5. **Assertion** (A) High productivity-low morale can be observed due to a fear of loss of job.

Reason (R) Low morale may lead to high productivity when there is good supervision and the work is machine-paced.

Ans (a) Both Assertion (A) and Reason (R) are true and Reason (R) is the correct explanation for Assertion (A)

Chapter 5 Staff Motivation

Direction (Q. No. 1 to 5) *There are two statements marked as Assertion (A) and Reason (R). Read the statements and choose the appropriate option from the options given below*

(a) Both Asssertion (A) and Reason (R) are true and Reason (R) is the correct explanation for Assertion (A)
(b) Both Assertion (A) and Reason (R) are true, but Reason (R) is not the correct explanation for Assertion (A)
(c) Assertion (A) is true, but Reason (R) is false
(d) Both Assertion (A) and Reason (R) are false

1. **Assertion** (A) Recognition and praise have great impact on staff motivation.

Reason (R) Employees are only motivated by tangible rewards, such as promotions or bonuses.

Ans (c) It is entirely not accurate that employees are only motivated by tangible rewards. While tangible rewards can indeed be powerful motivators, but recognition and praise also play a significant role in staff motivation.

2. **Assertion** (A) Creating a positive work environment has no impact on staff motivation.

Reason (R) Employees' motivation is solely influenced by their personal goals and ambitions.

Ans (c) Employees' motivation is not only influenced by their personal goals but also by organisational goals.

3. **Assertion** (A) Clear and attainable goals increase employee motivation.

Reason (R) When employees have a clear understanding of what they need to achieve and believe that the goals are achievable, they are more likely to be motivated.

Ans (a) Both Assertion (A) and Reason (R) are true and Reason (R) is the correct explanation for Assertion (A)

4. **Assertion** (A) According to Maslow's Hierarchy of Needs theory, individuals can only focus on one need at a time until it is satisfied.

Reason (R) The fulfillment of higher-level needs automatically leads to the satisfaction of lower-level needs.

Ans (b) Both Assertion (A) and Reason (R) are true, but Reason (R) is not the correct explanation for Assertion (A)

5. **Assertion** (A) Staff motivation helps to change negative or indifferent attitudes of employee to positive attitudes so as to achieve organisational goals.

Reason (R) Staff motivation helps to improve performance levels of employees as well as the organisation.

Ans (a) Both Assertion (A) and Reason (R) are true and Reason (R) is the correct explanation for Assertion (A)

Chapter 6 Staff Remuneration

Direction (Q. No. 1 to 5) *There are two statements marked as Assertion (A) and Reason (R). Read the statements and choose the appropriate option from the options given below*

(a) Both Asssertion (A) and Reason (R) are true and Reason (R) is the correct explanation for Assertion (A)
(b) Both Assertion (A) and Reason (R) are true, but Reason (R) is not the correct explanation for Assertion (A)
(c) Assertion (A) is true, but Reason (R) is false
(d) Both Assertion (A) and Reason (R) are false

1. **Assertion** (A) Employees benefits, such as health insurance and retirement plans, contribute to overall remuneration.

Reason (R) These benefits provide financial security and support the well-being of employees.

Ans (a) Both Assertion (A) and Reason (R) are true and Reason (R) is the correct explanation for Assertion (A)

2. **Assertion** (A) In time rate method, remuneration is directly linked with the time spent by an employee in the job.

Reason (R) There is no relation between the efficiency and reward in the time rate method.

Ans (a) The method states that even if employees work more efficiently and completes tasks faster, they will still receive the same remuneration as someone who takes longer to complete the same tasks.

3. **Assertion** (A) The piece rate method may lead to quality issues if employees focus solely on quantity.

Reason (R) Employees who receive remuneration based on piece rates, may sacrifice quality to maximise their earnings.

Ans (a) Both Assertion (A) and Reason (R) are true and Reason (R) is the correct explanation for Assertion (A)

4. **Assertion** (A) Employee Provident Fund (EPF) is a social security scheme that provides retirement benefits to employees.

Reason (R) Employee provident funds are solely funded by the employer and does not involve employee contributions.

Ans (c) Employee provident funds involve equal amount of fixed contribution from both the employer and the employee.

5. **Assertion** (A) Employee identification information, such as name and employee ID, is included on a payslip.

Reason (R) This information helps to ensure that payslip is accurately assigned to the correct employee.

Ans (a) Both Assertion (A) and Reason (R) are true and Reason (R) is the correct explanation for Assertion (A)

Chapter 7 Staff Leadership

Direction (Q. No. 1 to 5) *There are two statements marked as Assertion (A) and Reason (R). Read the statements and choose the appropriate option from the options given below*

(a) Both Assertion (A) and Reason (R) are true and Reason (R) is the correct explanation for Assertion (A)
(b) Both Assertion (A) and Reason (R) are true, but Reason (R) is not the correct explanation for Assertion (A)
(c) Assertion (A) is true, but Reason (R) is false
(d) Assertion (A) is false, but Reason (R) is true

1. **Assertion** (A) Democratic leaders make decisions without consulting their team members.

Reason (R) A democratic leadership style encourages participation, collaboration and input from team members.

Ans (d) Democratic leadership style takes decisions after consultation and encourages the participation of subordinates.

2. **Assertion** (A) Laissez-faire leadership allows employees to have maximum autonomy and freedom.

Reason (R) Laissez-faire leadership involves minimal interference and allows subordinates to make decisions independently.

Ans (a) Both Assertion (A) and Reason (R) are true and Reason (R) is the correct explanation for Assertion (A)

3. **Assertion** (A) The middle of the road leadership style, as defined by the managerial grid, represents a moderate level of concern for both people and production.

Reason (R) Middle of the road leaders strive for a balanced approach, compromising on both task accomplishment and employee satisfaction.

Ans (b) Both Assertion (A) and Reason (R) are true, but Reason (R) is not the correct explanation for Assertion (A)

4. **Assertion** (A) A situational leadership is a leadership theory that emphasizes on the need for leaders to adapt their leadership style based on the situation and the needs of their followers.

Reason (R) Different situations and followers require different leadership approaches to maximise effectiveness and achieve desired outcomes.

Ans (a) Both Asssertion (A) and Reason (R) are true and Reason (R) is the correct explanation for Assertion (A)

5. **Assertion** (A) Autocratic leadership style can result in quick decision-making.

Reason (R) Autocratic leaders have complete control over the decision-making process and make decisions without consulting others.

Ans (a) Both Assertion (A) and Reason (R) are true and Reason (R) is the correct explanation for Assertion (A)

Chapter 8 Staff Appraisal

Direction (Q. No. 1 to 5) *There are two statements marked as Assertion (A) and Reason (R). Read the statements and choose the appropriate option from the options given below*

(a) Both Assertion (A) and Reason (R) are true and Reason (R) is the correct explanation for Assertion (A)
(b) Both Assertion (A) and Reason (R) are true, but Reason (R) is not the correct explanation for Assertion (A)
(c) Assertion (A) is true, but Reason (R) is false
(d) Both Assertion (A) and Reason (R) are false

1. **Assertion** (A) Staff appraisal provides feedback and evaluates an employee's performance against pre-determined goals and standards.

Reason (R) Staff appraisal helps to identify areas of improvement and recognise achievements to enhance overall employee performance.

Ans (a) Both Assertion (A) and Reason (R) are true and Reason (R) is the correct explanation for Assertion (A)

2. **Assertion** (A) 360-degree feedback is a type of staff appraisal that involves input from multiple sources, such as peers, subordinates and supervisors.

Reason (R) 360-degree feedback provides a comprehensive and well-rounded assessment of an employee's performance and behaviours.

Ans (a) Both Assertion (A) and Reason (R) are true and Reason (R) is the correct explanation for Assertion (A)

3. **Assertion** (A) Evaluation of performance by the superior staff is generally one-way.

Reason (R) The personal relationship between the employee and the superior may negatively influence the evaluation and potentially impact objectivity.

Ans (a) Both Assertion (A) and Reason (R) are true and Reason (R) is the correct explanation for Assertion (A)

4. **Assertion** (A) Performance appraisals should only occur annually.

Reason (R) Conducting performance appraisals annually provides sufficient time to evaluate employee's performance accurately.

Ans (d) The performance appraisals can be conducted annually, but the frequency of appraisals can vary depending on organisational practices. Also, in some cases more frequent evaluations may be necessary to provide timely feedback and support employee development.

5. **Assertion** (A) Self-appraisal is typically conducted as a separate process from the regular performance review conducted by the supervisor.

Reason (R) Self-appraisal provides an opportunity to employees to evaluate on their own performance before engaging in a discussion with their supervisor.

Ans (a) By conducting self-appraisal before the discussion with the supervisor, employees can enter the conversation with a clearer understanding of their own performance, making the dialogue more productive and meaningful.

Chapter 9 Staff Promotion, Transfer and Separation

Direction (Q. No. 1 to 5) *There are two statements marked as Assertion (A) and Reason (R). Read the statements and choose the appropriate option from the options given below*

(a) Both Assertion (A) and Reason (R) are true and Reason (R) is the correct explanation for Assertion (A)
(b) Both Assertion (A) and Reason (R) are true, but Reason (R) is not the correct explanation for Assertion (A)
(c) Assertion (A) is true, but Reason (R) is false
(d) Both Assertion (A) and Reason (R) are false

1. **Assertion** (A) Staff transfer is a horizontal or lateral movement of an employee from one department to other or from one place to another with the same level of responsibility.

Reason (R) The purpose of staff transfer in a firm is only to punish an employee.

Ans (c) Staff transfers can occur for various reasons, such as organisational restructuring, talent development, or meeting specific operational needs. These transfers are often intended to leverage employees' skills, provide them with new experiences, or fill gaps within the organisation.

2. **Assertion** (A) Retrenchment is a permanent termination of an employee's service for economic reasons in a going concern.

Reason (R) Retrenchment usually occurs due to surplus staff, poor demand for the product, economic slowdown, etc.

Ans (a) Both Assertion (A) and Reason (R) are true and Reason (R) is the correct explanation for Assertion (A)

3. **Assertion** (A) Exit interview is the way of finding out why an employee wants to leave the organisation.

Reason (R) The purpose of exit interviews is to identify areas of improvement and address any concerns or issues raised by employees.

Ans (a) Both Assertion (A) and Reason (R) are true and Reason (R) is the correct explanation for Assertion (A)

4. **Assertion** (A) Promotion should be a transparent process with clear criteria and guidelines.

Reason (R) Transparent promotion process build trust among employees and reduce the perception of favouritism.

Ans (a) Both Assertion (A) and Reason (R) are true and Reason (R) is the correct explanation for Assertion (A)

5. **Assertion** (A) Promotion by seniority is a position which is granted to an employee on the basis of his/her seniority.

Reason (R) It fails to encourage the existing young employees for better performance.

Ans (b) Both Assertion (A) and Reason (R) are true, but Reason (R) is not the correct explanation for Assertion (A)

Chapter 10 Emerging Trends in Human Resources

Direction (Q. No. 1 to 3) *There are two statements marked as Assertion (A) and Reason (R). Read the statements and choose the appropriate option from the options given below*

(a) Both Assertion (A) and Reason (R) are true and Reason (R) is the correct explanation for Assertion (A)
(b) Both Assertion (A) and Reason (R) are true, but Reason (R) is not the correct explanation for Assertion (A)
(c) Assertion (A) is true, but Reason (R) is false
(d) Both Assertion (A) and Reason (R) are false

1. **Assertion** (A) Remote work and flexible work arrangements are getting popularity due to advancements in technology and changing work culture.

   Reason (R) Flexible hours allows employees to achieve a better work-life balance and reduces costs for employers.

Ans (a) Both Assertion (A) and Reason (R) are true and Reason (R) is the correct explanation for Assertion (A)

2. **Assertion** (A) Self-managing teams can lead to increased productivity.

   Reason (R) Self-managing teams eliminate the need for formal leadership and hierarchy.

Ans (b) Both Assertion (A) and Reason (R) are true, but Reason (R) is not the correct explanation for Assertion (A)

3. **Assertion** (A) Retainership agreements ensure a dedicated service for clients.

   Reason (R) Retainership agreements typically involve providing emergency or urgent assistance to clients.

Ans (c) Retainership agreements are contractual agreements between a professional (such as a lawyer, consultant or accountant) and a client. These agreements typically involve the professional providing ongoing services and advice to the client over a specified period of time. While some retainership agreements may indeed involve emergency or urgent assistance, it is not a defining characteristic of such agreements.

Chapter 11 Business Communication : Concept, Methods and Types

Direction (Q. No. 1 to 5) *There are two statements marked as Assertion (A) and Reason (R). Read the statements and choose the appropriate option from the options given below*

(a) Both Assertion (A) and Reason (R) are true and Reason (R) is the correct explanation for Assertion (A)
(b) Both Assertion (A) and Reason (R) are true, but Reason (R) is not the correct explanation for Assertion (A)
(c) Assertion (A) is true, but Reason (R) is false
(d) Both Assertion (A) and Reason (R) are false

1. **Assertion** (A) Gestural communication plays a significant role in business interactions.

   Reason (R) Body language, facial expressions and gestures can convey emotions, build rapport and enhance understanding in business communication.

Ans (a) Both Assertion (A) and Reason (R) are true and Reason (R) is the correct explanation for Assertion (A)

2. **Assertion** (A) Horizontal communication enhances collaboration and coordination between individuals and departments at the same hierarchial level.

   Reason (R) Horizontal communication is primarily used for transmitting information from superiors to subordinates.

Ans (c) Horizontal communication focuses on facilitating communication and information sharing among colleagues or peers at the same hierarchical level.

3. **Assertion** (A) Language barriers can impede effective communication.

   Reason (R) When individuals do not share a common language, it becomes difficult to convey and understand messages accurately.

Ans (a) Both Assertion (A) and Reason (R) are true and Reason (R) is the correct explanation for Assertion (A)

4. **Assertion** (A) Effective internal communication enhances employee engagement.

   Reason (R) When employees are well informed and involved, they feel a stronger sense of belonging and purpose.

Ans (a) Both Assertion (A) and Reason (R) are true and Reason (R) is the correct explanation for Assertion (A)

5. **Assertion** (A) Formal communication is less prone to misunderstandings as compared to informal communication.

   Reason (R) The use of precise language and professional tone minimises ambiguity.

Ans (b) Formal communication can help minimise misunderstandings to some extent, but it is not solely, due to the use of precise language and professional tone. Other factors like context, clarity and mutual understanding also play important role in effective communication, regardless of whether it is formal or informal.

Chapter 12 Business Correspondence and Current Trends

Direction (Q. No. 1 to 5) *There are two statements marked as Assertion (A) and Reason (R). Read the statements and choose the appropriate option from the options given below*

(a) Both Assertion (A) and Reason (R) are true and Reason (R) is the correct explanation for Assertion (A)
(b) Both Assertion (A) and Reason (R) are true, but Reason (R) is not the correct explanation for Assertion (A)
(c) Assertion (A) is true, but Reason (R) is false
(d) Both Assertion (A) and Reason (R) are false

1. **Assertion** (A) Video conferencing is an effective tool for remote teams.

Reason (R) Video conferencing allows for real-time communication and collaboration between individuals located at different geographical locations.

Ans (a) Both Assertion (A) and Reason (R) are true and Reason (R) is the correct explanation for Assertion (A)

2. **Assertion** (A) The use of passive voice is recommended in business letters.

Reason (R) Passive voice conveys a sense of formality and objectivity in professional communication.

Ans (d) The use of passive voice is discouraged in business letters as it can make sentences less clear and may come across as impersonal.

3. **Assertion** (A) Annual reports provide a comprehensive overview of a company's operations, finances and performance during a specific year.

Reason (R) Annual reports are prepared to communicate a company's financial information to stakeholders.

Ans (a) Both Assertion (A) and Reason (R) are true and Reason (R) is the correct explanation for Assertion (A)

4. **Assertion** (A) Non-statutory reports are prepared voluntarily by organisations.

Reason (R) Non-statutory reports provide additional information beyond what is legally required.

Ans (a) Both Assertion (A) and Reason (R) are true and Reason (R) is the correct explanation for Assertion (A)

5. **Assertion** (A) The interview letter should clearly state the date, time, location, authority before whom the candidate is to be appeared and other details of the interview.

Reason (R) Providing the interview details in the letter helps the candidate to plan and prepare accordingly.

Ans (a) Both Assertion (A) and Reason (R) are true and Reason (R) is the correct explanation for Assertion (A)

Chapter 13 Business Size and Finance

Direction (Q. No. 1 to 5) *There are two statements marked as Assertion (A) and Reason (R). Read the statements and choose the appropriate option from the options given below*

(a) Both Assertion (A) and Reason (R) are true and Reason (R) is the correct explanation for Assertion (A)
(b) Both Assertion (A) and Reason (R) are true, but Reason (R) is not the correct explanation for Assertion (A)
(c) Assertion (A) is true, but Reason (R) is false
(d) Both Assertion (A) and Reason (R) are false

1. **Assertion** (A) A sole proprietorship is the simplest form of business entity.

Reason (R) A sole proprietorship involves a single individual owning and operating the business.

Ans (a) Both Assertion (A) and Reason (R) are true and Reason (R) is the correct explanation for Assertion (A)

2. **Assertion** (A) Trade credit is a cost-effective source of short-term financing.

Reason (R) Trade credit allows businesses to delay the payment for goods and services purchased from suppliers.

Ans (a) Both Assertion (A) and Reason (R) are true and Reason (R) is the correct explanation for Assertion (A)

3. **Assertion** (A) Venture capitalists primarily target at established companies with stable revenue streams.

Reason (R) Venture capital firms prefer to invest in businesses that have access to equity markets.

Ans (d) Venture capital is a form of private equity investment where investors provide capital to high potential startups or supports small companies that wish to expand but do not have access to equity markets.

4. **Assertion** (A) Global Depository Receipts (GDRs) can be converted into underlying shares of the issuing company.

Reason (R) The conversion of GDRs into shares allows investors to benefit from potential capital appreciation.

Ans (a) Both Assertion (A) and Reason (R) are true and Reason (R) is the correct explanation for Assertion (A)

5. **Assertion** (A) Partnership firms do not have a separate legal entity from their partners.

Reason (R) In partnership firms, the owners are personally responsible for the debts and obligations of the business.

Ans (a) Both Assertion (A) and Reason (R) are true and Reason (R) is the correct explanation for Assertion (A)

Chapter 14 Globalisation and Recent Trends in Business

Direction (Q. No. 1 to 5) *There are two statements marked as Assertion (A) and Reason (R). Read the statements and choose the appropriate option from the options given below*

(a) Both Assertion (A) and Reason (R) are true and Reason (R) is the correct explanation for Assertion (A)
(b) Both Assertion (A) and Reason (R) are true, but Reason (R) is not the correct explanation for Assertion (A)
(c) Assertion (A) is true, but Reason (R) is false
(d) Assertion (A) is false, but Reason (R) is true

1. Assertion (A) Outsourcing has become a common practice in many businesses.

Reason (R) Outsourcing allows companies to reduce costs by delegating specific tasks or functions to external service providers.

Ans (a) Both Assertion (A) and Reason (R) are true and Reason (R) is the correct explanation for Assertion (A)

2. Assertion (A) Globalisation has led to increased competition among businesses.

Reason (R) Globalisation allows companies to expand their operations and reach new markets, leading to more competitors in the global market place.

Ans (a) Both Assertion (A) and Reason (R) are true and Reason (R) is the correct explanation for Assertion (A)

3. Assertion (R) E-business eliminates the need for physical storefronts completely.

Reason (R) E-business relies solely on online platforms for conducting business transactions.

Ans (d) While it is true that e-business reduces the dependency on physical storefronts, but it does not completely eliminate their need in all cases.

4. Assertion (A) Intra-business transactions involve the exchange of goods or services between different departments within the same company.

Reason (R) Intra-business transactions help to optimise resource allocation and streamline operations.

Ans (a) Both Assertion (A) and Reason (R) are true and Reason (R) is the correct explanation for Assertion (A)

5. Assertion (A) Knowledge Process Outsourcing (KPO) offers higher value additional as compared to BPO.

Reason (R) KPO provides primarily focus on knowledge-related work carried out by experts.

Ans (a) Both Assertion (A) and Reason (R) are true and Reason (R) is the correct explanation for Assertion (A)

Chapter 15 Business Regulators and Intermediaries

Direction (Q. No. 1 to 5) *There are two statements marked as Assertion (A) and Reason (R). Read the statements and choose the appropriate option from the options given below*

(a) Both Assertion (A) and Reason (R) are true and Reason (R) is the correct explanation for Assertion (A)
(b) Both Assertion (A) and Reason (R) are true, but Reason (R) is not the correct explanation for Assertion (A)
(c) Assertion (A) is true, but Reason (R) is false
(d) Both Assertion (A) and Reason (R) are false

1. Assertion (A) The RBI acts as the banker to the government in India.

Reason (R) The RBI provides short-term loans to the government to finance its budgetary deficits.

Ans (a) Both Assertion (A) and Reason (R) are true and Reason (R) is the correct explanation for Assertion (A)

2. Assertion (A) The presence of foreign banks can enhance competition and efficiency in domestic banking sectors.

Reason (R) Foreign banks bring in new technologies, practices and financial products, stimulating innovation and improving the overall efficiency of domestic banks.

Ans (a) Both Assertion (A) and Reason (R) are true and Reason (R) is the correct explanation for Assertion (A)

3. Assertion (A) FSSAI conducts regular inspections and audits of food establishments to ensure compliance with food safety regulations.

Reason (R) FSSAI aims to prevent foodborne illnesses and protect consumer health through effective monitoring and enforcement.

Ans (a) Both Assertion (A) and Reason (R) are true and Reason (R) is the correct explanation for Assertion (A)

4. Assertion (A) Depositories eliminate the risk of loss, theft or damange associated with physical securities.

Reason (R) Depositories enable investors to hold securities in electronic form and transfer them without the need for physical movement.

Ans (a) Both Assertion (A) and Reason (R) are true and Reason (R) is the correct explanation for Assertion (A)

5. Assertion (R) Stock exchanges are considered as barometer of the economy.

Reason (R) Every major change in country and economy is reflected in the prices of shares.

Ans (a) Both Assertion (A) and Reason (R) are true and Reason (R) is the correct explanation for Assertion (A)

ISC

Examination Paper 2024

Time : 3 hrs
Marks : 80

Business Studies XII

General Instructions

1. Candidates are allowed additional 15 minutes for only reading the paper. They must not start writing during this time.
2. Answer all questions in Section A, Section B and Section C.
3. Section A consists of objective/very short answer questions.
4. Section B consists of short answer questions.
5. Section C consists of long answer questions.
6. The intended marks for questions or parts of questions are given in brackets [ ].

Section A

(16 Marks)

1. (i) Name the leadership style that enables quick decision-making. [1]

(ii) Sneha works in a private company and has to report to office. According to the company's policy, she is allowed to report to office as per her convenience.
However, she needs to complete a set number of hours in office per week. Identify the emerging trend in human resources as exhibited in the above situation. [1]

(iii) Which method of performance appraisal reduces the bias on the part of raters so that ratings are not concentrated in a particular area on the rating scale? [1]

(iv) Give the expanded form of SMTs. [1]

(v) Human resource management is …… in nature as it involves the application of knowledge from Sociology, Anthropology, Psychology, Economics, etc. [1]

(vi) As per the Companies Act, a public limited company should have a minimum number of …. shareholders. [1]

(vii) …. refers to commercial transactions done *via* internet wherein goods or services are delivered in an electronic or a tangible form. [1]

(viii) ……. is the cheapest and fastest means of electronically transmitting written message which can also be used as legal evidence. [1]

(ix) Which one of the following is not a part of job specification? [1]

(a) Job title
(b) Job experience
(c) Physical appearance
(d) Communication skills

(x) The security guard of ABC Limited submits a report to the authorities on an incident of theft in the premises of the organisation. This report is an example of [1]

(a) interpretative, private, statutory and periodic report.
(b) information, public, statutory and periodic report.
(c) informational, private, non-statutory and special report.
(d) interpretative, public, non-statutory and periodic report.

(xi) Which one of the following types of transfers is done to stabilise employment when a particular department/branch of an organisation is understaffed? [1]

(a) Production transfer (b) Remedial transfer

(c) Versatility transfer (d) Replacement transfer

(xii) **Assertion** (A) Piece rate system of wage payment is suitable when the work is repetitive in nature and the output can be measured.

Reason (R) Piece rate system can cause insecurity among the workers as minimum wage is not guaranteed. [1]

Alternatives

(a) Both Assertion (A) and Reason (R) are true and Reason (R) is the correct explanation for Assertion (A)

(b) Both Assertion (A) and Reason (R) are true, but Reason (R) is not the correct explanation for Assertion (A)

(c) Assertion (A) is true and Reason (R) is false

(d) Both Assertion (A) and Reason (R) are false

(xiii) State whether the following true or false.

(a) The first step in the procedure for dismissal of an employee is to seek an explanation from the employee on their conduct. [1]

(b) SEBI regulates the securities market in India. [1]

(c) Refresher training in a type of training where the existing employees are trained in the latest methods and techniques of doing their work. [1]

(d) Globalisation has increased employment opportunities all over the world. [1]

Section B

(32 Marks)

2. (i) Cost of training is a major hindrance to a good training programme. State any two hindrances to training other than the cost. [2]

(ii) Briefly explain any two benefits of a training programme to the employer. [2]

Or (i) Discuss the following staff benefits.

(a) Group insurance [2]

(b) Gratuity [2]

3. (i) Give any two differences between performance appraisal and potential appraisal. [2]

(ii) Explain the concept of situational leadership. [2]

4. (i) State any four limitations of promotion. [4]

Or (ii) State any four ways in which globalisation has transformed the manner in which business is conducted.

5. Observe the picture given below and answer the questions that follow.

(i) Identify the factor indicated in the above image as per the two factor theory of Herzberg. [1]

(ii) Which need of Ms. Roy is being satisfied as per Maslow's Hierarchy of Human Needs? [1]

(iii) Briefly explain the need of Ms. Roy that is being satisfied. [2]

6. (i) What is meant by compulsory retirement? [2]

(ii) Briefly explain the concept of permanent part time as an emerging trend in human resources. [2]

7. (i) With reference to a report, explain appendix. State its role in a good report. [2]

(ii) Expand BIS. State any one role of BIS. [2]

8. Quite a few organisations outsource services instead of hiring people as a permanent staff. State any two advantages and any two disadvantages of this practice to the outsourcer. [4]

9. Briefly explain the following online means of conducting business.

(i) Intra B [2]

(ii) G2B [2]

Section C

(32 Marks)

10. Briefly explain the following sources of finance.

(i) Equity shares **[2]**

(ii) Debentures **[2]**

(iii) Trade credit **[2]**

(iv) Venture capitalist **[2]**

11. (i) Draw morale productivity matrix. By referring to the matrix, discuss any three situations to show the relation between moale and productivity. **[8]**

Or (i) Name and explain the two sources of e-recruitment. **[4]**

(ii) What is meant by staff selection? Given any two reasons to justify that it is a negative process. **[4]**

12. Anupriya Sport Store wants to place an order for the following sports equipment from Devesh Enterprise.

- 10 Cricket Bats @ ₹ 2,000 each.
- 30 Cricket Balls @ ₹ 300 each.
- 20 Hockey Sticks @ ₹ 1,000 each.
- 10 Hockey Balls @ ₹ 300 each.

Draft an order letter on behalf of Anupriya Sports Store. **[8]**

13. Read the passage given below and answer the questions that follow.

Annie and Naveen are fresh Engineering graduates who have been appointed by Scottish Automobile Ltd. Equipped with the latest information, Annie wants to introduce some changes in the production of automobiles. She is hesitant to discuss her ideas with her superior, Mr. Shah. Hence, she discusses it with Naveen.

Annie and Naveen make a power point presentation based on Annie's ideas. On behalf of Annie, Naveen presents it to Mr. Shah in the monthly review meeting.

(i) Identify the barrier to communication that exists between Annie and Mr. Shah. **[1]**

(ii) Suggest any three ways in which the barrier to communication between Annie and Mr. Shah can be overcome. **[3]**

(iii) Name and explain the type of communication between

(a) Annie and Naveen **[2]**

(b) Naveen and Mr. Shah **[2]**

Answers

1. (i) The leadership style that enables quick decision-making is authoritative or autocratic leadership.
   (ii) The emerging trend in human resources as exhibited in this situation is flexitime.
   (iii) Merit rating/Grading method of performance appraisal reduces the bias on the part of raters so that ratings are not concentrated in a particular area on the rating scale.
   (iv) SMTs stands for 'Self Managing Teams'.
   (v) inter-disciplinary
   (vi) seven (7)
   (vii) e-business
   (viii) e-mail
   (ix) (a) Job title
   (x) (c) informational, private, non-statutory and special report.
   (xi) (a) Production transfer
   (xii) (b) Both Assertion (A) and Reason (R) are true, but Reason (R) is not the correct explanation for Assertion (A)
   (xiii) (a) False. First step in the dismissal procedure is charge sheet.
   (b) True
   (c) True
   (d) True

2. (i) Two hindrances to staff training are stated below
   (a) Lack of resources on time.
   (b) Lack of support from supervisors or trainers.
   (ii) The benefits of training programme to the employer are
   (a) It enhances employee productivity both in terms of quantity and quality and leading to higher profits.
   (b) It increases employee morale, reduces absenteeism and employee turnover.

Or (i) (a) **Group insurance** It is an insurance policy where a group of employees is covered by a single insurance policy. Company is responsible for the payment of premium in respect of group insurance policy. There are two types of group insurance *viz.* group health insurance and group life insurance.
   (b) **Gratuity** It is the social security scheme which is applicable to every factory, mine, port, shop or establishment employing 10 or more employees. All employees are eligible for this, irrespective of salary provided if, they have rendered minimum 5 years of service in an organisation.

3. (i) Performance appraisal differ from potential appraisal in the following ways

Basis	Performance appraisal	Potential appraisal
Meaning	Performance appraisal is the process of evaluating the employee's performance on-the-job in terms of the requirements of the job.	Potential appraisal is the appraisal of the qualities of an employee to assess whether he is able to discharge higher responsibilities.
Perspective	It is backward-looking.	It is forward-looking.

   (ii) Situational leadership refers to the style of leadership in which leaders match their style with competence and commitment of subordinates. It was developed by Hershey and Blanchard which says that different situations demand different kinds of leadership. It has two components
   (a) **Leadership style** The leadership can be directive, coaching, participating or delegating.
   (b) **Follower's maturity** Level depending on competence and commitment, follower's maturity can be M_1, M_2, M_3 and M_4.
   Following leadership styles can be used with different maturity level
   M_1 = Directive Leadership
   M_2 = Coaching Leadership
   M_3 = Participating Leadership
   M_4 = Delegating Leadership

4. (i) The limitations of promotion can be summarised as follows
   (a) **Managers may reward their favourities rather than the best employees** Often, it is seen that supervisors select employees from their own choices which may be based on bias.
   (b) **Merit and ability are difficult to measure** It is a very difficult task to measure the merit and ability of employee in an objective and impartial way.

(c) **Lack of fresh ideas** The employees who are working in the organisation often lack a fresh perspective that only an outsider can bring.

(d) **Dissatisfaction at work** When one employee is promoted, bad feelings can result in the employees left behind. It can lead to dissatisfaction at work and poor work performance.

Or (ii) Ways in which business is transformed due to globalisation are

(a) Producers now can reap more benefit from economies of scale and division of labour.

(b) Competitive markets reduce monopoly and provide incentives for cost reduction.

(c) Globalisation facilitates free flow of goods, services, knowledge, technology, capital and people across national boundaries which led to higher productivity.

(d) Improved governance and capital markets also helps in transformation of business.

5. (i) As per the two factor theory of Herzberg, motivational or growth factor is indicated here.

(ii) Self-actualisation need of Ms. Roy is satisfied as per Maslow's Hierarchy of Human Needs.

(iii) Self-actualisation need is the highest level need in the 'need hierarchy' theory given by Maslow. These needs include needs for growth, self-fulfillment and achievement of goals. These needs represent what an individual wants to achieve after fulfilling the needs of his family and society. An individual strives to fulfill this need when he has been able to fulfill physiological needs, safety and security needs, love and belongingness needs and self-esteem needs.

6. (i) **Compulsory retirement** The employee retires automatic after attaining a specific age. The age of retirement set by the government varies from country to country. It generally varies from 50 to 70 year. In India, the retirement age is 60 years.

(ii) **Permanent part time** A permanent part time employee is an employee who works on a regular basis, but for fewer hours a week than a full time working employee.

An employee is to be considered as a permanent part time employee, if

(a) He/She works less than 38 hours in a week.

(b) He/She usually works regular hours each week.

(c) He/She is entitled to same benefits as a full time employee, but on a proportional basis.

(d) He/She is a permanent employee or on a fixed term contract.

7. (i) Appendix is a section at the end of report which include extra information that doesn't fit into the main text.

Advantages/Roles of an 'appendix' in a report are as follow

(a) It contains the information that is not essential to explain the findings, but that supports the analysis.

(b) It includes figures/tables/chart/graphs/questionnaires, which are directly related to the research problem or purpose.

(ii) BIS stands for 'Bureau of India Standards'. It is responsible for the harmonious development of the activities of standardisation, marking and quality certification of goods and for matters connected therewith or incidental thereto.

8. Advantages accrue to the outsourcer are

(i) **More profits** Generally, outsourcer has expertise in his work and he can earn more profits.

(ii) **Quality services** Outsourcers provide personalised quality services to their clients.

Disadvantages faced by the outsourcer are

(i) **High risk** The outsourcer faces high risk due to accountability of performing the required task.

(ii) **Sharing losses** In case of losses incurred by client, the outsourcer has to share the losses.

9. (i) **Intra Business** (Intra B) Here, parties involved in the electronic transactions are from within a given business firm only. It enables the smooth flow of transaction within the different departments (production, HR, accounts, marketing) of a specific firm.

(ii) **Government to Business** (G2B) G2B focuses on transactions between government and various business organisation, including contract bids, data collection and grants, sales of government services and goods along with procurement facilities.

10. (i) **Equity shares** The capital obtained by issue of equity shares is known as 'equity share capital'. It is considered as a permanent source of capital for a company, as it is not required to be returned during the life of the company. The return on equity shares is paid in the form of dividend.

The company pays dividend only in case of profits. The rate of dividend is not fixed and depends upon the surplus profit left after paying dividend to preference shareholders.

(ii) **Debentures** Debenture is an important instrument for raising long-term debt capital. Debenture is basically a written acknowledgement of the company, under its seal, that it has borrowed certain amount of money. In general, it refers to long-term loan to the company by the debentureholders on which they receive a fixed rate of interest.

(iii) **Trade credit** It is an agreement in which credit is extended by one trader to another for purchase of goods and services. It facilitates the purchase of supplies without immediate payment. It is a short-term (say, 30 days to 90 days) source of finance.

(iv) **Venture capitalist** These are private investors and venture capital firms who provide capital to start-up ventures or supports small companies that wish to expand but do not have access to equity markets. Venture capitalists are willing to invest in such companies because they can earn a massive return on their investments. Venture capital firm raise fund from different investors.

11. (i) An increase in morale may either cause increase or decrease in productivity. A high morale reflects a predisposition to be more productive, if attempts are made to provide effective leadership and coordinate various technical factors.

Miller and Form has given four combinations of productivity and morale. This is known as the morale productivity matrix and is illustrated below. It describes the relationship between morale and productivity.

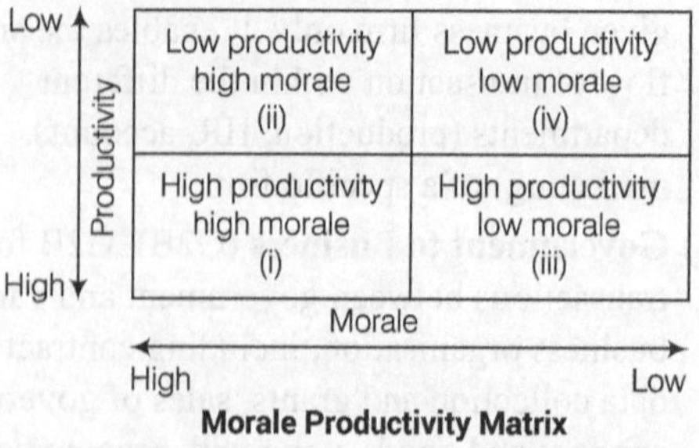

Morale Productivity Matrix

This matrix gives four combinations of morale and productivity (any three)

(a) **High productivity-high morale** Generally, high morale leads to higher productivity if it is backed with proper leadership and employees are offered financial and non-financial incentives.

Complete identity between organisation's goal and individual's goal leads to this situation.

(b) **Low productivity-high morale** This situation arises when employees spend their time and energy in fulfilling their individual objectives, totally unrelated with organisational objectives.

This situation can also arise due to faulty machinery, lack of training and ineffective supervision.

(c) **High productivity-low morale** In general, low morale does not lead to high productivity. However, in a short time period, this phenomenon can be observed due to fear of loss of job and good supervision.

(d) **Low productivity-low morale** This is a common phenomenon as low morale yields low productivity in the long-run.

So, it can be concluded that there is a complex relationship between morale and productivity.

Or

(i) Various sources of e-recruitment are as follow

(a) **Internet** (external source) It is a network of computers which is available for all. Internet is the main source of e-recruitment.

Following are the basic categories of the e-recruitment through internet

- **General purpose job board** It provides online recruiting solution to both employers and job-seekers, e.g. Monster, hot jobs, etc.
- **Niche job board** It provides highly specialised job markets, e.g. Journalismjobs.com, Marketingjobs.com, etc.
- **Social networking services** These are used by most job seekers and human resource professionals, e.g. Facebook, Linkedin, etc.
- **Video platforms** Now-a-days, video platforms are used for e-recruitment, e.g. Youtube.
- **Blogs** These are personal editorial spaces which allow company to publish job description.

- **Social professional networks** They provide potential employees to corporate, e.g. CA club India, MBA club India, etc.

(b) **Intranet** (internal source) It is private network available only to those with the company. It can be considered as internal source of e-recruitment. It is accessed through login details, i.e. user id, password, etc.

(ii) Staff selection is the process of choosing the right candidate from the pool of many individuals. In this process, all applicants are divided into two groups, *viz.* those selected in company and those rejected from process.

It is a negative process due to following reasons

(a) It involves rejection of candidates at every stage of it.

(b) In this process, more candidates are rejected than employed.

12. Anupriya Sports Store,
Seelampur, Delhi
Telephone....Fax......
15th April, 2024
To,
Devesh Enterprises
14, Pitampura
Mumbai
Subject Order for sports equipment
Dear Sir,
We thank you for your quotation for sports equipment dated 10th April, 2024. The prices are satisfactory, thus we are pleased to place a order with you for the following items at the prices and terms quoted

Description	Quantity	Unit Price	Total (₹)
Cricket Bats	10	2,000	20,000
Cricket Balls	30	300	9,000
Hockey Sticks	20	1,000	20,000
Hockey Balls	10	300	3,000
			52,000

Terms of payment, $2\frac{1}{2}$% one month, 7% 7 days.

Signed ....
Manager (Purchase)
Anupriya Sports Store

13. (i) Socio-psychological barrier exists between Annie and Mr. Shah.

(ii) Following are the ways in which the barrier to communication between Annie and Mr. Shah can be overcome

(a) Try to create a working environment where everyone has an equal opportunity to express their point of view.

(b) Develop your social skills with your all subordinates.

(c) Try to be as broad minded as possible.

(iii) (a) Annie and Naveen have horizontal communication between them.

Horizontal communication When employees of the same level or rank share information with each other, it is called horizontal communication.

(b) Naveen and Mr. Shah have vertical communication between them.

Vertical communication When information flows from higher authorities to subordinates and *vice-versa,* it is called Vertical communication.

ISC

Examination Paper 2025

Time : 3 hrs
Marks : 80

Business Studies XII

General Instructions

1. Candidates are allowed additional 15 minutes for only reading the paper. They must not start writing during this time.
2. There are thirteen questions in the paper. All questions are compulsory.
3. This paper is divided into three sections: A, B and C.
4. Section A has sixteen subparts which are very short answer questions. Each question carries 1 mark.
5. Section B has eight questions which are short answer questions. Each question carries 4 marks.
6. Section C has four questions which are long answer questions. Each question carries 8 marks.
7. Internal choices have been provided in two questions in Section B and in one question in Section C.
8. The intended marks for questions are given in brackets [ ].

Section A

(16 Marks)

1. (i) Mahima has joined XYZ Ltd. as a sales executive. She is a bright employee with good interpersonal skills. At a review meeting, the management feels that Mahima is promising and can be considered for a future leadership role in the company. Identify the method of appraisal that has led the management to this conclusion about Mahima. [1]

(ii) As per the Blake and Mouton Managerial Grid, name the 5,5 leadership style combination. [1]

(iii) Observe the relation between the first two phrases/terms and then fill in the fourth phrase/term.

(a) Monthly sales report : Routine report :: Report on theft : .... [1]

(b) Reserve Bank of India : Regulator :: State Bank of India : .... [1]

(iv) A movement to a higher pay scale without any change in the status of the employee is known as .... [1]

(v) As a source of finance, ... shares are considered best for cautious investors seeking steady dividends. [1]

(vi) Ex-employees are an .... source of recruitment. [1]

(vii) The .... significance of human resource management implies maximum utilisation of human resources by ensuring their physical and mental well-being. [1]

(viii) Organisational barriers to communication refer to those obstacles that hinder the flow of communication within an organisation.

Which one of the following scenarios correctly indicates an organisational barrier? [1]

(a) Rohit submits a report to his manager about a new consignment. The report is ambiguous, poorly worded and does not present all facts.

(b) Vidya has innovative ideas on product design but is hesitant to present them to her superior as she fears rejection.

(c) Tarun, an employee at Tarzan Associates urgently needs to meet the general manager. However, his immediate superior tells him to follow all the levels of hierarchy and then meet the general manager.

(d) Some employees at ABC Ltd. could not apply for the position of a manager within the company, due to a technical error in the internet server in their departments.

(ix) With reference to non-monetary incentives offered by an organisation, identify the odd one out from the following. [1]

(a) Appreciation of work
(b) Participation in management decisions
(c) Job security
(d) Medical reimbursement

(x) Select the preliminary step in the procedure of staff dismissal. [1]

(a) Holding of an enquiry
(b) Issuing of a written charge sheet
(c) Issuing of a notice of enquiry
(d) Receipt of an explanation

(xi) **Statement I** Pay slips help employees to understand their wage structure.

Statement II Since composition of wages is complicated, employees require a pay slip showing details of total wages, deductions and net wages. [1]

(a) Statement I is true and Statement II is false.
(b) Statement I is false and Statement II is true.
(c) Both Statements are true and Statement II is the correct explanation for Statement I.
(d) Both Statements are true but Statement II is not the correct explanation for Statement I.

(xii) State whether the following are true or false.

(a) A sole proprietorship firm has no legal existence separate from its owner. [1]
(b) Staff transfer refers to a vertical movement of an employee from one branch to another. [1]
(c) Though casual leave allows an employee to enjoy the leave, it results in deduction of pay during the period of leave. [1]
(d) Informal communication is completely authentic and reliable. [1]

Section B

(32 Marks)

2. State any two advantages and any two disadvantages of oral communication. [4]

Or State any four effects of globalisation on business around the world.

3. With reference to business correspondence, briefly explain each of the following

(i) Subject and Reference [2]
(ii) Complimentary close and Signature [2]

4. With reference to Herzberg's two-factor theory, explain the motivational and hygiene factors. [4]

5. Distinguish between training and education on the following bases [4]

(i) Nature (ii) Participants
(iii) Duration (iv) Contents

Or Distinguish between recruitment and selection on the following bases

(i) Nature (ii) Aim
(iii) Process (iv) Number

6. With reference to the morale productivity matrix, name the quadrant indicated in each of the following cases [4]

(i) Firoz, an efficient tailor in a garment factory, normally stitches 40 shirts in a week which is more than the average of 30 shirts stitched by the other tailors in the factory. However, his sewing machine broke down one day and he could stitch only 25 shirts in that week.

(ii) Natasha is working with a company that has laid off many employees in the past few months. The fear of losing her job makes Natasha work beyond fixed hours to achieve all her sales targets.

(iii) Gurdeep, a new employee at MN Sons Ltd., is a very dedicated and diligent worker. She strives relentlessly to achieve organisational goals for which she has received recognition by the company.

(iv) Prince has been working as a clerk at Ronald Bank. He has completed twenty-five years of service and is due for retirement. During his tenure, the management of the bank did not consider him for any promotion because of his laid-back attitude towards his work.

7. A 360° appraisal is inclusive and based on collection of feedback from a variety of sources.

With reference to the above statement, explain any two components of this method of appraisal. [4]

8. Observe the image shown below and answer the questions that follow

(i) Identify the type of training indicated in the image shown above. [1]

(ii) How often is this type of training conducted for employees? [1]

(iii) State any two reasons for conducting this type of training. [2]

9. Vasu, a sales executive at Sunshine Ltd., has been working with the organisation for fifteen years. He has a good track record. In recognition of his capabilities and long years of service in the organisation, the management promotes him to the post of sales manager.

Identify the basis on which Vasu has been promoted. Enurnerate any three advantages of this type of promotion. [4]

Section C

(32 Marks)

10. (i) Explain two types of retirement. [4]

(ii) With reference to staff benefits, briefly explain each of the following

(a) Encashment of leave [2]

(b) Maternity leave [2]

11. Briefly explain each of the following

(i) Human resource management [2]

(ii) B2B [2]

(iii) Loans [2]

(iv) Private limited company [2]

Or Briefly explain each of the following

(i) Job description

(ii) Refresher training

(iii) Retainership

(iv) EPF

12. Neeta Kumar, an entrepreneur, wants a modern look for her new office. She comes across a newspaper advertisement from Majestic Furniture that gives an overview of the furniture available with them.

Based on the above information, draft a letter from Neeta Kumar to Majestic Furniture seeking more information about the furniture. [8]

13. Read the passage given below and answer the questions that follow

Guardian Angels, a startup, offers childcare services for working parents. They have a set of trained caregivers and provide child and toddler care services at the client's residence. They offer two packages. Parents can opt for services in either the morning or the evening shift. Guardian Angels soon gains popularity and is flooded with demand for its services. However, it is understaffed and struggles to meet the growing demand.

Since it is a startup, Guardian Angels does not want to refuse the clients. Therefore, it decides to pay an additional amount to the employees who are now required to work in both the shifts. The increased work pressure leads to low morale among the employees.

(i) "However, it is understaffed and struggles to meet the growing demand."

Which area of job planning needs to be reconsidered by Guardian Angels? [1]

(ii) Name the method of remuneration followed by Guardian Angels. [1]

(iii) Outline any two roles that angel investors play in a startup venture. [2]

(iv) Discuss any two strategies that Guardian Angels can adopt to raise the morale of its employees. [4]

Answers

1. (i) Potential appraisal
   (ii) Middle of the road
   (iii) (a) Special Report
   (b) Intermediary
   (iv) Upgradation/Increment
   (v) Preference
   (vi) Internal
   (vii) Social
   (viii) (c) Tarun, an employee at Tarzan Associates urgently needs to meet the general manager. However, his immediate superior tells him to follow all the levels of hierarchy and then meet the general manager.
   (ix) (d) Medical reimbursement
   (x) (b) Issuing of written charge sheet
   (xi) (c) Both Statements are true and Statement II is the correct explanation for Statement I.
   (xii) (a) True
   (b) False – Staff transfer refers to the horizontal movement of an employee from one branch to another.
   (c) False – Casual leave does not result into deduction of pay.
   (d) False – Informal communication is spontaneous and not reliable. Formal communication is authentic and reliable.

2. The main **advantages** of oral/verbal communication are as follow
   (i) It is time saving communication.
   (ii) It creates healthy climate in the organisation.
   Oral communication suffers from the following **disadvantages**
   (i) Generally oral communication is not found in record so it is impossible to preserve the message for future.
   (ii) It has no legal validity.

Or Folowing are the four effects of globalisation on business around the world
   (i) Producers now can reap more benefit from economies of scale and division of labour.
   (ii) Competitive markets reduce monopoly and provide incentives for cost reduction.
   (iii) Globalisation facilitates free flow of goods, services, knowledge, technology, capital and people across national boundaries which led to higher productivity.
   (iv) Improved governance and capital markets also helps in transformation of business.

3. (i) **Subject and Reference** It is generally used in writing a formal letter. It can be written after the receiver's address or even after the salutation. It should be short and to the point. For example, **Subject** Application for the post of content writer.
   (ii) **Complimentary Close** It is a courteous way of ending the letter. The expression used must match the salutation.
   For example,
   (a) Yours affectionately/yours/with love for family and friends.
   (b) Yours sincerely/yours faithfully for principal, boss or for any other official purposes.
   Signature It is written just below the 'complimentary close' and includes the sender's name, designation (if applicable) and signature.
   For example,
   Yours truly/sincerely
   Ankita Chakravarti
   Editor

4. (i) **Motivational factors or growth factors** They provide job satisfaction to employees with better performance at work.
   Motivational factors include
   (a) **Responsibility** Employees should be assigned ownership of work with responsibility.
   (b) **Growth** There must be scope for growth and advancement opportunities in organisation for talented employees.
   (c) **Recognition** Employees should be praised and recognised for good work.
   (d) **Interesting work** Work should be interesting, meaningful and challenging for employees.
   (e) **Achievement** The employee must have a sense of work achievement.

(ii) **Hygiene factors or maintenance factors** They are required in organisation to avoid dissatisfaction among employees. Hygiene factors do not increase satisfaction among employees but that can increase dissatisfaction, if they are missing.

Hygiene factors include

(a) **Salary** Salary structure should be appropriate and reasonable in the organisation.

(b) **Company policies and administration** Company policies should be fair and clean. Administration should adopt flexible approach for workers.

(c) **Status** It should be familiar and retained.

(d) **Relationship with co-workers** There should not be conflict among co-workers in the organisation.

(e) **Good working conditions** There should be good working environment in organisation. It include

- Safety
- Cleanliness
- Hygiene

(f) **Job security** There should be job security in organisation for workers.

(g) **Working schedule** Working schedule should be flexible as per the need of employees.

5. Following are the differences between training and education

Basis	Training	Education
Nature	Training is practical and job-oriented, focusing on improving specific skills required for a particular job.	Education is theoretical and knowledge-based, providing a broad understanding of concepts and principles.
Participants	Training is mainly undertaken by employees or workers to enhance their job performance.	Education is pursued by students or learners to gain general knowledge and develop intellectual abilities.
Duration	Training is usually short-term and specific, designed to meet immediate job requirements.	Education is long-term and broader, aiming at overall personal and professional development.
Contents	The contents of training focus on improving job-related skills, techniques, and efficiency.	Education covers a wide range of subjects, theories and concepts that contribute to a person's overall growth and understanding.

Or Following are the differences between recruitment and selection

Basis	Recruitment	Selection
Nature	It is a positive process as it attracts people towards the organisation.	It is a negative process as it involves rejection of candidates at every stage of it.
Aim	The aim is to create a pool of potential candidates for the job.	The aim is to choose the best candidate who meets the job requirements.
Process	It is the process of identifying, attracting, and encouraging a large number of candidates to apply for a job.	It is the process of screening, evaluating and choosing the most suitable candidate from the pool of applicants.
Number	No restriction.	Only limited number of candidates are selected.

6. (i) **Low productivity-high morale** This situation arises when employees spend their time and energy in fulfilling their individual objectives, totally unrelated with organisational objectives. This situation can also arise due to faulty machinery, lack of training and ineffective supervision.

(ii) **High productivity-low morale** In general, low morale does not lead to high productivity. However, in a short time period, this phenomenon can be observed due to fear of loss of job and good supervision.

Generally, supervisors follow the penalty method to increase the productivity of employees in short period.

(iii) **High productivity-high morale** Generally, high morale leads to higher productivity if it is backed with proper leadership and employees are offered financial and non-financial incentives. Complete identity between organisation's goal and individual's goal leads to this situation.

(iv) **Low productivity-low morale** This is a common phenomenon as low morale yields low productivity in the long-run, where group goals and individual goals do not get satisfied.

So, it can be concluded that there is a complex relationship between morale and productivity.

7. Following are the components of 360 degree appraisal

(i) **Self-appraisal** It is a process by which employees get the clarity about where they currently stand in terms of their potential and contribution to the organisation. Employees evaluate their performance, reflecting on their strengths and areas for improvement. This helps employees to plan their career growth by developing required skills.

(ii) **Peer appraisal** This is a process where colleagues provide feedback, offering insights into the teamwork, communication and collaboration skills of an employee. The feedback not only contributes to an understanding of an employee's performance but also fosters a collaborative and supportive work environment, as it develops teamwork and mutual growth within the organisation.

8. (i) The type of training that is provided in the image is induction/orientation training.

(ii) Induction training is provided immediately after the selection of employees. An employee is required to undergo this training only once.

(iii) Two reasons for conducting induction training are as follows

(a) It helps in familiarising the employee with the ways of company and helps him to learn all aspects of his job.

(b) This training programme helps an employee to adjust easily in the working environment.

9. The basis on which Vasu has been promoted is 'seniority'.

Following are the advantages of this type of promotion

(i) It can essentially guarantee improvement and advancement in a job field.

(ii) It promotes the feeling of belongingness towards the organisation.

(iii) It promotes the feeling of job security among the employees.

10. (i) Retirement may be of the following types

(a) **Compulsory retirement** The employee retires automatic after attaining a specific age. The age of retirement set by the government varies from country to country. It generally varies from 50 to 70 years. In India, the retirement age is 60 years.

(b) **Voluntary retirement** Voluntary retirement is yet another type of separation. When organisations give option to its employees to retire even before superannuation, known as voluntary retirement. Under this scheme, an employee receives a lumpsum amount.

(ii) (a) **Encashment of leave** As per the service rule of organisation, eligible employees are provided leave for certain number of days. If leave is not utilised by employees, it may be lapsed, encashed or accumulated. Generally, organisation provides leave encashment to employee at the time of retirement or leaving the job.

(b) **Maternity/Paternity leave** Maternity leave is granted to regulate the employment of women in certain establishments for certain periods before and after child birth and to provide for maternity benefits and certain other benefits.

Every woman shall be entitled to, and her employer shall be liable for the payment of maternity benefit at the rate of average pay. Paternity leave is granted to male employee with less than two surviving children for a period of 15 days to take care of his wife and new born child.

11. (i) **Human resource management** It refers to that part of management which manages the people at work. It is the process which coordinates people within an organisation and helps both people and organisation to achieve each other's goals.

(ii) **B2B** These transactions take place between two business firms.

Hence, the name is B2B (business-to-business). A business interacts with a number of other business firms which may be suppliers or vendors of diverse inputs. Also they may be a part of the channel through which a firm distributes its products to the consumers.

(iii) **Loans** Commercial banks such as State Bank of India (SBI), Canara Bank, etc, advance money to the business firms for different purposes and different time periods.

Banks extend in many ways like, cash credits, overdrafts, discounting of bills of exchange and issue of letter of credit.

The repayment is made by the borrower in instalments as per the agreement between the bank and the borrower. Interest charged by banks depends upon a number of factors, such as nature of advance, period for which the loan is taken, etc.

Loan is generally offered by banks on the basis of security of assets.The loan can be repaid either in instalments or in lumpsum.

(iv) **Private Limited Company** According to **the Companies (Amendment) Act, 2013,** a private company means a company which

(a) restricts the right of its members to transfer shares.

(b) has minimum two members and maximum two hundred members, excluding present and past employees. A One Person Company (OPC) can be formed with only one member.

(c) does not invite public to subscribe to its share capital.

(d) have a minimum paid-up capital as may be prescribed.

It is necessary for a private company to use the words 'private limited' after its name.

Or (i) **Job description** It gives information about the scope of job activities, major responsibilities and positioning of the job in the organisation. This information gives the worker analyst and supervisor with a clear idea of what the worker must do to meet the demand of the job.

It includes

(a) Job title/name of the job

(b) Working hours

(c) Duties and responsibilities

(d) Working conditions

(e) Salary and incentives

(ii) **Refresher training** It is provided to familiarise the existing employees with the latest methods of performing their jobs and improve their efficiency.

It is also known as 'retraining programme'. It includes

(a) Up-to-date information about working procedures.

(b) Rapid technological changes.

(c) New pattern of demand for goods in market.

(iii) **Retainership** Under retainership, a retainer is a professional (consultant, freelancer, lawyer, etc), who is retained by a firm or a company for giving expert advice on some complex matters such as intellectual property issues, legal issues, tax issues, labour laws, etc.

A retainer would charge a retainership fee for his services. He does not have fixed working hours and is not required to put in daily attendance.

(iv) **Employee Provident Fund** (EPF) It is a retirement benefit applicable to salaried employees. Under this scheme, both the employer and employee contribute fixed amount in EPF account. This fund (i.e. fixed percentage of salary) is pre-set by the government. This fund is managed by Employees Provident Fund Organisation.

12. Neeta Kumar

42, Green Park Avenue

New Delhi - 110016

March 28th, 2025

The Manager

Majestic Furniture

12, Industrial Area

New Delhi - 110020

Subject Inquiry regarding modern office furniture

Sir,

I recently came across your advertisement in the newspaper regarding the range of modern office furniture available at Majestic Furniture. I am looking to furnish my new office with a modern and elegant look and your products seem quite appealing.

I would like to inquire about the various designs, materials and pricing of the available office furniture.

Additionally, it would be helpful to know if you provide customisation options and delivery services. Kindly send me the complete product catalog along with the price list and any ongoing offers.

I would appreciate a prompt response to my inquiry. You can contact me at the address mentioned above or *via* email at neetakumar@example.com.

Yours sincerely,

Neeta Kumar

13. (i) The area of job planning that needs to be reconsidered by Guardian Angels is 'manpower planning'.

(ii) The method of remuneration used by Guardian Angels is the 'time rate system'. The company decides to pay an additional amount to employees who are required to work in both shifts (morning and evening).

(iii) Angel investors can play the following two roles in a startup

(a) **Financial support** Angel investors provide the much-needed initial capital to startups, helping them kickstart their operations, develop products, or expand their business. This financial assistance is crucial for startups that might struggle to secure funding from traditional financial institutions.

(b) **Mentorship and guidance** Apart from funding, angel investors often offer valuable mentorship, business advice, and industry connections. They leverage their experience and networks to guide the startup through challenges, strategic decisions, and growth opportunities.

(iv) Following strategies can be adopted by Guardian Angels to raise the morale of its employees

(a) **Building responsibility** Everyone wants to feel that his or her work has higher value. One of the key requirement in this phase is to provide a feeling of responsibility to the employees, so that they feel that their work is more important than the other jobs.

(b) **Offer incentives** It stimulates employees to perform better, while at the same time helping them to feel that they are being appreciated by the organisation. Incentives can be offered in the form of money, appraisal, bonus, parking spaces, free meals, etc.

ISC

Sample Paper 01

Time : 3 hrs
Marks : 80

Business Studies XII

General Instructions

1. Candidates are allowed additional 15 minutes for only reading the paper. They must not start writing during this time.
2. There are thirteen questions in the paper. All questions are compulsory.
3. This paper is divided into three sections: A, B and C.
4. Section A has sixteen subparts which are very short answer questions. Each question carries 1 mark.
5. Section B has eight questions which are short answer questions. Each question carries 4 marks.
6. Section C has four questions which are long answer questions. Each question carries 8 marks.
7. Internal choices have been provided in two questions in Section B and in one question in Section C.
8. The intended marks for questions are given in brackets [ ].

Section A

(16 Marks)

1. (i) Name the future oriented appraisal that is used to measure and judge the potentiality of an employee. [1]

(ii) Observe the relation between the first two phrases/terms and then fill in the fourth phrase/term. [2]

(a) Positive process : Recruitment :: Negative process : ....

(b) Securities Market : SEBI :: Insurance market : ....

(iii) A to Z Publication's books are in great demand. As a result, the employees are always racing against time and have to work overtime. The work stress has led to dissatisfaction among the employees and managers.

Name the step of staffing process that has not been performed properly. [1]

(iv) When an outside expert is hired by an organisation to do a specialised work, it is called .... [1]

(v) .... involves planning the requirement for staff in near future by the organisation. [1]

(vi) .... refers to the learning opportunities designed to help employees grow. [1]

(vii) In .... leadership style, employees and leader collectively takes decision. [1]

(viii) Which one of the following scenarios correctly indicates a social need according to Maslow's need hierarchy? [1]

(a) Priya strives to achieve her personal goals and excel in her career, aiming for recognition and respect among her peers.

(b) Raj is looking for a safe and secure job that ensures his family's well-being and financial stability.

(c) Ankit enjoys participating in team-building activities at work and values the friendships he has formed with his colleagues.

(d) Naina is focused on self-improvement and personal growth by learning new skills and pursuing higher education.

(ix) Which of the following is not a method of training? [1]

(a) Vestibule training

(b) Apprenticeship training

(c) Refreshers training

(d) Off-the-job training

(x) Raouncoff Ltd. offers its directors certain benefits such as car, housing, medical facilities, etc., apart from salary.

Identify the incentive provided by the Raouncoff Ltd. to its directors. [1]

(a) Stock option
(b) Perquisites
(c) Bonus
(d) Job enrichment

(xi) **Statement I** Employees benefits, such as health insurance and retirement plans, contribute to overall remuneration.

Statement II These benefits provide financial security and support the well-being of employees. [1]

Alternatives

(a) Both statements are true and Statement II is the correct explanation of Statement I
(b) Both statements are true, but Statement II is not the correct explanation of Statement I
(c) Statement I is true, but Statement II is false
(d) Both statements are false

(xii) State whether these statements are true or false. [4]

(a) Training focuses on technical skills.
(b) Bio-data should be enclosed along with job letter.
(c) A public limited company should have minimum 3 members.
(d) Trade unions support piece rate system of wage payment.

Section B (32 Marks)

2. State any four differences between morale and motivation. [4]

Or State any four differences between oral communication and written communication.

3. Explain following components of job and manpower planning [4]

(i) Job description (ii) Job enrichment

4. Performance appraisal is the systematic evaluation of performance of the job. With reference to the above statement, explain any two methods of performance appraisal. [4]

5. Distinguish between time rate method and piece rate method on the following basis [4]

(i) Basis of payment
(ii) Nature of payment
(iii) Link with productivity
(iv) Quality of work

Or State four symptoms of high morale.

6. Riya has recently joined a reputed IT firm as a software developer. During her first week, she was introduced to the company policies, work culture, and team members. She was also briefed about her role and responsibilities to help her settle into the new work environment.

Identify and state the method of training used in the given situation. Discuss any three benefits of providing training to the employees. [4]

7. With reference to the types of business organisations, name the form of organisation indicated in each of the following cases [4]

(i) Ramesh runs a small grocery store in his neighbourhood. He is the sole owner, manages the business independently and bears all profits and losses.
(ii) Anita and Meera decided to open a boutique together. They have an agreement to share the responsibilities, profits and losses equally.
(iii) Techwave solutions is owned by a group of friends. The company restricts the transfer of shares and has only a limited number of shareholders, all of whom are known to each other.
(iv) Global Industries Ltd. has issued shares to the public through an IPO. The company's shares are traded openly on the stock exchange.

8.

(i) Identify the external source of staff recruitment depicted in the image above. [1]

(ii) Explain the source of staff recruitment identified in (i). [1]

(iii) State any two merits of external source of staff recruitment. [2]

9. A leader's approach to guiding and influencing team members can vary significantly based on their leadership style. With reference to the above statement, briefly explain any two types of leadership styles. [4]

Section C

(32 Marks)

10. (i) Briefly explain any two transactions, which come under the purview of e-business. [4]

(ii) With reference to e-business, explain each of the following

(a) Two benefits of e-business to the buyer [2]

(b) Two benefits of e-business to the seller [2]

11. Briefly explain each of the following

(i) Reports [2]

(ii) Statutory-reports [2]

(iii) Non-statutory reports [2]

(iv) Private reports [2]

Or Briefly explain each of the following

(i) Performance appraisal

(ii) Merit rating

(iii) Self-appraisal

(iv) Appraisal by results

12. As the manager of the company, write a letter of complaint to XYZ Furniture Ltd. for having delivered some chairs in a broken condition and asking them for replacement of the broken chairs. [8]

13. Pranay runs a medical shop started by his grandfather. As online business is becoming popular, Pranay's son Mitansh wants to stop physical sale of medicines and go for online website. By doing this, Pranay will be able to cover a wide area of its customers and customers can place orders at any time as per their convenience.

(i) If Pranay stops physical sale and starts online sale of medicines, then state any four benefits that will be available to Pranay. [4]

(ii) Identify the type of e-business highlighted in the above case. [1]

(iii) Explain the type of e-business identified in (ii). [1]

(iv) State any four points describing the nature of e-business. [2]

Answers

1. (i) Potential appraisal

(ii) (a) Selection

(b) Insurance Regulatory and Development Authority of India (IRDAI)

(iii) Manpower estimation

(iv) Retainership

(v) Manpower planning

(vi) Development

(vii) Democratic

(viii) (c) Ankit enjoys participating in team-building activities at work and values the friendships he has formed with his colleagues.

(ix) (c) Refreshers training

(x) (b) Perquisites

(xi) (a) Both statements are true and Statement II is the correct explanation of Statement I

(xii) (a) True (b) True

(c) False (d) False

ISC

Sample Paper 02

Time : 3 hrs
Marks : 80

Business Studies XII

General Instructions

1. Candidates are allowed additional 15 minutes for only reading the paper. They must not start writing during this time.
2. There are thirteen questions in the paper. All questions are compulsory.
3. This paper is divided into three sections: A, B and C.
4. Section A has sixteen subparts which are very short answer questions. Each question carries 1 mark.
5. Section B has eight questions which are short answer questions. Each question carries 4 marks.
6. Section C has four questions which are long answer questions. Each question carries 8 marks.
7. Internal choices have been provided in two questions in Section B and in one question in Section C.
8. The intended marks for questions are given in brackets [ ].

Section A

(16 Marks)

1. (i) Which of the job design tool is designed as a portrayal of the tasks, responsibilities, duties and functions of a job? [1]

(ii) Observe the relation between the first two phrases/ terms and then fill in the fourth phrase/term. [2]

(a) Knowledge related work : KPO :: Legal support services : ……………

(b) Time spent : Time rate method :: Units or pieces produced : ………………

(iii) Anshul was working under the guidance of Sumit, who encourages his subordinates to attempt and provide creative solutions. He also allows mistakes to occur without severe punishment. Identify the Maslow's hierarchy need of the Anshul that is fulfilled by Sumit in the above case. [1]

(iv) ………… is the process of stimulating people to apply through web-based resources for a vacant job position in the organisation. [1]

(v) A male employee is generally granted paternity leave for ………… days. [1]

(vi) ………… involves raise in wages or salary with a possible change in the designation. [1]

(vii) ………… is considered as the fastest mode of communication. [1]

(viii) For the purpose of recruiting employees, M/s X Ltd. placed a TV commercial on a leading channel.

This is an example of recruitment through [1]

(a) advertisement on electronic media

(b) advertisement on print media

(c) advertisement on web

(d) None of the above

(ix) Which of the following is a motivational factor according to Herzberg's two factor theory? [1]

(a) Status (b) Working conditions

(c) Salary (d) Challenging work

(x) Mr. R. Sarthi, the ex-chairman of Swadesh Ltd., built up his successor before retiring. Following the norms set up by himself, he handed over the reins of the company to the co-founder, Mr. Shravan, who had the potential to bring about change in the behaviour of others.

Name the concept of management which was the reason why Mr. Sarthi chose Mr. Shravan to be his successor. [1]

(a) The ability to inspire employees to work efficiently and with enthusiasm.

(b) The ability to influence the behaviour of others to achieve organisational goals.

(c) The process of exchanging information, ideas, and feelings effectively.

(d) The process of acquiring, deploying and retaining the workforce.

(xi) **Statement I** Staff motivation helps to change negative or indifferent attitudes of employee to positive attitudes so as to achieve organisational goals.

Statement II Staff motivation helps to improve performance levels of employees as well as the organisation. [1]

Alternatives

(a) Both statements are true and Statement II is the correct explanation of Statement I

(b) Both statements are true, but Statement II is not the correct explanation of Statement I

(c) Statement I is true, but Statement II is false

(d) Both statements are false

(xii) State whether these statements are true or false. [4]

(a) Job enrichment may require high level of skills.

(b) Bonus is a monetary incentive which motivates employees for better performance.

(c) Informal communication is also known as grapevine communication.

(d) Trade credit is an amount of money borrowed for a set period within an agreed repayment schedule.

Section B

(32 Marks)

2. State any four differences between training and development. [4]

Or State any four differences between internal communication and external communication.

3. With reference to the selection procedure, explain the significance of [4]

(i) Application blank (ii) Medical examination

4. Training plays an important role in the life of an employee. By stating any four points, prove the statement. [4]

5. Distinguish between performance appraisal and potential appraisal on the following basis [4]

(i) Meaning (ii) Process

(iii) Concept (iv) Appraisal

Or Give four roles of credit rating agencies in India.

6. Rajat runs a business where he sells electronic gadgets through an online platform. Customers place orders through his website, and payments are made digitally. Rajat also collaborates with suppliers through the internet to manage inventory efficiently.

Identify the type of business Rajat is engaged in and state its three types. [4]

7. With reference to the recruitment and selection process, name the source/step indicated in each of the following cases [4]

(i) Rahul visited a company without any prior appointment to inquire about job opportunities, leaving his resume with the receptionist.

(ii) Priya, an HR manager, visits universities and colleges to interview students for entry-level positions at her company.

(iii) Aman, an HR executive, quickly goes through the received applications to shortlist candidates who meet the basic qualifications.

(iv) Ritu fills out a standard form provided by the company, detailing her personal information, education and work experience.

8.

(i) Identify the type of communication depicted in the image given above. [1]

(ii) Explain the type of communication identified in (i). [1]

(iii) State any two advantages of the communication identified in (i). [2]

9. An employee separation occurs when the employment relationship between an employer and an employee comes to an end. It can take various forms, depending on the circumstances and reasons.

With reference to the above statement, briefly explain any two forms of employee separation. [4]

Section C

(32 Marks)

10. (i) Explain any two hindrances in training programmes. [4]

(ii) With reference to the types of staff training, briefly explain each of the following

(a) Remedial training [2]

(b) Safety training [2]

11. Briefly explain each of the following

(i) Communication [2]

(ii) Semantic barriers [2]

(iii) Socio-psychological barriers [2]

(iv) Organisational barriers [2]

Or Briefly explain each of the following

(i) Co-partnership/Stock option

(ii) Employee empowerment

(iii) Perquisites

(iv) Job enrichment

12. Draft a letter of order with the following details [8]

(i) 200 units of 60 watts tubelights @ ₹ 80 per unit.

(ii) 200 units of 100 watts bulbs @ ₹ 20 per unit.

(iii) 400 units of 40 watts bulbs @ ₹ 80 per unit.

13. Mr. Ramesh, after joining ABC Ltd. found himself in a situation where his boss Suresh doesn't show any interest in the opinions of her subordinates, initially, Ramesh was working for Giriraj, who would reward every attempt and innovative solution. Thus, at the end Ramesh lost all of his motivation due to lack of self-expression.

(i) Identify and explain the need of Ramesh not fulfilled. [2]

(ii) State importance of motivation to the employer and the employee. [4]

(iii) Define motivation. [1]

(iv) State any one characteristic of motivation. [1]

Answers

1. (i) Job analysis

(ii) (a) LPO (Legal Process Outsourcing)

(b) Piece rate method

(iii) Physiological and self-fulfillment needs

(iv) Recruitment

(v) 15

(vi) Upgrading

(vii) E-mail

(viii) (a) advertisement on electronic media

(ix) (d) Challenging work

(x) (b) The ability to influence the behaviour of others to achieve organisational goals.

(xi) (a) Both statements are true and Statement II is the correct explanation of Statement I.

(xii) (a) True (b) True

(c) True (d) False

ISC

Sample Paper 03

Time : 3 hrs
Marks : 80

Business Studies XII

General Instructions

1. Candidates are allowed additional 15 minutes for only reading the paper. They must not start writing during this time.
2. There are thirteen questions in the paper. All questions are compulsory.
3. This paper is divided into three sections: A, B and C.
4. Section A has sixteen subparts which are very short answer questions. Each question carries 1 mark.
5. Section B has eight questions which are short answer questions. Each question carries 4 marks.
6. Section C has four questions which are long answer questions. Each question carries 8 marks.
7. Internal choices have been provided in two questions in Section B and in one question in Section C.
8. The intended marks for questions are given in brackets [ ].

Section A

(16 Marks)

1. (i) At which stage of selection procedure is the minimum qualification of recruited candidates checked? [1]

(ii) Observe the relation between the first two phrases/terms and then fill in the fourth phrase/term. [2]

(a) Multimedia : Visual communication :: Waving of hand : ....

(b) Incorporated outside India : Foreign banks :: Accept deposits from general public : ....

(iii) Which method of communication involves the use of graphs, charts and diagrams? [1]

(iv) Job security creates .... morale among employees about their organisation. [1]

(v) Managerial grid theory was developed by .... [1]

(vi) A team consisting of employees working in different locations but connected through internet is called .... [1]

(vii) Trade credit is .... term source of finance. [1]

(viii) With reference to the types of training, select the odd one out from the following [1]

(a) Refresher training
(b) Remedial training
(c) Preliminary screening
(d) Induction training

(ix) Job specification is a written statement of the .... required for performing a job. [1]

(a) skills
(b) knowledge
(c) abilities
(d) All of these

(x) Promotion by seniority refers to the practice of granting a higher status or position to an employee based on their length of service within the organisation. This practice has both advantages and disadvantages.

Which of the following scenarios correctly indicates an advantage of seniority-based promotion? [1]

(a) An employee with high qualifications is promoted over a senior employee, boosting innovation.
(b) A senior employee is promoted, which instills a sense of job security among other employees.
(c) A junior employee is promoted due to exceptional performance, encouraging skill development.
(d) A senior employee is not promoted as the position requires specific technical expertise.

(xi) **Statement I** Staff transfer is a horizontal or lateral movement of an employee from one department to other or from one place to another.
Statement II The purpose of staff transfer in a firm is to punish an employee. **[1]**

Alternatives
(a) Both statements are true and Statement II is the correct explanation of Statement I
(b) Both statements are true, but Statement II is not the correct explanation of Statement I
(c) Statement I is true, but Statement II is false
(d) Both statements are false

(xii) State whether these statements are true or false. **[4]**
(a) SEBI regulates the security market in India.
(b) Crowdfunding is a source of finance.
(c) Shifting of an employee from one department to another is called separation.
(d) Motivation is the process of stimulating people to action to accomplish desired goals.

Section B **(32 Marks)**

2. State any four differences between equity share capital and preference share capital. **[4]**

Or State any four differences between horizontal and vertical communication.

3. In context to staff remuneration, explain the following
(i) Piece rate system (ii) Time rate system **[4]**

4. Leadership style is the result of leader's philosophy, personality, experience and value system. With reference to the above statement, briefly explain any two styles of leadership. **[4]**

5. Distinguish between recruitment and selection on the following basis **[4]**
(i) Meaning (ii) Objective
(iii) Nature (iv) Sequence

Or Distinguish between retrenchment and lay off on the following basis
(i) Meaning (ii) Nature
(iii) Reason (iv) Reappointment

6. A global team working on a project regularly collaborates despite being in different locations. They exchange detailed documents and updates through digital messages, while important discussions and collaborative meetings take place through virtual face-to-face interactions.
Identify the two trends in business communication indicated in the case and discuss their uses. **[4]**

7. With reference to human resource, name the process indicated in each of the following cases **[4]**
(i) Rahul, the HR manager of a multinational company, focuses on the efficient utilisation of the workforce and ensures a cordial relationship between employees and management. He regularly conducts employee engagement activities and addresses workplace grievances.
(ii) Priya is responsible for screening candidates based on their qualifications and experience. She conducts interviews and evaluates the skills of applicants to select the best fit for the job role.
(iii) Akash, working in the HR department of XYZ Ltd., is responsible for attracting a pool of qualified candidates through job portals, advertisements and campus recruitment drives.
(iv) Meera, an HR executive, organises workshops and training sessions to enhance the skills and competencies of employees, ensuring they stay updated with the latest industry practices.

8.

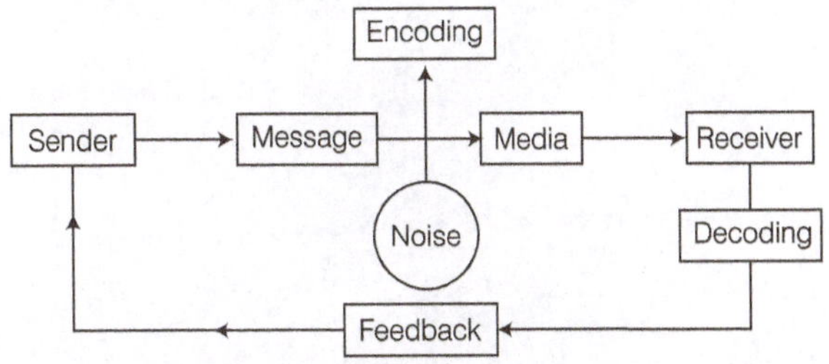

(i) Identify the process depicted in the above image. **[1]**

(ii) Explain the process identified in (i). [1]

(iii) Explain any two elements involved in the process identified in the (i) above. [2]

9. Business intermediary acts as a middlemen between lenders and borrowers. With reference to the above statement, explain any two intermediaries. [4]

Section C

(32 Marks)

10. (i) Explain any two sources of finance. [4]

(ii) With reference to the types of business entities, briefly explain each of the following

(a) Sole proprietorship [2]

(b) Public limited company [2]

11. Briefly explain each of the following

(i) Promotion [2]

(ii) Open system of promotion [2]

(iii) Closed system of promotion [2]

(iv) Dry promotion [2]

Or Briefly explain each of the following

(i) Business communication

(ii) Oral communication

(iii) Written communication

(iv) Visual communication

12. On behalf of a multinational company, draft an interview letter for the post of management trainee. [8]

13. Steve Jobs, the Co-founder of Apple, was known for his leadership style. He was known for being demanding and pushing his team to achieve the impossible. Despite his difficult personality, he was able to create products that revolutionsed the tech industry.

(i) Which leadership style did Steve Jobs follow? State its merits. [4]

(ii) State the meaning of leadership [1]

(iii) State any one benefit of leadership [1]

(iv) Distinguish between leadership and management. [2]

Answers

1. (i) Preliminary screening

(ii) (a) Gestural communication

(b) Commercial Banks

(iii) Formal

(iv) high

(v) Blake and Mouton

(vi) virtual team

(vii) short

(viii) (c) Preliminary screening

(ix) (d) All of these

(x) (b) A senior employee is promoted, which instills a sense of job security among other employees.

(xi) (c) Statement I is true, but Statement II is false

(xii) (a) True

(b) True

(c) False

(d) True

ISC

Latest ISC Specimen Paper

Business Studies XII

Time : 3 hrs
Marks : 80

General Instructions

1. You are allowed additional fifteen minutes for only reading the question paper. You must not start writing during reading time.
2. It is divided into three sections and has 13 questions in all.
3. All questions are compulsory. Answer all questions.
4. Section A has sixteen subparts which are very short answer questions. Each question carries 1 mark.
5. Section B has eight questions which are short answer questions. Each question carries 4 marks.
6. Section C has four questions which are long answer questions. Each question carries 8 marks.
7. Internal choices have been provided in two questions in Section B and in one question in Section C.
8. The intended marks for questions are given in brackets [ ].

Section A

(16 Marks)

1. (i) In order to adapt to changing work dynamics and provide flexibility to its employees, ABC Consulting Pvt. Ltd. decided to allocate a project to a group comprising employees in geographically dispersed settings.
Identify the emerging trend in human resources used by the ABC Consulting Pvt. Ltd. (Understanding) [1]

(ii) Which characteristic of human resource management deals with providing competent employees to an organisation, both now and in the future? (Recall) [1]

(iii) Observe the relation between the first two words and then fill in the fourth word. (Analysis) [2]
(a) Recruitment : Positive :: Selection : ....
(b) Verbal communication : Oral communication :: Non verbal communication : ....

(iv) As per Maslow's classification of human needs, safety needs consist of physical safety and .... safety. (Recall) [1]

(v) The Partnership Act limits the maximum number of partners in a non-banking partnership firm to .... (Recall) [1]

(vi) On the basis of ...., communication may be classified as internal and external. (Understanding) [1]

(vii) .... method of performance appraisal eliminates the subjective bias on the part of raters. (Understanding) [1]

(viii) Casual leave is a type of leave granted to an employee that can be availed in an unexpected situation or an unforeseen event.
Select the most appropriate instance for casual leave. (Application) [1]
(a) Mr. Aggarwal avails one week leave to take care of his wife who is in her last week of pregnancy.
(b) Ms. Khan takes one day leave to take her mother to the hospital as she had slipped and injured herself.
(c) Mr. D'Mello takes three days leave for his knee replacement surgery.
(d) Ms. Prabhjot takes four days leave to visit her parents in the village.

(ix) Mr. Rathi, CEO of a firm, frequently travels for work related to business. However, he ensures that he is present in office every Monday to monitor business operations. On his arrival, his personal assistant, Mr. Varma has to submit a report on the working of the previous week.

Which one of the following reports does Mr. Varma submit? (Understanding) [1]

(a) Routine report
(b) Special report
(c) Statutory report (d) Public report

(x) Staff dismissal involves permanent separation of an employee from the payroll. It is a drastic step and should therefore be resorted to with great care. Which one of the following situations indicates staff dismissal? (Application) [1]

(a) When an employee has reached the age of superannuation.
(b) When an employee fails to work according to the job requirements.
(c) When there is an acute shortage of raw material to continue work in the factory.
(d) When the employer relieves certain employees to reduce the cost of production.

(xi) **Statement I** In order to ensure effective learning, a teacher must minimise the barriers to communication.

Statement II Communication is incomplete without feedback. (Analysis) [1]

(a) Statement I is true but Statement II is false.
(b) Statement I is false but Statement II is true.
(c) Both statements are true and Statement II is the correct explanation for Statement I.
(d) Both statements are true but Statement II is not the correct explanation for Statement I.

(xii) State whether the following are true or false

(a) SEBI regulates the prices of the securities listed in the market. (Understanding) [1]
(b) A public deposit is a deposit made by public in the nationalised banks. (Understanding) [1]
(c) Human resource management is significant to an enterprise since it provides psychological satisfaction to people. (Understanding) [1]
(d) Venture capital is one of the primary sources of finance for start-ups. (Recall) [1]

Section B

(32 Marks)

2. Briefly explain any two limitations of e-recruitment as a source of staff recruitment. (Understanding) [4]

Or Briefly explain any two barriers to Communication. (Understanding)

3. With reference to staff selection, explain the significance of the following (Understanding)

(i) Application blank [2]
(ii) Placement [2]

4. State any four requirements of a sound promotion policy. (Recall) [4]

5. Distinguish between authoritative and democratic styles of leadership on the following basis (Analysis) [4]

(i) Effect on motivation and morale
(ii) Development of subordinates
(iii) Speed of work (iv) Resistance to change

Or Distinguish between piece rate system and time rate system of remuneration on the following basis (Analysis)

(i) Quality of work
(ii) Wastage of resources
(iii) Attitude of Trade Unions
(iv) Weightage to efficiency

6. What is meant by the following terms with reference to the sources of finance? (Understanding)

(i) Peer-to-peer funding [2]
(ii) Factoring [2]

7. Briefly outline the role of job analysis in the following processes (Understanding)

(i) Recruitment and selection [2]
(ii) Training and development [2]

8.

Elements of communication process

(i) Identify elements a, b, c and d in the communication process. (Understanding) [2]
(ii) Evaluate the significance of element 'e' in the communication process. (Analysis) [2]

9. ABC Ltd., a well-known IT firm has opened a new branch in Ahmednagar. In order to maintain their standards, the company is committed to hiring the best brains in the field.

As the HR manager of ABC Ltd., suggest any two strategies that the firm can use to attract suitable candidates. Justify your suggestion. (Evaluate) [4]

Section C (32 Marks)

10. (i) Name and explain any two types of training. (Understanding) [8]
(ii) Draw a specimen of a payslip. (Recall)

11. Briefly explain the following (Understanding)
(i) Outsourcing [2]
(ii) e-business [2]
(iii) Globalisation [2]
(iv) Communication [2]

Or

Briefly explain the following (Understanding)
(i) Business regulators
(ii) Business intermediaries
(iii) Reports
(iv) Group insurance

12. Ms. Chopra has applied for the post of an accountant in a firm in response to its advertisement in a daily newspaper.
Design the letter to be sent by the firm to Ms. Chopra, as she fulfils the criteria for recruitment. (Application) [8]

13. Read the passage given below and answer the questions that follow.
IBM's CEO, Arvind Krishna, says, employees' careers could suffer if they work from home. Krishna told Bloomberg in the Monday interview: "In the short term you probably can be equally productive, but your career does suffer. Moving from there to another role is probably less likely because nobody's observing them in another context," he said. "It will be tougher. Not impossible, but probably a lot tougher."
He added that remote workers do not acquire skills, such as dealing with difficult clients.
Source *(edited): https:// www. businessinsider.in/careers/news/ibm-chief-says-employees-careers-could-suffer-and-promotions-may-be-harder-to-achieve-if-they-work-from-home/articleshow/100013434.cms*
(i) Identify and explain the type of staff appraisal Arvind Krishna is referring to. (Understanding) [4]
(ii) What is meant by work from home? (Understanding) [2]
(iii) Explain the two ways by which an employee can be moved from one position/department to another in an organisation. (Understanding) [2]

Answers

1. (i) Virtual teams
(ii) Future-oriented
(iii) (a) Negative (b) Visual communication
(iv) economic
(v) 50 (vi) area of operation
(vii) Merit grading
(viii) (b) Ms. Khan takes one day leave to take her mother to the hospital as she had slipped and injured herself.
(ix) (a) Routine report
(x) (b) When an employee fails to work according to the job requirements.
(xi) (d) Both statements are true but Statement II is not the correct explanation for Statement I.
(xii) (a) False-SEBI does not regulate the prices of securities; it regulates the securities market and protects the interests of investors. Prices are determined by market forces.
(b) False-A public deposit is a deposit made by the public with companies, not with nationalised banks.
(c) False-Human resource management is significant to an enterprise, but it primarily focuses on managing people efficiently and effectively rather than providing psychological satisfaction. Psychological satisfaction is an indirect outcome rather than a primary focus.
(d) True

2. The following are the limitations of e-recruitment
(i) **Impersonal** E-recruitment lacks a personal touch between employers and job seekers. There are a lot of specialised jobs that require one-to-one meeting.
(ii) **Increasing number of applicants** Employers spend a great deal of time in screening the candidates through resumes.

Or Following are the two barriers to communication

(i) **Semantic barriers** Semantic barriers arise due to problems in the process of encoding and decoding a message. They occur when words and phrases are interpreted differently by the sender and receiver due to language differences, technical jargon, or the use of ambiguous words. This can lead to misunderstandings, as the intended meaning is not conveyed accurately.

(ii) **Socio-psychological barriers** These barriers arise from the social and psychological aspects of communication between individuals. Factors like emotions, perceptions, attitudes, and social values can distort the message. For instance, if the receiver has a biased opinion or preconceived notion, they may interpret the message differently than intended. Effective communication requires overcoming these personal and social influences.

3. (i) Following are the points of significance of application blank

(a) Helpful in providing a base of records about the candidate to the organisation.

(b) Helpful in shortlisting the candidates for tests and interview.

(ii) Following are the points of significance of placement

(a) Helpful in reducing labour turnover ratio in company.

(b) Helpful in improving the morale of employees.

4. The requirements of a sound promotion policy in the organisation can be summarised as follows

(i) **To distribute promotion opportunities** There should be equal ratio between internal promotion and external recruitment at various levels in all the departments.

(ii) **To promote morale among employees** Promotion system should be "open and not closed" so that eligible employees may get promotion at higher position.

(iii) **To establish a well defined system for promotion** There should be some definite system for the selection of employees who are to be promoted within the company. (i.e. criteria for promotion)

(iv) **To evaluate the employees** There must be a true and fair system for evaluation the efficiency and skills of employees for promotion.

5. Following are the differences between authoritative and democratic style of leadership

Basis	Authoritative	Democratic
Effect on motivation and morale	Often lowers motivation and morale as decisions are imposed by the leader without input from subordinates.	Boosts motivation and morale as subordinates feel valued and involved in decision-making.
Development of subordinates	Limited development as subordinates have little autonomy and are not encouraged to take initiative.	Encourages development by involving subordinates in decision-making and fostering responsibility.
Speed of work	Generally faster as the leader makes quick decisions without consulting others.	Relatively slower as the leader seeks input and consensus from the group.
Resistance to change	High resistance as subordinates may feel disengaged and reluctant to accept changes.	Low resistance as subordinates are more likely to support changes they have contributed to.

Or Following are the differences between piece rate system and time rate system

Basis	Piece Rate System	Time Rate System
Quality of work	Quality may suffer as workers focus on quantity.	Higher quality as workers focus on maintaining standards.
Wastage of resources	Higher wastage due to speed and quantity orientation.	Lower wastage as workers are not under pressure to produce more.
Attitude of Trade Unions	Generally opposed, as it may exploit workers.	Generally accepted, as it ensures fixed income.
Weightage to efficiency	High, as efficient workers earn more.	Low, as efficient and less efficient workers earn equally.

6. (i) **Peer-to-peer funding** It involves direct lending and borrowing between individuals without traditional financial institutions. It operates through online platforms connecting borrowers with individual lenders. Participants include borrowers (individuals or small businesses seeking loans) and lenders (individual investors or people willing to lend money for returns).

Lenders assume risk and earn returns through interest payments from borrowers. Interest rates are often determined by the borrower's creditworthiness. It connects individuals in need with a community of lenders, potentially benefiting those who may not meet traditional lending criteria.

(ii) **Factoring** It involves selling accounts receivable (invoices) to a third party, known as a factor. Businesses use factoring to receive immediate cash flow by converting invoices into cash. This financial strategy transfers the risk of non-payment by customers to the factor, which takes on the responsibility of collecting payment. Factors charge fees for their services, usually based on a percentage of the total invoice value, with the discount subtracted from the face value of the invoices. Factoring is commonly used in industries with extended payment terms, providing immediate cash flow for businesses in manufacturing, distribution and services.

7. (i) **Recruitment and selection** Job analysis serves as a realistic basis for hiring employees. It helps in guiding as to what an employee is expected to do on the job. It is a basis for meaningful forecast of job performance. It also helps in creating job related interview questions and tests that are tailored to evaluate candidates based on the specific requirements of the job. It aligns actual demands and expectations of the job roles within an organisation.

(ii) **Training and development** Job analysis identifies the skills and competencies required for a job, highlighting areas where employees may need additional training. It helps in designing training programmes to bridge the gap between current capabilities and job requirements. It helps in evaluation of training programme and further modifications.

8. (i) (a) Source (sender) (b) Encoding (message)
(c) Channel and medium (d) Receiver

(ii) Element 'e' is feedback.

Significance of Feedback Communication is the exchange and flow of information and ideas from one person to another. It involves a sender transmitting an idea, information or feeling to a receiver. Effective communication occurs only if the receiver understands the exact information or idea that the sender intended to transmit and this is possible only with feedback, as it would help in evaluating the effectiveness of our message. It makes communication meaningful.

9. Two strategies that the firm can use are

(i) **Advertisements** Large organisations usually prefer advertisements as a source of attracting large number of candidates for a vacant job position. It is useful when the company wants a wide choice for selection, fresh talent and employees for blue collar jobs. But it suffers from the limitation of high cost.
It also generates a large number of ineligible candidates, increasing cost and time involved in their screening.

(ii) **Educational institutions/Campus recruitment** Many big organisations have close contact with colleges, universities and institutions, from where they get fresh candidates in a cost-effective manner.

10. (i) Following are two types of training

(a) **Job Training** It is provided to employee to handle a specific job. It generates minimum skills and confidence among employees to do a specific job.
It includes
- All information about machines, equipments, etc.
- Instructions
- Process of production
- Methods
- Safety measures

(b) **Remedial training** It is provided to reduce the shortcomings in the behaviour and performance of old employees in the organisation due to the invention of new technology or process of production. Generally, such type of training is conducted by psychological experts or human resource experts.

(ii)

Specimen of Pay Slip

Name of Employee	Department ....
Designation	Month ....
Bank Name	Bank Account No. ....
Earnings	(₹)
1. Basic	....
2. Dearness Allowance	....
3. House Rent Allowance	....
4. Conveyance Allowance	....
5. Medical Allowance	....
6. Special Allowance	....
	Gross Salary
Deductions	
1. Professional Tax	....
2. Tax Deducted at Source	....
3. Employee Provident Fund	....
	Net Salary
Dated	.... Signature

11. (i) **Outsourcing** The term 'outsourcing' means having an external vendor, who provides such services on regular basis that would normally be performed within the organisation. It involves delegation of one or more business processes to an external service provider, who then manages the selected business process based on defined measures of performance.

(ii) **Electronic business or e-business** It refers to the conduct of industry and commerce using a computer network such as the internet.

Following is the nature of e-business

(a) It is very easy to set up e-business.

(b) There are no geographical boundaries to conduct business.

(iii) **Globalisation** It is the process of integration of the economy of a country with the world economy. It includes free flow of goods and services, knowledge, technology, capital and people across all boundaries. Economic activities are governed by domestic market and world market. There is absence of excessive government control over trade.

(iv) **Communication** It is as a process of exchange of ideas, facts, feelings, views, etc between two or more people to create common understanding. It involves a systematic and continuous cycle of listening and understanding.

Or (i) **Business regulators** The business regulators are organisations or government agencies which are established to regulate the business activities such as financing, investing, etc. In India, business activities are regulated with the help of independent regulators (i.e. SEBI).

On the other hand, the Indian Government is also known for playing a significant role in regulating the business activities.

(ii) **Business intermediaries** It refers to an institution, firm or individual who performs as middlemen between lenders and borrowers. They take money from the lenders and loan it directly or indirectly to the borrowers. In other words, the institutions which cannel funds from saver to borrowers are called business/financial intermediaries.

(iii) **Report** A report is written for a clear purpose and to a particular audience. Specific information and evidence are presented, analysed and applied to a particular problem or issue. The information is presented in a clearly structured format, making use of sections and headings, so that the information is easy to locate and follow.

(iv) **Group insurance** It is an insurance policy where a group of employees is covered by a single insurance policy. Company is responsible for the payment of premium in respect of group insurance policy.

There are two types of group insurance, viz. group health insurance and group life insurance.

12. Dear Ms. Chopra
Date [Insert Date]
Post Accountant

Madam,

With reference to your application for the post of Accountant, we are pleased to inform you that you have been shortlisted for an interview. Please come on [Date of Interview] at [Venue of Interview], telephone number [Contact Number], at [Time] for the interview.

The interview is scheduled to last approximately [Duration] and will take the form of a personal interview to assess your suitability for the role.

Please bring the following documents while coming for the interview

1. Resume/CV
2. Educational Certificates
3. Experience Certificates
4. Identity Proof
5. Passport-size Photographs

Thanking you

Yours sincerely,
For [Company Name]
[Name of Officer with Sign]
[Designation]

13. (i) The type of staff appraisal Arwind Krishna is referring to is 'potential appraisal'.

Potential appraisal is a future-oriented appraisal. It is used to measure and judge the potentiality of an employee for future higher positions. Most organisations include potential appraisal as a part of the performance appraisal.

Generally, it is done by employee's supervisor on annual basis. It updates training and recruitment activities in the organisation and informs to employees about their future prospects.

(ii) Work from home is a work arrangement where employees perform their job duties remotely, typically from their homes or other non-office locations. It heavily relies on technology such as internet connectivity, digital collaboration tools, etc.

(iii) The two ways by which an employee can be moved from one position/department to another in an organisation are

(a) **Promotion** It is an advancement of an employee's salary, status and responsibilities.

(b) **Transfer** The movement of an employee from one department, or location to another within the same organisation, without any significant change in salary, status and responsibilities is called transfer.